Werner Scholem

JEWISH CULTURE AND CONTEXTS

Published in association with the
Herbert D. Katz Center for Advanced Judaic Studies
of the University of Pennsylvania

Steven Weitzman, Series Editor

A complete list of books in the series
is available from the publisher.

Werner Scholem

A GERMAN LIFE

Mirjam Zadoff

Translated by Dona Geyer

PENN

UNIVERSITY OF PENNSYLVANIA PRESS

PHILADELPHIA

Publication of this volume was assisted by a grant from the
Herbert D. Katz Publications Fund of the Center for Advanced Judaic Studies
of the University of Pennsylvania.

The translation of this work was funded by
Geisteswissenschaften International—Translation Funding for Work in the Humanities
and Social Sciences from Germany, a joint initiative of the Fritz Thyssen Foundation,
the German Federal Foreign Office, the collecting society VG WORT and the Börsenverein des
Deutschen Buchhandels (German Publishers & Booksellers Association); and by
the Robert A. and Sandra S. Borns Jewish Studies Program of Indiana University.

Originally published as Der Rote Hiob: Das Leben des Werner Scholem
by Mirjam Zadoff © Carl Hanser Verlag München 2014

English translation copyright © 2018 University of Pennsylvania Press

Published by
University of Pennsylvania Press
Philadelphia, Pennsylvania 19104-4112
www.upenn.edu/pennpress

Printed in the United States of America
on acid-free paper

1 3 5 7 9 10 8 6 4 2

Library of Congress Cataloging-in-Publication Data

Names: Triendl-Zadoff, Mirjam, author. | Geyer, Dona, translator.
Title: Werner Scholem : a German life / Mirjam Zadoff ; translated by Dona Geyer.
Other titles: Rote Hiob English | Jewish culture and contexts.
Description: 1st edition. | Philadelphia : University of Pennsylvania Press, [2018] | Series: Jewish
  culture and contexts | "Published in association with the Herbert D. Katz Center for Advanced
  Judaic Studies of the University of Pennsylvania." | Includes bibliographical references and
  index.
Identifiers: LCCN 2017026905 | ISBN 9780812249699 (hardcover : alk. paper)
Subjects: LCSH: Scholem, Werner, 1895–1940. | Jewish communists—Germany—Biography. |
  Jews—Germany—Biography. | Jews—Persecutions—Germany. | Holocaust, Jewish
  (1939–1945)—Germany.
Classification: LCC DS134.42.S374 Z3313 2018 | DDC 940.53/18092 [B]—dc23
LC record available at https://lccn.loc.gov/2017026905

I stand for the reform of municipal morals and the
plain ten commandments. New worlds for old. Union
of all, jew, moslem and gentile. Three acres and a
cow for all children of nature. Saloon motor hearses.
Compulsory manual labour for all. All parks open
to the public day and night. Electric dishscrubbers.
Tuberculosis, lunacy, war and mendicancy must now
cease. General amnesty, weekly carnival with masked
licence, bonuses for all, esperanto the universal
language with universal brotherhood. No more
patriotism of barspongers and dropsical impostors.
Free money, free rent, free love and a free lay church
in a free lay state. . . . Mixed races and mixed marriage.

—Leopold Bloom in James Joyce, *Ulysses*, 1918–1920

CONTENTS

ABBREVIATIONS

BAB	National Archives, Berlin (Bundesarchiv Berlin)
BAB SAPMO	Foundation Archives of Parties and Mass Organizations of the GDR in the Federal Archives, Berlin (Bundesarchiv Berlin, Stiftung Archiv der Parteien und Massenorganisationen der DDR)
Comintern	Communist International
CV	Central Association of German Citizens of Jewish Faith, Central Verein (Centralverein deutscher Staatsbürger jüdischen Glaubens)
DDP	German Democratic Party (Deutsche Demokratische Partei)
DNVP	German National People's Party (Deutschnationale Volkspartei)
DVP	German People's Party (Deutsche Volkspartei)
EKKI	Executive Committee of the Communist International (Exekutivkomitee der Kommunistischen Internationale)
IfZ	Institute of Contemporary History, Munich (Institut für Zeitgeschichte, München)
IISG	International Institute of Social History, Amsterdam (Internationaal Instituut voor Sociale Geschiedenis, Amsterdam)
INL	Israeli National Library
IPW	Institute for Political Science, Leibniz University Hannover (Institut für Politische Wissenschaft, Leibniz Universität Hannover)
ISC	Institute for the Study of Capitalism, Genua (Istituto di Studi sul Capitalismo, Genua)
ITS	International Tracing Service
KAPD	Communist Worker's Party of Germany (Kommunistische Arbeiterpartei Deutschlands)
KPD	Communist Party of Germany (Kommunistische Partei Deutschlands)
KPdSU	Communist Party of the Soviet Union (Kommunistische Partei der Sowjetunion)
MSPD	Majority Social Democratic Party of Germany (Mehrheitssozialdemokratische Partei Deutschlands)

NLA   Lower Saxony State Archives (Niedersächsisches Landesarchiv –
             Hauptstaatsarchiv Hannover)
NSDAP   National Socialist German Workers' Party (Nationalsozialistische
             Deutsche Arbeiterpartei)
ÖNB   Austrian National Library (Österreichische Nationalbibliothek)
PMZ   Private archive of Mirjam Zadoff
PRG   Private archive of Renee Goddard
RGASPI   Russian State Archive of Socio-Political History (Russisches
             Staatsarchiv für Sozialpolitische Studien)
SPD   Social Democratic Party of Germany (Sozialdemokratische Partei
             Deutschlands)
USPD   Independent Social Democratic Party of Germany (Unabhängige
             Sozialdemokratische Partei Deutschlands)
VKPD   United Communist Party of Germany (Vereinigte Kommunistische
             Partei Deutschlands)

PROLOGUE

THE POLITICS OF LOVE

Marriage is but the union of free individuals based
on erotic affection. Thoroughly liberated from the
torturous earthly residue of material prerequisites,
usufruct, and consequences. All freedom and love.

—Otto Rühle, *Die Sozialisierung der Frau*, 1922

We'll make a twosome
That just can't go wrong. Hear me—
He loves and she loves and they love,
So won't you
Love me as I love you?

—Ira Gershwin, lyrics, "He Loves and She Loves," 1927

A Wartime Wedding in Hanover

On New Year's Eve in 1917, a young couple married at the registry office
in Linden, a town on the outskirts of Hanover. The marriage of the twenty-
two-year-old student from Berlin and the one-year-younger office clerk
from Linden was attended by a small gathering. A metalworker, the uncle
of the bride, acted as a witness, as did a local carpenter, a friend of the
couple.[1] While the newlyweds celebrated their wedding with a group of

family and friends in the proletarian community of Linden, the event caused a scandal in distant Berlin: there it was viewed as an affront that Werner Scholem, the son of a bourgeois Jewish family, had married the illegitimate daughter of a household servant who had formally renounced her membership in the church just recently.[2] Therefore, no member of the Scholem family showed up to celebrate with Werner and his bride, Emmy, née Wiechelt. Werner's younger brother Gerhard congratulated the couple by mail only a month later, and his new sister-in-law responded: "Thank you for your congratulations on our wedding; yours were the first, and I was very happy to receive them."[3]

Werner's father, Arthur Scholem, was enraged by this union and refused to meet his son ever again. It goes without saying that he also shunned his daughter-in-law, whom he had met briefly by chance a few months before.[4] He expected his family, and particularly his wife, Betty, to spurn this rebellious son as well. Nevertheless, some time after the wedding, Hans Hirsch, Betty's brother, sent presents to the couple and was subsequently struck by what he is said to have jocularly called an "Arthur Scholem thunderbolt."[5] So great was the paternal rancor that Arthur Scholem revised his will, reducing Werner's inheritance to the minimum amount required by law.[6]

The wedding that took place in the fourth year of the First World War was the climax of a dispute between father and son that had begun years before. Arthur Scholem could forgive his son for everything but this marriage to the pretty young office clerk. Whether Arthur knew it or not, he had played a role in the course of events leading to this wedding: with the decision to marry, Werner had professed not only the love and loyalty he felt for his girlfriend Emmy but also his rejection of his father and his father's worldview. "This is also why I am marrying," Werner had written his brother Gerhard several months earlier, "I want to burn all my bridges to the bourgeoisie."[7] It was an intentional decision to bring about a breach he knew would be irreversible. The events of the previous ten years and the experiences of his youth, cut short so abruptly by the war, made it easier for him to take the radical step of publicly celebrating the feelings that he and Emmy shared for one another.

Of Versatile Disposition

Werner Scholem was born in 1895, the third of four sons of Arthur Scholem, the owner of a successful Berlin printing business, and his wife, Betty.

FIGURE 1. Werner Scholem, 1896. Private archive of Renee Goddard.

When he was two years old, his mother gave birth to his brother Gerhard, who, throughout Werner's life, would remain the relative he felt closest to, next to their mother.

Decades later, this younger brother, who had long since taken the name "Gershom" and was then at the end of a long life as a professor for Jewish mysticism in Jerusalem, included a very personal portrait of the Scholem family in his autobiography.[8] He described the relationship between the sons and their father as "not a particularly close one" and explained this situation with the laconic remark that their father had suffered from heart disease and had therefore gone away for rather long stays in health spas every year. His wife Betty spent her days outside the home and attended to the bookkeeping of the family business. Still, she was quite close to the children, especially the two youngest, who spent a great deal of time buried in their books and often accompanied her on her frequent vacation trips.[9]

In many respects, the Scholems were a typical German Jewish family of the early twentieth century. Arthur's and Betty's parents had already advanced into the educated and propertied bourgeoisie by the middle of the preceding century. The Scholems lived well on the profits of a flourishing family business that allowed them to go on spa and leisure trips regularly and also to give the best education possible to the four sons: Reinhold, Erich, Werner, and Gerhard. Theirs was a childhood with all the amenities offered by the urban, bourgeois world of Berlin around 1900. The family apartment and the printing business were located only a few meters from one another near the Leipzigerstrasse, a street lined with department stores such as Tietz, Wertheimer, and Jandorf. The city surrounding them was a modern bustling metropolis, in which electric trams and the city railway were beginning to replace horse-drawn cars. Museums were being built, parks were laid out everywhere, and the Circus Busch opened its doors at Hackescher Markt.[10] Every Friday evening the family dined together with several close relatives, although these meals no longer had any religious content. Jewish holidays like Passover and Rosh Hashanah were only celebrated as large family gatherings, and on Yom Kippur, the holiest of Jewish holidays, Arthur Scholem went to work. "We were a typical, liberal, middle-class family in which assimilation to things German, as people put it at the time, had progressed quite far," noted Gershom Scholem.[11] Their Jewishness was merely the expression of the cultural and social network of friends and family in which they happened to live.

Little is known about Werner Scholem's childhood. Although Betty Scholem jotted down several of her recollections in 1931 during a trip to Jerusalem, these were primarily about the childhood of her youngest son, Gerhard.[12] When he was five years old, Werner took part in a series of scientific experiments conducted by the psychologist Arthur Wreschner, who was probably acquainted with the Scholems, showing his parents' openness to modern science. Wreschner had selected twenty-two people of various ages and levels of education in order to study "the reproduction and association of ideas" based on these people's reactions. The experiments required of the child were probably conducted in his parents' apartment. To no great surprise, the results of Werner's tests reflected the imagination of a five-year-old.[13]

Whereas the two oldest sons, Reinhold and Erich, lived up to their father's expectations and developed the same active interest in the family business and the German empire, the third son differed from the rest at a very early age. In his father's view, Werner was a defiant spirit and exhibited "a very versatile disposition," according to Gershom Scholem. "While I shot up to a considerable height, my brother remained rather small, but at an early age he developed sharp intellectual facial features which clearly reflected his nature. During our adolescent years we were to be faced with various shocks and conflicts. They pointed us in entirely different directions, yet again and again they brought us closer to each other." During their childhood and youth, the two younger brothers felt as close to one another as they felt distant from the two older ones. Gershom Scholem could not recall ever having had "a real conversation" with his elder brothers, Erich and Reinhold, and it is highly probable that this was also the case for Werner, who did not care much for his two older brothers then.[14]

Werner's "versatile disposition" prompted his parents to remove him from his school in Berlin, the Dorotheenstädtisches Realgymnasium, at the age of twelve and send him to Jewish boarding school in Wolfenbüttel, where he remained for nearly four years.[15] This school, the Samson-Freischule, grew out of a Talmud Torah school. Since the beginning of the nineteenth century, it had been considered an important Jewish institution of the Reform movement, where prominent figures of progressive German Judaism like Leopold Zunz and Isaak Marcus Jost were taught the ideals of the Enlightenment. However, in the course of the nineteenth century, the school developed into an educational institution in which the children with little Jewish background were raised as future members of the bourgeoisie.[16] Around 1900, when a great majority of the German Jewish population had successfully achieved social and economic advancement, the heads of the Samson-Freischule set a new educational goal. No longer would the school teach its pupils strictly within a context of Jewish religion and ethics, but it would also strive to awaken and cultivate in them a deep love for their fatherland and emperor.[17]

Forced to leave liberal Berlin for the oppressive and confining atmosphere of this provincial school, to which, as Gershom Scholem noted laconically, mainly "Jewish businessmen, cattle dealers, and master butchers in Western Germany" sent their children, Werner was confronted with a "considerable amount of religious hypocrisy and false patriotism, which he found quite repulsive. The school was run along strict German nationalistic lines, but some major aspects of the Jewish ritual, daily prayer, and a kosher kitchen, were maintained. During school vacations I would be treated to cynical lectures and outpourings on the subject of his school by my brother, who was beginning to test his rhetorical skills on me even then."[18] As the annual reports of the school confirm, the pupils enrolled there were indeed the sons of Jewish merchants, cattle traders, and butchers from the provinces, but also from Berlin. Very few of them sought to continue their education following *Realschule*, a six-year secondary school. With few exceptions, the 150 pupils were Jewish, and the number of non-Jewish pupils continued to decline in the years prior to the First World War, so it became essentially an exclusively Jewish institution. The curriculum included three hours each week for Hebrew and religion lessons, which was the only concession to the Jewishness of the school. The pupils' classes and essay topics dealt primarily with Schiller, Homer, and the *Nibelungenlied*. As in other German schools, commemoration days were celebrated with gymnastic events and flag parades, and the school honored the birthday of the emperor and the Duke of Braunschweig, the battles of Sedan and Quatre-Bras, and no less so the centennial of the 1812 Prussian Edict of Emancipation for German Jews.[19] It was here that Werner Scholem, who had lived until then in an almost completely secular world, was now involuntarily and intensively confronted with a German Jewish culture, which appeared incoherent and repulsive to him; in fact, this experience would shape his lifelong ambivalence toward Judaism.

These years in Wolfenbüttel probably caused the first major rupture between father and son. Werner subsequently rejected his father's Germanness as well as his bourgeois way of life, interspersed with randomly handed-down fragments of Jewish tradition. Arthur Scholem was a "short and stocky man, near-sighted and completely bald by the age of forty," who was enthusiastically involved in the Berlin gymnastics association, an athletics club, and showed little interest in Jewish religion and culture, even though he called baptism an "unprincipled and servile act" and disapproved of "mixed marriages."[20] He accepted printing jobs with Jewish content at his business from time to time, such as printing the Jewish weekly publication *Israelitische Wochenschrift*, but he categorically rejected having anything to do with Zionism—in contrast to his brother Theobald, whose print shop worked almost exclusively for the Zionist organization.[21]

The conflict between Arthur Scholem and his obstinate third son, which emerged in the years before the war, was characteristic of the rebellion of the generation of young Germans born around 1890, which was so widespread that it soon "became a cliché," as Peter Gay writes. Even though this conflict would not climax until the Weimar era, rebellion against the authority of the fathers hung long in the air.[22]

Most likely in early 1911, but possibly not until 1912, Werner Scholem had pressured his parents to the point where they agreed to take him out of the school in Wolfenbüttel before earning a diploma and bring him back to Berlin.[23] What awaited the fifteen-year-old in the metropolis was a growing center of Jewish culture with academic, literary, cultural, and political organizations, on the one hand, and an active Socialist movement in and around the working class districts of Neukölln and Wedding, on the other.[24] Between these two innovative and lively poles, Werner initially chose to become active in the Zionist movement. His brother felt that the political aspect of Zionism had attracted Werner, but that he never delved any deeper into Zionism.[25] In any case, it was through Werner that Gerhard first came into contact with Zionism. The Zionist organization Werner chose to become involved in was the oppositional youth group Jung Juda, which Gerhard later adopted as his political and ideological home. For a while the brothers attended together the events of the small group, which had been founded by Zionist student organizations and to which twenty to thirty youths of various backgrounds belonged: some came from the German bourgeoisie and others had Orthodox and often Eastern Jewish backgrounds. There, for the first time, the two brothers met observant Jews, whose Judaism was rooted in religious tradition.[26]

At the end of 1912, Werner announced that he had "found a broader, more comprehensive sphere of activity" and became a member of the Sozialdemokratische Arbeiterjugend (Young Social Democratic Workers).[27] Gershom Scholem noted with amusement that, between him and his brother, things sometimes "came to blows because he tried to force me to listen to Socialist speeches of his own devising, which he delivered to an imaginary audience while standing on a chair—an enterprise that I resolutely opposed." The younger brother had other interests apart from those of historical materialism, "the most massive forms of which made so much sense to my brother that he would have loved to pound them into me."[28] At the time Gerhard was interested in Orthodox Judaism, attended religious services regularly, and began to study Hebrew and traditional religious literature, the Mishnah, Gemara, and Torah. He even became a member of the Agudat Israel, an organization of Orthodox Judaism, which he left in 1914 for Zionist reasons. So it happened that the two brothers had already begun to develop in opposite directions at the respective ages of fifteen and seventeen. "Why was the one brother fascinated by German social democracy, while the other was captivated by the Jewish cause?" asked Gershom Scholem in an interview he gave in the winter of 1973–1974. "I don't have an answer to this. These are personal decisions, the secret of which one can hardly fathom."[29]

Werner's political activities soon led to open conflict with his father. "One day in 1913, my father came into his office and found that one of his typesetters had placed on his desk a clipping of an item from the socialist daily *Vorwärts*," recalls Gershom Scholem in his memoirs. The newspaper story reported on "my brother's activity in the Arbeiterjugend [Young Social Democratic Workers]. Coming from his own firm, this act, which was evidently intended as an ironic comment on the 'capitalist employer,' made my father very angry." The employee, Ebel, himself a Social Democrat, had "wanted to put one over on his old master," so he pointed out a notice in the newspaper to him, announcing that his son would be speaking before nightshift workers. A quarrel ensued, in which once again the rebellious son was bossed about or, as his father saw it, made to see reason.[30] "If I had been Werner," noted Gerhard in his diary, "I would have already run away ten times and would have tried to survive without the 'family.' You see, for us, nothing remains of the Jewish family. . . . Hopefully things go differently for me someday."[31]

Defiant Love

In the fall of 1913, after less than two years in Berlin, Werner Scholem was again sent to a boarding school. This time his parents chose a private school in Hanover, where he was to prepare as a day pupil for the graduation exams required to earn his secondary school diploma (*Abitur*). However, the paternal banishment to the seemingly apolitical province did not have the desired

FIGURE 2. An outing to Tegel by functionaries of the Young Social Democrats of Berlin
in the spring of 1913 (Werner Scholem, standing, third from left).
Private archive of Renee Goddard.

effect. Instead of waning, Werner Scholem's political activism began to take
on real contour and content in Hanover. Soon after his arrival in the city, he
felt himself drawn away from the school on Leopoldstrasse and his apartment
on Sophienstrasse, both located in the middle-class center of Hanover, and
attracted instead to the east side, to Linden,[32] a community that had once
been on the outskirts of the city but by then had grown together with it and
was years later incorporated into it. It was there, in Linden, that Werner
found his first political stage—and met Emmy Wiechelt.

Separated from the former royal capital of the Hanoverian kings by a
river, Linden was a completely different world. Although otherwise rich in

detail, the 1921 Baedeker guidebook on Hanover and the German North
Sea coast mentions the relatively large quarter only briefly. In the "commercial city district of Linden" the visitor could climb to "the panoramic sum-
mit of the Lindener Berg [the area's highest hilltop] in a few minutes."[33]
The guidebook did not find it necessary to mention the view the visiting
tourist strolling about the city would encounter there, namely, a densely
built industrial settlement, in which row upon row of crowded four-story
brick structures were separated from one another only by narrow, dark
courtyards; a quarter with no room for gardens, avenues, boulevards, or
squares.

This residential area was surrounded by a ring of smokestacks. In close
proximity factories were producing tires, machinery, woodwork, rubber,
corsets, asphalt, meat, sausage, and bed feathers. There were weaving and
spinning mills, a lime kiln, an iron foundry, and a brewery. In the middle
of the nineteenth century, what had been a farming settlement rapidly
developed into an industrial village intended to spare the bourgeois villas,
palaces, and parks of Hanover the noise and pollution of industrialization.
With each new factory more company-owned housing was built for the
workers, with each unit no larger than fifty to sixty square meters. Once
the entrepreneurs built these houses, they invested little in their upkeep,
and the buildings quickly fell into disrepair.[34]

Within sixty years, from 1852 to 1910, the population in Linden mush-
roomed from 5,000 to 73,000 inhabitants. With this rapid increase in population, the labor movement also experienced growing popularity starting at
the end of the nineteenth century. When Werner Scholem first arrived in
1913, he did not find the famous "Red Linden" of the Weimar Republic,
but a number of associations, cooperatives, and meeting houses already
existed there,[35] and in early October, Werner met a young woman who was
active in the Linden labor movement: Emmy Wiechelt.[36]

Emmy was born on 20 December 1896 in Braunschweig, where she had
a difficult childhood. Her father, a pastor's son, had refused to marry her
mother, Emma Martha Rock, a seventeen-year-old household servant.[37] So
her mother left daughter Emmy in the care of a neighboring family until
she finally found a man who was willing to marry her and accept her illegitimate child, a worker in the Continentale Reifen- und Gummifabrik, a rubber and tire manufacturer. Thus, at the age of nine, Emmy, who had until
then been known simply as "the illegitimate one," moved to Linden with
her mother and stepfather. Reportedly, she was never happy there.[38]

FIGURE 3. Emmy and her mother, Emma Rock, around 1900.
Private archive of Renee Goddard.

When Emmy Wiechelt met the Jewish pupil from Berlin in the fall of
1913, she had already been a member of the Young Social Democratic
Workers for two years. She became the head of the local Linden group
when she was sixteen and a member of the organization's leadership in the
Hanover city and rural district a year later. Emmy, who had a business-
school diploma and worked as an employee in a fish shop, attended evening
courses and lectures in order to earn her *Abitur* degree and thus qualify
herself for university study. In 1913 she became the head of the education
section of the young workers and met Werner Scholem in this capacity,
having recruited him to give presentations and lectures. The two young
people fell in love and, after only a few weeks, became engaged on Christmas of that same year.[39]

Werner Scholem kept this thoroughly unacceptable liaison secret from
his family and even his younger brother for months. Not until September

1914 did he inform Gerhard in a letter that, "by the way, in eight days I am moving to my mother-in-law's—I became engaged last Christmas—in Linden, Struckmeyerstr. 6, IVe. Please send your scribbles there from here on in." In answer to the curiosity expressed in his brother's reply, Werner wrote that his "babe" was a "nice and clever girl," interesting, with a tendency toward anarchism, and possessing "amazing writing talent. That she is pretty is proven by the fact that yesterday she was doggedly chatted up and chased-after six times within the space of an hour, including by a colonel in front of whom she spat!"[40]

Despite the secrecy, the news of Werner's move into the small, cramped working-class apartment where Emmy lived with her mother, her stepfather, and her stepsister soon reached the ears of Arthur Scholem. On 14 November 1914, Werner wrote Gerhard, who apparently had not been able to keep this scandalous news to himself: "You will know that, through one of the spies he uses to watch me, our Lord of Beuthstr. 6 smelled a rat concerning my whereabouts. He reacted angrily to this and stated in a letter that the intention had been to 'catch' me and 'I, in my stupidity' let it happen."[41] What enraged the father was not the fact that the son lived as a subtenant with his future mother-in-law and had not told him about this development. Was his main concern about Werner's intention to marry a non-Jewish woman the disapproval that this would meet with the Scholem relatives? Gershom Scholem saw a contradiction in this and maintained in retrospect that the paternal ideology "ought to have made him welcome a mixed marriage."[42] For his part, Werner was convinced that the real reason for the paternal anger was, as he noted in a letter to his brother, quoting a popular song of the time: "Sure, since my bride has no money, it was all about the good old saying: We need no mama-mom-in-law . . . without money, without money . . . ?! If she, the mama-mom-in-law, had dough, then I, 'a son from a good family' as our Lord officially called me, would have been able to keep living there. As it is, out of that house! I, the son from a good family . . . , hereby vamoose officially."[43]

The decision to "vamoose" officially did not come out of thin air two months after the outbreak of the First World War, which had abruptly changed the sense and reality of life for an entire generation. Having just been a middle-class secondary-school pupil anticipating a parentally financed education in a German university city, Werner Scholem now found himself confronted with a future in the trenches. For him and countless other young men who enthusiastically entered the war or were drafted

FIGURE 4. Emmy Wiechelt, 1914. Private archive of Renee Goddard.

against their will, this future meant the loss of self-determination, of perspectives, and of everyday normality. The war, which polarized and radicalized German society, also became the backdrop for Werner's decision to move to proletarian Linden and to break with the warmongering bourgeoisie and, not the least, with his patriotic father.

Emmy Wiechelt was Werner Scholem's way out of the bourgeois world, which he detested increasingly, while he represented her rescue from the working-class quarter that she had been trying to flee. Together they saw their future in the Socialist revolution and a new social order; or as their daughter would put it years later: "It was natural that she should be attracted to the young, brilliant firebrand of a socialist orator and that he should fall for his vision of the working class girl—blond, hard-nosed, neat, with her clean white collars. He believed that the future lay with her class, not his."[44]

This love story started in the fall of 1913 and was officially consecrated four years later when Werner and Emmy married on New Year's Eve 1917. They chose to enter the bourgeois institution of marriage, while many of their party comrades and role models like Rosa Luxemburg had decided to live in nonmarital love relationships. It is somewhat ironic that Werner Scholem accomplished the desired, irreversible break with the bourgeois German Jewish world of his parents by entering into the bourgeois bond of matrimony. Nevertheless, this marital union was never exclusively monogamous, in accordance with the Communist sexual ethic and—with the birth of two daughters, Edith and Renate, in 1918 and 1923, respectively—Communist family politics and child-rearing practices. The discrepancy between tradition and innovation clung to this marriage from the day the couple was united at the registry office, and it had a lasting impact on its nature.

A shared political utopia was the binding force of this romantic relationship, but, like all utopias, it proved very difficult to implement in daily reality and in family life. Not surprisingly, Werner Scholem defined his marital and family life as the exact opposite of what he had seen and experienced in his parental home. Nevertheless, gender-specific roles were adopted in his new family, as were conventional guidelines for raising children. Gerhard once remarked that almost nothing about his parental home reflected the ideals of Jewish family life, while bourgeois conventions permeated its each and every thread.[45] Werner Scholem instinctively brought this heritage to his new life and new family, whereas the proletarian and far less self-assured traditions of his wife played a subordinate role.

FIGURE 5. Renate (on the left) and Edith Scholem in English exile in 1936.
Private archive of Renee Goddard.

Werner and Emmy Scholem invested all their strength, creativity, and imagination in their shared political utopia. They gave no thought to the way in which their private lives and that of their children would play out in a postrevolutionary society. Yet the shadow cast by the expected and anticipated revolution, along with its messianic potential, proved to be a heavy burden. Since it was not clear which social realities would change and what the new world would look like, all that really counted was the present; the future, even the near future, remained uncertain and seemed utopian. This time vacuum was filled with frenetic activity and impatient expectation: the revolution would come, had to come! However, the years passed, the children grew older, and the relationship between their parents began to suffer from the discrepancies of a life deeply preoccupied with the future and simultaneously devoid of one.

Once the National Socialist dictatorship began and all revolutionary energies in Germany were channeled into a nationalist counterrevolution, these hopes for the future were relegated to the past. When Emmy and Werner Scholem were arrested by the Gestapo in the spring of 1933, their relationship and family, like their hopes, became part of the past. They existed only in memories, and the couple was robbed of nearly all artifacts, insignia, and material props of a shared life. As active revolutionaries, Werner and Emmy Scholem lived from the start, even during the First World War, in constant fear of house searches; therefore they regularly destroyed personal and political documents. Everything that remained, which amounted to the harmless and not incriminatory belongings of the family, was confiscated and very probably destroyed by the Gestapo in 1933.

Despite many difficulties, their marriage lasted for twenty-seven years, during which its form and meaning changed, as did its orientation between tradition and reform. What today appears to be a generally conservative allocation of roles—Werner pursued a career while his wife's activities remained in the shadows—reveals itself upon closer examination to have been a complex constellation, one that the couple itself perceived as being modern, in keeping with the times, and individualistic. Werner described his family's state in a letter written in March 1931 to his brother in Palestine: "Personally there is otherwise nothing to report. Mother will faithfully give you an account. I am continually concerned about Emmy, who for years has not been actually sick but also never truly well. She really ought to take a break from the constant work at the office, which she has been doing for twenty years, and to recuperate. If she can just survive the next few years.—Edith is already a real *Backfisch* [literally, "baked fish," slang for a teenage girl], unfortunately without any interest in the sciences, although she is not stupid. The little one, Renate, is a *Goite ohne Beimischung* [unmixed gentile]. Don't yet know what will turn out there. This, a portrait of a family of today. I feel alive in the summer when I go climbing."[46]

The family Werner describes is a typical "new family" of the Weimar Republic, in which the "new married woman," besides being gainfully employed, was usually the mother of at most two children.[47] Emmy's years of uninterrupted employment, which sometimes provided the sole income for the family and from which she took only a few days off at the births of her daughters, were also consistent with this image, as were her catastrophic experiences with abortion and birth control, which made her chronically ill. On the other hand, Werner's portrait points to the aspects of this family that did not correspond with the Communist ideal of a social utopia. For example, although he considered his Jewish background immaterial, he described his small blond daughter as a *Goite ohne Beimischung*, and he mentioned mountain climbing, his regular escapes into the Tyrolean Alps, which he undertook as a member of the Jewish section of the alpine associa-tion Deutscher Alpenverein Berlin.

The central figure in this book must be seen and understood against the background of his complex and contradictory family—bourgeois Jewish and proletarian gentile. Werner Scholem was an extremely prominent Ger-man politician for a short time in the 1920s and then thoroughly forgotten in the postwar period, a man whose biography does not fit neatly into the German, Jewish, or Communist Party narratives of the first half of the last century. Therefore it sheds light in various directions.

Prominently Forgotten

In his biography of the German general and opponent of Hitler Kurt von Hammerstein, Hans Magnus Enzensberger presents a fictional dialogue between his subject and Werner Scholem. It begins: "Herr Scholem, I've come to see you because your name still means something in Germany." Scholem answers, "That must be a mistake. You're probably confusing me with my brother Gershom. He was cleverer than me and emigrated in good time. I can well imagine that he made something of himself in Palestine."[48] Once the most famous member of the Scholem family—a child star, as it were, of the Weimar Republic and the youth revolts of the early 1920s—the journalist and politician Werner Scholem fell into oblivion after 1945. Denounced as a Trotskyist and party enemy in East Germany and regarded as an unwelcome reminder of the radical Communists of the Weimar Republic in West Germany, Werner Scholem slipped out of the collective German memory almost entirely.[49] However, in West German research on the labor movement, the historian and political scientist Hermann Weber, starting in the 1960s, mentioned Werner Scholem time and again in his writings on the KPD and outlined his biography.

In 1973 the long-forgotten Scholem caught the attention of Martin Broszat, who had recently become the director of the Munich Institut für

Zeitgeschichte. At that time Broszat said in his introduction to a talk being
given by Gershom Scholem that his brother's history was "for long stretches
of time [a] still unknown, unwritten chapter of contemporary history."[50] In
1980, a biography of Ernst Thälmann appeared in the German Democratic
Republic (GDR), depicting him as a hero of the workers' state. In this hagi-
ography of the non-Jewish, Stalinst proletarian, Werner Scholem, almost
his direct antithesis, appears but does not come off well. The authors
described him as a nonobjective and unrealistic petit bourgeois who ended
as a left-wing sectarian.[51] It took another ten years, on the fiftieth anniversary of his death, before a short article appeared with the title "The Fate of
Werner Scholem" in the East German newspaper *Neues Deutschland*. In this
piece, the historian Reiner Zilkenat attributed this neglect to the East German dictatorship, which he argued had deliberately concealed the history
of the Jewish Trotskyist. He also urged for the writing of a biography of this
German revolutionary, whose name was mentioned only when "argument
occurred about the political self-image" in the young KPD.[52]

The fact that Werner Scholem began to find his way into both public
German memory and Jewish Israeli memory starting in the late 1960s is
primarily due to his brother and his autobiographical writings.[53] Gershom
Scholem opens the famous and widely read memoir of his youth, *From
Berlin to Jerusalem*, with the following dedication: "To the memory of my
brother Werner, born in December 1895 in Berlin, murdered in June 1940
in Buchenwald." Of the many friends and relatives whom he had lost
because of the Nazi regime and the world war, he decided to dedicate the
book to his older brother, because he symbolized the loss of his homeland,
the place where they shared their youth as members of the generation that
turned away from their fathers and toward the utopias of Zionism and
Socialism. Werner and Gerhard started in the same place and distanced
themselves from it over the years, each in his own direction. Despite the
differences in their life experiences and the opposing decisions that they
made, they were linked by a nostalgic memory of their youth.

Along with Gershom Scholem's unavoidably one-sided depiction of his
elder brother in his memoirs, their correspondence and Gershom's diary
entries about Werner offer a fuller and more nuanced picture of their relationship, which continued to develop after Gershom departed for Palestine.
Later, their mother, Betty Scholem, came to play a key role as family chron-
icler. Expressing irony, criticism, and concern, but also great affection, she
documented the rise, fall, and tragic end of her son and the fate of his

family. These reports, which she sent in her regular letters to Gershom in Palestine, bear extraordinary witness to Werner Scholem's story—especially for the period between 1933 and 1940, the years of his persecution, arrest, and eventual murder. Itta Shedletsky, who prepared these letters for publication, assumes that Gershom Scholem wanted them to be published for just this reason. However, they were published posthumously.[54]

Quiet Heroines

"Set up new heroes for our admiration," demanded Virginia Woolf in 1939 in her programmatic text on writing biography.[55] Werner Scholem, whose meteoric career and brief good fortune plummeted into a series of tragic events when he was only thirty-seven years old, was a modern Job, whose suffering occurred unspectacularly and quietly. Fully in the sense advocated by Virginia Woolf, he was surrounded by "new heroines" who played a key role in his biography. Granted, they left behind even fewer traces of themselves than the main protagonist, and, as a result, their voices are quieter and even harder to register. Often their stories are found mirrored or recalled only in the texts of others.

Nevertheless, the few letters and documents that still exist in Emmy Scholem's meticulous handwriting show that she was a self-confident and intelligent woman who summoned great courage to overcome the obstacles posed by her birth and background. At times she acted as the wife alongside her husband, keeping him free of obligations, writing his articles when he was busy standing at the speaker's podium, and deciding what was to happen with their children. At the same time, she was one of the women who shaped and changed Germany and particular Berlin of the 1920s, women who were "brave, innovative, sometimes also witty and shrewd."[56] Serving for years as a secretary in the Communist Party headquarters, she felt at home in the Communist milieu of these years and pursued her own commitment and her own interests within the party. With her braided hair neatly wrapped around her head and no makeup, she was the perfect exemplar of the Communist woman, as the more rustic agitator, a head of the German Communist Party in the mid-1920s, Ruth Fischer embodied it. Her features were, however, finer, her wardrobe more elegant, and her smile shy in a coquettish way, contrary to that of "Comrade Ruth."

The catastrophic events of 1933 placed the active role of the partnership in her hands, and she played it in her own headstrong way, greatly influencing the lives of her husband and two daughters. The relationship between Werner and Emmy Scholem is extraordinarily well documented for the more than seven years he spent in prison and concentration camps. Even though her numerous letters were written with the censor in mind, they reveal insight into the partnership, the handling of the children, the family structure, and possible plans for a shared future shadowed by persecution rather than imbued with hope for revolution.[57] The deeply ingrained fear of revealing any personal or political information influenced the life of the family after Emmy and her daughters fled to London in 1934, after Werner's murder in July 1940, and even after the war ended in Europe in the spring of 1945. Emmy Scholem never broke her silence and had trained her older daughter, Edith, early in her life to "keep mum": name no names, reveal no details. Not until shortly before her death did Edith Capon, née Scholem, who as a teenager in Berlin had been well informed about the political and private lives of her parents, agree to give an interview in which she revealed much about her family history.[58]

The younger daughter, Renate—or Renee, the name she later gave herself as an actress in England—had spent the greater part of her childhood living with Emmy's mother and stepfather in Hanover and, according to her, had stubbornly rebelled against this educational measure imposed by her parents. Since she was not willing "to keep her mouth shut," neither her parents nor her sister told her anything—not telling anything to the child, who was with her parents and sister only for limited periods of time in Berlin, but also not to the grown woman, who was given the letters written by her father in prison and concentration camp only after her mother's death. In radio plays and essays, she began to work through her memories to make the history of her family plausible and tellable—not the least for herself. Since Renee is the last living protagonist, her account of the family history—things expressed, remembered, kept silent, and forgotten—as well as her own story as the continuation of her family's history have been an invaluable source for this biography.[59]

Insights, remembered and recounted, and also factual, as well as family photographs enhance this portrait, too. Among the few documents of Werner's in the Scholem papers is a photo album he made during or shortly after the First World War. The arrangement and choice of photos in this album reflects his perspective on the women in the family and on a few friends; thus it is an important supplement to the narrative sources.[60]

Like the photo album, the structure of this book is an arrangement of public and private views of Werner Scholem the politician, father, husband, brother, son, and friend. Those aspects of his biography that are of interest to cultural history focus both on the "figure" created by Scholem's own view of himself and the perspective of others and also on the relations and feelings that link the various protagonists to one another. What results is an unusual picture of German Jewish experience in the early twentieth century, one that serves as a reminder of the multifold possibilities and experiences that were available in a country during times of revolution.

On the Biographical Intention

"I like biography far better than fiction myself: fiction is too free. In biography you have your little handful of facts, little bits of a puzzle, and you sit and think and fit 'em together this way and that, and get up and throw 'em down, and say damn, and go out for a walk. And it's really soothing; and when done, gives an idea of finish to the writer that is very peaceful. Of course, it's not really so finished as quite a rotten novel; it always has and always must have the incurable illogicalities of life about it. . . . Still, that's where the fun comes in."[61] With these words, the Scottish writer Robert Louis Stevenson described in June 1893 the pleasure he got from the "incurable illogicalities," those internal processes that are usually not reflected upon during the course of events in a person's life: changes, revisions, doubts, and reorientations. Yet it is precisely these inadvertent and incoherent aspects that pose difficulties for the biographer; not only must they be addressed and given structure, but a possible inherent sense should also be divined from them. Ultimately, however, the endeavor to bestow meaning to the whole of another person's actions and being is illusory.[62]

Like every historiographic undertaking, biographical writing involves conjecture and construct. There is always the danger that one piece or another of the puzzle will not lie where it should. What distinguishes a biography from a novel is the fact that the set pieces are not dreamed up. Only their arrangement and interpretation lie in the hands of the biographer, who feels bound to uphold the rules of historiography. However, unlike her protagonists, the biographer knows how the story ends and must be careful neither to interpret a life teleologically nor to employ a premature explanatory model in light of the subject's known successes and failures. Therefore, much speaks for unfurling a life primarily in chronological order and for describing—or at least attempting to describe—directional changes, corrections, or retrospection from the perspective of the protagonist.[63]

Writing biography has been repeatedly referred to as an art.[64] Indeed, from time to time it does resemble an effort to paint a portrait with the model absent, meaning that the model and the corresponding environment have to be (re)constructed using every available detail. Therefore, the finished portrait not only is a result of this process but is at the same time influenced by the style of the painter and the painter's own times.

This biography is a work of cultural history, due, first, to the personality and interests of the author, and, second, to the zeitgeist that prevailed at its writing. The culturally historical nature of the work results from the diversity of sources and perspectives used and from the effort to locate Werner Scholem in the dense social network of his manifold relations, particularly in his contacts with relatives and friends. The emotional bonds that a person enters into, changes, ends, or redefines over a lifetime reflect that individual's own changeable identities, just as they also influence them. The diversity of these relations points to the changing roles people assume in social contexts. Precisely in light of the theatrical quality of life—especially a public one—the interaction between small details of private life and the large stages of the Weimar Republic is a major focus here. In this way, this biography is a prism of the history of both a generation and a milieu.[65]

Werner Scholem's biography could be told in many ways. However, two alternative perspectives are likely to be particularly fruitful when used together: that of the politician and revolutionary, a prominent public figure created by Werner himself and redefined by his public, and that of his networks of friends and family members, networks that in the precarious years of the First World War, the Weimar Republic, and the National Socialist dictatorship compose the fabric of his life.

One of the inescapable anomalies of Werner Scholem's life was that, while he had broken with his Jewish heritage, as had many other Jewish Communists, nonetheless he was perceived first and foremost as a Jew by the public—his opponents, followers, and comrades alike. As a consequence, a complex identity emerged as an amalgam of his self-perception and the perceptions of him by others. For example, Scholem saw himself as a German Communist, while in the eyes of others he was the perfect example of a Jewish revolutionary. Another such inner contradiction was that he had made much ado about distancing himself from his father and Judaism but continued to maintain close contact with his brother, his mother, other family members, and Jewish friends. The manifold tensions created by the coexistence of Werner Scholem's different sides, private and public, are thus the theme of this book.

The years 1914–1920, the period in Werner Scholem's life when he formed and developed his political self, are those first examined here. Important for his development was the intense exchange of ideas with his brother Gerhard. For both brothers, the roots of radicalism lay in the dramatic years of the First World War, which deprived them of hopes for a future. The structure of this radicalism drew them close together while at the same time their views became increasingly incompatible. In order to understand adequately the importance of both their mutual influence and their differentiation, the first part of this book focuses on the brothers' development. This approach also compensates for the fact that little is known about Werner's youth, and few sources are available, with the exception of the letters to his brother Gerhard. As a result, this first part often presents itself as a biography of *both* brothers.

The second part takes a look at the public figure of the young and successful politician Scholem, who was constantly forced to negotiate his self-image as a Communist with his outward image as a Jew. Not only was he accused of being too young and inexperienced, he was also criticized for his Jewish origins, which were apparently evident in both his name and his purportedly "typical" Jewish physiognomy. Even though he went on the offensive in countering each of these anti-Semitic attacks, they did not abate. On the contrary, they only became more encompassing and universal. Werner Scholem's early and massive criticism of the Stalinization of the German Communist movement not only resulted in his expulsion from the party but also saddled him with the reputation of a dissident incapable of allegiance, loyalty, and party discipline, much like that of his role model Leon Trotsky.

The third and final part of this book starts in the winter of 1933. Werner Scholem was among the first to be arrested under the National Socialist dictatorship, a circumstance that was very much a consequence of his political role in the Weimar Republic, as was his extraordinarily complex and grievous story of persecution. Ostracized as a dissident by a great majority of his former comrades, he could count almost solely on his wife, his children, and the Scholem family: Emmy, Betty, and Gershom Scholem sought help in every conceivable direction in their effort to secure his release.

The epilogue of his story—and hence the conclusion of this book—begins with his murder in Buchenwald concentration camp in June 1940. For Emmy Scholem and her two daughters, the memory of the man who was her husband and their father played and plays a defining role. This was also true for Gershom Scholem, whose affinity with the messianic movements of the seventeenth century was rooted to no small degree in the fascination that his numerous Jewish contemporaries felt for Communism.[66]

The finished puzzle of this biography is now ready to be presented. After being shifted around a bit, the various pieces have each found their proper place. To return to Stevenson, a biography can never be completed in the way that a novel comes to its definite end. However—with a nod to our constant fascination with the "incurable illogicalities" of a life—in any event such an ending would not be in line with the biographical intention of this book.

I

TWO UTOPIAS SEATED
AT ONE TABLE

To find it, to find the right thing, for which it is worthy
to live, to be organized, and to have time: that is why
we go, why we cut new, metaphysically constitutive
paths, summon what is not, build into the blue, and
build ourselves into the blue, and there seek the true,
the real, where the merely factual disappears.

—Ernst Bloch, *The Spirit of Utopia*, 1915–1917

There's so many different worlds
So many different suns
And we have just one world
But we live in different ones

—Dire Straits, "Brothers in Arms," 1985

Betty's Premonition

Perhaps Betty Scholem had a premonition when she wrote a skit called *Ex Oriente Lux* in November 1904 on the occasion of the wedding of her brother-in-law Theobald Scholem. Her sprightly pen, her Berlin humor, and her great interest in books show she had the makings of a journalist or editor. But the wife of the printer Arthur Scholem, like many bourgeois women at the turn of the century, if she worked at all, was expected to work in the family business. She expressed her creativity and wit in other contexts: in letters, poems, and skits, which reflected her empathetic, sometimes ironic interest in close and distant relatives. Particularly the skits she wrote for weddings and other festivities in the years 1903 to 1908 earned her the reputation of the "indispensable family poet." The theatricals were performed by her four sons, whose ages ranged from barely seven to thirteen at the time of Theobold's marriage to Hedwig Levy.[1]

Appropriate to the occasion, *Ex Oriente Lux* pokes a bit of fun at Theobald Scholem's greatest passions: orientalism in general and Zionism in particular. His bookshelves were filled with studies on the Far East, Japan, China, India, and Tibet. The most important customer of his printing business was the Zionist Association for Germany, and his enthusiasm also extended to the Jewish gymnastic club Bar-Kochba, of which he was a founding member and in whose ranks he had performed for Theodor Herzl and the Basel Zionist Congress in 1903. Though his primarily anti-Zionist relatives thought of Theobald, who was ten years younger than Arthur, as the black sheep of the family, he enjoyed being the odd man out.[2]

Betty's skit, printed in the family shop for the wedding party, is a parody of Theobald's passions: an Arab, an Indian, a Chinese, and a Jew from Palestine appear in the play to congratulate the newlyweds.

Betty dressed her sons in imaginative costumes for these roles. As the Arab, thirteen-year-old Reinhold wore harem pants and a turban; Erich, who was about to celebrate his eleventh birthday, played the Chinese with a long braid, paper umbrella, and peacock feather; Werner, who would soon turn nine, wore a long curly wig and carried a shepherd's crook to play the Palestinian Jew; and Gerhard, the youngest at not quite seven, appeared as the Indian, dressed in a cloak and feather turban. These were the four illustrious figures who were journeying to Berlin to pay their respects to the "learned The-o-phil."

At one point the Arab, the Chinese, and the Indian get into a discussion about whether the honorable scholar is Confucian, Muslim, or Buddhist. But then "the Jewish lad" appears, a farmer from "the homeland of our ancestors," from the "country for which we mourn," and congratulates the "national Zionist." He ends the argument over Theobald's confessional membership in just a few words:

> What you all say is not true,
> Not true, not true, absolutely out-of-the-blue,
> For he has in his reachings
> Only but your fine teachings,
> From each the best to secure;
> So all things stay as they were.
> Theobald, as a modern Jew,
> Is naturally a Zionist, too.
> On his tie flaunts, highly bekoved
> The Mogen Doved—
> Round his belly on a chain
> There it is again!
> In the pocket of the coat
> Is a pad of notes;
> Some are empty and some, in turn,
> Are fully filled-out Schekelblätter

> (Was ihr alle sagt, das stimmt nicht,
> Stimmt nicht, stimmt nicht, ganz bestimmt nicht,
> Denn er hat ja unbeirrt
> Eure Lehren nur studiert,
> Um das Beste zu behalten;
> So bleibt alles hübsch beim alten.
> Als moderner Jude ist
> Theobald ein Zionist.
> Auf dem Schlips prangt höchst bekowed[3]
> S' Mogen-Dowed[4]—
> An der Kette, auf dem Bauch
> Sitzt es auch!

FIGURE 6. The Scholem brothers in *Ex Oriente Lux*, 1904. From left to right: Gerhard, Reinhold, Erich, and Werner. Israeli National Library, Archive Gershom Scholem.

In der Tasche von dem Rock
Steckt ein Block
Teils mit leeren, teils mit nettern
Schon beschriebenen Schekelblättern)[5]

Teasing her brother-in-law, Betty deliberately made Zionism, rather than Judaism, the fourth religion alongside the three "oriental" ones and at the same time satirized anti-Semites by having Gerhard ask, as he glances at the leather pouch hanging on Werner's side: "Do you have your pearls and diamond gemstones in the pouch?" Whereupon Werner answers in a broad Berlin dialect: "Tfillim[6] sinds, verstehste mich. Theo aber legt se nicht" (They're tefillin, you understand. But Theo doesn't put them on). Like many Zionists, Theobald Scholem was not religious and rejected traditional rites, including the use of phylacteries. At last, the four travelers from the Orient offer their congratulations to the bridal couple, whereby the Palestinian farmer concludes his greetings from the "old new land" by urging the couple to move there very soon and build a "good Jewish gymnasium"—since Jews in Berlin were at the time being thrown out of just such a sports facility.[7]

Betty Scholem could not have known that one of her four sons would follow a path similar to the one taken by his eccentric uncle and become a Zionist. Yet, that fall, a few months after the death of the author of *Alt-Neuland* (Old New Land) and the founder of political Zionism, Theodor Herzl, she might have been expressing a premonition about the conflicts that would someday affect her family, when, unlike Theobald, one of her sons, not content with representing Zionism in Germany, would actually immigrate to Palestine.[8] However, Betty apparently thought that the rebellious Werner, whom she had lovingly dressed as the biblical shepherd, would be the one who turned his back on Germany, as he was always butting heads with his father. Rather, her youngest son, Gerhard, was the one who, in mid-September 1923, packed his 2,000-book library, some tropical clothing, a mosquito net, and ten pounds sterling and made his way to Palestine, which had already changed so much that he didn't have to make a living either as a farmer or a shepherd. By then, Werner had become a nationally known politician in Germany. He was disappointed by Gerhard's decision in favor of the Orient over Germany and is reported to have said to him upon his departure: "It's too bad that a young person like you should waste his strength on such a thing, instead of offering to serve on behalf of the world revolution that is just around the corner."[9]

By then, fierce arguments over the revolutionary ideologies of the time—Communism and Zionism—had occurred in the Scholem household, not only leaving the parents alienated from their children, but also leaving the brothers alienated from each other. For as close as Werner and Gerhard had been during the Great War in their mutual opposition to it, their political concepts and their personal plans for their lives had pushed them apart. Nevertheless, Betty's premonition had been accurate: even if Werner felt less drawn to the mountains of Galilee than he did to the summits of the Tyrolean Alps, he was by far the most radical of her four sons, waged grim battles with his father, and was thus for a time a major role model for his younger brother. Werner's great love for extreme landscapes and for climbing in the Alps reflects his penchant for great challenges and radical aims.

Memories of the Summer of 1914

In February 1975, a few weeks before his eightieth birthday, the conservative, nationalist German writer Ernst Jünger sent a postcard to Jerusalem. The addressee was Gershom Scholem, who was a few years younger and whom he did not know personally. Jünger wrote that he often came across the name Scholem in the press; therefore he wondered whether "you are identical with my schoolmate (Hanover 1914)?"[10]

Gershom Scholem took his time to answer the postcard from Tübingen. A month and a half later he finally wrote a friendly letter in which he mentioned that he had "attentively studied" two of Jünger's books. He also congratulated him on his milestone birthday. In answer to Jünger's question, he added that he was not the same person as the schoolmate in question. "But strangely enough, my *brother* Werner, later a member of the Reichstag (who was murdered in 1940 in Buchenwald), did indeed live in Hanover from the fall of 1913 to the end of 1914, where he attended a so-called 'cram' school in preparation for the *Abitur* and was active in the Social Democratic 'young workers' (where he also found his later wife)." Did Jünger remember the appearance of his schoolmate? Werner "was small, also had (like me) a small, *scharfjüdisch* face, and was quite thin back then."[11]

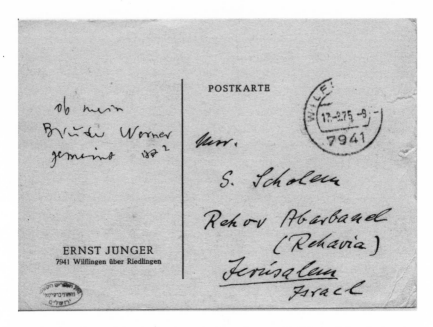

FIGURE 7. Copy of the postcard sent by Ernst Jünger with Scholem's handwritten notation "whether he means my brother Werner?" Israeli National Library, Archive Gershom Scholem.

Jünger responded immediately that the person he meant was "indeed" Werner Scholem. "With the exception of one other schoolmate, your brother is the only person whom I remember. He did not seem to me to be particularly small or lean, as you write, but unusually 'adult'—which may have been due above all to the intelligent physiognomy and a skeptical smile. Our relationship was one of ironical sympathy." The "intelligent physiognomy" of his former schoolmate prompted Jünger to express not only distress but also surprise at the news of Werner's murder in a concentration camp: "With the sound assessment of the situation that I credited him with, I assumed that he, apparently like others in his family, had not missed the last train out."[12] Scholem reacted promptly and crossly to this remark, which demonstrated Jünger's ignorance, by writing that he himself had left Germany already in 1923—and not, as Jünger implied, at the last moment. "You are surprised that he did not get away in time 'apparently like others in his family.' It wasn't like that. He was one of the first to be arrested in the night of the Reichstag fire. . . . My brother, the radical Socialist, was convinced that, as a veteran of the world war, nothing could happen to him. This is now difficult to imagine, but these ideas were widely held. Everyone who corresponded at the time with family members in Germany has a sad story to tell."[13]

After this letter, the correspondence broke off until Ernst Jünger again contacted Gershom Scholem a year later in June 1976, writing that he had seen Scholem on German television and had discovered, "even after sixty-two years," how closely Gershom resembled his brother: "His image is branded in my mind much more clearly than those of the other classmates. This may well be because he was an adult compared to us pubertal boys and, as I have now discovered to my astonishment from his vita, already politically active. Only the teacher noticed it, apparently in a type of anxious sympathy. I can imagine the concerns it must have caused your father."[14] Gershom Scholem answered with a polite letter, saying that he had only realized in "advanced age" that he was beginning to resemble Werner.[15]

Once again the correspondence came to a halt until 1981 when Gershom Scholem took the initiative in order to address a topic that mattered a great deal to him, prompted by a letter from Theodor Adorno, written in 1951, which he came across while perusing old correspondence. Adorno wrote that, in the summer of 1940, members of the German General Staff in Paris, in which Ernst Jünger served, had devised a plan to save Walter Benjamin.[16] Gershom Scholem asked Jünger about the plan, but the latter was evasive in his response, noting only that it was indeed possible but he could no longer remember. "Thus, I can hardly contribute anything to your investigation," wrote Jünger toward the end of his letter and changed the subject. Although his memory did not serve him well concerning his military assignment in Paris during the Second World War, he could not stop thinking about Werner Scholem and the brief time they spent together in the same classroom. "Hopefully you are doing well. It is strange how the early years of youth push to the fore in advanced age—so I see your brother ever more clearly, as if he were sitting next to me on the school bench in Hanover."[17]

A little more than six months later, Gershom Scholem died. He had mentioned the correspondence with Jünger in his autobiography, published in 1977, shortly after their first written contact. In it he had written that Jünger had been one of Werner's schoolmates. Several years later in the

Hebrew edition he added that after the war Jünger had become "one of the best writers of the German right."[18]

Ernst Jünger also mentioned his former classmate in the final volume of his diary, which was published several months before his death. On 4 July 1995, just days before the fifty-fifth anniversary of Werner Scholem's death, Jünger, who was now a century old, noted in his diary: "Why did Werner Scholem appear before me this morning—his presence was more than dreamlike."[19] This is followed by a sentimental depiction of his former classmate, one that adds little to anything previously written by Gershom Scholem.[20] Why indeed did Werner Scholem, a Jewish Communist murdered by the Nazis, appear regularly and even more frequently with age in the dreams of this prominent man of the intellectual right? Perhaps it is due to Werner's tragic fate, of which Jünger learned in his correspondence with Gershom, as well as to the German Jewish story he represented. Certainly the memory of Werner Scholem was closely linked to a formative and decisive period in the lives of Jünger and his entire generation: the First World War.

Ernst Jünger, who was six months older than Werner Scholem and had also changed schools several times, spent a month at the end of 1913 in the French Foreign Legion in North Africa. Upon his return, his father sent him to Hanover to the Gildemeister Institute, where he was to prepare for his *Abitur*. As he later recalled, this boarding school was a "cram school for students who had been either chucked out of the state schools or had flunked them."[21] In an autobiographical novel, in which he calls the facility the Tegtmayer Institute, Jünger describes the place as also being a catch basin for teachers who were just as unsuccessful as their students: "School fees were high; so you only saw the children of wealthy parents at Tegtmayer—this was yet another thorn in the side of the teachers who, on top of it all, taught sullenly. They had one thing in common with the students: they felt out of place there. So, the hours were limited to cramming. Success was not to be denied for the reputation of the Institute was based on that."[22] Jünger remembered Werner Scholem, with whom he shared a school bench, particularly well. Among other things, he recalled an incident in German literature class when one day the teacher handed Werner back his essay with the following words: "Scholem—I am warning you for the last time." At the time, the incident made no sense to Jünger, but in retrospect he came to the following conclusion: "Probably Scholem, who was much further developed intellectually than we were, had used the essay to inject nihilistic or Communist slogans, which was not tolerated even at cram school."[23]

In the warmongering atmosphere of these months, Ernst Jünger read Friedrich Nietzsche's *The Will to Power* and was introduced to the concept of the *Übermensch*, which was highly influential in forming his political opinions. In contrast, Werner Scholem was in contact with proletarians in Hanover and spent his after-school hours with party comrades, friends, and his fiancée Emmy in the town of Linden. The students at the Gildemeister Institute immediately returned to Hanover in response to the general mobilization, which took place during the summer break.[24] There they found their German literature teacher rather despondent; he could neither share nor understand the euphoria of his students. "The outbreak of war," wrote Jünger in his memoirs, "was the last day of school for most of us; it was buzzing in the classroom like a swarm of bees. Schmidtchen was sad—he said: 'You don't know the horrors of war.'"[25] For the majority of the boys, who—like Jünger—had checkered school careers behind them, the war meant the long-sought-after release from school life; volunteers were expected to be given what was known as "emergency" *Abitur* exams, an easier, simplified version of the graduation exams that was usually not hard to pass. One of the few who wanted nothing to do with all of this was Werner Scholem. He turned his back on the war enthusiasm of his classmates and advocated unconditional pacifism. At that juncture, in Jünger's words, "We saw each other for the last time after war was declared. We deregistered from Gildemeister in order to scatter ourselves in the caserns. . . . On that day I had just come from the barber; he took note of that with a skeptical smile: 'The Germanic lad anoints his hair before the fight.'"[26]

Werner Scholem's pacifism was contrary not only to the attitude of his classmates but also to the majority opinion of his party and its supporters. In late July, the Social Democrats had still been holding antiwar demonstrations throughout Germany.[27] At the same time, representatives of the Social Democratic Party of Germany (SPD, Sozialdemokratische Partei Deutschlands) participated in a meeting of the International Socialist Office in Brussels. There, the majority of the European left appeared confident that the war could still be prevented. The German government, it was wrongly believed, wanted to avoid war and maintain peace.[28] However, only a few days later, in early August when Germany mobilized and declared war on France, it became clear that they had been deceiving themselves. In the frenzy of war enthusiasm the bulk of Social Democrats did not want to be

"men without a fatherland" (*vaterlandlose Gesellen*). They succumbed to
the pressure of the emperor and the bourgeois parties and fell in line behind
the official stance of the government, according to which Germany found
itself in a defensive war and all means were legitimate.[29] As one of the few
opponents of the war within Social Democratic circles, Karl Liebknecht
chose to refer to it instead as a war of conquest by the Great Powers. At a
meeting of the Social Democratic faction in the Reichstag, he demanded an
internal party vote on the approval of war loans. The number of opposing
votes was so low that unanimous approval by the SPD of the war loans in
the Reichstag session the following afternoon was considered a done deal.
This situation, in which even the fierce opponent of war Karl Liebknecht
was obligated to vote in favor of the war loans in order to uphold party
policy, plunged the SPD into a crisis that later would result in the split of
the left.[30] Enthusiasm for the war penetrated "deep into the circles even of
the left wing of the Social Democratic Party."[31] Thus, the young Werner
Scholem found himself isolated with his pacifism as a member of a tiny
minority centered around Rosa Luxemburg and Karl Liebknecht in distant
Berlin. For in his immediate environment, his schoolmates were not the
only ones who streamed to the caserns; the Hanoverian working class also
took up arms with enthusiasm.

Now the war was reality and began to influence everyone's lives, perspectives, and possibilities, be they supporter or opponent. "Today it is hard
to imagine," explained Gershom Scholem, "how profoundly everyone was
affected by it, even one who had an entirely negative attitude toward its
events." The outbreak of the war had caught him "high up in the Made-
raner Valley" in Switzerland, where he had been vacationing with his
mother.[32] The sixteen-year-old, who in Betty's words was "nervous, lanky,
with his nose only in books a[nd] not to be had for any sort of sport," was
spending a medically prescribed four-week stay at the health spa.[33] As different as the two younger Scholem brothers were and as divergent as the
paths of their respective political convictions had already taken them, in
August 1914 they found themselves once again unexpectedly in alliance.
"At the outbreak of the war," wrote Gershom Scholem, "which I rejected
so completely from the beginning that I was completely untouched by the
waves of emotion that were sweeping over the nation, I unexpectedly found
myself in the same political camp as my brother Werner, my elder by a few
years, who had already joined the Social Democratic Party but was a member of its resolute pacifist minority."[34] At this point, Gerhard also found

himself in the minority, because the German Jews and even the Zionists approved of the war. Since Kaiser Wilhelm II had declared in August 1914 that he knew only Germans, a people who "stand together without difference of party, without difference of class and religious affiliation," there was hardly a Jewish voice that spoke out against the war.[35] Therefore, in the years that followed, 96,000 Jewish soldiers would march to war for Germany and usually fought on the front lines. They did this not only as Jews, but also as Zionists.[36] Even in the basically oppositional youth organization Jung Juda, to which Gerhard belonged, fierce discussions broke out between supporters and opponents of the war, in which the latter found themselves commonly accused of "cowardice, shirking, and a lack of loyalty."[37]

The two brothers were also very close personally during this period. A bundle of letters from Werner in Hanover awaited Gerhard upon his return from Switzerland, offering him an opportunity to establish contact with his brother.[38] Thus began an intense correspondence between the brothers that lasted throughout the war. The binding interest was their opposition to the war and criticism of the ideals held by their father and older brothers, who supported the war as ardent patriots. Their letters reveal the intellectual development of two youths, whose political and personal coming of age occurred while a war of unparalleled cruelty raged in Europe. At the heart of their debate stood their playful, humorous, yet also serious interest in each other's weltanschauung: Zionism and Socialism. With regard to their utopian redemptive promise, both ideologies still appeared mutually compatible.

Even though the brothers, in their individualism and their radicalism, were not representative of the majority of young German Jews, their letters did mirror precisely the "confusion" that, according to Gershom Scholem, divided the Jewish youth,[39] among whom decision-making processes, changes in direction, and areas of possibility in the political and social landscape of Germany were discussed. Out of their mutual fondness, they developed ideas for common projects and activities, most of which materialized only when the two of them were briefly in the same place, usually in their parent's apartment in Berlin. Many of Gerhard's letters have not survived, but his answers are found indirectly both in his journals and also in other correspondence with friends.[40] They show how seriously he took the discussions with his brother. Since their written dialogue was replaced by direct personal conversation during regularly occurring visits, the correspondence is fragmentary. Still, it offers insight into their close and intense brotherly relationship, a continual and emotional dialogue that waxed and waned but lasted for years.

The war played a major role in these letters. It injected a serious, sometimes cynical tone into the give and take and bestowed existential import on decisions. It unified the brothers in their shared opposition to the belligerent environment and at the same time alienated them from each other over the years, not the least as a consequence of the thoroughly different realities of their two lives, which at some point became impossible to explain or convey in letters or even in conversation.

Send the Old Men to War Instead

On 7 September 1914, Gerhard began his first letter to Werner with the following words: "Dear to-be-esteemed Brother! You may indeed be bewildered to receive a letter from me. Mama's boy! Fanatical Jew! Dreadful . . . but there is a reason for everything. Over the last three months, I have often intended to write you—and you will learn why later. Now the time has come to open up. Yesterday I read your letters from August, and behold, all that I saw was good. There are various reasons why I hold you in rather high esteem, but now my admiration for you has risen quite a bit."[41] Since the content of Werner's letters is not known, conjecture can only be offered about why the older brother had called the younger one "mama's boy" and "fanatical Jew." Probably the first reference was prompted by Gerhard's trip to Switzerland with their mother, while the second poked fun at his attitude toward Judaism at the time. Not long before this, Gerhard had begun to learn Hebrew and to study the canonical texts of Judaism: the Bible, Talmud, and Midrash. According to his autobiography, during this period he even played with the idea of leading an Orthodox Jewish life.[42]

Why had his esteem for Werner risen? Gerhard explained that he was pleasantly surprised to learn that his brother rejected the SPD's patriotic support for the war and the idea of volunteering, and that Werner reacted with "a cool head and heart" regarding "this mass murder, also known as *Kulturkrieg*." This was without doubt a reason to express his happiness and esteem. However, the actual reason for his letter was different: Gerhard asked for information about social democracy that he had searched for in vain despite his regular reading of the *Vorwärts*, the SPD's central organ.

He, Gerhard, supported the Marxist Erfurt Party Program of the SPD yet still did not call himself a Social Democrat, "because you all are 'organized.' I don't like any organization. The organization is like a murky sea into which flow beautiful, powerful streams of ideas that are never again allowed to leave it." Organization seemed synonymous with death for him; Gerhard emphasized his individualistic standpoint and distanced himself from the "bickering" in the party.[43] Without mentioning Mikhail Bakunin, this line of argumentation reflected his sympathy for the Russian anarchist and his radical rejection of all organization.[44] The questions that then followed were to be understood not so much as real questions but were instead meant to challenge his brother, the organized party member, to an intellectual debate: What was the party's position on anarchism and the question of "good" and "evil"? Did it consider morality to be something inherent in people or something devised? Perhaps Werner had already heard of the Hasidim in Galicia, the mystic Jewish sect that teaches "Socialism *sans phrase*" and is planted firmly "on the ground of unity and mythos"? Does Socialism have such a mythos as can be found in all religions? He added that much depended on Werner's answers, and he would await them impatiently: "I believe in Socialism and the path it is taking. I believe in the will to happiness, but I do not believe that either you all or we will bring about that happiness."[45]

In Hanover, Werner answered Gerhard the very next day with a lengthy letter that was serious and—true to his role as the older brother—a bit ironic: "Your letter did not astonish me as much as you think, because I have been expecting something like this for a long time. Every thinking Jew becomes a Socialist, which you are, too, since you stand firmly grounded in the Erfurt Program." He defended the party against Gerhard's accusations by arguing that it had no alternative to approving the war loans because the majority of its followers supported the war enthusiastically. He himself had seen that many comrades had threatened to resign; the Hanoverian workers' movement still belonged to that moderate wing of the party, which not only adopted a stance far from the left-wing opposition to the war but was quite seriously afflicted with "war madness" and "blood lust." However, his own position on the war had not changed, wrote Werner in defense of himself. "By the way, the reason I avoided answering Father's letter demanding that I volunteer, instead of answering him obediently, is because I am very tired and sick and just don't feel like being kicked out onto the street right now. You can see from this that I, too, am

gradually acquiring a 'sensible' weltanschauung." Then he jested about his
financial dependence, which contradicted his ideology: "Who knows, perhaps I will yet become a junior partner in Arthur Scholem, Printer of Stationery and Lithographs."[46]

Following these "grovelingly down-to-earth remarks," Werner declared,
not without a touch of irony, his wish to follow his brother "into the rare-
fied heights of the mind" and to answer his questions—an undertaking that
he would find hard to accomplish since he had "gone to pot intellectually"
and had not read a single scholarly book for months outside his preparation
for the *Abitur*. Like Gerhard, he hated organization but also considered it
necessary, therefore it had to be anchored in the Erfurt Program. He, however, rejected anarchism because it represented the greatest contradiction
to Socialism through its propensity toward violence and simultaneous over-
emphasis on the individual. At the same time, nothing could be said against
morality as long as one understood "social drives" as a type of morality.
Only the last of Gerhard's questions, the one about the mythos of social
democracy, was one he did not want to answer; it appeared to him to be
confused and unclear. As a concomitant effect, Socialism would bring
about the "ennoblement and liberation of people," but he doubted it would
bestow complete happiness upon each person. "Happiness is inner balance
for one person, tumultuous longing for another, generally something different for everyone. For most, the greatest happiness means to have a full
stomach. It's nonsense to rack my brains any longer about 'happiness,' and
I advise you not to do it either!"[47]

The Socialist rhetoric and party-political pragmatism in this statement
demonstrates the differences that already existed between the brothers.
Werner Scholem's proximity to the classic clientele of the SPD—the working class and all of those whose bellies were usually empty—underscored
this difference, as did his growing impatience with his brother's theoretical,
intellectual games and with the prerequisites for pursuing them, namely, a
well-organized bourgeois world providing sufficient time, room, education,
and food. Yet, despite the connection that Werner described between his
brother as a "thinking Jew" and Socialism, and despite the fact that he told
Gerhard to join the party, he ended his letter with a resigned warning that
also expressed his own doubts: "It's better not to concern yourself with the
workers' movement—it only looks grand from a distance—and don't follow in my footsteps. A person can hit the rocks and eventually go meshuga,
which is certainly not a blissful state to be in. W."[48] Werner's use of the

Yiddish word "meshuga" (crazy) draws on the brothers' shared Jewish background, and his reference to the danger of madness is indicative of his evaluation of the state of Germany in 1914. Soon Werner would report to his brother about anti-Semitism in the working class.

A few days later Werner received an answer from Gerhard, who had discovered how dangerously close he was to being conscripted. Their father had chided him for being a coward, and the relationship between the two had "reached the famous impasse not unknown to you," he reported. Still, he preferred to stay in the parental apartment in Berlin than move to a backwater like Werner and avoid open conflict with their father. Continuing their discussion, Gerhard claimed that he called himself a Socialist and not a Social Democrat despite and not because of his rejection of philosophical materialism. He spurned all philosophies of history and denied the existence of historical laws. If any lesson was to be drawn from history, it was at most an argument for anarchism. Still, he pursued the same aim as Werner: "Socialism is the belief in the future, among us Jews—occasionally also among others—augmented by the belief in the regenerating power of revolution. *Not evolution, but revolution.*"[49] He seemed amazed by Werner's agreement with his criticism of organization and suspected that it was prompted in good measure by disappointment with the Hanoverian labor movement. Had this experience changed Werner's view of Zionism, or did he still think so "*rachmonus*-like" about it? He assumed that his brother's pity for the Zionist movement blinded him to the existence of a Marxist-Zionist party.[50]

Gerhard did not have to wait long for a response. Werner responded with amusement to the news that Gerhard and their father had argued. "So, you are also an incorrigible little rogue; you sit off by yourself and growl for a drawn-out period, but still you eat your 'grub' in a dining room and not in your 'dog house'; consequently, it will still take a while before you consider fresh air to be a more pleasant residence than the cozy home life at Neue Grünstrasse 26. By the way, the fight will be worse for you, because you are the second little rogue!" In his letter, Werner ignored Gerhard's request to clarify his position and did not write one word about Zionism or the link between it and Socialism. However, Werner did react strongly to the younger brother's provocations and the doubts he expressed about the seriousness of Werner's convictions: "I am not an evolutionary, but a revolutionary, because I do indeed stand where Rosa Luxemburg stands, or, who knows, stood until the war." Disappointed? No, he was not disappointed, even if he found the

Hanoverian unions thoroughly to his disliking because they were only interested in material issues. On the contrary, he said that, since being thrown out of his parental home, he had been very successful and had become well liked and well respected in the leadership circles of the Berlin SPD as a result of his political activity. He claimed to have long established himself in Hanover and had been "the Spiritus Rector of the youth" until the war: "honored and respected by the radical minority, feared and hated by the leading union bosses, a stunner at the meeting of the election association, a whiz at regional agitation." The situation had only changed with the war and with an outbreak of chronic neurasthenia that occurred, not accidentally, at the same time. Consequently, he was not in the doldrums, as Gerhard assumed, but suffered from torturous headaches and insomnia and felt as if he were at the end of his rope. Werner was silent on Gerhard's question about his knowledge of Zionism, and there the correspondence stopped. With his affirmation of Socialism, Gerhard had reached out to his brother, even though it was ultimately Zionism that was important to him. Since his brother demonstrated no willingness to meet him halfway, Gerhard did not write back this time.[51]

Nearly two months later, on 14 November, Werner wrote again to his brother in Berlin, using military jargon that had become commonplace everywhere since the war started. He reported that he had concentrated the "army corps of his mind" one hundred kilometers rearward and his intellectual niveau had sunk to the depths of school mathematics; he hardly had the chance to read anymore. At the same time, family problems preoccupied him, namely, an argument with his father because the latter had learned that a few weeks earlier Werner had moved into Emmy's parents' apartment.[52]

A day later, Gerhard noted in his diary: "Brrrr! The clashes that will take place in our house in the next few years threaten to be delightful." Werner's turbulent life preoccupied his thoughts, and not only because of the possible consequences it would have for himself. His brother's autonomy, his decision in favor of Emmy and a life with her family, and his successes as a politician impressed Gerhard and caused him to doubt himself: "I sit here in my cloud cuckoo land and read. Have to read, because I don't have anything else except my ruminations. And how does that help me? I am awfully highly regarded by everyone as the most educated and such other niceties, which might be right—yet what does it take to know a bit more about things than what's in the headlines?—but for me it is all insubstantial." He was thirsting, he wrote, for a life beyond the school desk and university, a life that he didn't know how to find.[53]

After Werner moved to Linden, the daily lives of the Scholem brothers began to differ significantly even though they both still sat in classrooms, and so they had to try harder to understand each other's lives. The differences, which had begun to emerge years before, when Werner had been forced by his parents into the oppressive atmosphere of the Samson School, and which continued after his transfer to Hanover, increasingly defined their relationship. Whereas Gerhard felt committed to the educational ideal of humanism and worked diligently on his intellectual growth, his rebellious brother turned his back on it all: his Jewish origins, the bourgeois world of his parents, and the educational ideal of German Jews.[54] He acted out his rebellion with his premarital relationship with Emmy Wiechelt and his move to proletarian Linden.

At this point, Werner's behavior could still be interpreted as a provocation against his parents and as experimentation with another type of life, because all the while he kept a door open to the family. He enjoyed his role as a black (or red) sheep of the Scholem family, as well as all the comforts of the family bond, which he did not intend to give up. Thus in November, barely two months after moving into the Wiechelts' home, he wrote to Betty: "Dear Mother, I received a card from you on Repentance Day[55] in which you talk delightfully of canned goods and soups. I then sensed something good might happen, and behold, your magnanimous package sailed in on Thursday, for which I thank you very much. You met my tastes splendidly, and particularly the pheasant with sauerkraut I ate with a rapt look on my face." Werner not only devoured the pheasant with relish, but also the other delicacies that Betty had sent him. Smoked sausage spread, crab soup, and oxtail soup seldom appeared on the dinner table during the war years and certainly never in proletarian Hanover-Linden. So the revolutionary ate well, and in the same letter he announced the imminent appearance of his "bookkeeping," in which his mother would see that the goods she sent had reduced his expenses. He asked her not to forget to pay the bills for his books. Though contumacious, Werner was still a part of the family and expected to receive the same treatment as his three brothers. As long as he fulfilled his parents' essential requirement and continued his education, they chose to view his political activity and love life as youthful escapades.[56]

However, the war called into question his freedom of choice and his prospects for the future. The news of the first deaths among their friends had reached the brothers and abruptly dispelled the complacency of their daily lives. One of Werner's old friends was killed in the first battle of Ypres near Dixmuiden and with him a group of other acquaintances—all on the same day. "Send the old men to war instead, so that they beat each other to death," wrote Gerhard angrily in his diary when he learned of the deaths, "but don't rob us of young blood."[57]

Soon Werner received word that he would have to undergo his medical examination for military service. He reported the news to his brother in early December 1914, with black humor:

> I will soon be called up and shot dead. The physical examination of the '95 cohort will be in January, then emergency *Abitur*, February: outfitting, April:
> "He died a heroic death for the Fatherland in the western theater of war on the . . .th of April, our beloved son, Fusilier (Musketeer, Cannoneer) in the . . .th Regiment
>> Werner Scholem
>>> In grief and pride
>>>> Arthur Scholem and Wife Betty, née Hirsch."
>
> That's what's coming, you can bet on it. So, "carpe diem!" I will make arrangements for my inheritance. Are you interested in my books? My bride will inherit most of it in memory of me.[58]

In the same letter, Werner unexpectedly answered the question that Gerhard had asked him three months earlier about his position on Zionism and the Marxist-Zionist party. Did he still think so "rachmonus-like" about Zionism? Yes, he answered without offering any further explanation, he was still a " 'rachmonus Zionist,' " that is, a Zionist albeit a pitiful one. He conceded that the SPD was permeated with strong anti-Semitic sentiments, of which people themselves were unaware, but this changed nothing. The war had shifted his view "leftward . . . but I certainly do not give up all hope. I tell you, after the war (which naturally will end undecided!), militarism will demand everything it wants even more greedily than before." Then he hurriedly and very excitedly added a postscript: "The news just arrived that Liebknecht has refused [to endorse] the means of murder." What he had learned from internal party channels would appear the next day as a short press statement in the *Vorwärts*.[59]

Throughout the fall, Karl Liebknecht had been working to make up for the calamity that he felt had been caused in August 1914 by the SPD vote in favor of war credits. In his eyes this was what actually triggered the French, Russian, and English enthusiasm for war. In order to rehabilitate German—and international—Socialism, he tried to whip up resistance within the SPD faction in the Reichstag against approving the second war credit bill. He declared the alleged "defense of the Fatherland" to be clever propaganda meant only to mask imperialistic expansionist efforts. Although a minority of the SPD faction had pledged Liebknecht support, in the vote taken on 2 December 1914, that minority surprisingly abandoned him, and in the end he alone voted against approving any additional war credit.[60]

After reading Werner's letter, Gerhard also declared his approval of Liebknecht's act, which was condemned or ridiculed everywhere. What made an even greater impression on Gerhard, who was a studious observer of the situation of Jews in Germany, was the anti-Semitism in the Socialist Party, about which Werner had written. "That interested and moved me quite a bit. Still, I don't know which circles Werner means, whether the proletarians or the leadership. I presume the former. That is striking proof for the validity of the Zionist doctrines. Everywhere, even where we were first and involved the most, we are tossed out. Whether it's the capitalists or the workers makes no difference. Socialism will just have to be carried out within each of the national borders, only then will it become truly international." Convinced that Werner's loyalty to Germany and his belief in the salvation offered by internationalism were nothing but false hopes, Gerhard noted in his diary that he intended to inform his older brother about his own views.[61]

Shortly thereafter, in his daily journal entry, Gerhard described an incident that had taken place the day before in the *Vorwärts* bookstore in Berlin: He had visited the shop, which Werner had once recommended to him, and purchased an edition of Karl Marx's *The Poverty of Philosophy*. He talked with the shop employee, an acquaintance of Werner's, about anti-Semitism in the party, an issue in which he was keenly interested. The bookseller noted bitterly that "all of the leading positions are occupied by Jews" and admitted frankly that he and many other SPD members were anti-Semites. "But it appears to me to be very illogical of people who swear by Marxism," commented Gerhard on the incident. "If I say to them: You will yet again throw the Jews out of the party, they start to laugh, but they still believe themselves to be anti-Semites. . . . Yes, these are bad times for orthodox believers from whatever orthodoxy they may be."[62] He soon received a letter from his brother, whose straightforward description of anti-Semitism in the Hanoverian SPD strengthened this impression: "*Rishes* [anti-Semitism] in the Social Democratic Party is naturally not to be found among the leaders, for there are many Jews, but among the masses. In Berlin this is all not so noticeable because anti-Semitism there is anyway null, which one only notices when one gets out of there. But here it is bad!"[63]

In the same letter, which Werner wrote the day after New Year's 1915, he informed Gerhard that he would volunteer to serve in the army. "This is not a matter of principles," he justified, "but otherwise they will stick me mercilessly in the infantry." By volunteering he could select a less dangerous branch of the armed service and at the same time register for the emergency *Abitur* exam—a great relief for a mediocre student. Either way, he would be inducted into service.[64] Gerhard wrote back also on behalf of his mother, who lay sick in bed, and he chided Werner for complaining to his mother about his grades, which only reflected his lack of effort. Moreover, Gerhard accused Werner of devoting too much energy to his love life and his political career and too little to his academic work. "Although I consider it illogical that you are volunteering now," he added, "one can hardly also expect you to be rational in your position. It is just that you should already have been illogical three months ago, because the fact that you would be called up is one that you could have thought of." He himself was also facing a similar fate.[65]

Gerhard wrote this letter over the course of nearly two weeks, and it probably was never sent, for the reproachful tone would not have sat well with Werner. Before Gerhard could finish the letter, his brother had arrived in Berlin and, on 16 January 1915, he took the emergency graduation exams as an external pupil at the Luisenstädtisches Realgymnasium, his former school and also that of all the Scholem men.[66]

A Proletariat of Longing

Werner Scholem stayed at his parents' apartment in Berlin while he awaited his draft notice, which was due to arrive any day. For the first time since Werner had been sent to Hanover a year and a half earlier, he and Gerhard found themselves together in one place for an extended time. Immediately after his arrival in Berlin, Werner invited his brother to accompany him to Rixdorf. That notorious working-class neighborhood, which had officially been named Neukölln in 1912, was developing into the center of internal opposition within the SPD in Berlin at the time. In the Hasenheide, the local public park in Neukölln, there was a widely known entertainment establishment called the Karlsgarten, which featured a theater, a dance hall, and clubrooms. Illegal biweekly meetings of the young revolutionary workers' movement had been taking place at the Karlsgarten since September 1914. Leading opponents of the war attended, including Rosa Luxemburg, Wilhelm Pieck, and especially Karl Liebknecht, and eventually the Karlsgarten developed into a meeting place for the Gruppe Internationale, which was renamed the "Spartakus Gruppe" in 1916. Following the lectures and discussions, illegal publications on the question of German war guilt were distributed among the participants. Werner and Gerhard were among the members of the group who later distributed the pamphlets throughout the city. These publications also included the magazine *Die Internationale*, published by Rosa Luxemburg and Franz Mehring, which appeared for the first and, for the time being, last time in April 1915 and was immediately banned because it demanded the resurrection of the International, which the war had destroyed.[67]

A few days after the first meeting, the seventeen-year-old Gerhard noticed a change in himself, which was prompted by the influence of his brother and the time they spent together. He began to feel estranged from the Zionist youth group Jung Juda of which he was a member. To counter this, he composed a speech with the title "Über das Wesen der Jung Juda" (On the Essence of Jung Juda), in which he integrated the radical rhetoric of the extreme left into his Zionist ideology. With this polemic, he sought to radicalize Jung Juda and push it toward the left. He called for a revolution in all aspects of life: in families and parental homes, and above all in Judaism. The aim and mission of the Jung Juda should be to build a free, anarchist society in Palestine, and not a nation in the sense propagated by Theodor Herzl. In his enthusiastic vision, the Orient metamorphosed into the romantic, fresh antithesis of the ailing, war-torn Europe and, at the same time, the only place where a Jewish revolution could take place in all its political, social, and emotional dimensions. Whether this revolution would be a Socialist or a Zionist one was all the same to him. Those who carried out this revolution would be the members of a new and better breed of people, namely Zionists who rejected the war not only because it wasn't theirs but also because they did not want to share in its depravity and ignobility and who thought of themselves as the representatives of a "proletariat of longing" (*Sehnsucht*).[68] Meanwhile, he spent more and more time away from the group, choosing instead to talk with his brother about historical materialism and other key topics of the left. Although Werner had originally warned him about the workers' movement, he now encouraged Gerhard to begin organizing in the party. And so one of the first joint political actions of the brothers came about.[69]

On 5 February 1915, an article appeared in the *Jüdische Rundschau*, the organ of the Zionist Association for Germany, with the title "Der Krieg der Zurückbleibenden" (The war of those left behind) by Heinrich Margulies.[70] In response, a letter to the editor of the *Rundschau* was composed by the undersigned Zionists, who expressed deep regret over the article, to which they gave the satirical title "Der Krieg der Zurückgebliebenen" (The war of the retarded): "Dear Editor: This article, which culminated in the words 'And so we went to war—not despite our being Jews, but because of our being Zionists!' this article is the most deplorable product of Zionist journalism that has appeared during the war period." The signatories particularly criticized the German feeling of community, which Margulies had asserted that the war had elicited and by which Jews and Zionists had let themselves be seduced. This letter to the editor was signed by sixteen members of the Jung Juda group, and the list was headed by Gerhard and Werner Scholem. It is surprising to see the latter—the Socialist and "rachmonus Zionist"—take a public position of such avowed Zionist nature. As a former member of Jung Juda, he had been again attending the group's meetings upon his return to Berlin— perhaps to reciprocate for Gerhard's participation in the Rixdorf events. Ultimately it is no surprise that Werner Scholem took part in such an unquestionably revolutionary action against the war.[71]

This letter was never published in the *Jüdische Rundschau*. Even before it was sent, the entire affair blew open at the Luisenstädter Gymnasium. The school administration, which was proud of its voluntary paramilitary training units and its students' contributions to the war effort, reacted immediately. The known opponent to the war Gerhard Scholem, along with three other pupils whom he had convinced to participate, was subjected by the school to a four-week-long investigation, which had the character of a tribunal, on the charge of "unpatriotic sentiments."[72] When the contents of the letter were made known to the board of the Zionist Association for Germany, it was appalled and feared serious difficulties for the Zionist movement in Germany. Not surprisingly, Gerhard was expelled because, according to the principal, he caused polarization between the Jews and Germans at the school. However, he was not denied the right of taking the matriculation examinations. Arthur Scholem was exceedingly angry at his son, saying he had had enough of his youngest and that Gerhard would be sent "to Stettin or Greifswald to be apprenticed to a '*Heringsbändiger*' [herring tamer]—Berlin slang for a grocer." It was only the persuasive arguments of relatives and a special regulation at Berlin University, discovered by chance, that enabled Gerhard to begin studying there before his eighteenth birthday and to make up his *Abitur* afterward as an external student at another school.[73]

After the commotion over the letter subsided, Gerhard learned that Heinrich Margulies was "one of Buber's intimate friends" and that his article had thus also reflected Buber's convictions—which, Gerhard noted, "would be very sad if, as I fear, that is true." Should Margulies ever be invited to a Jung Juda evening on the topic of Zionism and war, then it would actually be "Buber to stand in the dock."[74] This realization must have been a great disappointment. For years, Gerhard, like many other Zionists of his generation, felt an enthusiastic although not uncritical attachment to Martin Buber, whom he knew from his writings and lectures but had never met personally. Buber fascinated his Jewish readers with his revelation of the mystical realm of eastern European Hasidism and even more with his concept of Zionism, which was conceived not as defense against anti-Semitism but as Jewish spiritual rebirth. By linking Jewish tradition and a Zionist future, he imparted to the Jewish youth movement that specifically Jewish identity and authenticity, which distinguished it from organized German youth.[75]

It is unclear whether Werner Scholem, studying for the matriculation examinations at the Luisenstädter Gymnasium, was also thought to be responsible for the protest letter to the *Jüdische Rundschau*.[76] During these weeks he mainly stayed in Berlin, awaiting his imminent mobilization. In the end of March he spent the Passover holiday with the whole family in Neue Grünstrasse, as Erich, who was serving in German-occupied Ghent, had received leave from the front and had come home, too. Gerhard, the only nonsoldier, made fun of his proud father and even more of his mother, who had hosted a "heroic mother afternoon," which, in his eyes, was highly comic. Because of the ceaseless arguments with his youngest son, the Zionist, Arthur Scholem refused to hold a seder altogether, and the holidays passed laden with conflict.[77]

Werner remained in Berlin until mid-April and continued to attend the Rixdorf meetings accompanied by his brother. Then he returned to Emmy in Hanover and enrolled in the nearby University of Göttingen to study history at the end of April.[78] He had completed his first semester when he was finally called up for duty in mid-September 1915 and sent to the front. At the end of November, the family was informed that he had been sent to a military hospital due to illness, but they were not told where it was located. Werner soon recovered, but was severely wounded in the spring of 1916 on the eastern front and was transferred to a Berlin military hospital three months later.[79]

Werner and Gerhard were out of contact with one another for an entire year, from June 1915 to June 1916. Sometimes Gerhard mentioned Werner in his diaries, usually in connection with his own constantly reconsidered and questioned position regarding social democracy, a topic that preoccupied him over the course of that year. Although he was still in contact with Social Democratic circles, since the departure of his brother Werner, he missed the presence of one key person with whom he could discuss these matters. However, in July 1915, he encountered someone who was in a position to fill this void: Walter Benjamin, then a student of philosophy, German literature, and art history at the Berlin University. With him, Gerhard took up the dialogue, begun with his brother, and in the initial weeks their conversations concentrated especially on the question of the incompatibility of Socialism and Zionism. For the most part, Benjamin agreed with Gerhard, especially about his opposition to the war and his sympathy with the left, particularly Karl Liebknecht. He read the publications of the leftist opposition enthusiastically and listened to stories about the brothers' antiwar activities, in which he wanted to participate actively himself.[80] Particularly in that first year, Gerhard's friendship with Walter Benjamin was similar to his relationship with Werner, parallels of which Gerhard was aware. Like Werner, Walter Benjamin was a few years older than Gerhard, and his future was not yet clear. Benjamin also already had a fiancée whom he always called "my wife," just as Werner called Emmy, and, also like Werner, he viewed Zionism skeptically. So Gerhard harbored similar missionary hopes that both men might indeed embrace Judaism someday and no longer be "just 'somehow' a Jew."[81]

FIGURE 8. Werner Scholem in uniform, 1915. Private archive of Renee Goddard.

Confused

During Werner's absence, Gerhard decided to channel the radicalism he had developed during the past months into the project of creating his own magazine. Hardly had the idea for the *Blau-Weiße Brille: Ein Blatt für Quertreiber* (Blue-white eyeglasses: A paper for troublemakers) been conceived when it became a done deal. Together with Erich Brauer, a friend from Jung Juda, Gerhard planned a critical and satirical paper that was to use commentaries, poems, articles, and caricatures to voice "the opposition of the radical Zionist youth against the war and the Zionist circles afflicted with war psychosis." The first issue appeared in August 1915 with a print run of fifty copies, lithographed secretly in his father's printing shop; the second issue followed one month later.[82] At the heart of the criticism was the Jewish youth movement, which Gerhard accused of immobility and the lack of a strong Jewish identity. In a half-ironic, half-serious *Laienpredigt* (lay sermon) on the first year of the war, he again demanded the drawing of a "dividing line between Europe and Judah." He urged German Jews to think about the consequences of their support for the war, because the struggle being waged on European battlefields was not their own. He admonished them for their nationalism and encouraged them to defend themselves with cheerfulness and joy against the gloom of the *golus* and the war. In a letter addressed to Werner a year earlier, Gerhard had already expressed what he now made public, namely, that, unlike most German Jews, he saw his future in Zion.[83]

At the height of his involvement in publishing the *Blau-Weiße Brille* came the news that Gerhard's cohort was about to be called up for military medical examination, and he made the decision for which he had criticized his brother at the beginning of the year: he volunteered in order to avoid serving in the infantry, something he fails to mention in his autobiographical writings. This way he was able to take his graduation exams as an external pupil at the Königsstädter Gymnasium on 18 October 1915. One month later he was ordered to appear in Lower Saxony, where, on the evidence of several stays in a health spa during his youth, he claimed to be high-strung and to suffer from fainting spells during long periods of marching. He was tentatively declared unfit for service and released. When he was called up for a second medical examination in early December, his performance as a neurasthenic was so convincing that he was temporarily deferred.[84]

Thus Gerhard was ensured a quiet life for a while. He attended lectures in mathematics, religious philosophy, and theology at the Berlin University and had time to sleep long and read much. "Naturally I have it far better than those who automatically have to take part in the war; I can quietly work here and so gain [a] year or years of my life, which are valuable," he noted in his diary. He did, however, have a bad conscience about avoiding the war so easily, so he joined a small group of German students and academics holding strong antimilitary views. This group campaigned against the plans much discussed at the time to create a "Reichsjugendwehr," preparatory military training for children and youth starting at the age of six. The group was successful.[85]

In addition, Gerhard worked with Erich Brauer on the third issue of the *Blau-Weiße Brille*, which appeared on the last day of 1915 with a print run of seventy-five, because of increased demand. In it he once again criticized German Zionism, arguing that only one deed, namely, "to go to Erez Israel"—the Land of Israel—would bring about change. In response to his own call to burn all bridges to Europe and to prepare for emigration, Gerhard began to study modern Hebrew and, shortly thereafter, Arabic. He even considered joining the Berlin Zionist organization, about which he now appeared not to harbor any of the doubts that had plagued him about the SPD, in which he was still interested.[86] Werner's influence had undeniably fostered this interest in social democracy, but it was not the sole reason for it.[87] The Rixdorf meetings had made him "significantly more appreciative of and receptive to" proletarian anger. He continued to follow all developments within the leftist opposition and was favorably disposed toward it, not the least because it had considerable Jewish support.[88] Thus, Werner, despite his absence still played a major role in his thinking. Time and again, Gerhard considered joining the SPD because, he reasoned, didn't a clear and public commitment to both ideologies mean true radicalism? Shouldn't publicly declared support for Socialism be followed up by the deeds of true Zionism and thus by the emigration to Palestine? In this way, both ideologies would be combined meaningfully. At the same time, however, he had come to the conclusion that the wonderful people of the leftist opposition, among them Gustav Landauer, the anarchist whom Gerhard revered highly, made up only a dwindling minority in the SPD and that they would not be helped much if he joined the party.[89]

While engaged in wrestling with the need to make political and ideological decisions, Gerhard led an increasingly solitary life of a scholar. More and more young men were being called up for active duty; the university, clubs, and organizations emptied out. To escape the dreariness of Berlin and the feeling of being one of the few left behind, he set out on a journey in April 1916. He did so on the recommendation of the family physician, Gerhard's uncle, who had diagnosed him with neurasthenia as a result of his strenuous studies and had recommended a few months of travel. Gerhard was not to touch a book for half a year or do anything but eat, sleep, and take walks. After extended visits with friends all over Germany, he arrived at the end of June 1916 at the spa Oberstdorf in the Allgäu region of Bavaria, where he was to relax for six weeks in the fresh mountain air.[90]

Upon his arrival in the upper Allgäu, Gerhard received—probably to his great surprise—a long letter from his brother Werner, who had only recently arrived back in Berlin and was living at their parent's home: "Man!" he wrote without any polite opening address, "let's ax from my life the period from the 15th of September '15 to the 24th of March '16 as being unworthy of mention, forget the twilight state lasting until 31 May when I—*tace!*—went on vacation to see dear little Emmy in Hanover, and start at the place where we were interrupted on the 11th of June '15."[91] In March of 1916, Werner had suffered a bad leg wound on the eastern front and subsequently spent two and a half months in a military hospital in Graudenz, West Prussia.[92] By late May he had recovered enough so he could visit Emmy in Hanover for two weeks, a fact he kept from his parents. Since an operation on his leg still had to be performed, he was billeted for the time being in a Berlin military hospital. Despite the strictly regulated routine of hospital life, he was allowed to spend a few hours in his parents' apartment during the day. Happy to have escaped the front, he often thought of the Russian gunner who had fired a fifteen-centimeter-long projectile into his leg during the Lake Naroch offensive and whom he had to thank for the fact that he was now sitting at Gerhard's desk.[93] "I hope that you have nothing against it if I use your room as an office and use your library (oh, my!) a bit. Everything will be properly treated. Where should I go otherwise? At Erich's, our dear brother, it stinks like semen, pajamas, and intellectual wasteland!"[94]

There was little to report about the past year, he added, and instead drew a graph charting his state of mind over a period of time. The various possible mental states on the y-axis ranged from "übermensch, mensch, humanity, hope" downward to "brutish, bestial, swine, warmonger." His own development started out in the spring of 1915 at the point "humanity,"

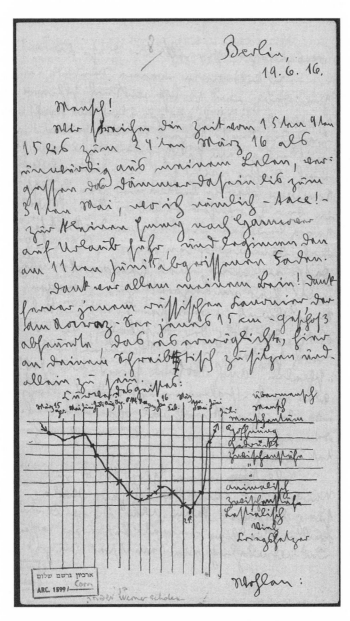

FIGURE 9. "State of Mind," Werner Scholem to Gerhard Scholem, 19 June 1916.
Israeli National Library, Archive Gershom Scholem.

from which it fell steadily until it reached the level "bestial" in March 1916, after which it began to climb steeply again in the direction of "hope," his current state of mind.

What there was to say was told in this curve, he wrote, except that his wound had really gotten bad. "I hobble horribly with a cane, and the people gaze admiringly-pityingly after the field-gray hero, who will shirk [his duties] in Berlin at least for the summer and in the barracks in the autumn." He felt it was such a stroke of luck not to be sent back to the front immediately that he did not want to waste any more time than necessary dwelling on the events of the foregone months. No sooner had he arrived in Berlin than he procured a visitor's card for the university that allowed him to attend lectures without being enrolled. Although classes had long started, he still attended several lectures in the history department and another on the topic of "hygiene in the male sex life." After all, he surmised, he had studied the "unhygiene" during his first semester on the battlefield.[95]

Werner expressed his enthusiasm about the third issue of the *Blau-Weiße Brille*. Why not continue it? Had the potential authors from the Jewish youth movement also been sacrificed to Moloch, like the people of promise in the Socialist youth movement?[96] More than before being inducted into the military, Werner now spoke about Jewish issues, which he knew particularly interested his brother but which had also gained new significance for him. For example, he wrote Gerhard about an old friend, Heinz Jansen, who lay in the infirmary of Breslau with frozen feet and from there had written a "slimy letter" to Emmy. In it "he—he, the Jew Jansen" attacked

my hapless Jewish way to think and express myself . . . as a very pitiful trait ("poor Werner, may he find happiness!"). He called me "Jew" and referred to himself as "we Germans." He spoke of the German way, of the wealth of ideas in Christianity, of Paul (!) and Augustine. I had written him that I had been subjected to an appalling hatred of Jews in the field, whereof he wrote, always to Emmy, that it was due to my Jewish manner. Oh, what ingenious revelation! In addition, he praised them to heaven, the "dear, magnificent" German people, these "simple, honest" people whom he had met. Well, whoever considers these pigheaded *Boches* (superb and precise expression!) to be magnificent people, he is dead for me.[97]

FIGURE 10. Gerhard Scholem in Oberstdorf, standing with arms crossed, summer 1916. Israeli National Library, Archive Gershom Scholem.

Werner experienced similar disappointment in an acquaintance of Gerhard from the Jung Juda group, Gotthold Kalischer, "the Jew, the Zionist, the dialectician, the orthodox Marxist, the clear mind." In 1915, Kalischer had signed the protest letter to the *Jüdische Rundschau* but was now serving as an Austrian cadet and reportedly viewed the military campaign as a liberating deed. "Am I just dumb?" asked Werner, "because I don't reeducate myself when all are reeducating themselves, or am I clever? It can't be Jewish, no, as examples teach!"[98]

The lengthy letter ends with an appeal to his brother to reestablish close contact: "Hey! Write me! Enjoy your life, in case they still come for you, because the war won't be over before the fall of 1917. I calculate that by then Germany will have wagered every last drop and every last morsel and every last man. But it will certainly take so long. Three years, as the *Times* wrote very prophetically in August 1914. I read your Darwin! The *mishpokhe* all scramble to be near me. Father is moved: 'Hero!' 'Reinhold has the Cross!' *Nebikh!* I have again given up guzzling schnapps already. Werner."[99]

Finally Arthur Scholem could be proud of more than just his oldest sons Reinhold and Erich, who had turned out so well and lived up to his expectations in both peacetime and wartime. Even the rebellious Werner was a war hero who enjoyed being welcomed back into the family with open arms, although he was careful not to breathe a word about his connection in Hanover. The language he had picked up in the trenches was harsh and crude; at the same time, he now used Yiddish expressions that the Scholem household frowned upon and otherwise were only ever used by his Zionist brother.[100]

Before Gerhard answered this letter from his vacation spot in Oberstdorf, he wrote to his friend Erich Brauer. His letter closed with the request to contact Werner and "revive his Jewishness." The hopeful, almost missionary tone of this request was reminiscent of a similar remark about Walter Benjamin that Gerhard had made a few days earlier. Gerhard reacted immediately to his brother's apparent turn toward Judaism, which seemed to have been prompted by his experiences on the war front.[101]

Gerhard's letter to Werner has not survived, but most probably it conveyed his approval of the recent development. Werner responded with a long praise for the reinvigorated leftist opposition. While the leaders of the workers' movement had been sent to the front, he wrote, the remaining youth had joined forces with the educational associations (*Bildungsvereine*) influenced by the Spartacus Group.

Since you are a man of a youth movement, I hardly need to tell you what that means. Imagine if the entire Jewish youth were again a movement in your radical sense; no standstill! Yet this is how it is with the working-class youth. My sense of hope, suppressed by the horrible *Boche*-hood of the German people at war, was gleefully restored once I realized that the work for the Socialist youth movement had not been for naught. When you think that this youth, tinged with the beauty of action, this guard of Liebknecht and Rosa Luxemburg, will direct the party of tomorrow—for the functionaries and go-getters of the party will emerge from it—then it will move you all the more to learn that the circles of the movement have not suffered during the general demise of the organization but have increased in strength. I have written to many about this because it is important to emphasize all things hopeful, be they of a Socialist or Zionist nature.

He was concerned with anything that gave the German and German Jewish youth hope—hope to be freed from the burden of war, from social expectations, and from fathers. In this way, Werner also declared his belief in the *Blau-Weiße Brille* as a factor and indication of such hope: "That's why the blau-weiße Brille also inspires me, for isn't it a factor of hope for the Jewish future? Is it really important that I am '*m'bulbal*' [*mebulbal* (Hebrew): confused] when it comes to Judaism? I am sympathetic to every wonderful future, in particular any life in general. Zionism itself is living proof of Judaism, the blau-weiße Brille is living proof of the Jewish youth, and Jewish youth living proof of Zionism. Long live the proof of holy life!" Gerhard's magazine appeared to Werner to be the adequate answer to the arrogant German silence, and he gladly announced his willingness to contribute something about the Socialist and Zionist youth movement, when the next *Blau-Weiße Brille* was placed on "the noses of the Jewish youth."[102]

Meanwhile, Gerhard had started his spa treatment in Oberstdorf. Amid the peaceful and still rich life in the upper Allgäu region, he was completely unprepared for the latest news from Berlin, for the war had become visible and tangible in the capital. Wounded and crippled soldiers like his brother walked the streets, and food was rationed. In the idyllic Alpine surroundings, Gerhard fought his loneliness by corresponding with fifteen to twenty men and women and by thinking about the fourth issue of the *Brille* during long hikes. He also worked on an article about the Jewish youth movement for Martin Buber's newly founded publication *Der Jude*, in which he emphasized Alfred Kerr's call to "remain unconfused" as the solution for what appeared to him to be the aimless and confused Jewish youth.[103]

Werner's renewed presence in Gerhard's life is mirrored in the younger brother's daily journal entries. In articulating his feeling of distance toward Germany, Gerhard now used the derogatory French expression *Boches* and claimed to have become more of a Marxist, because Marxism alone guaranteed the "perpetual rebirth of the movement." In spring Gerhard had been thoroughly enthusiastic about the split within the SPD in which many leaders who opposed the war left to establish the Sozialdemokratische Arbeitsgemeinschaft (Social Democratic Workers' Association) under the leadership of Hugo Haase. Haase now joined Karl Liebknecht and Eduard Bernstein in Gerhard's pantheon of role models, which, in his opinion, Zionism lacked. Both Haase and Bernstein were Jewish, prompting him to indulge in nearly messianic hope.[104] He also wrote his brother about his rekindled enthusiasm for Marxism. "Your opinion of Marxism as a movement is also mine," answered Werner in early July, "but it seems to me that you are mistaken if you believe that I didn't think this way earlier. On the contrary, you have slowly but surely shifted to the left from regions that smelled very rightist."[105]

Now the main topics in the correspondence between the brothers were the Jewish youth movement and a joint project: the fourth issue of the *Blau-Weiße Brille*. Even though the third issue had been a flop, Gerhard Scholem and Erich Brauer had decided to publish a fourth issue that would be both a type of final issue and a eulogy.[106] Werner now convinced his brother to let him work on the next issue. Like Gerhard at his spa in Oberstdorf, Werner spent his time in the military hospital thinking about the Jewish youth movement. "Once I am again wearing the coat of a respectable person," he wrote, "I will have to inform myself about the current state of the Jewish movement in order to see if I can open my big mouth here in addition to the Socialist arena. It should actually be possible to work together or indeed think together. I have been unsure about this since 1912. I have to reach a decision if I want to lay a solid foundation for a fruitful life. But right now, this is impossible, isn't it? I cannot use this summer intermezzo for such important decisions."[107] He was certain he would be sent back to the front once he had recovered. Therefore he postponed any further deliberations on the topic of the compatibility of Socialism and Communism until after the war was over. However, he had reached a decision regarding religion, he wrote, and had turned his back on radical atheism: "I talked this over with Emmy—this is important for me—when I was in Hanover. She is strangely nonreligious, but this also lies in her development so far. I told her of my final resolve *not* to leave the Jewish community and eventually to raise my children in a Jewish sense. Not only did she agree to this, she seemed to be quite moved by the idea."[108] Werner stated emphatically that he did not want this development to be attributed to his war experience. Despite the supposedly leveling and community-building experience of the trenches, there was indeed something like a specifically Jewish war experience.[109] On the one hand, Jewish soldiers had encountered strong anti-Semitism among the troops; and, on the other, they had celebrated Jewish holidays together, enjoying copious meals and generous donations of cash and commodities by Jewish organizations. However, stated Werner ironically, the soldier's life did not even come close to influencing his return to Judaism as much as had the lessons gleaned from Darwin's *On the Origin of Species*, which he had borrowed from Gerhard's library.[110]

Shortly after this, Werner underwent the operation on his leg. During the three weeks he was required to recuperate in his military hospital bed, he read other books that he had found in his brother's room: Georg Simmel, Kurt Hiller's *Ziel*, Otto Weininger, Søren Kierkegaard, and Martin Buber's *Legende des Baalschem*. Two of these books confronted him with questions he felt to be highly existential and "damned important" for his identity. One was Weininger's book *Sex and Character*, about which Werner wrote that he "would really like to find the mistakes in this book, there must be one in there. But you can't get around this man, everything is so solidly proven that you become concerned that he might be right. I fear that it is very possible for me to adjust to Weininger's train of thought!" Werner was probably referring to Weininger's low estimation of women, which he shared to a point, and to his criticism of Judaism—Weininger argued that Judaism was something to be overcome, a comfortable idea for Werner. Naturally, Gerhard did not share these sympathies. He saw Weininger, a Viennese philosopher who had committed suicide in 1903 at the age of twenty-three, as a man who failed to reconcile with Judaism, and, in fact, Weininger has come to be seen as a paradigmatic figure of Jewish self-hatred.[111]

It might seem surprising that *Legende des Baalschem*, a collection of Hasidic tales translated by Martin Buber, was as important to Werner as

Weininger's *Sex and Character*. Two years previously, Gerhard had written
to his brother, urging him to study Hasidism as a mystical Jewish sect
teaching true Socialism, and now he finally turned his attention to it. In
this book he discovered existential insights regarding his self-perception
and his future. Rather amused, Werner reported to his brother that he was
not the only one to be fascinated by this book: a soldier in the hospital had
begun to read it while Werner was sleeping. "He was enraptured and said
that he had never read anything like it. Since then he has become completely absorbed in Buber. And the man is otherwise a total *boche*! I see that
it is a remarkable book." Obviously, Werner missed his brother's compan-
ionship for discussion of the topics that preoccupied him, from Spartacus
to Weininger and Hasidism, and finally to Zionism, because he closed this
letter with the following demand: "See to it that you return soon! Are you
brooding in silence in Oberstdorf?—I am thinking about Palestine!"[112]

While Gerhard was out on lonely hikes through the mountains, enthusiastically making plans for further issues of the *Blau-Weiße Brille*, his
copublisher and his coauthor in Berlin were developing little liking for one
another. Erich Brauer had visited Werner in the hospital following the latter's operation and had gained the impression, as he subsequently reported
to Gerhard, that Werner was someone who was "not particularly logical or
certain of his opinions." Brauer added: "It might be wrong, but I feel as if
his Socialism is ostentatious. It stands out starkly that Zionism means to us
something else by far than Socialism means to him. By the way, I do not
believe that he can be the *Jew* we can be—regardless how he positions himself. I consider his position to be very precarious in light of the current state
of Judaism." Evidently unaware of the negative impression he had made,
Werner greatly wanted to contribute to the *Blau-Weiße Brille*, and he wrote
another letter to Brauer from his "crypt of mattresses," asking him to visit
him again.[113]

Gerhard answered his friend in a long letter in which he emphasized
how much it meant to him to publish this issue as a joint venture. In
an unusually emotional passage with many single- and double-underlined
words, he expressed his unconditional solidarity with his brother to Erich
Brauer:

> I do believe that your opinion of my brother is unjustified in essen-
> tial ways, because—even if everything was indeed as you say—there
> is one thing you should not forget: *he is on the right path*. Four years

ago he left us; now he is coming back again. He wrote me that he has to take a *good look* at the Jewish movement after the war in order to possibly play an active role in it. His Jewishness is "corrigible," which unfortunately isn't the case for so many "Zionists," because he is not self-satisfied. The more you work on him—and I intend to win him over *fully* to our side later—the more he will ever more consciously turn to the *one* path. I know, e.g., that he has undergone a religious change; I know that he already wants to raise his children as *Jewish*; I am convinced that he will soon arrive at Hebrew. *Basically the two of us see eye to eye*: we both have a truly straightforward ideal concerning the "movement" and "radicalism." You are definitely mistaken about his Socialism, I know that *for certain*, and precisely *because* I know this, I know that [it] will lead him to Zion. He changes his opinions just as we all do: we who slide to the left. You, I, and he. And everyone.

Gerhard ended his defense by noting that Werner had willingly and on his own initiative found his way to the *Blau-Weiße Brille*, even against his own resistance at first.[114] A few days later, he received the first draft of Werner's contribution. The article carried the title "Zur Unbedingtheit einer Jugend: Einige Regeln" (On the unconditionality of youth: A few rules). It used a language noticeably inspired by the activist and unconventional language of the first three issues of the *Blau-Weiße Brille*, but at the same time his tone was even blunter. Still, Gerhard was very happy with the article because it outlined the concept not of a Socialist youth movement but of a radical Jewish one. " 'Get thee out of thy country, and from thy kindred, and from thy father's house, unto the land that I will show thee.' You will someday have a fatherland! We point you in the right direction. But you must go by yourself. Always try to run your head through the wall. A Jewish skull is harder than most walls! Don't ready your handkerchiefs for German snotnoses, because that's the job of the Socialist youth movement! You fight Jewish snot!" This unexpected exhortation to Jewish nationalism from Werner's pen was followed by a less surprising criticism of the enthusiasm for the war by the Jewish youth and a call to unconditional pacifism: "Should someone talk to you of world war, barf three times until your mouth is full of green bile! . . . Then go and buy a butcher's knife or perhaps a stink bomb for that person who spoke to you about world war!"

Opposition to the war represented the link to the Socialist youth movement, to which, in his opinion, the Jewish youth movement should draw closer. "Be fanatic! Be ascetic! Be loud-mouthed! Revere the dreams of youth, and sacrifice your holy future at the altars of the present! That is the meaning of a youth movement! Say: 'These are people!' when you hear of the Socialist youth movement. Grow, and they will be your brothers! Honor the man Liebknecht! His name is the symbol of unconditionality!"[115] It was important to Werner to see the name Liebknecht mentioned in the *Blau-Weiße Brille*. He believed that this man—were he to become a role model for the Jewish youth—had the potential to bring the Zionist and Socialist youth movements closer together and to use their common opposition to the warmongering establishment to unite them into a powerful force.

If we read Werner's text for the *Blau-Weiße Brille* against the background of his relationship with his younger brother, we find that he not only links Socialists and Zionists, but he also expresses the hope for further rapprochement between them in the future. In this light, his interest in Judaism, which now shows up regularly in his letters to Gerhard, comes across as an invitation to discussion and perhaps also to joint agitation. But these posed no serious challenge to Werner's identity and ideological roots in the workers' movement and his dreams for the postwar period. (He intended to work on a new Social Democratic youth magazine in Braunschweig.) The networks and friendships he maintained were still mainly in Socialist circles. Thus, he lived his life, just as he had written to his brother back in June, with two pairs of eyeglasses on one and the same nose: "In this context I really like something you said, which is consubstantial with what I believe: 'Courage to true dogmatism.' But can true dogmatism for me only be seen through Jewish glasses? Of course I look, even consciously, through Jewish glasses, but I see, e.g., the dogma of historical materialism, which is rooted in me stronger than ever. I want to observe history with its eyes."[116]

Moreover, his brother's growing political resoluteness encouraged Werner to espouse, more seriously than before, the idea that the two movements find a platform for cooperation and cocontemplation. When he sent Gerhard the copy of his manuscript, he therefore also asked his brother to send him the article entitled "Jüdische Jugendbewegung" that Gerhard had finished recently for Buber's magazine *Der Jude*.[117] In this article, Gerhard expressed regret that various organizations existed that referred to themselves and their programs as the "bodies and flags of the Jewish youth movement," although what they lacked was "often not only Judaism and youth, but time and again the movement. Without exception, all of them, big and small, lack the insignia of the movement: wholeness, esprit, and greatness." Just two years earlier, he had told Werner in a letter that he wanted nothing to do with organization. Now he complained that no mobilizing and organizing of the Jewish youth was taking place. This appeared to him to reflect one thing above all: confusion. In his mind, this had been evident from the moment Jewish youth had expressed enthusiasm for the war. Not even longing—a feeling that had always been and was still present among the Jewish youth—could change this in any way, he felt. Longing alone would not bring about renewal; it had to be about totality, totality in the commitment to Zion. Jewish youth, however, were not wholly committed; they were confused.[118]

Confusion was Gerhard's favorite word at the time, both in regard to the Jewish youth as well as to himself. After going through much inner conflict, during the lonesome weeks in Oberstdorf he had resolved to leave the ranks of the confused, because he felt "soil, Jewish soil" under his feet.[119] He posed the challenge of overcoming his own confusion and dedicating himself to a life of active Zionism to himself and to Jewish youth in general. This is probably why he was so enthusiastic about having Werner contribute to the magazine and so excited by Werner's willingness to view—temporarily—the world through blue-white spectacles. While languishing in the military hospital, Werner did indeed appear to be impressed that his brother had found such solid ground under his feet. "My hospital deliberations about the youth movement are only illustrations with respect to my 'path,'" he wrote on 7 July 1916 to his brother. "This path is apparently unclear. I read good words about it in the *Ziel*: 'Get thee out of thy country, and from thy kindred, and from thy father's house, unto the land that I will show thee.'" However, in Werner's perception, this land had as little in common with the Land of Israel as the speaker had with his God or the addressee with Abraham. Rather he read the quotation from the Bible in the context of the philosopher Hans Blüher, who cited it in his text, in order to lend expression to his dreams of a different Germany.[120] Blüher's article appeared in one of the most influential books published in Germany during the war, which Werner discovered in his brother's library in 1916: *Das Ziel: Aufrufe zu tätigem Geist* (The goal: A summons for an active spirit). The editor, Kurt Hiller, brought together a number of German-speaking intellectuals from different generations in his battle cry for activism. These included Heinrich Mann, Max Brod, Walter Benjamin, Franz Werfel, and Alfred Kerr.

The censors did not take notice when the book first appeared in February 1916 but banned it shortly thereafter because of its radical pacifism. By then, however, it was already widely discussed and had been reviewed in the country's most important newspapers. In March 1916, Gerhard enthusiastically noted the radical opposition to the war expressed in *Das Ziel*: "It is—second only to the *Internationale* of Rosa Luxemburg, who, by the way, has since been released from prison—the most outstanding publication of the war years: with the true force of the opposition (understandable since the majority are Jews!!), the future is being pursued. If we Zionists had such people among us, things would be much better. It is up to us Jews to be such people!" The fact that the various authors expressed in part contradicting opinions did not bother him. In the end it did not matter "what path one took to revolution as long as it is imbued with spirit." The activism advocated by *Das Ziel* appealed to both Gerhard and Werner Scholem, unlike Walter Benjamin, for example, who explicitly rejected it even though he was one of the contributors to the book.[121] For the Scholem brothers, the youth movement was a matter of deeds, and the *Blau-Weiße Brille* was meant to express precisely that.

However, the project fell through. In August, Gerhard's euphoria for the *Brille* succumbed to the terribly beautiful weather in the upper Allgäu, as he wrote. Even though he had wished "out loud and silently" for rainy weather, he spent his days hiking and taking walks, writing a poem every now and then, and dreaming at night "about the magnificence of the coming *Brille*," through which their true radicalism would be voiced. In the meantime, he learned that Brauer had not taken his appeal on Werner's behalf seriously and had cut off all contact with him. Gerhard wanted to pursue the project even without his brother, but soon it became quite clear that the *Blau-Weiße Brille* was dead, and he never mentioned it again. Until the end of the summer, Werner assumed they would push forward with the project and that the fourth issue would appear, but once he had recuperated from his leg operation and had to return to the barracks, he also said no more about the matter.[122]

The proposed fourth issue of the *Blau-Weiß Brille* was the brothers' last cooperative effort. Their shared rejection of the war, of their father's generation, and of the bourgeois establishment led them briefly to believe they could reconcile their ideologies and youth movements. They hoped to form a joint opposition under the symbolic banner of Karl Liebknecht, who was falsely rumored to be of Jewish descent. For this purpose, one brother embraced Marxism and the other at least began to consider Palestine. The failure of the project was also the first major break in the close bond of family and friendship between them. From then on, they grew steadily more estranged until 1933. While Gerhard was to put Jewish soil beneath his feet, the ground on which Werner stood—despite his strong criticism of the *Boches*—continued to be German.

Against Kaiser and Father

While Werner was confined to his bed, assigned small tasks in the military hospital, or spending time at the desk in Gerhard's room, he thought about more than the *Blau-Weiße Brille*. In fact, he spent most of his time attempting to reconstruct his lost war diary. The original had gone missing during his delousing in the army infirmary, and he wanted to replace it quickly, as long as his memories were still fresh.[123] In early July, he sent a thick envelope to Gerhard in Oberstdorf containing the latest *Spartakusbriefe* of the leftist opposition and the first chapter of his war diary *Nokturno meines Lebens*.[124] Gerhard was fascinated by the report of Werner's war experiences in the two months from 15 September to 2 November 1915; he referred to it as a "first-rate *documentum humanum*." After reading Werner's reconstructed diary, Gerhard realized that the so-called "culture war," the propaganda effort to present Germany as the representative of high culture, in combat against barbarism, was entirely specious. "In fact: Were it not for the love of neutrality, a person could turn into a first-class enemy of Germany. There can be no doubt that the diary is reporting the truth. That *Boche*-hood looks like this is something I had thought was almost impossible. But every rape of a Russian girl by a German soldier is announced to the world as documented fact." Gerhard had not been prepared to read about anything more than the general barbarity of wartime in Werner's diary, and he was surprised that "such Cossacks" lived in "sacred Germany." However, Gerhard did not call German soldiers "Cossacks" just because they had raped Russian women; he was evoking a key topos in collective Jewish memory. After the murder of thousands of Ukrainian Jews during the Cossack uprising under Bohdan Khmelnytsky in the seventeenth century, Russian and Ukrainian Cossack tribes had been responsible for so many more pogroms that, in Jewish parlance, they came to symbolize all violent and brutal anti-Semitism.[125]

The war diary, later lost, apparently described anti-Semitism in the German army in particular, which Werner had already mentioned in his letters to his brother.[126] If these stories were told to other German Jews, noted Gerhard, they would definitely declare the author himself as the guilty party: "Yes, he had indeed made רשעות!"—he provoked anti-Semitism. Gerhard wrote the Hebrew word, rish'ut, pronounced rishes in Yiddish, and used as a synonym for anti-Semitism. He continued: "Those who don't make רשעות hide their Jewishness as much as possible and reveal it at most in camp worship service! Otherwise, you make רשעות. Oh God, if I would land in the military!!! God save me from this fate."[127]

Gerhard hoped that Werner would continue rewriting his diary, describing his experiences up to the hour when he was wounded, because there was, in Gerhard's mind, "no better means to propagandize the unbourgeois in oneself," which was—according to Werner—the main purpose of his report. Since the Blau-Weiße Brille project was still alive at this point, Gerhard made plans to print parts of the diary in it.[128] However, Werner would probably not have approved this. Indeed, Gerhard's failure to acknowledge the arrival of his package immediately alarmed Werner, because he feared that this valuable text—the only copy of his notes—had been lost in the post or landed in the wrong hands.[129] Since he was still in military service, there would have been serious consequences for him had the text become known, as did indeed happen a year later.

Direct or indirect experience of anti-Semitism played a major role in the lives of both brothers. While Werner was rewriting his personal war diary, anti-Semitism in German society was becoming increasingly visible. At the start of the war, the emperor had promulgated a policy of Burgfrieden (civil peace), but during 1916, social solidarity crumbled steadily, and accusations were increasingly voiced against so-called Jewish "war profiteers." During that summer, Jews were accused of shirking military service, leading, in October 1916, to the infamous "Jewish census" in the German army.[130] This measure was a reaction to widespread anti-Jewish resentments in the German officers corps and to growing anti-Semitic propaganda among various groups and parties in Germany. This was the background against which Werner was rewriting his diary. Even if, as he had once written Gerhard, the war experience had no influence on his growing interest in Judaism, perhaps anti-Semitism did. For his part, Gerhard reacted to the anti-Jewish developments with inner emigration; he detached himself from all things German and devoted himself instead to pursuing an idealized Judaism. The insights into a soldier's life that he had gained by reading Werner's journal showed him, on the one hand, that a German Jewish existence after the war would be problematic if not impossible and, on the other, that—strictly pragmatically speaking—he had to avoid going to war for this Germany unconditionally and by all means.

In July 1916, Werner still hoped to be dismissed from the army as a war invalid and dreamed of resuming his studies soon in tranquil Göttingen with Gerhard. "The stay in Göttingen, which the future hopefully holds for us in its lap, will be very necessary and decisive for our lives," he wrote. "We definitely have to dedicate ourselves to the final things in this quiet nest, a year untouched by the noise of the Berlin intellectual hub. For Göttingen is a lost cause both for Socialism and for Judaism."[131] As it was, things turned out quite differently.

In early August, one month after the beginning of the Battle of the Somme, the bloodiest battle of the First World War, it was clear that the war would drag on for a long time and more men would soon be called up. Both brothers had to face the fearful prospects of being ordered to the front, and so Werner sent his brother a warning: if he returned from the Allgäu healthy and recovered, he would certainly be drafted,

> and you do not yet know what it means to be swallowed up by the Moloch; that can only be judged by someone to whom it has happened. I am warning you because it would be a real shame if you were to get a bullet in the head. And it is a long time until the autumn of 1917. One of us has to remain behind so that the gens Scholem can create new humans. I am doing all that is possible, running around for all that it's worth, despite incredible pain, against the strict orders of the doctor, but who knows? The wound is not festering much and it appears as if I will get caught up in it all again next year. Therefore, again: do harm to your health, for then you are doing the best you can for it. Get used to smoking like crazy and, last but not least, return to Berlin as soon as possible. Don't be imprudent.[132]

Shortly afterward it was determined that Werner's wound had healed completely. He became thoroughly distraught at the news that he did not even need to wear a bandage. He knew he would soon be called up again in order to "take up quarters in the mass grave. This summer dream is soon over." Likewise, an idyllic summer was coming to an end for Gerhard. He was forced abruptly to end his stay at the health spa when the newspapers reported that all cohorts were to be called up for medical reexamination. He arrived in Berlin at the end of August, where the war was much closer and had become evident in everyday matters like the temporary insolvency of his father's business. To Gerhard's great fortune, the medical examination went as hoped, and he was deferred from military service as a neurasthenic.[133]

In Berlin the brothers just missed each other. Werner was released from the hospital and left the city just as Gerhard set out on his return trip to Berlin. The recovered soldier had been given two weeks leave, which he wanted to spend with Emmy in Hanover. He told his parents that he was traveling to Bad Rehburg to rest in the small spa town near Hanover. Only Gerhard was privy to Werner's actual whereabouts, and he was instructed to destroy all letters that could betray Werner's secret—which Gerhard did not do. To avoid arguments with his parents or, even worse, their refusal of financial support, Werner had not let it be known that his relationship to Emmy was still intact. Although he had been getting along better with his father than with his mother, for a while, the two of them still fought adamantly time and again. "Meanwhile, the old man has decided again that I am a swine and has forbidden me to show myself to relatives, so I don't do anything stupid and embarrass him!" reported Werner to his brother. "You see, I (1) made fun of Mr. Reinhold's Iron Cross (!!) and (2) read the *Vorwärts* in the military hospital. But this time I really let the old man have a piece of my mind, and afterward he was also subdued." Arthur Scholem was proud of his two oldest sons, patriotic war heroes, whereas the two younger ones still appeared to make fun of everything he held sacred.[134]

By this point, the relationship between Werner and Emmy had lasted nearly three years. Though he kept it a secret from his parents after his return from the front, Emmy visited him regularly in the military hospital and assured him of her great love in daily letters from Hanover.[135] Since their correspondence no longer exists, the nature of their romance can only be gleaned from Werner's depiction of it in his letters to his brother, one-sided and often polemic as they are. Although he expressed concern for Emmy as well as pride and feelings he had for her, he also chose to express a degree of male chauvinism when writing to his still unattached brother.[136]

He reported with some enthusiasm, for example, that his "little Emmy" was doing well and that she had "gained wisdom and knowledge" while he had been off fighting. The young woman had decided to take private lessons and earn her *Abitur* diploma while simultaneously holding down a job. To Werner, a poor student who had worked hard just to earn his emergency *Abitur* diploma, her ambition and her talent made him proud, but it also disturbed him. He wrote to Gerhard:

> I certainly do not look at her with honeymoon eyes, although I love and need her as much as is humanly possible. She is what one calls a very bright girl, that is, she learns easily and even has a certain drive to learn something. She is certainly better than me in all the school stuff. And still, I don't think she is capable of following my thoughts; I don't presume she can comprehend the slowly but very surely grinding mills of my reason, and therefore I still have a great edge over her. . . . Be that as it may! We need these halves of ourselves, not only sexually—alone that would be an absurdity—but as complements to ourselves: And here I have chosen well for myself, because she does not spout the shoots of vengeance typical of a Berlin Jewish flower or a Linden working-class plant. She is built well, inside and out, and will, once she had learned something, make a very good mother, unlike what we know on this topic.

It did not bother him that Emmy was not Jewish. If he so wanted, she would even convert to Judaism, but because she appeared to him to be "free of Christian spirit and free of Germanic flaws," he saw no reason for her conversion.

Werner's remarks about his fiancée reveal a certain ambivalence, both male and educated middle-class chauvinism and love and esteem for Emmy. He wrote to Gerhard that he had found one of the cleverer girls in Emmy but that she was slow and uncomprehending compared to him. Once he said he believed in monogamy and proudly declared that he had not touched any other woman during his years as a soldier; another time he spoke in favor of introducing polygamy in Palestine. Likewise, he described Emmy as that "creature with whom, according to the Zohar, I should unite into one being," and he worried incessantly about her health, which suffered from the double burden of work and study.[137] Precisely this ambivalence between esteem and arrogance as well as his commitment to

monogamy and fantasies about polygamy influenced his relationship to
Emmy throughout their marriage.

After spending two weeks in September 1916 with Emmy in Hanover,
Werner had to report to a barracks in Diemitz, one of the city districts of
Halle an der Saale. He suffered from the strenuous duty he was assigned to in
an *Ersatz* (replacement) company and hoped that his petition to be discharged
from the military as a war invalid would be granted. He used what little leisure
time he had to continue rewriting his war diary. He also asked Gerhard to
send him the magazine *Der Jude* and other publications that he could not get
in provincial Saxony. He continued to read the *Vorwärts* and, once the paper
was banned again, Halle's Social Democratic newspaper *Volksblatt*. He felt it
would be unwise to engage in more political activity than this in his current
situation. Instead he took a course in the university in Halle, resuming the
study of history, which he had started in Göttingen. Emmy's regular visits in
Halle were to remain a secret, which is why Gerhard was asked to prevent as
many unannounced visits by their Berlin relatives as he could. Under no
circumstances did Werner want to forgo the monthly support he received
from his parents, which alleviated the discomfort of life in the barracks. Furthermore, he asked his brother to send him a chess set and to give his mother
a list of further necessities: "Please do prompt Mother to send me another 2
underpants, 1 nightshirt and if possible 1 necktie. As for the underpants, she
should not take such long things that go up to the chest!"[138]

Contact between the brothers was becoming less frequent. During the
autumn, Gerhard had again delved into the study of Orthodox Judaism;
however, this time he was motivated by his Zionist convictions. He
explained his growing interest in traditional literature by arguing that Judaism could not be modernized without robbing it of its soul. In addition to
the main religious texts such as Talmud and Mishnah, he now also read
Kabbalistic and Hasidic literature, as well as modern Hebrew prose and
poetry, and composed his own translations for the first time. "Jewishifica-
tion" (*Verjüdischung*), he noted in his diary, "grows proportionally to the
square of familiarity with all things Hebraic, but makes a quantum leap at
the point where the heart of the Hebrew language suddenly reveals its
soul."[139] This inner development occurred in parallel to an external one, in
which the city all around him began to metamorphose into a center of
Jewish and Hebrew culture. War refugees from eastern Europe, rising inflation, and declining printing costs started a process that would reach its
climax early in the Weimar era.[140]

After Emmy's visit to Halle over the Christmas holidays in 1916, Gerhard arrived at New Year's to spend three days with Werner. Contrary to his original intentions, Werner had again become politically active and asked his brother to give a talk at a meeting of the local young workers' group during his visit. The members were looking forward to hearing the great theoretician from Berlin with excitement, he let Gerhard know with a chuckle.[141] In his journal, Gerhard described his visit to Halle, without mentioning the lecture, as an experience of growing distance: "I was able to make many observations about Werner in these last three days," he noted bitterly, "and did not conceal from him that when it comes down to it, he is simply bourgeois. When I said that Liebknecht was supranational [*übernational*] and he subnational [*unternational*], he was quite outraged."[142] Such accusations were not new. Gerhard had repeatedly reproached his brother in past years for being bourgeois and lacking political radicalism. But now his remarks expressed a greater alienation, almost contempt. Although both brothers were mainly interested in youth movements, this interest no longer had the power to bond them.

For Gerhard, Jung Juda had developed into a group of like-minded people who expressed their commitment to their common political goal of Zionism through deliberation and debate. Working with several other members, he drafted a program for a secret society that closely resembled Gustav Landauer's Socialist Federation (Sozialistischer Bund). Before the group undertook the practical work of building a community in Palestine, it first dedicated itself primarily to the intensive study of Hebrew as the origin and essence of every Zionist activity and to the recruitment of new members. This missionary impulse emerged from an interpretation of Zionism as the call "to become a holy people." Therefore, friends and acquaintances were to be converted, in a quasi-religious sense, to membership in the Jung Juda and thus to radical Zionism.[143]

After Gerhard's hopes to make his brother a member of this association were dashed, and Werner's interest in Zionism proved to be a nonserious flirtation, Gerhard withdrew from the correspondence in disappointment. However, Werner stubbornly pursued his brother's friendship and closeness and made final efforts to convert him to Socialism.

After spending New Year's 1917 together, there was silence between the brothers, until the beginning of February, when Gerhard received an unexpected letter from Halle containing a warning:

As I sit down to write you, I find myself in a strange situation. In short, I am standing at the edge of the abyss that will certainly engulf me. There was a Socialist demonstration here on the emperor's birthday in which I was denounced. At first, nothing happened, so I carelessly let down my guard. Today the criminal police searched my things with the permission of the garrison command, and unfortunately found a great deal. I expect to be arrested today or tomorrow. At any rate, my university study just went down the drain, and you can imagine the punishment that a military court will slap on me. I cannot write you in more detail; at any rate my immediate fate is sealed. My bride knows. Don't say anything to the parents right now; I will let it be known if I am put in custody. But keep in mind that they found letters in my possession from you and take the appropriate steps immediately.[144]

The action for which Werner was denounced took place on 27 January 1917 at a public event in Halle celebrating the emperor's birthday. About forty demonstrators interrupted the celebration and called out "Long live Liebknecht!" and "Down with the war!" before scattering in all directions. The police intervened immediately yet were unable to apprehend any of the demonstrators. However, Werner Scholem, who had been wearing his uniform while taking part in the protest, was denounced by a woman student.[145] Before the war, while attending the Samson School in Wolfenbüttel, he had been forced to observe the emperor's birthday year after year in a nationalistic school celebration, and he had resented it.[146] In an effort to give the emperor's birthday new significance, Werner and his co-demonstrators followed the example of Karl Liebknecht, who had led an antiwar demonstration at Potsdamer Platz in May 1916. Liebknecht was charged not only with civil disobedience but also with treason. Following seven months in custody in Berlin-Moabit, he was sentenced to four years in the workhouse.[147] Even though Werner was a small fish compared with the great enemy of the state Liebknecht, he had reason to assume that he would also be charged with treason.

Werner's letter was the last he sent from Halle for the next five months; nor did he receive any word from his brother, who was apparently quite frightened. Gerhard had reacted immediately to the possibility of a house search and deposited all incriminating papers, especially his diaries, in a

friend's apartment. Shortly afterward, their father received the official notification of Werner's arrest, and, as Gershom Scholem recalls in his autobiography, there ensued "a terrible scene . . . at the dinner table. When I
raised a mild objection to one of my father's assertions, he flew into a rage
and said he had now had enough of the two of us, that Social Democracy
and Zionism were all the same, anti-German activities which he would no
longer tolerate in his house."[148]

To have his son accused of treason deeply wounded the ardently patriotic father. The very next day, Gerhard received a registered letter from his
father's printing business in which Arthur Scholem banned him from his
house as of 1 March and announced that all forms of financial support
would cease. So as not to leave his son broke and on the street, the father
gave him one hundred marks and recommended that he register for civilian
duty at the war office in order to earn an income.[149] Gerhard did not wait
until 1 March but moved out immediately. The episode caused great excitement among his friends, who now treated him as a "martyr of Zionism"
even though his exile from the parental home had basically been a result of
Werner's arrest.[150] A dwelling for Gerhard was quickly organized in a cheap
boardinghouse in Berlin-Wilmersdorf. For the next four months, until
mid-June, he lived in Pension Struck, a strictly kosher boardinghouse with
a nearly exclusively "eastern Jewish" clientele. During this period well-
meaning relatives supported him, and, behind his father's back, Betty
arranged to have a friend secretly bring food and money to the hotel for
him.[151] He was also helped by his friend and next-door neighbor in the
boardinghouse Zalman Rubashov, who would later become Israeli president Zalman Shazar. Rubashov arranged for Gerhard to be paid for trans-
lating a Yiddish book memorializing the fallen heroes of Zionism.[152]

Against his own better judgment, Gerhard approached his father in
early May and asked him for money. Arthur brusquely turned him down,
saying that, if he were Gerhard, he would be ashamed to accept handouts
at the age of nineteen. He called his son's academic interests in Judaism a
game, a preoccupation with mere abstractions, and declared that he was
only willing to pay Gerhard's tuition costs. "Whether I will grant you an
allowance as soon as you are drafted into the army remains to be decided,"
he added, for this would be dependent on Gerhard's future behavior.
"Should you, however, express your anti-German views in any recognizable
form, then I will cut you off just as I have—unfortunately too late—cut off
Werner." This threat did not have the desired effect on his son, who refused

to accept the unconditional reconciliation he demanded. Gerhard complained to his friends that his father, who was not ashamed of having someone spy on him, had systematically bred bitterness in Werner and him. So, he would just have to live without his father for a while. He then declared the matter closed.[153]

Gerhard took Werner's warning about a possible house search very seriously and stopped writing in his diary for three months. He resumed in early May 1917 with a positive remark about his new living arrangements. Later, in his autobiography, Gershom Scholem also recalled his life at Pension Struck and fellow boarders, most of whom belonged to the Russian Jewish intelligentsia, as a thoroughly positive experience.[154] However, his diary mentions some negative aspects of those four months. For example, he wrote on 19 May that he was so disgusted by his landlady, Mrs. Struck, that not a single word passed his lips the entire day. "They now all think that something has happened to me, and no one has any idea what the real reason is: *that this boardinghouse nauseates me just as my parents' house did.*" He also called the other boarders, with the possible exception of Rubashov, "really disgusting citizens" for whom he had lost all respect. He explained that he retreated into himself instead of simply moving out because he was complacent and bourgeois. Still, in the future it would be *"anything but a boardinghouse again!!* I have learned that lesson *well."*[155]

There had been no communication between the brothers since Werner's arrest in February. Then, in June, a long letter arrived for Gerhard from the prison where Werner was detained. Almost bitterly he asked why Gerhard had not written to him or visited him in prison. Had he been deterred by cowardice and fear for his own skin? Werner appeared to be proud that his brother could no longer accuse him of triviality and a lack of radicalism. He recalled how Gerhard had told him at Christmas that Karl Liebknecht was "supranational," while he, Werner, could only be called "subnational": "Let me remind you of the conversation we had during your last visit to Halle, in which you wanted with a vengeance to label me as subnat[ional], as opposed to other people whose merits had also been to affirm the totality of their ideas behind prison walls. I have been doing the same for four months and am convinced that I will still be doing it for some time. I hope that my actions now appear to you to be supran[ational], even though I never repudiated my beliefs through my deeds earlier." While he himself was in prison, affirming the totality of his ideas, Gerhard was living a life of compromise. It was pathetic, Werner wrote, that he still took money from their father after being thrown out of the house. Werner, on the contrary, had finally decided never again to dip his fingers into the parental pot. Could Gerhard maintain his principles even without paternal support, as a "proletarian and especially also as a Prussian soldier"?[156] These accusations certainly hit the younger brother hard, since Gerhard was often plagued with existential self-doubt at that time and, he confessed in his diary, even too hypocritical to commit suicide.[157]

Werner also wanted to know what political position his brother had taken and whether he was a member of the new party, which had been founded in April. In the absence of the two prominent leaders Karl Liebknecht and Rosa Luxemburg, who were both incarcerated, a split developed in the ranks of the SPD, and the antiwar faction had been expelled from the party. In April, those who had been expelled convened a national conference of the Social Democratic opposition in Gotha, during which a diverse group of politicians, including Hugo Haase, Kurt Eisner, and the reform-minded revisionist Eduard Bernstein, founded the Independent Social Democratic Party of Germany (USPD, Unabhängige Sozialdemokratische Partei Deutschlands). Werner, who had been a member of the SPD since reaching majority, reported that he had joined the new party from his prison cell. At the same time, he said that he was intently watching war developments in the Near East, where Allied forces were engaged in fierce battles with the Ottoman Empire over Palestine. "I would have also liked to ask you what Jews and Jewish comrades were saying about the recent events in Palestine?"[158]

At the end of this letter, Werner reported that, more than anything else, the pacifism and criticism of the government expressed in his war diaries were the reason for the sixteen-month sentence he had received in his first trial. In the upcoming appeal, he wanted "to give a big speech and then, with a happy heart, to lodge an appeal to the Reich Military Court, so that I will certainly sit here until fall. Should you, against all expectations, find yourself in the vicinity, do visit me. Then I will be able to say: *Et tu, Brute!*"[159]

This long letter reached Gerhard just before he himself was conscripted. Already at the end of March he had received the news that he had been classified as physically and mentally fit for military service, and in May the draft notice arrived. Now he found himself waiting to be called up at any time.[160] Although Gerhard's letter is not extant, Werner's answer enables us to divine its contents. Werner complained that Gerhard had distanced himself from his brother's political life and ideas: "Earlier you had completely different views with regard to connections to a party, and I know that only last year you said that you would join the left wing should a split occur among the Social Democrats. And back then you did not think any differently about the relationship of revolution to politics." He was sorry that his brother had not felt drawn to the opposition, even though it was fighting precisely what they all suffered from, namely the war. In light of Gerhard's future career as a soldier, Werner noted bitterly: "The exalted regions in which you care to dwell appear to have somewhat pulled the rug from underneath you. Perhaps the next two or three years are apt to rudely remind you of the situation you are in, and before then I will not give up the hope of meeting you in my hunting grounds."[161]

Most of all, Werner's letter expressed indignation about the manner in which Gerhard had written about his trial, for Gerhard had accused him once again of un-Socialist behavior. After all, Werner wrote, Gerhard had only received sporadic information about the trial, and how did he even know what little he did? It could only be from the "*mishpokhe*, who merely disseminated *what our begetter so wisely and deliberately propagated.* It seems to me that this clever man has achieved part of what he intended, because he knows that, among certain people, he can only belittle me [i.e., his ideas] by praising my behavior before the court." Yet how could he— Gerhard, who had no available source but the poisoned well of Arthur Scholem—come to condemn his brother, whose behavior was described as correct and honorable by every friend? In a certain sense, he continued, this unexpected attack from his brother's pen suited his purposes, because it would help him prepare for the appeal trial in Magdeburg. There he planned to deliver such a strong plea in his defense that no one would be able to malign him for un-Socialist behavior ever again—unless they wanted to slander him. Werner expressly urged Gerhard to attend the trial together with Emmy in order to see for himself. Despite his hurt and indignation, he ended the letter on a conciliatory note: disregarding the fact that he had spent the last four months behind bars, he was doing well. Halle had maintained its role as a stronghold of Marxism, and he felt surrounded by friends. He inquired about Gerhard's impending entry into military service and asked his brother to keep either Emmy or himself informed of his current address, because they could "so easily lose sight of each other and ahead of us still lie glorious years! Greetings, Werner."[162]

Gerhard probably received this second letter after he had moved into the army barracks on General Pape Strasse in Berlin on 18 June 1917. His friend Zalman Rubashov had accompanied him to the barrack gates very early that morning, embraced him "Russian style," kissed him farewell on both cheeks, and given him a miniature edition of the Psalms in Hebrew to take along. In the barracks, the new recruits were informed that they were to be shipped to the reserve infantry in the military camp of the Twentieth Army Corps in Allenstein, East Prussia.[163] Once there, Gerhard experienced the daily absurdities of military life, about which he wrote in a letter to his friend Erich Brauer: Every Sunday all divisions were allowed outside the barracks to take walks, but under the strict orders that "they are forbidden to go into the city, to enter taverns, meet with civilians, or pick blueberries, yet they must 'take walks.' So they race around like mad sheep in the forest, spouting their smutty talk (with the junior officer leading the way), and amusing themselves in all sorts of ways."[164] While Gerhard was also amused by this situation, he shared it for less than two weeks, as he was soon exempted from duty because of his apparent poor state of health and his recalcitrance. Subsequently he was assigned to easy duty in the mail room and later in the latrines, where he sat for hours and made sure that the soldiers washed their hands with carbolic soap because dysentery had broken out in the camp.[165]

At the end of July, after a nervous breakdown, Gerhard was placed in the psychiatric ward for six weeks of observation. There he experienced a relatively comfortable period in which his peace was not disturbed either by examinations or treatments. In letters to friends, he said that he truly needed this peace and quiet because his mental state was very precarious. Sometimes he would feel unable to think, read, and write for days, and he apologized for the illegibility of his writing, caused by his shaking hand. After only two weeks, the psychiatric observation was ended, and Gerhard was discharged on 21 August on the grounds of being temporarily unfit for military service.[166]

Months later, Gerhard confided to his friend Werner Kraft that the everyday craziness of military camp, the feigned breakdowns, and his actual psychic instability had been enormously traumatizing: "Have you ever imagined, deeply and truly imagined, in a most truthful way, what unprecedented command of greatest intellectual vigor had to be exerted in my struggles with the military, what image [*Gestalt*] I, *with eyes wide open* (and

FIGURE 11. Gerhard Scholem as a soldier, summer 1917 (first row, second from left). Israeli National Library, Archive Gershom Scholem.

that is precisely the most terrible), had to give my life in order to remain pure."[167] Ultimately, he said it was his Zionist convictions that had enabled him to effect this metamorphosis and thus obtain his discharge.[168]

However, Gerhard had no idea that his quick and relatively painless discharge from the military was attributable less to his talent for feigning mental illness than to a nearly unparalleled stroke of luck. Conscientious objection to military service was not recognized during the First World War on either side of the conflict. Very rarely did anyone refuse to serve in the army for political reasons in Germany, and the judicial distinction between conscientious objection and desertion was so vague that both offenses were severely punished. All conscientious objectors were subjected to psychiatric evaluation, as they were regarded as mentally ill. The consensus in psychiatry at the time was that both objectors and malingerers were rarely to be found among the mentally healthy population, so most of them were labeled "hysterics, imbeciles, psychopaths, inferiors" and confined in psychiatric institutions. The rest were imprisoned as draft dodgers. Only a few doctors declared the soldiers in question to be healthy and sent them back to their units, often with a request for a mild punishment. There most of them were quickly tried and sentenced to prison for terms of varying length.[169]

Gerhard proved to be a rare exception to this rule because he had the good fortune of falling into the hands of a sympathetic physician. As Gerhard wrote, the military hospital in Allenstein was teeming with Jewish doctors, who had to deal with aggressive anti-Semitism. The most prominent was the psychoanalyst Karl Abraham, who built the psychiatric ward of the hospital and worked primarily on the treatment of shell shock. Abraham had been a student of C. G. Jung and Sigmund Freud before working in Berlin as a registered neurologist and psychoanalyst. Toward the end of the war, Abraham invited several colleagues to Budapest to exchange views on the psychoanalysis of war neurosis. At this congress, the key speaker, Ernst Simmel, argued that even mentally healthy people could be traumatized by the war, contrary to the scientific consensus at the time. It is likely that Gerhard was prematurely discharged from military service on the basis of this opinion. Abraham diagnosed dementia praecox in Gerhard as a result of the crisis with his father. A few years before the war, this disorder had been redefined and grouped under the general heading of schizophrenic psychosis. For other psychiatrists this would have been a reason to commit him to an institution. But Abraham did not do so, nor did he order any treatment, not even psychoanalysis. He recognized Gerhard's behavior as a result of the young man's Zionist convictions, that "visionary state" in which Gerhard had found himself for years. So, Abraham exempted him from fighting in a war for Germany.[170]

Gerhard had achieved his goal. Even if he was traumatized by the episode, at least he would not have to go to war for Germany under any circumstances. What is more, a fortunate solution had been found not only for his relationship to the German emperor but also for his relationship to his father. Meanwhile, his brother Werner, who had gone to war for emperor and fatherland and now sat behind bars on the charge of lèse-majesté, had thoroughly ruined his relationships to both Wilhelm II and Arthur Scholem. While Gerhard was still in the military hospital, he received a card from Emmy Wiechelt in which she told him how Werner's appeal trial in Magdeburg had gone. Shortly afterward, an extensive letter arrived from Werner, who reported that the original prison sentence of sixteen months had been reduced to nine, of which four had already been spent in pretrial detention. Werner had said from the start that he did not want to be reprieved or pardoned only to have to be sent back to the vale of tears of the front lines. Gerhard was overjoyed by the outcome of the Magdeburg trial.[171]

During what turned out to be six months in solitary confinement, Werner had reached one definite decision: he wanted to marry Emmy as soon as possible. As expected, Arthur Scholem rejected his future daughter-in-law because he opposed marriage between Jews and non-Jews despite his German patriotism. Somewhat surprisingly, Betty was also not at all pleased. Later Gershom Scholem would write that his mother had accepted this decision "indifferently and even with a certain benevolence," but this is not how Werner described her reaction. "I don't know why Mother is upset about my intention to marry at Christmas," he complained to his younger brother. "First she kicks me out and then she wonders why I draw consequences from that. By the way, the thing is imperative. You will be invited to the wedding, but that means without any money, because I now definitely mingle with the plebs. . . . I hope that you do not return to Neue Grünstr. once you are free, only to let yourself be thrown out again at their next whim! I could also now *zoppen* if I would scrap the marriage project, but I have finally had enough. I will cross the Rubicon."[172]

The day after Gerhard's discharge from the army, Werner wrote the long letter from his cell, mentioned above, in which he described the course of the Magdeburg trial in great detail. In order to circumvent the censor, he had this letter to his brother smuggled out of prison:

> Accept my congratulations, you poor emotionally disturbed man! Yes, if the psychiatrists who observed you were really capable and truly astute, then how could they have come to any other diagnosis! Unfortunately in my case, as one who is also in conflict with military authority, they didn't accept any hallucinations but unmercifully put me there where the weeping and gnashing of teeth prevail. Seriously, dear boy, I have soon been sitting here in solitary confinement with nothing to do for seven months! How that eats away at a person is only something that can be judged by someone who has gone through it himself.

His comrades from Halle—among them Reinhold Schönlank, the brother of the poet Bruno Schönlank—sent him food and books, but the latter were restricted rigorously. Scholarly and political subjects were not permitted, only thoroughly apolitical prose and poetry. He wrote that the trial had so

FIGURE 12. Emmy Wiechelt,
1917, in Halle. Private archive
of Renee Goddard.

far changed little about his situation and that he had been sitting in the
same cell, staring at the same four walls, for two hundred days. He expected
to be transferred soon to Spandau, where he would remain until December,
after which he would return to Halle and be sent to a convalescent company. Then, as plans stood currently, he and Emmy wanted to marry over
the 1917 Christmas holidays. "Only the gods know what will happen to me
later. Probably they will stick me in some filthy backcountry dump. They
will hardly let me go to revolutionary Halle."[173]

Then Werner began his promised report on his trial before the High
Military Court, a report in which he spared no detail, for fear someone
would preempt him—that someone being Arthur Scholem—and lie to Gerhard once again. As was common in trials for political crimes, the proceedings were not open to the public for reasons of security. Not even Emmy

was allowed in. The only one to appear was Arthur Scholem, who had petitioned to be present at the trial in which the charge was lèse-majesté. Astonishingly, the key witness in Werner's first trial, the student who had denounced him, was not even called upon to testify. Instead, the arguments presented in this trial centered on the war diaries as the key evidence of the prosecution. As Werner wrote, the three-hour plea of the prosecuting state attorney and that of the defense attorney focused primarily on the frequently used pejorative appellation *Boches* and also on a single controversial sentence. The charge of lèse-majesté was difficult to substantiate, since it could not be proven that Werner's action had been "malicious, deliberate, and committed with the intent to insult." "You would have died laughing," wrote Werner, quite amused, "if you had read in the judgment of the first trial how they justified the charge of maliciousness. No one could prove that I had acted deliberately, which is indeed not the case, because I certainly did not want to deny the emperor his personal honor. For that he is too indifferent to me! The prosecutor asked me why I did not simply go to Social Democratic meetings if I wanted to demonstrate, to which I countered by saying that he should tell me when a meeting of the radical Socialists had ever been permitted in the vicinity of the Fourth Corps."[174]

Werner assumed that the judges were in agreement that his was not a case of lèse-majesté. However, since he could still be charged with "breaching the peace" (*Landfriedensbruch*) or "disorderly conduct" (*grober Unfug*)—of which the first carried too much weight and the second too little—the case would be decided on the charge of lèse-majesté. In his speech to the court, the prosecutor described Werner as an intriguer, conspirator, and traitor, yet he often contradicted himself in his drastic description of Werner. "One time he described me in the most luminous colors as a highly intelligent person; another time, when he spoke about the diary, as a greenhorn and parrot," Werner wrote. "Then he asserted that I was a practiced crook and a skillful tactician, because I had now changed my tactic by admitting to have sung. In doing so he spoke continually about the 'great role models' that I had had, whereby he foolishly always implied Liebknecht, whose strength it was that he never compromised." After the defense had made its final plea, Werner himself addressed the court and began, as he noted, "a roaring speech that must have been heard throughout the entire building. Inwardly, I was immensely amused by doing this, while I mimed Danton. By the way, among the old gentlemen sitting on the High Military Court, mouths went agape and eyes widened. This was not something that they experienced very often. But they still remained decorous, because they did not interrupt me although I swore frightfully. My defense attorney had assured me that the speech cost me at least two months more! Meaning, it was good!" He described the horrors he had experienced as a soldier during the Serbian campaign in lurid detail. When the court finally passed its verdict, Werner was greatly surprised how mild it was and that the prison sentence handed down in the first trial had been reduced by seven months.[175] Of small build but with a strong voice, Werner Scholem had given the court a taste of the politician he was to become. He probably acquired his theatrical ability while going to plays with his mother when he was younger; he had also had the opportunity to develop his talent and try out his skills before a private audience in the skits that she wrote.

After the trial, Emmy accompanied her fiancé back to Halle, and it was, as Werner summed up, a good day all in all. The only disturbing factor was the presence of his father, who met Emmy on this occasion for the first and only time. Werner offended his father terribly by refusing the money that Arthur offered him at the train station in Emmy's presence, but the son saw no reason to reconcile with his parents again. He had come to the conclusion that it was time to assert his own political and social intransigence radically and uncompromisingly. The marriage with Emmy would make this decision public. Werner closed his long letter, which he successfully smuggled past the censor, with a strong political statement: "Until now I had held the view that the war must and would end undecided. But now I hope and believe that it will have to end with the complete smashing of Germany. No other way out is possible, no other is desirable, either for the international proletarian or for the Jewish people. And only with England's complete victory would Palestine become Jewish!"[176]

Werner was already transferred to Spandau in September, when his brother decided to study mathematics and philosophy in Jena. Originally Gerhard had wanted to follow Walter Benjamin and his wife Dora to Switzerland, as the two of them had succeeded in leaving Germany with the help of a medical certificate enabling Benjamin to avoid the draft. However, Gerhard was only temporarily relieved from military duty and in financial straits during the final war years, making such travel impossible. Arthur Scholem sent his son a monthly allowance and paid for his books, while Betty Scholem ensured the regular delivery of food packages. When it came to expenses for his university studies, Gerhard's father proved generous, prompting his mother to note ironically: "We are sending you the spent 27, along with 3M for feasting on cake, but extras *every* month is bitter (if it were up to me, you wouldn't get one book more!!). . . . You are devouring books again!" Gerhard was aware that he had managed to obtain everything he wanted from his father pertaining to both ideas and finances. Nevertheless, during these months in Jena he suffered from hunger, cold, and a shortage of funds, like all his fellow students.[177]

The University of Jena was a disappointment. The only ray of hope Gerhard found there was Paul F. Linke, a former student of Edmund Husserl who was one of the few academic philosophers who opposed the war energetically, and Gerhard soon established a friendly relationship with him. Other than that, he spent a lot of time thinking and reading in his room or in the library and devoted his attention particularly to the work of Edmund Husserl and Hermann Cohen. He criticized the latter for his rationalism, but at the same time valued him as one of the "priests" of Judaism, whose teachings would someday find their place in Zionism. Gerhard quickly formed a circle of friends, including women he had known for a long time, who were Jews or interested in Judaism. He taught them Hebrew or gathered with them in his room on Friday evenings for the weekly Torah reading. Still, Gerhard felt lonesome during these months in Jena: his friends from the Jung Juda were either in Berlin or had been drafted, and Walter Benjamin was in Switzerland. Since his time in Allenstein, he had been a close friend of Werner Kraft, who served as a combat paramedic in Hanover. Benjamin, who was concerned about Kraft's melancholic state, introduced them, and soon they had engaged in an intensive correspondence. Unlike Gerhard, Werner Kraft had little interest in Judaism or Zionism but was fascinated by the distinctly Jewish identity of his friend.[178]

In November 1917, a political incident sparked Gerhard's passionate attention. It was not the promise made by the British government early in the month to advocate the establishment of a "national home for the Jewish people" in Palestine. As a supporter of Achad Haam's concept of a spiritual center in Palestine, Gerhard acknowledged the Balfour Declaration merely with a good bit of irony. However, he responded enthusiastically to the Bolshevik Revolution and its intention to pull Russia out of the war. He felt that a quick end to the war would be particularly important for the Jewish and Zionist cause, while at the same time he also supported the content and aims of the revolution and wrote that, in his entire life, he had "never seen such a humanly moving and authentic political tract as the documents of the maximalist revolution."[179] Yet his consideration of a possible end to the fighting and the transition to a revolutionary society also brought him to acknowledge the enormous effect of the war: many friends and acquaintances had been drafted, and he saw himself as one of the few who remained, a survivor surrounded primarily by women friends. If that wasn't enough, more and more soldiers were returning from the front, turning up in train cars and on city streets in wounded, crippled, and confused condition, as one sees in the painful paintings of Otto Dix.

In response, Gerhard began to translate the book of Lamentations from Hebrew at the end of November 1917. For him, this work symbolized grief over alienation from Judaism and particularly the Hebrew language, while expressing his intention to embrace both. The work also reflected the melancholy and loneliness he was feeling when he lamented over those who had fallen and those who would or could not return to Judaism after the end of such fratricidal war. "How can we look into each other's eyes," he wondered in his diary in early December, "once the friends are back again and the new work commences. Only then will we see who are not there, not only those killed, I mean, but the others, who have slipped off somewhere in these years, gone off in bitterness, and no longer want to see—and have returned to a *Hatschi* life—ah, there are indeed all too many of the latter."[180] Among those embittered people for whom Zionism was not a very serious episode in their lives—complacent *Hatschi* Zionists, as he called them—he probably counted Werner, who had disappointed him with his halfhearted interest in Judaism and Zionism and whose war and prison experiences had estranged the two brothers.[181]

In "Orcus"—the Underworld

Werner spent the entire autumn in his cell in the Spandau military prison. Only once a week, always on Sunday, he was permitted to write a single letter. For this reason, he asked his family to write and visit regularly and regretted that his brother did not find the time to do either. In his autobiography, Gershom Scholem recalls having undertaken the trip from Jena to Halle regularly to visit Werner; according to his brother, these visits never occurred. In fact, Werner had already been transferred to Spandau when Gerhard moved to Jena.[182] The most important event to occur that autumn found no mention in Werner's letters, probably because of the prison censor: the Russian Revolution. The news that suddenly, like magic, this horrific war could end and a new era would begin had certainly reached him right away. While imprisoned in Breslau, Rosa Luxemburg, whom Werner so admired, described this change: "I have the feeling that all this moral filth through which we are wading, this huge madhouse in which we live, may all of a sudden, between one day and the next, be transformed into its very opposite, as if by the stroke of a magician's wand may become something stupendously great and heroic; must inevitably be so transformed, if only the war lasts a few years longer."[183]

On 9 December, one day before his release, Werner addressed his last Sunday letter to his brother. "Our pleasant sojourn in Aranjuez is over now," he wrote, ironically quoting the first line of Schiller's *Don Carlos* but omitting the similarly pertinent sentences of the drama that followed it: "And yet your highness quits these joyous scenes no happier than before. Our visit hath been fruitless." Instead he wrote that he would long think about the dreadful months in Spandau. Not much good news awaited Werner upon his release. From Berlin he was to return directly to Halle to a new battalion and back to the daily life in the garrison. Furthermore, all of his friends had been arrested, and the University of Halle had initiated expulsion proceedings against him. If he were indeed expelled, then it would not only be from the University of Halle, but from all other German universities as well.[184]

Yet there was also good news to report: "It has now been definitely decided that we will marry at Christmas or as soon as possible, if the battalion grants me permission. Emmy has already sent off the application to marry to Halle, so that I can delight you with a sister-in-law maybe even next week. Mother is appalled, of course, but I am adamant about burning all my bridges behind me. United together, Emmy and I will find a way so that I can study eventually. I am fed up with eternally quarreling with the *mishpokhe*."[185]

Very shortly before the Christmas holidays Gerhard came from Jena to visit. The brothers' last and emotionally tense meeting had been a year before, almost to the day. Yet Werner now showed how pleased he was to be in contact with his brother once again and how happy it made him that Gerhard was visiting. He listened with great interest as Gerhard reported on his time in the military. "I only wish," he wrote soon afterward, "that I were granted the chance to be free soon, because if I have to play soldier for another three years, then what little guts that I have perhaps been able to salvage will certainly be gone completely, and the creature that will some-day again wear civilian clothes will be one that feeds, talks, and—fucks, *last not least* [in English in original], brooding darkly all the while that every-thing could have been different. Can you tell me how to protect oneself against Prussian militarism? I wish that I was also mentally ill."[186]

On 29 January 1918, Werner traveled to Hanover to get married. Ger-hard wanted to accompany him and at the same time visit his friend Werner Kraft, who was stationed there. But, as he realized shortly before the wed-ding, he didn't have enough money to make the trip, nor could he expect help from his parents, who were so vehemently against this marriage. He did not send a congratulatory note to the newlyweds until quite a while after the wedding, but in early December, a few weeks before it was to take place, he did relate the news about the happy event—punctuated with sev-eral exclamation marks—to his friend Harry Heymann. Although Werner's active days as a member of the Jung Juda lay several years behind him, Gerhard called Werner the first Jung Juda member to marry.[187]

The relationship between the brothers did indeed appear to have improved a bit. At Werner's request, Gerhard intervened on his behalf in the matter of the university expulsion proceeding, which was to be decided on 7 January. In his memoirs, Gershom Scholem remembers meeting with the rector of the University of Halle, the philosopher Hans Vaihinger, twice on this matter. According to Gerhard, Vaihinger was not disinclined to grant him his request and entered into a friendly conversation with the young student. As it turned out, the Senate agreed on 7 January 1918 to grant a *consilium abeundi* [literally, "advice to go away"], a recommenda-tion that Werner leave the University of Halle and, should he choose to continue his studies, enroll in another university. Hence, all the other Ger-man universities remained open to Werner. He accepted the decision with delight, very thankful for his brother's intervention on his behalf.[188]

A short time later, Gerhard himself received unexpectedly favorable tidings from another commission: based on the findings of his military examination in Jena, he was discharged from the army on 14 January 1918 as being "permanently unfit for military service, no further examinations." This was, to put it mildly, a huge relief. Time and again in the preceding months, there had been moments in which he might have and almost did tell the story of his successful simulation of mental illness to friends and acquaintances who were facing military examination. Had it become known, he would have had to face a prison sentence or serve time fighting on the front. With the final discharge, this threat was now removed.[189]

In early February, Gerhard received a letter from his sister-in-law in Hanover in answer to his letter congratulating Werner and her on their marriage. The two had still not met, but Emmy's letter was sincere and friendly. She had always read Gerhard's letters to Werner and therefore thought she knew him rather well. In the previous week she had been with Werner in Halle and, though he had not been denied access to all German universities, he was doing poorly. Upon his return to Halle, he had learned that all of the couple's party friends were incarcerated and that a few of the younger comrades had testified that Werner had given antiwar speeches in the winter of 1916. Therefore, the authorities sought to bring the charge of treason against him, but it was eventually dropped because of lack of evidence. As if this wasn't enough, as Emmy continued to report: "Now they have tried to take him out another way; they simply listed him as k.v. [*kriegsverwendungsfähig*, fit for military duty] and it is very well possible that he will be deployed to the field this week. Of course this is nothing but harassment because Werner has long been unfit for the infantry, he is no longer able to march great distances, etc., and anyone else would have been able to dodge service for years with such a wound. Unfortunately, in our blessed Germany Werner has no alternative but to go into the field—or into prison." Werner expected to be shipped out to the field as a fusilier on a moment's notice, but the newly married couple managed to enjoy a week together in Halle. Werner was allowed to spend his nights and that entire Sunday outside the barracks with his wife, as long as he remained in the city.[190]

Shortly afterward, Gerhard received a very distraught letter from Werner, which confirmed Emmy's report: he might face trial for treason. The fact that he was again experiencing the same fate as his role model Liebknecht was apparently no consolation. He said that he had tried unsuccessfully to have himself declared sick, but nothing helped because the entire deal was a frame-up. Arthur Scholem had taken the news of his marriage and the subsequent treason charge badly. According to Betty, he was terribly nervous and could not calm down even after the charge had been dropped. He let his son know that he was going to separate from Betty if she did not immediately break all ties to him. "Mother is too weak to resist, of course," commented Werner, "which you can't blame her for. So, she sent me a farewell letter and asked me not to write her anymore. Well, fine by me." Since that last source of financial support had now dried up, and Betty Scholem's food packages no longer arrived, Werner asked his brother for five reichsmarks that he still owed him. As a rich student, suggested Werner, Gerhard might even double the amount and thereby do a good deed.[191]

In early March, Gerhard came from Jena to visit and, after he had returned, described the relationship to Werner as being very bad: Werner dreamed of being admitted into the Bolshevik Red Guard and beheading Baltic barons, he noted in his diary. "It is actually sad, but I have to admit: between us has opened up such a *gigantic* permanent chasm as cannot be overcome. He lives in a sphere that I condemn, condemn, condemn. Were he not my brother, I would never be in contact with him. These are the people who make the revolution fail (or rather, a priori *impossible*) time and again. For Werner, it is enough to be famous as a demagogue. He is political in the worst sense. It is sad. He has become a stranger." For Gerhard, who was retreating more and more into the worlds of metaphysics and philology, to be political had become reprehensible.[192] As several times in the past, Werner reacted to the growing alienation between him and his brother by denying it. He wrote numerous letters asking Gerhard to send him books and telling him about his currently easy and comfortable life in the barracks. He also asked Gerhard to let their mother know he was doing well but that every now and then he did not have enough to satisfy his hunger. Since he could no longer expect any more from her, he borrowed small sums of money from his brother.[193]

Arthur and Betty Scholem spent the Easter and Passover holidays not far from Jena in Kösen, where Gerhard visited them. After that, Betty planned to spend a few days with him in Jena. Despite Werner's repeated request that she also visit him in Halle, unbeknownst to his father, she didn't feel she could, and he chided her for her cowardice. Still, the holidays passed pleasantly for Werner, and he was able to eat his fill on Passover, thanks to the local Jewish community and a Jewish welfare organization.[194]

In early May 1918, Gerhard moved to Switzerland after having convinced his parents that he needed to do so for the complete recovery of his health. He was to remain there for a year and a half, far from the war and its conclusion, the capitulation, and the German revolution. At the tranquil university in Bern he studied mathematics, theoretical physics, philosophy, Old Testament, and Arabic. He spent his leisure time with Walter Benjamin, his wife Dora, and their infant son Stefan, who had been born in

April. Actually, these three were the real reason for Gerhard's move to Bern. Soon they all moved together to Muri, a village with 2,500 inhabitants not far from the city, in which they could lead a more comfortable and less expensive life than in Bern. There they founded their own "University of Muri," whose curriculum was the daily study of the philosophical writings of Hermann Cohen.[195]

Meanwhile, Werner had also moved, albeit not voluntarily. First classified as a fusilier and then as an artilleryman, at the end of April he was assigned to a light artillery unit. Gerhard continued to be his only family contact, so Werner asked him to let Betty Scholem know before he was transferred to the western front. What awaited him there would be worse than anything he had yet experienced, because by then the German army was only suffering defeat. From the trenches of this war of attrition, he wrote his brother one or two letters a month, always in the hope of reaching his mother through him. Like nearly all soldiers, he imposed self-censorship on his letters to avoid military censorship. He wrote neither about the details of the fighting nor about political subjects. At the same time, when writing to his brother he never felt it was necessary to whitewash the situation and reassure him, as he probably did with Emmy.[196]

Gerhard answered regularly, but his letters have been lost. As he wrote one of his friends on the front lines, he suffered from a bad conscience since being discharged, and he viewed the freedom given to him as a liability and responsibility for the coming years. Without knowing how it felt to be in the field, he empathized with his friend by writing that he had recently "heard a wonderful, infinitely deep soldier's expression: to sit in the ass of eternity. Do you know it?"[197] His brother was now sitting right there, in the mud and dirt of the trenches and bivouacs, battling fatigue, vermin, undernourishment, diarrhea, and the Allies.

Werner did not hesitate to express to his brother the injustice he felt in the different fates that had been dealt them. He congratulated Gerhard on his move to beautiful Bern, while he himself was currently sitting in delightful Flanders. But before he offered a description of this wondrous stretch of land, he wanted to know everything about Gerhard's life and studies in Switzerland. Following several meanderings with a light artillery convoy, he had been assigned to the field artillery, where so far he found himself better off than in the garrison, because he could finally eat his full. However, he was soon assigned to a battery where he had to man a firing position. In order to avoid that, he had immediately reported sick. Since he rejected the war on moral grounds and was also convinced that he was there unjustly, he did not hesitate to avoid the fighting wherever he could. For a while he had been assigned "a very stimulating post as the librarian and supervisor of a reading room," which his artillery detachment had set up. In this case, it was to his advantage to be uncommonly well educated for a simple soldier. Although his social status qualified him for an officer's rank, his political background made this impossible. As a simple soldier, he had to put up with poor accommodations and the often insufficient and monotonous troop rations. Unlike other soldiers, Werner did not receive packages from home. Emmy had nothing herself at the time, and nothing was sent by his parents and brothers. Only his aunts Hedwig Scholem and Käthe Schiepan and his uncle Hans Schiepan sent him a little money.[198]

At the end of July, Gerhard received another letter, this time from the Champagne region of France. Following numerous rainy nights camping in the open, Werner was currently living in the relatively human conditions of a barracks and was writing his letter very comfortably at a real table. Shortly before, while serving as an ammunitions driver, he had come under very heavy fire. He thanked Gerhard for the description of his daily life in Switzerland, which appeared to Werner like the land of milk and honey: "I found the description of your life there interesting, because it shows that there still are human beings who live like civilized people. I soon forgot that one could live differently—than a hounded animal." Gerhard would finish his studies long before he himself had even begun. His own occupational future, should the war someday come to an end, lay in the hands of his wife. That is why he was relieved that she had once again found well-paid work. Without such a financial cushion, all that remained open for him was a career as a party journalist—not a rosy prospect, as he noted bitterly: "I already see myself as the local editor praising the founding of a workers' bicycle club in Kleinschingelsheim. I could even now argue why one should not ride bicycles with the bourgeoisie, but that will probably interest you little." In the meantime, Werner had received news from another member of the Scholem family: to his surprise, his eldest brother Reinhold had contacted him. The reason was Käthe Wagner, a young gentile woman, with whom Reinhold had fallen in love, much to the anger of his father. "Probably the row over the *Geheimrat*'s daughter filled his soul with somewhat more understanding for my situation," Werner reported to Gerhard, referring to Käthe Wagner's father by the honorific title he bore.[199] "By the way, the old man in Neue Grünstraße appears to be truly afflicted with megalomania. Apparently the *Geheimrat*'s daughter had no money, because I hardly believe that denomination would have been a hindrance if the dowry was large." After a while, Arthur Scholem did indeed learn to accept his second non-Jewish daughter-in-law, who came from a bourgeois family whose social prestige was beneficial to the family.[200]

In the night of 19 August 1918, Werner's detachment was relocated on the front and put at the heart of "Foch's Offensive." "I have terrible days behind me, the end of which is not in sight," he reported to his brother. "Barely had we arrived when I was ordered again to join the 2nd battery of our regiment, an accompanying infantry battery, where I had to endure 6 days under very heavy fire." Afterward he had to drive ammunition trucks through the front lines and said that he was lucky to still be alive. His old wound had again opened and occasionally became infected, yet there was no hope of being discharged from the army for that reason. "If this letter seems stuporous to you, please keep in mind the fact that since the 9th of June I have been bivouacking *57 days and nights*, i.e., have been lying in filth and still lie in it. E.g., right now I am writing you on the ground, sitting, while at any moment it could start to rain yet again. This bivouacking is the greatest exertion in my current life. I would rather lie on the muck in a pigpen than in the nicest bivouac." To offset this all too blatant criticism of military life, he added a sentence meant to placate a censoring official who, scanning it quickly, would not notice its irony: "I hope you will believe me that, despite this, my patriotism as you know it has not suffered. The idea of fighting here for a *just cause* reduces the hardships somewhat. Oh, how wonderful it is indeed, etc., etc."[201]

On 23 October 1918, the day Karl Liebknecht was released from Luckau Prison after more than two years, Werner wrote his last letter to Gerhard from the front. He described the army's retreat as an experience that made his worst days on the Serbian front seem harmless. He again disregarded the risk and kept a diary, documenting "the daily trouble that I have here in the convoy. Yesterday I had to call on the help of military authorities against a brute who actually attacked me. Apparently I have not become completely stupid, otherwise the local dumbheads would not be so angry with me." His fellow soldiers tended to be both anti-intellectual and anti-Semitic, resentments that were exacerbated in Werner's case by his political activism and not least by his belief, evidently no secret to the men around him, that he had been unjustly sent to fight in this futile war. At any rate, the ideal of the community of the trenches was primarily propagated by officers from bourgeois backgrounds, and it did not figure in reports by simple soldiers.[202]

In late October Werner was convinced that the end of the war was in sight, but he feared that the effort to defend Germany would prolong combat for another year, although, as it turned out, the German naval fleet mutinied only days later, ending the war for Germany. When expressing his hopes for a revolution in Germany, he joked that he thought himself lucky to know how to fire a G98, a German bolt-action Mauser rifle, and, if necessary, also cannons. "Most likely I will soon leave the *UIndependents* [in English in the original, including the correction] and join the newly founded party. However, I first have to become a bit more informed and the entire matter has to be postponed until peacetime. Today I am outright lazy about writing. The conditions for writing—lying on half-rotten hay in a drafty shed, by candlelight, are unfortunately also not really conducive to motivating me." The party of which Werner spoke did not yet exist; he was referring to the illegal national conference of the Spartacus Group that had taken place in Berlin on 7 October 1918. Although a new party had not been established, a revolutionary program was promulgated.[203]

While the First World War ended on 11 November 1918 with the Armistice of Compiègne, it was far from over for many soldiers. Werner did not reach the home of his wife and parents-in-law in Linden until Christmas, after a harrowing march from the Champagne region. "I arrived here early on the 24th, the past years have disappeared in Orcus and before me lies a rather dark future," he wrote his brother. "Besides certain other things, I found waiting for me here my little girl and your congratulations. My, what should I say about this fact!" This fact was named Edith Elisabeth Charlotte Scholem, his tiny, three-month-old daughter, born on 27 September 1918.[204]

As difficult as the past months had been for Werner, life had also not been easy for Emmy. She had such severe health problems at the beginning of her pregnancy that she was forced to quit her job, and for a long time she had to live on the welfare provided to the wives of soldiers. Later she was healthy enough to find a new job and worked until three weeks before her daughter's birth. The birth went so smoothly that Emmy was able to return to work after only fourteen days. The only member of the Scholem family to learn about the birth from Emmy was her brother-in-law, whose discretion she trusted. On 14 October she wrote to Gerhard:

You have to excuse me for not having answered your card until now, but your timing was bad since I was sick, that is, not actually sick, I was *just* giving birth to a little girl, a little delicate black thing, a real "Scholem." There's nothing about me in her, at least not outwardly, except the cheekiness and energy and persistence. It is almost too wonderful to have a little child. Honestly, I would have preferred a boy, but Werner was more for a girl. Actually, no one was supposed to know, but I couldn't hold back and the news is safe with you. I assume that you share our happiness, even if in general there is no special cause for celebration; but everything has two sides and I am sincerely glad that it has happened.[205]

Emmy was unable to celebrate because Werner was still in the combat zone, and she had received no word from him in quite a while. She also thought that the Scholem grandparents would not be happy about the birth of their first grandchild. However, when Betty Scholem learned about the existence of her granddaughter through an indiscretion on Gerhard's part, she immediately sent her congratulations and a package with baby clothes to Hanover.[206] The young uncle was enthusiastic about the new family member and let his friends Walter and Dora Benjamin know that he had found a wife for their small son Stefan. So now, he beamed, nothing more stood in the way of a *shidduch* between the families Scholem and Benjamin, even if this lay in the distant future.[207]

The "fact" of Edith may—or may not—have helped Werner Scholem get through the difficulties facing him upon his return home, a few days before his twenty-third birthday. The future prospects of the ex-soldier and ex-convict were not very rosy: nearly four years had passed since he had been drafted into the army, and Werner had become hard and bitter. He had no university education or professional training and no one to finance it for him. What would happen now? In his famous war novel *All Quiet on the Western Front*, Erich Maria Remarque described Werner Scholem's situation as a veteran perfectly:

Now if we go back we will be weary, broken, burnt out, rootless, and without hope. We will not be able to find our way anymore.

And men will not understand us—for the generation that grew up before us, though it has passed these years with us already had a home and a calling; now it will return to its old occupations, and the war will be forgotten—and the generation that has grown up after us will be strange to us and push us aside. We will be superfluous even to ourselves, we will grow older, a few will adapt themselves, some others will merely submit, and most will be bewildered;—the years will pass by and in the end we shall fall into ruin.[208]

Family Systems

In truth, Betty Scholem had only one major ambition, to live in peace and quiet, and she was ready to sacrifice a great deal to make that wish a reality. Unfortunately, luck was not always on her side, and she would often have to bear the brunt of the bitter conflicts between the two youngest sons and Arthur Scholem. Arguments over political ideologies, court trials, conscientious objection, and an unwanted daughter-in-law dominated family life for several years. Rarely did Betty feel compelled to take sides, with the possible exception of her son Werner's early marriage. Generally she could sympathize with each person's standpoint but was reluctant to commit herself to one. Werner and Gerhard resented this, though she was the one who intervened on their behalf and saw to it that they received money, food, and letters, even "at the risk of bitter marital arguments."[209]

Compared with the drama in the lives of Werner and Gerhard, the biographies of the couple's two oldest sons paled; they left behind few papers and only played a minor role in the memoirs of Gershom Scholem. The oldest, Reinhold, developed as his father had expected and became a German patriot. However, he displayed even stronger assimilationist tendencies than Arthur Scholem and became even more German than his father. The relationship between him and his two youngest brothers was marked by mutual incomprehension and indifference, although he was only six years older than Gerhard. Erich, the second oldest son, was actually the only one who resembled Betty. Like his mother, all he wanted was a quiet life and to remain as noncommittal as possible; yet unlike her, he lacked ideals.[210]

"Perhaps one can say that the very different directions in which we four brothers developed in the ensuing years were typical of the world of the Jewish bourgeoisie and demonstrated what little influence a seemingly

FIGURE 13. Betty Scholem.
Israeli National Library,
Archive Gershom Scholem.

common environment has on the path taken by an individual young person," wrote Gershom Scholem in his memoirs about the way the four
brothers' diverse development reflected the heterogeneity of the German
Jewish bourgeoisie in the final years of imperial Germany.[211] Although their
background clearly did not dictate their fate, it did offer a certain range of
possibilities and opportunities, which each of them exploited in his own
way.[212] Although the extreme differences among the brothers in the Scholem family is exceptional, conflicting political outlooks in Jewish families
of the time were not uncommon.[213] For example, Walter Benjamin, whose
work was influenced by historical materialism and—under Gerhard's
influence—also by Jewish thought, had a brother, Georg, whose biography
is uncannily similar to that of Werner Scholem.[214]

Without doubt, the personality of their domineering father played a key
role in the development of the four Scholem brothers. Arthur Scholem did

FIGURE 14. The four Scholem brothers: from left to right, Reinhold, Erich, Werner, and Gerhard. Israeli National Library, Archive Gershom Scholem.

not aim to assimilate unconditionally into German culture. Instead he sought to maintain the status quo of a specific German Jewish identity, one tailor-made for his life but not transferable to that of his younger sons. Therefore, on the one hand, he opposed any observance of Jewish ritual, banned Yiddish or typically Jewish expressions from his vocabulary, and tolerated only the necessary minimum of religious symbols in his house. On the other hand, not unusually, his circle of friends and relatives all belonged to the Jewish middle class. From time to time he lectured his sons on the mission of Judaism "to proclaim to the world pure monotheism and a purely rational morality." He was also vehemently against marriage between Jews and non-Jews and called baptism "an unprincipled and servile act." Even friendships with non-Jews were not cultivated in the Scholem household.[215]

Much like Hermann Kafka, another man who became well known as the father of a famous member of this generation, Arthur Scholem had made a livable, perhaps even comfortable place for himself and could not comprehend why his younger sons rejected the prospect of such a life. He did not understand their skepticism about his bourgeois values, which they first expressed even before the war began. Yet by the time the war ended,

FIGURE 15. Arthur Scholem. Israeli National Library, Archive Gershom Scholem.

their skepticism had been confirmed, because all hope on the part of German Jews "to be finally accepted into the German *Volksgemeinschaft*" had been de facto obliterated by the "trauma of the First World War."[216] In the same situation, Franz Kafka wrote *Letter to His Father*, in which he accused his father of being weak and of capitulating to German culture. Like Werner and Gerhard Scholem and many others, Kafka sought authenticity, which they could not find in their father's bourgeois conformist values and way of life.[217]

When the war broke out, both of the younger Scholem brothers turned away from their father, whose concept of life seemed irrelevant to their needs and concerns, and they turned toward other role models. In the immediate neighborhood of their parents' home, in the Scheunenviertel and in Neukölln, they found numerous opportunities to discuss Judaism or Socialism with like-minded peers. In this environment of political associations, youth movements, libraries, and bookstores, the two brothers came of age politically and intellectually; an exposure interrupted for Werner by the early and forced stays in provincial towns. The difficulty of choosing one's own path among such diversity certainly contributed more than a little to the "confusion" Gerhard had described as a characteristic of the disoriented Jewish youth. The "Jewish question" played a major role in this search because "everyone found themselves in a degree of turmoil over this issue" and defined themselves through their affirmation or rejection of Judaism.[218]

Both of the younger Scholem brothers tried out various groups and movements before deciding on their own paths. Werner joined the Zionist Jung Juda, only to abandon it shortly afterward for the Socialist youth movement, and Gerhard belonged to the youth group of the Orthodox Agudat Israel until he discovered oppositional Zionism. The decisions they made in these early years were as important for the course of their lives as the following years would be. For Gerhard began a period of intensive and in part lonely study, which he described as one of "very stimulated thinking."[219] Meanwhile, Werner postponed his intellectual development to an indefinite "later day" after the war. Between barracks, prison cell, and trenches, he only had short breaks in which he could visit Hanover or Berlin and read what he wanted and what interested him. As differently as their lives unfolded, the brothers shared a determination to commit to a path of constant, antibourgeois rebellion. Their choices to join oppositional and minority groups—the Jung Juda and the Spartacus League—expressed their rejection of any closed or defined structure, an attitude that they essentially retained as long as they lived.[220]

As Gershom Scholem later put it, this rebellion was a renunciation of the self-deception in which, in their opinion, the "milieu of liberal, assimilated-German Judaism" lived. The Jewish youth revolted against a seemingly flourishing but actually decaying society by joining the ranks either of the Zionists or of the leftist revolution.[221] Gerhard's resolve to distance himself permanently from German Jews matured during the long summer of the war year 1916, which he spent in the seclusion of the upper Allgäu region. By embracing radical Zionism—which his mother described as a battle cry causing great strife in the family—Gerhard turned away from his father even before they came into open conflict. He ceased seeking a way to become rooted in Germany and instead envisioned his future in Palestine. At the time, this "Zion" appeared to him to be less a geographic location than a metaphysical space that united the origins and utopian goal of Judaism.[222]

While fighting in a war in the service of the German empire, which he abhorred, Werner also reached a personal decision. Though he expressed fleeting interest in Palestine, he increasingly saw radical internationalism like that advocated by Rosa Luxemburg as the solution to all Jewish—and other—matters. Like Karl Marx, Rosa Luxemburg claimed there was "no 'Jewish question' as a race or religious question" for the working class. There was only a societal and political one, which, once solved, would also thereby eradicate anti-Semitism. This was the position that Werner espoused.[223] In the final analysis, this could only mean assimilation, possibly that "revolutionary noble-minded assimilation" of the kind associated with unwavering Europeanism, which Gerhard enthusiastically described in his diary in late 1915, albeit not as a solution for himself but for Walter Benjamin and others.[224] Despite the deep aversion to Germans that Werner developed during the war, such assimilation would have to play out—in the absence of a postrevolutionary society—precisely in Germany.

Despite his evident importance, Arthur Scholem, the patriarch, was only one factor in the self-formation and self-definition of his two youngest sons.[225] In the complex equilibrium of the family system, the sons also influenced each other, differentiating their own political and social identity from that of the other: as Werner became increasingly politicized, his brother withdrew from politics into the world of philology and metaphysics. Naturally both sons were also influenced by factors outside of the family, especially by their friends.

Once the war was finally over, having forced both brothers into their respective radicalized political positions, thereby alienating them from one another, the Scholem family system broke down, particularly for Werner. Arthur Scholem had ceased all contact with Werner and Emmy, refusing to see his son again. He also denied him any further financial support. This decision was cemented by a will that he wrote in 1921, four years before his death. According to the will, the family estate was to be divided into three parts after Betty's death; Werner's inheritance was to be limited to the minimum amount required by law. The printing business was to be turned over to Reinhold and Erich, who were each to pay out fifty thousand reichsmarks to their younger brothers after Betty died.[226]

Meanwhile, Betty only acquiesced to her husband's dictate for the short time between Werner's wedding and the birth of her granddaughter; once Edith was born, she resumed contact. With very few exceptions, Betty now became the hub of family relations, especially between Werner and Gerhard/Gershom. Edith's birth had placed Werner in a new family system. For want of positive role models—Werner would hardly have looked to his father for inspiration and Emmy had spent her childhood in a foster family—both were rather at a loss about how to handle this new challenge. So they concentrated their energy and activity on politics and the German revolution, which, they assumed, would fundamentally alter German society. Only then would the time come to translate and integrate political utopia into daily family life. This now became the work ahead of them.

2

IN THE SHADOW
OF REVOLUTION

I was thirty.
My hair had turned gray.
I was not tired.

—Ernst Toller, *I Was a German*, 1933

If you want a future, darlin',
Why don't you get a past?

—Cole Porter, "Let's Misbehave," 1927

Red Flags Waving Above the Old Palace

"Dear Child! Let me reassure you that so far everything is happening with the greatest calm & there has not yet been any sort of disorder." On 9 November 1918, Betty Scholem quickly dashed off a letter to her son Gerhard in Switzerland to inform him about the revolution, which had reached Berlin that morning. During the day, the news of the emperor's abdication circulated throughout the city, whereupon the SPD politician Philipp Scheidemann proclaimed the founding of the republic from the balcony of the Reichstag. Still, all remained calm. No street fighting occurred, unlike other German cities during the previous two days. Betty felt there was reason to hope that everything would remain calm; after all, the soldiers and Social Democrats were supposed to be "in agreement about maintaining order." That afternoon she went for a walk with her sister in the immediate vicinity of her apartment in the city district Berlin-Mitte in order to discover what had not yet appeared in the newspapers. "I strolled with Käthe from 3 o'clock to half past four down the Leipziger, Königgrätzer & Linden streets & with astonished nostrils [*sic*] we saw red flags waving above the old palace. Peace is coming, everything will be fine!" she reported cheerfully. Only a few days earlier, the armistice had seemed to her little more than a distant hope, because people's daily reality was still being dictated by a war that did not want to end. What is more, the Spanish flu, a ghastly epidemic, had come in its wake and was plaguing all of Europe.[1]

After she had finished her short note to Gerhard and sent it off, she left the house once again, this time with her husband. "Since all appeared calm," the couple walked "a little toward the revolution," which was taking place in the immediate vicinity of Neue Grünstrasse, the street where they lived. In front of the occupied palace, where that afternoon Karl Liebknecht had proclaimed the founding of the republic for the second time, specifically the "Free Socialist Republic of Germany," the couple suddenly found themselves in the middle of a shoot-out. Full of irony and a bit of pride, Betty reported to Gerhard about the adventure his parents had involuntarily wandered into: "As we guilelessly approached Lustgarten, shots rang out from Schlossplatz, which quickly turned into massive rattle and machine-gun fire. Everyone scurried to flee over the palace bridge, with us right in the middle of them. That this should happen to me! My legs are

FIGURE 16. Machine-gun post at the palace fountain, 9 November 1918. Bundesarchiv, photo 146-2007-0005. Photographer: L. Marmulla

still shaking. . . . Naturally Father teases me about how I ran and stood trembling behind the cover of a poster pillar, yet he skedaddled just like me!"[2]

The initial calm dissipated as the conflict in Berlin escalated. In letters sent to Gerhard in distant and peaceful Switzerland at regular intervals during the following days and weeks, Betty described how the family increasingly suffered from the chaos and food shortages. In Berlin, the French chiefs of staff imposed a strict blockade of goods into the city as long as Germany did not meet its reparation payments, and the effects of this blockade were quickly felt. Everywhere in the city, strikes were both threatened and carried out, so that on one day there was no electricity, on the next no public transportation. The print shop of Arthur Scholem, which had long since grown from a small business into a sizable enterprise of sixty-five employees, was hit by the political upheaval. The eight-hour workday for which the labor movement had fought so long was now introduced by law, with no reduction of the hourly rate. Since it was also stipulated that no worker was allowed to be fired and no returning war veteran denied his old job, Arthur Scholem increasingly found himself in financial difficulty. According to Betty, her fifty-five-year-old husband aged considerably during the days and weeks of the German revolution. He appeared quite relieved when his oldest son, Reinhold, returned from the trenches in Belgium and took over a part of the family business with his brother Erich.[3]

There was also support for the German republic in the Scholem household. For her part, Betty immediately exercised her newly granted right to vote. Like her husband, she backed the recently founded liberal German Democratic Party, which was highly favored among middle-class Jews and closely affiliated with the Central Association of German Citizens of Jewish Faith (Centralverein deutscher Staatsbürger jüdischen Glaubens, abbreviated as Central Verein or CV). Like the majority of the German—and especially the Jewish—middle class, Betty Scholem was highly disturbed by the activities of the Spartacus League, which she viewed as a threat to the stability of a society that was still reeling from the harsh demands made upon it in the armistice. She criticized the group's relish for demonstrations, its propensity for violence, and the "reign of terror" that it spread—in her mind all "criminals, scatterbrains & wild bucks who tag along!" At the same time, she knew very well that her son Werner would have joined the Spartacists had he not been retreating from the Champagne region with the army. Instead he had joined the soldiers' council of his military unit.[4]

In essence, Betty echoed the prevailing opinion in the liberal Jewish middle class at the time concerning the connection between the terroristic activities of the Spartacus League and the growth of anti-Semitism. This was particularly evident in fliers found on Berlin streets that "called for Jew-baiting" and, according to Betty, were surely the product of right-wing parties "who want to divert the anger of the people, [thus using] the old historical ruse."[5] They accused the German Jews for the general unrest. In defensive response, the Jewish newspapers expressed skepticism about the revolution, and people were worried about the possibility of pogroms and violent riots. A majority of German Jews also feared that the revolutionaries, having suddenly acquired political power, would misuse it, and this would give rise to anti-Semitic sentiments.[6] As a voice for the Jewish middle class, the Central Verein had "moderately approved the liberalization of the German system of government" but continued to argue for "preservation" and against "violent change." Actually, the question about how the new political situation would affect the situation of the Jewish population concerned the CV only in the early phase of the revolution. Soon the organization became preoccupied solely with damage control and fending off the negative effects of this upheaval on Jewish life in Germany.[7]

Looking back years later, Golo Mann felt as if the "anti-Semitic passion in Germany" had never, not even in the 1930s, been "fiercer" than in the months following November 1918. In fact, anti-Semitism did become more radical, with frequent attacks on Jews.[8] In response, the Central Verein reaffirmed incessantly that there could be no specifically Jewish responsibility for the revolution—moreover, that the very assumption was absurd. How could it be that, as the Berlin newspaper *Deutsche Zeitung* wrote, "the current government of Germany is thoroughly *verjudet* [Jewified], that Germany is currently ruled only by Jews," while at the same time, the Spartacus League, which was agitating against the government, was also said to be thoroughly Jewish? This would mean that a Jewish government was being challenged by a Jewish, leftist opposition. Anti-Semitic accusations led to yet a further paradox: such a deep political split within the Jewish community ran counter to the extraordinarily strong feeling of solidarity attributed to German Jews. Thus, as the CV monthly *Im deutschen Reich* stressed, the entire argument was utter nonsense. Therefore the Jews should ignore anti-Semitism and the phenomenon should be downplayed and marginalized.[9]

Even though anti-Semitic propaganda exaggerated the number of German Jews participating in the German revolution, compared to the percentage of Jews in the general populace, a disproportionate number of the revolutionaries were of Jewish descent. Sometimes it was mere pragmatism that led Jews to join revolutionary bodies, since the social upheaval opened doors that had previously been shut to them. For example, a disproportionately large number of Jewish soldiers joined the soldiers' councils in the fall of 1918, probably because, as Jews, they had been denied entry in the officer corps, although their high level of education should have qualified them for it.[10]

However, the revolutionary movements in Russia in 1905 and 1917 and in Berlin and Munich in 1918 and 1919 attracted Jews for deeper reasons.[11] In the December 1919 issue of the *Neue jüdische Monatshefte*, the Berlin historian of literature Rudolf Kayser wrote: "As grossly exaggerated as it is by the anti-Semites, and as anxiously denied as it is by the Jewish bourgeoisie, the large Jewish participation in the current revolutionary movement is a fact; it is, after all, so large that it cannot be coincidence. Rather, an innate tendency dictates it: it is the consequence of Jewish existence in a modern political context." Kayser depicted the twentieth-century Jewish Socialists and Communists as the reincarnation of historic messianic figures: martyrs and prophets, who remained undeterred as they traveled a path that inevitably ended tragically.

> Even though, in thought and deed, they enter into a most fervent community with their comrades from other backgrounds, these true Jewish revolutionaries are very different from them. They usually have it harder in two respects: they lack the natural opposition of the suppressed class, the proletariat (they are always "intellectuals"), and second, [they lack] the broad national support evolving from the fact that leaders and their following are of the same folkish [völkisch] origins. The latter point will probably be challenged by referring to the international character of Socialism, as it is in every modern revolutionary ideology: still the fact remains that the Russian and the German revolutions have a strong nationalist element.

According to Kayser, these two factors explain the inevitable solitude of Jewish revolutionaries, who seldom subscribe to an orthodox revolutionary catechism, but more frequently are found among the heretics. Their role model was none other than the great mystic and false messiah Sabbatai Zevi, who had stirred the Jewish world of the seventeenth century into an eschatological frenzy. Kayser was convinced that he recognized the same excessiveness "in hope and being out of touch with reality" exhibited by Sabbatai Zevi that he saw in the political utopianism embraced by the professional revolutionaries of his time. By referring to Jewish messianism, this interpretation integrated Jewish social revolutionaries in both the historical and religious traditions. For their part, the Jewish revolutionaries would dismiss this explanation of their radicalism and deny its connection with any traditional essence that could be attributed to them solely through the fact of their ethnicity.[12]

Nevertheless, what Kayser called the "uncritical equation of revolutionary politics with messianism" was widespread among German Jews at the time.[13] Indeed, we find a similar position in Jakob Wasserman's autobiography, published in 1921: "Where the unconditional is demanded, where the slate was wiped clean, where the idea of governmental reformation was to be implemented with frantic earnestness, there were Jews, Jews are the leaders. Jews are the Jacobins of the age." Wasserman also thought the affinity between Jews and revolutionaries was the result of a "transplantation of the messiah idea, conceived in Judaism, from the religious realm to the social one."[14] In their theoretical writings, Walter Benjamin, Ernst Bloch, and Martin Buber all reflected on the possibility of such an affinity and developed philosophical, literary, and theological perspectives about it.

Although many Jews, particularly young people, were largely indifferent to their Jewishness, the German public, especially anti-Semites, saw them primarily as Jews. "Those operating as openly Jewish never interested the German public," wrote Werner T. Angress, a historian who grew up in Berlin, "That was irrelevant in their eyes. Only the 'disguised' Jews who took part in German political life as German individuals without a Jewish mandate were noticed."[15] Thus, not only did anti-Semites emphasize Jewish participation in the revolution, but they also postulated a universal affinity between Jewish intellectuals and this type of radicalism, and this insidious, ostensibly Jewish trait was depicted as more offensive than the actual practice of Judaism itself.[16]

Right-wing demagogues emphasized the presence of Jews in the Spartacus League and the Bavarian Soviet Republic whenever they could and turned prominent gentile revolutionaries into Jews—particularly Karl Liebknecht, who, as Arnold Zweig noted, "was considered a Jew throughout the entire army, naturally."[17] By the summer of 1914, Liebknecht had advanced to the position of public enemy number one, thanks to his pacifist activities. Later on, together with Rosa Luxemburg, he was even blamed for the strikes and unrest at the turn of the year 1917–1918. After he openly turned against the government once again, now in the position as the leader of the Spartacus revolt, he became the key figure in the myth of Germany's "stab-in-the-back" defeat.[18] In near desperation, the newspaper *Im deutschen Reich*, the voice of the Central Verein, denied Liebknecht's Jewish background and published family trees and excerpts from the registry of births to prove his thoroughly "Aryan descent."[19]

Naturally there was also open support for the revolution on the part of Jewish institutions and organizations. Although Zionists had not opposed the war at its start, groups of German Zionists now demonstrated goodwill toward the revolution and hoped that a democratic government would support their Zionist aims.[20] Even Martin Buber, who had conformed to the patriotic consensus during the war, publicly expressed support for the revolution in his newspaper *Der Jude*. It appeared as if he was seeking to compensate for his error in 1914, for which Gerhard Scholem, at the time still in school, had strongly criticized him. "For its own sake, not for the sake of any kind of side effects from which we profit, not as beneficiaries but as fellow combatants and backers, we welcome the revolution," wrote Buber in early 1919. He expressed his pride in the Jewish contribution to the revolution and his hopes that this was the start of a utopian period. "A new Socialism, which continues and implements the old, is emerging from the creative spirit of the age—not the least the Jewish. Perhaps the creative period of the Socialist idea is now truly beginning."[21] Buber thus described the predominant mood among many citizens of the young republic, the sense of being at the beginning of a new era, despite setbacks, famines, and political murders.

Werner Scholem immersed himself in this hopeful and visionary atmosphere as he, like hundreds of thousands of others, emerged from his wartime experience of living with no future. Now that the war was over, they could focus entirely on the future, on making a radically new start, and this moment only seemed possible because of the total war that preceded it. The break with the past produced a chance for a new world, which had to be established rapidly and with great energy. The future was beginning now, with dreams of political utopias.[22]

Revolutionaries and Kabbalists

"I will never in my lifetime get over the fact that I did not participate in the revolution in Germany," noted Werner Scholem bitterly in December 1918, two days after his return from the war. "Such bad luck to be stuck far away from all that was happening at the time, while at home every person who had previously been halfway active became a minister." He complained about his constant misfortune of being in the wrong place at the wrong time. Now the war was over, and Germany had entered the storm of revolutionary events that he had longed for since 1914. Back then, in December of the first war year, he had written his brother: "I hope for a revolution that makes 1789 look like child's play, just as the wars of that period are child's play compared to today. We will then be great bogeymen, should I still be alive."[23]

He was indeed still alive and in a few days would celebrate his twenty-third birthday. In the capital, the bloody Christmas battles at the Berlin City Palace had come to an end. Now the time had come for Werner Scholem to find a place in the new system and to rethink his own ideological position. Contrary to what might be expected, he did not immediately and uncompromisingly identify with the Spartacus League. His feelings, he wrote, did pull him in the direction of the Spartacists, who were staunchly supported by his wife and his friends. But he had to admit that "my reason enables me . . . to recognize the futility and absurdity of such politics far too clearly to let me join it. The Independents are right now on the brink of breaking up. Only in nuances does the left wing differ from the Spartacists and the right from the old party. This party will thus disband."[24] Although he predicted the split within the USPD, which did indeed occur a year and a half later, he still remained a party member. This coalition, born out of opposition to the war, was his political home, and for the time being he remained loyal to it. Moreover, the Independent Social Democrats still wielded power and influence despite the tensions within the party, while the newly formed Communist Party, which had evolved out of the Spartacus League at the very beginning of 1919, was not yet an alternative to take seriously.

So, now that he had answered the question about party affiliation, where should he begin his political involvement and how should he feed his family? If it had been solely up to him, Werner Scholem may have returned to Halle, where he had made important political connections while in the barracks and in prison for many months. Or perhaps he would have chosen Berlin, where he could have joined the revolutionary movements and resumed his university studies. Furthermore, in Berlin Emmy, who was the breadwinner of the family at the time, could probably find a job. But who would look after four-month-old Edith? Werner saw little hope for his political career in Hanover-Linden, but his wife had a good position, and his mother-in-law would assume the care of the baby. So, they decided to stay in Linden temporarily: Werner hoped this arrangement would last no longer than Easter. In early January 1919, the couple moved out of Werner's in-laws' small apartment and rented a place of their own in a brick building at Nieschlagstrasse 26 in the center of Linden. "We have 2 nice rooms with a comrade who lives alone," reported Werner, "and Emmy is developing astonishing talents as a housewife. Luckily she does not have to go into the office because there is nothing to do, although she continues to be paid." Edith remained in the care of her grandmother, whose apartment in the northern part of Linden was not very far away.[25]

While waiting out the war in the trenches in Champagne during the summer of 1918, Werner Scholem had imagined a dismal postwar future as a local reporter covering stories like the founding of workers' bicycle clubs. In the winter of 1919, since Arthur Scholem showed no inclination to forgive his son for the unwanted wedding and birth of a grandchild, Werner took a job with the *Braunschweiger Volksfreund*, one of the oldest Socialist newspapers in the country, which now aligned itself closely with the USPD. "I had to give up the idea of studying, whether I liked it or not," he reported to his brother in Switzerland, "because I have no money to study and could not keep my head above water in a university town under the current circumstances, not even with the help of my wife. Still, I have been lucky enough to quickly find a permanent job, one that I like whole-heartedly."[26]

In contrast to Braunschweig, the Independent Social Democrats in Hanover had distanced themselves from the Spartacus League, but Werner was certain that when the party finally decided on the direction it was to take, it would not be in favor of the majority Socialists, meaning the SPD. This assumption proved to be partially correct. Although the soviet model never really gained a strong foothold in Hanover and the SPD remained in power, the USPD increasingly became a political force to reckon with in Hanover-Linden, something for which Werner, among others, was respon-sible. In early 1919, he made his first major appearances as a political agita-tor. "I shoulder the entire burden of agitation in Hanover," he reported, "because I am the only one responsible for everything, so I have to work as my own reporter in the mornings, as an editor in the afternoons, and as a speaker in the evenings." By giving talks and speeches every evening in Linden and the immediate vicinity, he hoped to improve his chances to be elected to the city council in the elections scheduled in February.[27] His rapid success was remarkable but not surprising. As a convicted pacifist who had been forced to serve in the war against his will and who had been convinced by this experience of the necessity of unconditional radicalness, Werner Scholem embodied the ideal representative of this new party born out of opposition to the war.

Soon after his return from France, Werner made a short trip to Berlin. With the birth of her granddaughter, Betty flouted the ban that her hus-band had issued against his son and daughter-in-law. Arthur Scholem was probably traveling when his son "was very well received by Mother, who gave me all sorts of things for our new household. The *mishpokha* were also very nice toward me, but had changed little and now railed against Sparta-cus. Good old Reinhold, whom I did not see, thank God, works on behalf of the German People's Party." Clearly, the Scholem family had split politically in several directions, starting with Werner, followed on his heels by Gerhard, and now the oldest, Reinhold, who had moved to the right and proudly announced his membership in the national-liberal German People's Party (Deutsche Volkspartei, DVP). Erich was the only one who continued to represent the parents' position, and he did so quite nonpolitically.[28]

Once again Werner established contact with Gerhard, the only member of the family whom he considered reasonable. For nine months the brothers corresponded regularly. Werner wrote extensively about his political hopes and initial successes. Although Gerhard's replies are missing, their content may be inferred in part from diary entries and letters to third parties. As he had done earlier, Werner taunted Gerhard to discover where he currently stood politically. For example, Werner asked him immediately upon his return from the army in December 1918 how things stood with the "realization of the Zionist 'war aims' in Palestine"? Did there already exist "a Jewish annexation party that, following a famous pattern, also seeks to occupy Syria and the Sinai Peninsula, because historically these regions once belonged to the crown of David"?[29] Although he could not have known how serious Gerhard had become about Zionism, the provocative nature of his comment hit the mark directly at a highly sensitive point in Gerhard's own criticism of the Zionist policy in Palestine. On 29 December 1918, Gerhard wrote an entry in his diary that could well be in response to the content of Werner's letter: "Today is Werner's birthday. I did not even write him. Between us are mountains of unfamiliarity [*Unbekanntschaft*], of course: *what* can get more extreme about him? He is ruled by terrible demonic laws deep within. But we will die without having spoken to each other. I do not know him, I do not know his wife, I do not know with what right he has her—toward him I am basically what I generously call neutral. That is, I live, extending credit of goodwill toward him."[30]

The existence of demonic laws and their impact on human existence was a subject that had been preoccupying Gerhard increasingly for several months as a result of his intensive study of Jewish mysticism. A few months earlier, he had written in his diary that man takes on demonic characteristics in the dark of night and far from God's revelation, but that it is precisely in this moment that the opportunity arises for true redemption.[31] Perhaps, when he said that Werner was ruled by demonic laws, he meant that his brother did indeed live in darkness outside divine—that is,

Zionist—revelation, but at the same time, a chance for renewal and conversion existed.

Without a doubt, the incomprehension and unfamiliarity between the brothers had grown over the preceding months. After moving to Switzerland, Gerhard had increasingly withdrawn political concerns and devoted himself to academic study, an internal emigration that paralleled his physical exile to Bern, which had removed him from the war. He had turned his back on his radical and passionate opposition to the war and now felt as if his earlier resistance in connection with Jung Juda was light years away from his current pursuits. Nothing distracted him from these pursuits, not even the revolution, in which he had been involved at the very start in 1915 in Neukölln, or its key figure Karl Liebknecht, whom Gerhard had believed for years to be a "truly historic, invisible power." On the contrary, Gerhard refused to attribute any messianic quality to the German revolution of 1918 and thus any potential for far-reaching and radical change. The real objective, he wrote, had to be a thoroughly different movement, whose central concept would be the court, a movement that combined "indictment, evidence, and verdict" and whose ideal lay in realization of the Zionist idea of revolutionary life.[32] Gerhard felt justified in his rejection of Socialism in favor of anarchism—an opinion he had expressed even at the beginning of the war—because he regarded anarchism as nothing but a preliminary step to theocracy and thus the only acceptable "societal structure and therefore form of government for humanity." Not only was political Socialism to be rejected, he wrote, it also had to be fought, because in the end the messianic kingdom could "not be confirmed by elections. Community, the highest for which we strive, is not a political idea."[33]

Gerhard's attitude toward Bolshevism was completely different after the October Revolution as well. He noted that, among his circle, he was considered to be very Bolshevik friendly. Indeed, he did attribute a certain revolutionary magic to the movement, which originated from the central idea that a messianic empire could only develop out of a dictatorship of poverty. He argued that "even though the Bolshevik revolution will be caught up in bloodshed . . . it will nevertheless serve as the only high point of the history of the world war and, however saddening it may be, the messianic reaction against it." The revolution brought about the redemption from war, but it was simultaneously a result of that war's bloodshed and therefore could only take place through violence. Thus, in his opinion, everyone who professed allegiance to Europe was also called upon to approve the revolution, as had the friends of the Bolshevists in German prisons: Karl Liebknecht, Rosa Luxemburg, and—Werner Scholem. This conclusion might have applied to Jewish revolutionaries, but not to Zionism and Judaism and therefore also not to Gerhard himself. Revolution was found "where the messianic kingdom is to be established without the teachings," whereas for Judaism the true revolution has to be "reconnected to the teachings." Thus, the world war offered no argument for Jewish messianism similar to the one it offered Bolshevism, because Zionism turned away from war and therefore did not react to it. As for the Bolshevist revolutionaries, their ideological claim to be acting both historically and for the future was an impossible one to fulfill. "Bolshevism tries—perhaps with grandeur but surely in vain—to avoid submitting to judgment on itself through the permanence of its singular point of *Gewalt* [violence], which must appear to be in the future that it anticipates." As Gerhard saw it, by postponing judgment to the future, Bolshevism becomes unjust and thus reprehensible.[34]

It is not clear to what extent, if at all, Gerhard shared these thoughts with his brother. What does appear certain is that he accused Werner of lacking radicalism, just as he had done in prior years. Whatever Gerhard wrote, it prompted Werner, as before, to justify his decision to remain in the USPD for the time being and not to join the KPD: "But you are wrong, and if you consider it a mistake to be 'independent' as revolutionary, then this erroneous conclusion can be explained by your distance from events. I'm telling you now that this party is nothing permanent; it is one standing at the crossroads. I also now consider a Socialist middle to be superfluous, but it must first become clear what stands left of us. Then our party as such will most likely join the radical left unified front."[35] Despite these disagreements, Werner's letters were engaging and friendly. He still hoped to study with Gerhard in Göttingen and apologized for having little time right then, but the "massive load of daily work" prevented him from reading and studying. Furthermore, the gas in their two rented rooms was turned off at 10:00 p.m., more or less forcing them to go to bed early.

"You may not be aware," Werner wrote to Gerhard in May, "that we are in a 'revolution' here in Germany, and politicians in times of revolution have damn little time to write letters. You, on your blissful island there, do not have a very accurate picture of what is happening here. In fact, I even have the impression that it is not at all important to you to get such a picture." The tone of the letters becomes impatient, almost snide, which leads one to assume that Gerhard's letters had become increasingly critical.

Perhaps someday, wrote Werner ironically, his brother would understand him; perhaps someday he, Gerhard, would even find himself in "a revolutionary maelstrom," namely, "if you all establish the Jewish state, and your fat cats commit the decisive stupidity of setting up a capitalistic branch of London there with a Jewish proletariat. A Jewish Communist proletarian in Palestine, then you would experience something!"[36] This letter reached Gerhard just as he informed his parents of his plans to emigrate to Palestine upon completion of his studies. Within the period of only a few months, one brother had completely dedicated himself to a political career in revolutionary Germany, while the other had decided during his Swiss exile to leave not only Germany but also all of Europe behind him, a Europe he found so corrupted by war.[37]

Despite this dissonance, Werner told his brother proudly and self-mockingly about his own political successes, about his work as a city councillor and simultaneously as the chairman of the USPD Linden, about his speeches, and about his work as a commissioner, most recently in the Commission for Secondary Schools—a special triumph for someone who had formerly been a very poor pupil. He laughed about his antics before his mirror, where he practiced putting "parliamentary wrinkles" in his face in order to be taken seriously despite being an up-and-coming politician of only twenty-three years of age. "Besides I have a task that I take far more seriously, namely, the organization of revolutionary-minded elements in the city and province of Hanover. Here we have met with such success, it is really astonishing. Places where we were thrashed and decried only last January, where the appearance of an Independent was nearly impossible, people now cheer us." Both in Hanover and in several cities in the area, where the USPD had had few supporters up until then, laborers now stood firmly behind the program of the Independents. Parallel to the rise of the party, Werner Scholem's fame rose as a charismatic speaker and provocative politician. Almost surprised, he reported that he had already become the icon of the enemy and was being "railed at in all rags of Hanover province." The *Volkswille*, the Hanover Socialist daily, founded in 1890, had even bestowed upon him the title of "inexperienced," noted Werner. It wrote: "One has to have heard how this inexperienced young man treated the old, established leaders of the proletariat amid the clamorous applause of his supporters!" In March, Werner served as a delegate to the USPD party conference, during which a confrontation ensued between the moderate and the radical leftist wings. He described this confrontation using the rhetoric of war: "The Independent Social Democrats entered the Communist camp with drums beating and trumpets sounding, as was their duty. This march alone made it possible for me to remain in this party." Once the party had decided to head in this direction, Werner thought there was no longer much of a difference between Independents and Communists, especially because the USPD had decided in favor of the soviet system and had thus handed down its death sentence on parliamentarism.[38]

For just a few weeks, Werner had been able to concentrate solely on his career as a professional revolutionary, which would have been nearly impossible without the help of his wife. She ran the household and was in charge of most of their income. Once again he proudly pointed out that she demonstrated "remarkable talents as a housewife, is basically highly unpolitical and wishes I would be a street cleaner and not a politician. In these times, the thing is indeed highly dangerous, but I don't see why I should be afraid after having spent 4 years being forced to put my neck on the line for absolutely nothing."[39] Indeed it was perilous to be a leftist German revolutionary at that time. Rosa Luxemburg and Karl Liebknecht were murdered in January 1919, and their deaths were followed in February by that of yet another revolutionary, Kurt Eisner, the first president of the Bavarian Soviet Republic. In March Leo Jogiches was murdered; in May, Gustav Landauer; in June, Eugen Leviné; and, finally, in November, Hugo Haase.[40] The entire leadership of the left was assassinated that year and in the following three years. Four out of five of these murders remained unsolved and unpunished.[41] Hence, it was quite understandable that Emmy Scholem feared for the life of her husband.

While his brother pursued his career as a politician, Gerhard lived in Switzerland and contemplated his vision of ideal Communism, to which he attributed, on the one hand, a religious dimension and, on the other, a radical way of life that would structure the way young men and women lived together.[42] All this had very little to do with the everyday concerns of City Councillor Scholem, and Gerhard offered little acknowledgment of his brother's accomplishments. Nonetheless he was a bit curious. In April 1919, he wrote Werner Kraft in Hanover and suggested that he visit Werner and Emmy sometime. As Gerhard's friend, he would certainly be welcome. "Personally, I would encourage you to go, for one (may you forgive me), to see how he behaves—whether he delves completely into a not quite pure phraseology or whether he doesn't, as I would like to hope, but also because I hold his wife in *very* high esteem. I think you could even discuss your own poetry with her."[43] He advised Werner Kraft to visit his brother only when the latter was not giving a speech and wrote, "Incidentally, you should know him by now through the press, for he's supposed to be the roaring lion of the Independents for the entire province. Moreover, he is (at 23!!) the chairman of the Linden Independent Socialist faction and of the workers' council in Hanover, and editor at the *Volksstimme* in Braunschweig. Should you now be interested in Socialism, he can perhaps be of some help. Naturally, he is a 'Communist.'" Werner Kraft was not to be taken aback by the "robust language" of the long-serving soldier. "He regards me highly," concluded Gerhard, "because he believes or even knows that I am 'more leftist' than he is, if one can still call it that."[44] After all this time, the brothers were still competing to be the most radical, the most "leftist," the least compromising of the two.

The Language of the Barricades

The reputation of the eloquent young city councilor and journalist preceded Werner Scholem, and so early in the summer of 1919 he received a telegram with a job offer: would he be interested in working as an editor at the *Hallesches Volksblatt*? The decision was not an easy one. On the one hand, Werner had experienced great success in Hanover in just a few months, and now there was a chance that he might be elected as the party secretary. On the other hand, the *Volksblatt* was an SPD publication with a long tradition that had backed the Independent Socialists as early as 1917 and in the meantime had become one of the largest party newspapers. "If I were an ambitious show-off, I would have remained in Hanover, where I was already known all over town and was dragged through the muck nearly every day in the paper of the majority Socialist bigwigs," remarked Werner after he had decided in favor of Halle, which was a center of proletarian power, against the "little bit of regional fame in Hanover." With great pleasure he gave up his laurels as city councillor, he wrote to Gerhard. "*Nebikh*"—so what![45]

What finally convinced him to take the job in Halle were the prospects of working at a major newspaper and of learning party journalism from the bottom up. Although his position was at the bottom rungs of the *Volksblatt*, namely at the regional desk, the situation at the paper was so chaotic and the shortage of editors was so great that the opportunities for advancement could only be good. Furthermore, Halle and the administrative district of Merseburg were now considered the center of the left wing of the labor movement. In Werner's estimation, the party leadership and electorate here were "independent and truly revolutionary-minded" with only a very few "right-wing Socialists" among them.[46] There had been a tradition of left-wing Socialism there, ever since a majority of the membership had opposed the SPD's approval of war in the summer of 1914. For this reason, the left-wing district organization had been expelled from the SPD in March 1916, and their leaders had been among the founders of the Independent Social-ists in the spring of 1917. Werner Scholem, who was in detention in Halle at the time, became a member of the USPD immediately after it was estab-lished; by summer, 90 percent of the Social Democrats in the district had followed suit.[47]

For Werner Scholem, the move to Halle was a return to the scene of his very first political triumph, where comrades and friends had witnessed his trial and supplied him with books, food packages, and information during the months he spent in solitary confinement. One such person was Rein-hold Schönlank, the brother of the poet Bruno Schönlank, who had set up the local section of the newly founded Communist Party (KPD) in early 1919. Even though the KPD was "not much more than a revolutionary sect" compared to the powerful USPD at the time, his initiative represented an important step for the left wing of the labor movement in Halle.[48]

Werner had his hands full in his new position since he was solely responsible for the local and regional section of the *Volksblatt*.[49] As in Han-over, he traveled a great deal and reported from Halle and other small towns in the area—sometimes he even reported on his own frequent speak-ing engagements. For example, he wrote about an evening in the small town of Zörbig not far from Halle, where he had given a speech on the question of "peace and the political situation." An anonymous newspaper story, undoubtedly his own work, reported that "in an impressive, nearly two-hour talk, [Comrade Scholem] proved that the U.S.P. [USPD] was the only party that clearly and distinctly represented its standpoint on this issue. He unrelentingly criticized the people who seek to recreate the tumul-tuous mood of 1914 and likewise the governing Socialists, whose fault it is that, after three quarters of the year, the capitalists, Junkers, and clerics now hold the reins of power in their hands again and that the 'Noske'teers' want to force workers with machine guns and hand grenades to work." Since the summer of 1914, when the SPD supported the war, the party had been his declared enemy, and this attitude hardened after the Social Democrat Gustav Noske, as Reichswehr minister, repressed the Spartacist uprising in January 1919, during which Karl Liebknecht and Rosa Luxemburg were murdered. Werner ended the item by calling on all workers to participate in the international protest strike, planned for the coming Monday, against efforts to dismantle the hard-won rights of labor.[50] He thus advocated the local program of the USPD, which was working with the KPD in these months to initiate strikes and insurgencies in order to promote the revolutionary potential of the local labor movement. The *Volksblatt* energetically supported this undertaking, railed against the "counterrevolution" wherever the opportunity arose, and endeavored to "keep alive the tough fighting spirit of Halle's proletariat, to show the opponents that it exists and can and will use its power on the day of the revolution."[51]

In early July, Werner made sure that the *Volksblatt* was sent to his brother in Bern. "From now on, read Halle's *Volksblatt* with a critical eye," he advised Gerhard in a friendly tone. "In it you will recognize the lion's claw." He described his political position to Gerhard as being the most extreme within the Independent Social Democrats (USPD), since he openly spoke in favor of a speedy annexation into the Comintern, the Third International, which had been founded in March on Lenin's initiative. "Since having the opportunity to exercise real influence on the paper in my position, I have truly endeavored not to produce lies and, as you will have seen, being the attentive reader that you are, not to spare our own people when it was necessary." Despite the failure of the Bavarian Soviet Republic, Werner still believed in the soviet system and especially in the imminent advent of the revolution. He asked Gerhard if he thought the soviet system would be introduced into Palestine.[52]

Werner's letters to his brother imply that he was accompanied by his wife, leaving their seven-month-old daughter with Emmy's mother. Even though Emmy often said that she didn't like Linden and was probably happy to leave the place, she also said, as one would expect, that it was hard for her to be separated from her seven-month-old daughter. In Halle, she sometimes did not see her husband for days at a time since he worked continuously. So, she helped him where she could and assumed the job of writing smaller stories for the newspaper on a regular basis. But she did not leave it at that. Before long, she was pursuing her own interests. As Werner told his brother with a bit of pride but also a bit of regret, she had again become "rebellious" and no longer wanted to do any housework "although

she is a cute housewife. On the first of September she goes to [work at]
Halle's district miners' council, a very influential body. By the way, we will
then earn rather a lot of money, together about 900 marks, but that will
also be spent in a flash." Emmy also volunteered at the local social welfare
organization, taught courses for youths, and schooled women in the evening. She was often asked to speak at political meetings in Halle and the
surrounding areas.[53]

The couple moved into a small apartment in the Giebichenstein quarter
in early September 1919, not far from Halle's Volkspark, the main gathering
place of the local labor movement.[54] Werner cautioned his brother not to
think of their new dwelling in terms of any "cultivated home decor and
similar beautiful things" for they still had absolutely nothing and would
have to slowly accumulate a simple household. He asked Gerhard to keep
what he knew about their joint income from his mother—"for reasons," he
explained in a somewhat conspiratorial tone, "that are closely connected to
the still existing capitalistic social order." All he meant by this was that he
did not want to give up the financial support he had once again been getting
from Betty Scholem without his father's knowledge.[55]

In Bern, Gerhard read the *Volksblatt* for a month before he said anything about it to his brother. As he did with all letters that he considered
important, Gerhard included a draft of it in his diary. However, the text
stops midway and it is impossible to know whether he actually finished and
sent it. Had Werner indeed read this letter, it would explain the irreversible
break between the brothers. Gerhard's text is exceptionally critical and
emotional, and the many exclamation marks and double underlines set it
apart from the rest of his correspondence. Never before has he been so
unrelenting and devastating in his assessment, so angry in asserting his right
to pass moral judgment.

"I have done my best to read your newspaper," he writes in the letter,
"to find in it that which could attest to a sincere, exceptional (also in the
moral sense of exceptionally unmalicious) and forward-looking, pure spirit.
In these four weeks I have not only found nothing of the sort, but, on the
contrary, all I take from it is the saddest and most depressing evidence of
mendacity, . . . of impurity and, in a simple and direct sense, of inhuman-
ity." He could say a lot about the newspaper, but nothing inspiring; except
for its cover, the paper did not differ from the "most diabolical bourgeois
scandal sheet." What angered the sensitive and learned philologist above all
else was the language, the "*appalling* baseness" of the language used by the

journalists. At first, he was irked by the meaningless use of "quickly out-worn words and superlatives for the paltriest things" and thought about how much better he himself would do it. But now, after an intensive four-week study he could not remain so mild in his judgment. Nowhere does Marx state that it is appropriate to lie, which is exactly what he accuses his brother and the editorial staff of the *Volksblatt* of doing. So how dare they speak of the "Partei der *Niemals Umgefallenen*" when—and he himself was present in Rixdorf—"*four-fifths*" (underlined six times) of exactly this party decided in favor of the war in 1914. The fact that the Independent Social Democrats defined themselves as the predecessors of the Rixdorf war opponents was not something Gerhard could let stand.[56]

As if that was not enough, he announced, he had abandoned all the hope he had once placed in the Independent Social Democrats after having read the *Volksblatt*. Each article offered more proof that Communism could not be expected to evolve from this party, which he accused of seeking power as the major emerging opposition. One hundred thousand people and more were being educated by the content of the *Volksblatt*, a responsibility of which the editorial staff was apparently not aware. And what would happen—as definitely lay in the realm of possibility—if the USPD ever came to power? Then "the impurity, demagogy, and all the bad that you all unnecessarily injected into the workers, who trust you, through your barrage of phrases, which do indeed eventually have an effect, all this will then turn against any attempt to be serious, because nothing can be more ruinous for human community than demagogy." Last of all, he had no choice but to address the question of his brother's personal responsibility: "I don't know how much you have tried to influence these hyenas who publish your political section or how much you find yourself under their influence. Your editorial in your column does not enthrall me. For me, you use too much profiteer jargon, my friend. I implore you: write clean or don't write at all. The lowliest work is noble compared with that of an editor who destroys human language with his empty words."[57]

Mercilessly, Gerhard expressed his moral judgment, accusing his brother of irresponsibility in dealing with people and language. He reacted soberly and disappointedly to the way the radical Socialist parties were working to create a Communist utopia in Germany, pointing to party rhetoric and demagogy as the greatest weaknesses of the movement. But these, in fact, were the main talents and interests of his brother, whose career had advanced because of his radical and populist rhetoric as a journalist and speaker.

Although Gerhard might not have sent this harsh letter, the strong criticism of Werner's actions and opinions expressed in the draft found in his diary provide a sufficient explanation for the cessation of correspondence between the brothers and thus their political discussions. Gerhard spent the month of September in Berlin before he left for Munich, where he planned to earn his doctoral degree. From there he visited Emmy and Werner for two days in Halle. Since Werner was usually busy, Gerhard spent most of the time with his sister-in-law.[58] Later, Gershom Scholem recalled that the discussion between him and his brother centered primarily on the question of "whether a man like himself could really appear as a representative of the proletariat." Could the educated offspring of a bourgeois Jewish family, without even a hint of a Social Democratic origin about him, be accepted in a stronghold of the labor movement? In order to find that out, Gerhard accompanied Werner to one of his regular evening rallies and listened to him speak. Werner was "not untalented as a demagogue," but the reactions of the public were directed at his weaknesses. And so, as Gershom Scholem recalled in his memoirs, he went up to him at the end of the evening to make this point: " 'Don't fool yourself,' I told him, 'they'll applaud your speech and probably they'll elect you to be a deputy at the next election [which was his ambition], but behind your back nothing will change.' I heard one of the workers say to his colleagues: 'The Jew [not 'our Comrade'] makes a nice speech.' "[59] Werner didn't want to hear Gerhard's observations or advice—anti-Semitism in the labor movement was certainly not foreign to him and he had learned to ignore it. But Gerhard accused him of betraying himself just as their father had. He would never really be a representative of the exploited worker but always be a son from the Jewish middle class. In an interview during the early 1970s, Gershom Scholem noted that his brother had believed the solution to all problems—including the national problem—was the revolution. "At the time we did not know—we were not clever enough, neither I nor he—that as a historic reality the revolution as we introduced it into our lives solved absolutely nothing."[60]

No exchange of letters followed that visit in Halle, as in the past, and no entry in Gerhard's diary mentions the event. Thus, Emmy felt it became her duty to maintain contact and sent a letter in December congratulating her brother-in-law on his twenty-second birthday. In this letter she made sure to mention Werner several times: just then he was attending the USPD party conference in Leipzig, was "incredibly busy," and could therefore not write himself. Since she had to finish the work he left behind in Halle, she had to postpone her planned trip to Hanover to visit her baby daughter. Proudly Emmy wrote that her little girl had "developed mightily," and she hoped to bring her to Halle in the coming spring. She expressed great affection for Gerhard and thus ignored the conflict and distance between the brothers. "Dear Gerhard," she wrote, "unfortunately I am too dumb to be able to express my congratulations well. I expect a lot from you and your life. You are the person dearest to me, as a person I cherish you more than Werner, but naturally that has nothing to do with Werner being my husband. You understand that, don't you? I believe that many people like you very much. My wish is that you will disappoint no one."[61] After that, Gerhard remained a true friend to her and, time and again, also a close confident; she confided her fears, weaknesses, and hopes to him after Werner's death, and she asked him for his opinion and accepted his judgment.

In the next four years prior to Gershom Scholem's immigration to Palestine, the brothers met every once in a while in Berlin. Their relationship remained distant but friendly. The political differences between them were no longer recorded on paper but continued to be emotionally laden. In his memoirs about Walter Benjamin, Gershom Scholem noted that the letters he wrote to his friend during these years conveyed a calm tone that did not reflect his emotional state at the time, for he wrote about "neither the passions that were agitating me nor my conflicts with my brother Werner, who saw his ideal in political demagogy."[62] Gerhard had little patience for the repositioning of the extreme left and therefore for the career of his brother that was linked to it. With his advocacy for joining the Comintern, despite the split it caused within the USPD, Werner Scholem turned away from the radical opposition that once brought him close to his brother.

The Revolution Devours Its Fathers

The spring of 1920 was a turbulent time for German politicians, especially in Halle. In response to the attempted counterrevolutionary putsch by the Kapp-Lüttwitz group, both the USPD and the SPD called for a general strike. During the attempted coup, newspapers were banned, and editors, functionaries, and union members of the German Democratic Party and the leftist parties were arrested, including Werner Scholem. Members of the KPD (Communist Party) and the leftist faction in Halle took advantage of the moment and rallied their comrades to launch a revolution. The crisis escalated, the radicalized workers could no longer be brought under control, and violent confrontations ensued. In the shadow of these events, elections for the Reichstag were held in June, and although the Independent Socialists had been mistaken in thinking the time was ripe for revolution, the party still received 45.2 percent of the vote in Halle and Merseburg, making this one of their most important centers of political power.[63]

During the summer, the Independent Socialists began to negotiate admission to the Comintern, whose Second World Congress was to take place in July and August 1920. In light of the unstable situation in Russia, the Comintern showed a great interest in bringing the revolution to Germany and gaining the support of that highly industrialized country. One of the most vocal advocates for joining was the journalist Werner Scholem. In early August 1920, the *Volksblatt* printed his talk "The Political Revolution and the USP [Independent Socialists]," which he had given before a large audience gathered in Halle's Volkspark.[64]

The Volkspark, an art nouveau building erected in 1907 from labor-movement funds, contained the largest hall in the city, in which all important meetings of the local left were held. In his speech, Werner called upon the workers' movement in Halle to "return to the intellectual well of scientific Socialism in order to draw from it inspiration for present-day tactics and politics." From the start, radicalism had been a driving force of the workers' movement, he claimed. Even Marx had called for "forceful overthrow." Today, radicalism meant revolution, but not just political revolution. It should also be a social movement, he argued, borrowing from Karl Kautsky, who had been the intellectual authority of the Socialists until the end of the war.[65] The path to forceful overthrow, he argued, demanded a clear commitment to the Third International, which had already accepted the USPD into its governing bodies in an advisory role. Therefore, the coming party congress would definitely have to decide in favor of joining the Comintern and unifying with the KPD, to make the further "shift to the left, which each of our party congresses have instigated until now. Then, the German influence, which was so strong in the old International, will perhaps once again also be decisive in the 3rd International, and the German workers movement will become the vanguard of the fighting International."[66] This last sentence was met with enthusiastic applause. If the German workers' movement was to play a leading role in the new International, membership in the Comintern was necessary. The rhetoric of the speaker was one of force, shaped by the world war from which the revolution emerged and in which the politician Werner Scholem was born.

On 14 August, ten days after this speech in the Volkspark, the official "Conditions of Admission to the Communist International," known generally as the "Twenty-One Conditions," were announced. Lenin demanded immediate compliance with these conditions from all active parties within the Comintern as well as the new applicants: strict measures for disciplining and centralizing all parties in the Comintern, a declaration of their loyalty to the Communist Party of Russia, and subordination to its decisions. Furthermore, all party officials who voted against these conditions were to be expelled, as were all reform-oriented parties and those unwilling to undergo revolution. In this way, Lenin sought to create parties of a new type, which were regimented and centrally organized and followed Moscow's dictates unconditionally. He also used these conditions to justify the practice of defamation and denunciation, and from then on the Communist Party experienced wave upon wave of political purges.[67]

In Germany, the reaction of the Independent Socialists to Lenin's synchronization policy was overwhelmingly negative, and more than two-thirds of the party press rejected membership in the Comintern under these conditions.[68] Werner Scholem belonged to a minority of journalists who spoke out in favor of it, and he reported regularly on party officials who took the same position. At this juncture, the previously unknown young man was now seen throughout Germany as one of the masterminds behind the split in the workers' movement. His radicalism won prominence for him, and his political pieces appeared ever more frequently in the *Volksblatt*.[69]

In early September, his article on the future of the Independent Socialists appeared. In it, he did not attempt to mediate in the controversy that threatened to split the party; instead he depicted it as an unresolvable generational conflict that was splitting the party in half: "Being half the continuation of an old era and half the beginning of a new one in the German workers' movement, the USP is the party of those who want to revive the old radical oppositionist party, but also of those who want to make out of it the revolutionary party of today and a leader in the country of the future. Tradition and youthful passion wrestle within it, and this struggle will be and has to be fought out." He wanted his generation, the new radical youth, to be rooted in the history of the workers' movement and therefore emphasized their affinity to the formerly radical SPD opposition under the leadership of August Bebel, who belonged to the generation of the deserving and prudent elders, who now stood against accepting Lenin's demands. Consequently, together with the labor unions, they figured as "the Capua of the radicals" for him, thus making themselves the image of their sons and daughters' enemy. He wanted to see this generational conflict fought out in order to end "the unsustainable state of affairs blocking the entire revolutionary struggle in Germany, the state of affairs in which our party is made up of two parties, a unique situation in which the left wing of the USP is actually closer to the Communist Party than to its own party comrades from the right wing of the USP." For this reason, he also welcomed the strict conditions stipulated by the Communist International, which he believed would not cause the further splitting of the German workers' movement, as some feared, but would create clarity among the four leftist parties.[70] He believed that only if the anti-Communists left the USPD, would it be possible to unite leftist forces into a "unified revolutionary party that, for all practical purposes, will put an end to the division within the German workers' movement. . . . In the debates preceding the coming party congress, may the radical elements of the party be buoyed by hopeful optimism and push for the clarification of opposing stances with ruthless severity. Developments will prove them right by creating that party of the future, which will be the future of our party!"[71] As always, his language became very theatrical when he talked about the future. He was not a theoretician but a party orator and prophet of its secular utopia.

A short time later, on 6 September 1920, the *Volksblatt* published a reply by the veteran SPD politician Fritz Kunert to Werner Scholem's militant article. Kunert bitterly asserted that Scholem wanted to "do away mercilessly, even cruelly, with the old leaders of traditional radicalism. Regardless how very radical a person is—in the sense of this new era—one can still be unfortunate enough to have someone else show up who is even more radical and maintains: I am taking it a step further. I personally demand that the party select an official Shylock who, with knife in hand, is to claim according to the law of historical development—loosely adapted from William Shakespeare—a kilogram of flesh 'first from the heart' of the old traditionally radical leaders."[72] Kunert dealt a deeply anti-Semitic blow here, by placing his young colleague in the role of Shylock, Shakespeare's Jewish moneylender from *The Merchant of Venice*. Like him, Werner Scholem allegedly had nothing better to do than to rip the Social Democratic heart out of the party. On the one hand, the literary figure of Shylock bears witness to centuries of anti-Semitism, and, on the other, this tradition also presents an exception: the Venetian moneylender acts with self-awareness and claims to be using the same methods as the Christians, from whose precedent he has learned.[73] Thereby Kunert was also rebuking the young Jew, Scholem, for not acting with foresight and restraint, which was to be expected of him on the grounds of his defect—and which Jewish politicians ordinarily displayed.

Werner Scholem was insulted by the ostensibly facetious, ad hominem literary allusion, which was used in place of a debate on the issues. In his reply, he called Kunert the mouthpiece of the old guard "who attempt leisurely to continue the traditional vocal radicalism of the prewar period." He labeled Kunert a representative of the right wing in the USPD and thus identified him as a member of the group to be excluded from the party should the USPD join the Comintern.[74] Certainly, the anti-Semitic tone of Kunert's remarks had been highly uncalled-for. Nevertheless, he pointed to a major danger posed by membership in the Comintern: namely, that the demand for ever-increasing radicalism as the characteristic of a true revolutionary would trigger a spiral of defamations, a never-ending series of beheadings, whereby the revolution would devour not its children but its fathers.

This generational conflict was impossible to ignore at the national conference of the Independent Social Democrats on 1 September 1920, in Berlin, which was meant to bring about a "healing process of the party in the period of revolutionary struggle." The Reichstag faction and the extended Central Committee discussed membership in the Comintern with district representatives and editors from the party newspapers. While the younger party members were all in favor of joining, the older ones expressed prudent reservations, warning that Lenin's conditions were intended to establish the "*dictatorship of a brother party* over all other parties." The elder statesmen, as it were, dismissed those advocating membership as young and inexperienced. However, some of those in favor of joining the Comintern were prominent and well-established politicians.[75] In the heated debate, opponents of adhesion spoke of enslavement and the loss of autonomy, arguing that the different conditions existing in all European countries and societies could not simply be organized according to the Russian model. Meanwhile, those in favor of joining dreamed of Berlin as the future capital of the world revolution, where the Executive Committee of the Comintern (EKKI) would move following the USPD's admission. The general consensus opposed joining, and it was recommended that the party should wait until the end of the civil war in Russia to see how the problems there were solved.[76]

Werner Scholem, who had been a delegate at the national conference, vehemently attacked the established labor leader Wilhelm Dittmann in a speech that was published in the *Volksblatt* a few days later. In two articles that appeared in *Freiheit,* the organ of the USPD, Dittmann had described the precarious situation of the Russian economy, in order to stop the mass exodus of German workers to Russia, many of whom had returned in disappointment on account of the economic crisis there.[77] Werner Scholem therefore accused Dittmann of lack of solidarity with Russia and agitation against Russia, since the political right could make enthusiastic use of his articles in anti-Soviet polemics. For him, the Dittmann case proved the necessity of Lenin's demands for unconditional solidarity and control.[78] Dittmann's articles had resulted from embitterment over Lenin's conditions. But his effort backfired. He was declared to be an anti-Bolshevik and became de facto one of the first victims of Lenin's purge policy.[79]

As a vehement advocate for joining the Comintern, Werner Scholem was in the minority at the *Volksblatt,* where three of the four political editors were against it. In his articles he was blatantly critical of the party leadership and simultaneously reported on the leftward shift of the working class in Halle. Indeed, they had passed a public resolution, which Werner had promoted, in favor of joining the Comintern.[80] His new political prominence also exposed him to much criticism. In September he published a statement, "on my own account," in which he defended himself against the slander that representatives of the left USPD—particularly he himself—felt was being mongered against them: "So far, I have smiled about the vulgarities being spread to gullible ears in all the taverns of the city; but now the humbug has spread to the entire Saal district, and because many comrades who support our standpoint are perplexed by our continued silence, I see myself forced to issue the following statement." It was incorrect, he wrote, that he had only been "politically organized" since 1918; the correct date was 1912. As early as 1917 he had been imprisoned for a year on behalf of the workers' movement, a fact that robbed him of the chance to study and pursue a bourgeois career; further, neither he nor his wife and daughter belonged to any religious congregation. He did not offer any defense for the final point of defamation but issued the following statement: "I consider it beneath my dignity to answer the insults concerning my Jewish background. May those fellows who employ such means immediately leave the

USPD and join the German Nationalist Protection and Defiance Federation [Deutschvölkischer Schutz- und Trutzbund]."[81] It was rare to address the topic of anti-Semitism in the workers' movement so directly and openly, and his reaction is evidence of his growing political self-confidence, as well as his wish to emphasize that the values of the workers' movement were distinctly different from those of the German nationalist movement.

Meanwhile, his political agenda was successful. There was a great deal of support for soviet Russia in the workers' movement in Halle and just as great a hope for the speedy advent of world revolution. Every USPD meeting in Halle and Merseburg declared the membership's approval for admission into the Comintern—as did the election of delegates to the extraordinary party conference, where a final vote was to be taken on the issue. It hardly mattered anymore that the majority of the party leadership in Berlin were against it.[82] In a special issue of the *Volksblatt* dedicated to the extraordinary party conference to be held in Halle, Werner Scholem continued to campaign for admission by emphasizing the importance of Halle's proletariat as the radical avant-garde—one that had been against the war in 1914, voted now in favor of the Comintern, and would thereby take Germany a decisive step closer to revolution.[83]

The election of delegates to the conference had settled the issue of joining the Comintern even before it convened on 16 October in Halle. The large hall of the Volkspark was decorated with soviet emblems and propaganda posters. Grigory Zinoviev, people's commissar of the interior and the first chairman of the Comintern, had traveled from Russia with Nikolai Bukharin, in order to advocate admission. It was the first visit of Bolshevik functionaries to a western European party. Zinoviev's four-hour speech in halting German was a shining example of the new Soviet influence abroad, although the decision on Comintern membership had already been made before his arrival: 156 delegates voted against admission; 236 delegates— among them the journalist Werner Scholem—in favor and thus also for the split of the Independent Social Democrats from their right wing. This dividing party conference was followed in early December by a unifying one in Berlin, in which more than two-thirds of the USPD members from the Merseburg administrative district joined the United Communist Party of Germany (VKPD), an amalgamation of the USPD and KPD.[84]

At the *Volksblatt*, the first wave of purges occurred as early as October. All three political editors who had voted against the Comintern were suspended. The paper called in Victor Stern from Austria to head the political editorial staff, but he was deported from Germany shortly afterward. After this unsuccessful change of direction, the *Volksblatt* ceased being the party journal of the USPD.[85] But until that happened, Werner Scholem wrote most of the political articles for the newspaper. Although he did not add his byline, his authorship is revealed by the content of the pieces, by frequent use of catchwords such as "social revolution," "unconditionality," and "radicalism," and by the language, which differed conspicuously from that of other journalists in its frequent use of Latin terms—a remnant of his humanistic education.[86] He and his wife participated in the unification party conference in Berlin as delegates and joined the new party immediately in December.[87] Like other officials of the old USPD in Halle, who had played major roles in creating the first mass Communist party in Germany, Werner Scholem assumed key functions in the United Communist Party. During the preceding three months, he had earned respect as a mover and shaker in instigating the change that took place on the political left.

Deputy *Judenbengel*

In late December 1920, Werner Scholem celebrated his twenty-fifth birthday in Berlin. After more than seven years' absence, he returned to the city of his childhood and youth, accompanied by his wife. They decided to leave their daughter Edith in Hanover, and Emmy and Werner Scholem moved into an apartment in the rear house at Waldenserstrasse 15 in Berlin-Moabit. The apartment was in the immediate vicinity of the neighborhoods Roter Beusselkiez and Rostockkiez, two strongholds of Berlin's revolutionary workers' movement. As Edith Capon (née Scholem) later noted, it was consistent with her father's ideals to live in the big city slums near the supporters of his party.[88]

In early January 1921, the ambitious young politician became the political editor of what had been the organ of the Spartacus League, *Die Rote Fahne*, the Red Flag.[89] Until December 1920, this newspaper had been largely irrelevant, as was the Communist Party from the time of its emergence out of the Spartacus League until it unified with the leftist Social Democrats. However, the newly founded mass party decided to make the young but highly symbolic publication its mouthpiece, because the *Rote Fahne* had been established by Rosa Luxemburg and Karl Liebknecht as a forum of the revolution on 9 November 1918, the day the republic was declared. Starting in January 1921, the new party newspaper appeared with a larger circulation twice a day, except on Sundays and Mondays when only one issue was published. The party claimed there were 330,000 to 500,000 subscriptions to the *Rote Fahne* at various times during the Weimer Republic, but these figures are probably exaggerated. Indeed, the paper's primary aim was not to reach the electorate directly but to serve as a political instrument for "conditioning perceptions and controlling language use among the active members." As a party publication, the newspaper largely mirrored the opinion of the respective KPD leadership.[90]

The executive editors of the *Rote Fahne* changed in rapid succession because, for one, it was a job that entailed some danger and, for another, they frequently had to serve time in prison since they were responsible for the content of the paper. Werner Scholem was notably younger than his colleagues, who were, on average, thirty years old when they started working at the paper. Nevertheless, shortly after arriving at the *Rote Fahne*, he took what became a relatively long turn at being the executive editor, namely, from 3 March to 3 June 1921.[91] This astonishingly fast promotion was a compliment to Werner's rhetorical abilities and judgment, but it also entailed great responsibility.

Starting on 20 February 1921, Werner Scholem served the Communist Party as a deputy of the Prussian Landtag, the legislature of the Free State of Prussia, established in 1918 and the most important state in the Weimar Republic. Because of Scholem's youth, this caused a small sensation in the honorable institution.[92] By the end of March, the name of Deputy Scholem was already mentioned prominently at a meeting of the Reich cabinet with the Prussian Ministry of State, in which it was decided what further steps the government would take in connection with the so-called "March Action," the Communist uprising in central Germany that had just been repressed. At the end of this meeting, it was recommended to have the young deputy arrested in his capacity as executive editor of the *Rote Fahne* and to try him in a special court created just for this purpose. As a deputy of the Prussian Landtag, he enjoyed immunity, but it could be rescinded if he was "arrested while perpetuating the act or in the course of the following day, at the latest." Although it could not be proven that he had played an active role in the armed uprising, it was decided at another meeting to take legal steps against him "with a vengeance." What prompted this was the desire to take action not only against the initiators of the uprising but also against the Communist Party as such, which was held responsible for the escalation of the events.[93]

A month earlier, in February 1921, power had changed hands in the KPD after Paul Levi resigned as party chairman. Levi, who had been one of the founders of the Spartacus League in 1918, rejected the aggressive policy of synchronization now being dictated by Lenin to Communist parties outside of Russia. Levi claimed that armed revolutionary uprising outside the Soviet Union was intended to distract attention from the stalling of the revolutionary process there and the country's increasing isolation. Once rid of Levi, with support of the Comintern, the party staged an uprising in central Germany, where it had the largest base of support. This action was a departure from the maxim of Rosa Luxemburg: first win over the workers and then start a revolution. A provocation by the police triggered the uprising prematurely, and the battles—poorly organized and coordinated by the Communists—escalated, leaving 145 dead among the rebels and 34 from the ranks of the police. The KPD emerged greatly weakened by the events.[94]

On 18 March, an article appeared in the *Rote Fahne* written by the Hungarian Comintern commissioner Béla Kun, in which he called upon workers to take up arms and fight.[95] The executive editor, that is, Werner Scholem, was held blamed for this article. In his absence, the Prussian Landtag debated in early June 1921 whether the immunity of the accused deputy should be lifted, so that he could be put on trial. A parliamentary legal committee examined the case and came to the conclusion that Werner Scholem, as executive editor, did indeed have to take responsibility for the revolutionary agitation published in the *Rote Fahne*. The committee recommended to the Landtag not to treat his deed as a political offense, for which a deputy could not be charged, but as a call for treason and thus a crime.[96] The Landtag was to decide what action was to be taken next.

Werner Scholem's first defender was Hugo Eberlein, of all people. Eberlein was the head of the recently founded illegal military apparatus of the KPD, and he actually had been involved in the uprising.[97] Eberlein directed the debate away from the individual Scholem and described the affair as an attack against the Communist Party itself—a futile endeavor, he assured legislators: for every silenced Communist politician, two would emerge. He argued that parliamentary immunity provided one of the last places where Communist politicians could speak publicly without repercussion. The special individual courts that were being set up, however, to prosecute the protagonists of the "March Action" were nothing more than legalized Communist hounding. Yet, at the same time, the murders of numerous Communist leaders went unpunished, and the perpetrators were free as birds to travel throughout the country for years, as the cases of Luxemburg, Liebknecht, Jogiches, and Eisner proved.[98]

Eberlein's accusations were ignored by the Catholic Center Party, whose criticism was directed solely at the person Werner Scholem himself, to whom "blind obedience" was attributed. Eduard Beyer, the deputy from Upper Silesia, not only accused him of being the actual instigator of the uprising, but also charged him with deliberately acting irresponsibly: as an academically trained person he ought to have been able to predict the consequences of his actions—meaning the escalation of the fighting. With regard to parliamentary immunity, Beyer demanded that an example be made out of him, since the KPD would deliberately appoint their deputies as editors in order to guarantee their immunity before the law. "Now I clearly understand the reason," he said, "why we have Mr. Scholem here in Parliament. He may wield the pen sharply to excite your workers; but he has not been sent here to do any parliamentary work; he has been elected to ensure himself immunity.[99]

Despite the antagonism between the SPD and the KPD, the Berlin Social Democrat Ernst Heilmann, a cousin of Erich Mühsam, also came to Werner Scholem's defense. If one were to believe what was being said by the German People's Party (DVP) and the Center Party, he argued, then one could assume straightaway "that Colleague Scholem is the equivalent to Trotsky in Russia, and yet Colleague Scholem is the same person whom you here have called *Bubi* [little boy]." No one could seriously hold Werner Scholem responsible for the events in central Germany. Heilmann stated that the young deputy exemplified the "typical case of a Communist agitator," who had "arrived at his theory on violence under the impact of the war." However, it did not seem to him to have been a wise decision to make such a young man the executive editor of the party publication and to burden him with such a monstrous responsibility.[100] Oscar Cohn, who spoke on behalf of the few remaining members of the USPD in parliament, also stood up with determination for his Communist colleague. Despite all the criticism that he could level against Scholem, it should not be forgotten that some of the glory "of the Socialist spirit" had also settled "upon the youthful head of Deputy Scholem."[101]

At the end of the long debate, a vote was taken: 189 deputies from the middle-right parties voted for lifting Werner's immunity, while 122 members of the left parties voted against it.[102] On the following day, 3 June 1921, Werner Scholem resigned from his position as executive editor of the *Rote*

Fahne, and a day later a warrant for his arrest was issued. The police tried to apprehend him by sending an informer disguised as a political colleague to Emmy Scholem at their apartment and by sending fake telegrams. But they were out of luck. The wanted man spent the summer in hiding outside of Berlin. The police did not catch up with him until the morning of 14 September, when he was finally arrested at the Anhalter Bahnhof. He subsequently resigned his mandate and was imprisoned for several months.[103]

In February 1922, Werner Scholem was permitted to resume his seat in the Prussian Landtag; however, the *Rote Fahne* reported in early March that his immunity had not been restored and that a trial for treason still hung above his head.[104] Despite the threat of prosecution, the speeches he gave over the next two years established his reputation as a provocative and radical politician. The Social Democrat Carl Severing, minister of the interior at the time, once stated that he had "a healthy respect" for the talents of Deputy Scholem as a speaker. Scholem's response was: "Are you kidding?"[105]

Among the issues particularly important to the young deputy was reform of all aspects of the existing university system. He believed this reform was long overdue and denounced the reactionary spirit of both professors and students, making the universities into incubators of nationalistic and militant attitudes. Further, he called for the complete revamping of the internal structures of universities and demanded that *Privatdozenten*, those holding a type of unpaid adjunct professorship, be given equal status and pay as full professorships. While this attack on the rigid, hierarchical university system in Germany was consistent with the KPD political line, implicit in it but evident to people at the time was concern for the welfare of the numerous, usually Jewish *Privatdozenten* who did the same teaching work as full professors but at minimal pay and for whom the door to a permanent position remained closed.[106] Scholem sought to create an alliance between the proletariat and the "sinking classes of the former bourgeoisie, those intellectuals, doctors, and freelance scientists, all of these people who earlier could keep up a bourgeois standard of living and have now become proletarian."[107] Werner Scholem saw them as future allies of the proletarian revolution, whose concerns must be addressed in order to raise their class consciousness.

He took his ideas for university reform farther by demanding that the doors to university study be opened to all, German nationals and foreigners alike. By the former he meant the German working class and by the latter, an undefined group of immigrants. Whereas his advocacy on behalf of the *Privatdozenten* had not caused much of a stir in the Landtag, these demands now prompted deputies of the German National People's Party (DNVP) to voice their disapproval loudly during his speeches. Deputy Scholem commented on this offhandedly and then asked the hecklers to state their apparently pressing reservations against free access to university: "If, however, your objections are only directed against the so-called 'Galicians,' then you have to declare that clearly and honestly. Then you have to say: actually, we don't really care who comes to the universities; the main thing is that no Jews end up there." He openly accused the DNVP of anti-Semitism, which, in true Social Democratic tradition, he attributed to economic causes. In his further analysis, he referred to August Bebel's famous speech at the SPD party congress in Cologne in October 1893, in which Bebel described how economics were the true source of anti-Semitism. The success of many Jews in the capitalist system, thanks to their own hard work, prompted jealousy and aversion toward Jews among less successful non-Jews, said Bebel.[108] Werner Scholem was pursuing this logic when he maintained that opposition to offering university access to Jewish students from eastern Europe was nothing more than the expression of "the naked fear within certain circles of German nationalists, the landed aristocracy [Junker], and high-level state officials that they will be thrown out of their saddles by this competition" and the sheer anxiety "that the trifling talent of their up-and-coming successors could be overshadowed by the quite considerable talent of the *Ostjuden*." As if suddenly recalling his role as a representative of the proletariat, he closed his remarks by noting that Jewish students should be neither privileged nor discriminated against compared with other immigrants who wished to study at German universities.[109]

As a member of parliament, Scholem was often told that his radical demands reflected his youth and inexperience. Eugen Leidig from the German People's Party alleged that his intellectual level was that of an infant. Scholem countered by remarking that "we, the young, were old enough to defend the so-called Fatherland of Mr. Leidig in the trenches during the war," and therefore they were now old enough to participate in the country's politics. In particular, he included those who had experienced the world war as children and now constituted the youth of the young republic. Despite his own difficult school career, he let himself be elected to the school committee of the Prussian Landtag and warned against glorifying war when teaching children and youth. He criticized the history curriculum as outdated and quoted from textbooks then in use that painted a heroic and nationalistic picture of the world war. The militarism among teachers and professors, still very prevalent, was for him a particularly sharp thorn in his side due to his own difficult and painful war experiences and his conviction that the root of all evil in the young republic lay in continued militarism.[110]

The speeches of Deputy Scholem were often interrupted by ironic or sarcastic heckling, almost always of an anti-Semitic nature. When he argued against forcing primary-school children to learn Latin, the heckling came from the right: Why not Hebrew instead? Never at a loss for words, he answered: "How about Old Gothic? Hebrew is already being taught at the higher schools of learning." When he advocated a strict division between church and state, he was said to be insolent and foreign. When he participated in the debate about the pay for clergy, which the KPD wanted to see financed by church congregations and not the state, he was accused by those in the German nationalist faction of intervening in a discussion that was none of his business; furthermore, he was said to be doing so in an "unbelievably tasteless" manner, which was "only understandable in light of his oriental opinions." He was accused of dragging everything that most deputies found holy through the mire. Such accusations were not directed at Scholem as an atheist Communist but as a Communist Jew. His adversaries claimed that he did not at all acknowledge Germany as his fatherland, and thus he was alien and foreign.[111] These accusations smacked of the old anti-Jewish stereotype of the homeless Jew as well as the new stereotype of Jewish Bolshevism and internationalism, hence he had no right to sit in parliament. Should he be allowed to represent the citizens of a country that he did not acknowledge and, even worse, that, as an alien, he was unable to acknowledge?

Only a few of the attacks leveled from the right when Scholem took to the floor are noted verbatim in the protocols of the Prussian Landtag, usually the words "Unverschämter Jude!" (Impertinent Jew!), yet usually such commentary was noted only as "heckling from the right." But every once in a while similar commentary was heard from the left, as when the USPD deputy Theodor Ulmer called him "Judenbengel," Jewish rascal. Nearly always, Werner Scholem responded to such remarks caustically and immediately in these or similar words: "I understand that, naturally, one must resort to anti-Semitic comments when one has no factual arguments. Idiots—and I know I run the danger of receiving a second call to order by saying this again—anti-Semitic idiots are too dumb to be able to discuss factually. That is indeed the root of anti-Semitism!"[112]

One of the most controversial debates in the Prussian Landtag was the so-called "Ostjudendebatte" (Debate on eastern Jews) of 1921 and 1922, in which the Prussian legislators addressed the matter of the state's handling of Jews stemming from eastern Europe who resided in Prussia and were not German citizens. During the "Ostjudendebatte," coarse anti-Semitic language was used, seldom meeting with reprimands or calls to order, and this became "a key element of political confrontation and language."[113] During Germany's worst hyperinflation, the "Ostjudendebatte" centered on the lack of food, housing, and jobs—scarce resources that should not be shared with foreigners. The debates in parliament focused on the deportation of refugees to eastern Europe, on the poor conditions in the Prussian detention camps for eastern European Jewish immigrants, and not least on the question of whether the eastern border of the Prussian state should be closed to immigrants. When the debate began in July 1921, Werner Scholem himself was in hiding. But when an inquiry by the German National People's Party (DNVP) led to further debate lasting several days at the end of 1922, he participated intensively.[114]

Wilhelm von Kaehler, a professor for national economics at the University of Greifswald and a deputy for the DNVP, began the major inquiry of his party on 19 November 1922 with an attack against the Communists in attendance:

Ladies and Gentlemen, since the revolution the issue of eastern Jews in Germany has not quieted down. While it possessed political significance during the revolution, this political importance alone does not sufficiently explain its entire nature and hence the tasks that it makes necessary. There is no question that, still today, Bolshevism both in Russia and here among us is infiltrated with eastern Jewish elements in the leadership and rank and file. Within Communist circles, we also have a good number of names that clearly indicate here the existence of relations, both old and new types, to eastern Judaism.[115]

At this point, Kaehler was interrupted by the Communist Party deputy Rosi Wolfstein, who asked whether Kaehler had conducted his study in the German nationalist, right-leaning newspaper *Deutsche Tageszeitung*. No, answered Kaehler, he had conducted it here in parliament over the past few years, and he thus based his observations explicitly on Rosi Wolfstein herself and all other Jews among the Communist deputies in parliament. The nationalist economist attempted to plant a horrifying scenario in the heads of his colleagues: Germany was being overrun by thousands of Jewish immigrants from eastern Europe, all of whom were profiteers and usurers and who entered the West by way of Vienna. Furthermore, thousands upon thousands were waiting in eastern Europe to make the same journey westward. The next man to take the speaker's stand was the Prussian minister of the interior, Carl Severing, who argued against Kaehler, stating that both Jews and "Aryans" were guilty of the poor state of affairs currently being experienced in the country. Severing refuted Kaehler's crass exaggerations and falsehoods, and at the same time he defended the Prussian—and thus his own—refugee policy.[116]

The only KPD deputy to address parliament extensively in this debate was Werner Scholem. He agreed with the speaker who preceded him, a deputy from the German People's Party, that a great deal of resentment toward immigrants also existed among German Jews. Hence, he argued, the subject of debate here was "not a national issue but a proletarian issue, in fact, an international proletarian issue."[117] He explained that Germans, including German Jews, opposed immigration because they feared the intelligence and possible competition of the immigrants—the same materialist argument he had used in the debate on the universities. When a delegate, probably from the right, interrupted his speech, asking whether he considered himself a representative of this group, he jovially countered by saying how flattered he felt by this question. However, he was not there as a representative of any Jewish constituency but of the proletariat. For this reason he did not speak exclusively about eastern European Jews in his speech but about all eastern European migrants who lived in or were immigrating to Germany. His party, he noted, sought to act forcefully against nationals and foreigners alike "who lived off the misery of the people, who practiced usury, profiteering, or other pleasant pursuits," a category in which he also included "the German agrarian." At the same time, he pointed out to his colleagues in the Prussian Landtag that penniless Jewish immigrants were particularly weak and vulnerable as the target of aggressive anti-Semitism among representatives of the Prussian executive. "This is the danger when the problem of eastern Jews is handled directly as a Jewish problem and when the focus of debate does not remain solely on the fight against the profiteering and usury of nationals and foreigners."[118]

Thus, he categorically opposed any prohibition or restriction of immigration to Germany for eastern European Jews. A heckler from the right expressed doubt that an eastern European proletariat even existed. Werner Scholem did not let this unnerve him; instead he simply reminded the Landtag that in fact Wilhelmine Germany had brought thousands of eastern Jewish proletarians into the country, referring to the call to Polish Jews issued by the Army High Command in the fall of 1914 and reading the German translation of the Yiddish original.[119] He described in detail how thousands of Jewish workers were forcefully recruited from Polish villages during the final years of the war and deported to the Ruhr region, where they worked in empty munition factories, because the German workforce had been sent to the front. Today 55,000 eastern Jewish proletarians lived in Germany, he calculated for the Landtag, and of these people, the great majority still worked in the Ruhr region, many of them as miners. The others worked primarily as farmworkers in Pomerania for employers who valued their industriousness but would support a popular and anti-Semitic policy to repatriate them to their homeland.[120]

He concluded:

> It has to be noted that even today, in this debate, no one here in this house again dared to stand openly by their anti-Semitism, because it is still feared that the consequences would be too dear. Yet is quite clear that anti-Semitism is prompting this maneuver by the German nationalists. The opposition to eastern Jews is not because they are big profiteers and usurers, but because it is feared they could pose a competitive threat that would impinge upon the work of German nationalist usurers and profiteers against the populace. We see here one of the roots of anti-Semitism overall: the fear of the intelligence, of the acuteness of mind of those circles against whom lies and defamations are spread.

His speech was repeatedly interrupted by deputies from the German National People's Party who were, however, unable to refute his statements on the forced recruitment of eastern workers and their deployment in the Ruhr region and in Pomerania.[121] For this reason, most of the heckling was directed at the deputy Werner Scholem himself, who was accused of being foreign to Germany and who was asked when he finally planned to return home—after all, the war was over.[122]

The debate on Jewish emigration from eastern Europe reflected one of the problems of parliamentary debate during this period. Rather than seeking a consensus in order to pass legislation, speakers stated their political opinions in absolute terms. The heated environment of the Weimar Republic and the turbulent, fast-paced, crisis-ridden daily life in Berlin could not be shut out behind the doors to the Prussian Landtag, nor could the propensity toward violence in a militarized society.[123]

The role of the KPD in the Landtag was that of a young and radical party, whose officials were nearly all under the age of forty; in fact, a third were even younger than thirty. It was their mission to challenge established politicians and established structures. Many of them had fought in the world war as very young men. Their radicalism was rooted in the trenches as much as in the forceful suppression of the Spartacist uprising and the Bavarian Soviet Republic. They channeled this radicalism in their revolt against older, successful politicians and introduced a new type of provocation and protest to the Landtag.[124]

In a parliamentary debate on a motion of no confidence against Carl Severing, the SPD minister of the interior, provocations by the Communist deputy Ivan Katz led to a fistfight. Like Werner Scholem, Katz had been elected to the Prussian Landtag in 1921, and the two men knew each other from Hanover, where they had served as city councillors in 1919. In the Landtag, Katz had quickly made a name for himself by making brash remarks rather frequently, and this time he had called the USPD a "sleazy bunch." He was therefore banned from the Landtag for fifteen sessions while the USPD rowdies who had started the fistfight went unpunished. At the next session, the KPD deputies protested the presence of the police, who had been called in as a result of the altercation, and nearly all of them were banned from the building and for the following eight sessions. Among them was Werner Scholem, although he had apparently not participated at all in the protests. As the *Rote Fahne* reported, he was arrested together with Rosi Wolfstein and another comrade despite their immunity in the plenum.[125]

A few days later, the party paper printed a report written by Werner Scholem in which he declared his innocence, also documented by other sources.

As the police forced their way into the plenum, in order to throw out Comrade Paul Hoffmann, I was standing in an aisle next to the seat of Comrade Menzel. So as to avoid any detour, several police officers fell over me and pulled me in the roughest way out of the aisle. I thought that this glorious action was then over but I was wrong, because the police immediately pulled me with force from the plenum, through several hallways of the building, to a room that once before had been proposed as a possible detention room for obstinate deputies. During the removal I was pushed in the most brutal manner.

Because no cause could be found for the arrest of the three deputies, they were soon released. Indignant, Werner Scholem stated that the action taken by police represented "an egregious and unprecedented violation of the constitution. No police officer has the right to remove a deputy from any seat or location in the parliamentary building."[126]

For him and many other party comrades, the incident symbolized the irrelevance of Weimar parliamentarism. The Prussian Landtag manifested not only a form of government that they as Communists rejected, but it also stood for a system in which the old elite still ruled, a system whose unvaried rigidity had to be challenged anew every day. The KPD sought to make up for its numerical weakness in the regional and national legislatures by using a strategy of public protest in legislative debate. Yet, the true political stage of the KPD was the public realm of big city streets, where protests and demonstrations took place, and their politics was a politics of spectacle and display, one making use of the press in a new way. When they entered the country's provincial diets and the Reichstag, the young Communist deputies introduced something that seemed like anarchist street theater, which, as they knew very well, the press would be very glad to report on.[127]

With the "Kommunistens"

The early 1920s were turbulent times for German revolutionaries. Whenever Betty Scholem heard nothing from her son for several weeks, she wondered whether he was imprisoned or had disappeared underground because he was being threatened with a court trial.[128] In September 1922, Werner

Scholem again found himself charged with treason. This time the charge was based on the publication in the *Rote Fahne* of allegedly falsified documents on a weapons depot in Silesia. Although witnesses could prove that Werner Scholem had been in Czechoslovakia at the time of the publication, and he proved convincingly that he was not the executive editor when the documents were published, he was not released from detention until the end of the year.[129] This incident prompted Walter Benjamin to consider and reject the possibility of admitting Werner Scholem into the exclusive "Muri Academy." In the summer of 1918, during their studies together in the town of Muri, just outside of Bern, Benjamin and Gerhard Scholem had come up with this satirical challenge to the existing academic world. The two friends continued to discuss the Muri university for several years, especially when classifying the positive and negative aspects of the academic world. Benjamin concluded that Werner Scholem did not deserve to be counted among the chosen few admitted to "Muri" because "the efforts of certain gentlemen to appoint Deputy Scholem dean of the Bacteriology Faculty after his release from jail" had met with "serious opposition.[130] Benjamin knew of Deputy Scholem primarily from the stories Gerhard told and from the press, but the wayward son, who seemed to spend most of his time in prison, amused him. Benjamin evidently picked bacteriology because Werner Scholem would have been able to study the practical aspects of the discipline in depth under the poor hygienic conditions of the Berlin prisons. Indeed, Werner made another hopeful but unrealistic attempt to earn an academic degree by matriculating to study *Staatswissenschaften*, a combination of political science and law, rather than history, at the Berlin University. Yet, as before, in the light of his many other commitments, nothing much came from this effort and his enrollment was suspended a year and a half later due to a "lack of application" to his studies.[131]

Political science theory had to yield to the practical work of party politics, for at the end of 1922 Werner, while still a deputy in the Prussian Landtag and a newspaper editor, also assumed the job as organizational head of the important KPD district Berlin and Brandenburg. Furthermore, as a top orator among the Berlin Communists, he was being talked about by everyone.[132] Gerhard, who spent a year in Berlin starting in April 1922, refused to attend one of his brother's appearances. As he noted in his memoirs:

I could not bring myself to go there even once. Our discussions were quite stormy, but we remained friends nonetheless. Werner told me quite a bit about the behind-the-scenes activities of the leaders sent from Moscow; of these, Radek and Guralsky in particular played a deadly role. Like so many believers of the time, my brother defended the "revolutionary necessities" (read: the terror that shrank from nothing), which had played a central role in the debates since the Halle convention at which the split was decided. To be sure, as was the custom, my brother, like Grigoryi Zinoviev himself in that notorious Halle speech, simply denied most facts, though he accepted the theory supplied along with them. In this he may have been acting in good faith; I have never been able to determine that. I found the whole thing indigestible.[133]

Although Gerhard did not attend the public appearances of the politician Werner Scholem, the brothers met privately, sometimes under unusual circumstances. Such was the case in the spring of 1922. Dora and Walter Benjamin had asked their friend Gerhard to organize a traditional Passover celebration for them, to which he willingly agreed. Moses Marx, the Orthodox brother-in-law of the author Samuel Joseph Agnon, agreed to host it. Werner Scholem also attended this seder evening, making the small gathering of friends a very heterogeneous group. Still, as Gershom Scholem recalled much later in his life, "this company represented many contrasts, but held together by the ancient ritual, it made for a very pleasant evening."[134]

Except for such excursions, the social circles in which Emmy and Werner Scholem moved in Berlin were those of like-minded revolutionaries of their age. Looking back on those times, Arthur Rosenberg referred to "our left" as the group including himself, Werner Scholem, Ruth Fischer, and Arkadi Maslow.[135] By 1922 and 1923 they all held key political positions but were no older than their mid-twenties to early thirties. Both their contemporaries and later historians considered the group to be greenhorns, who lacked not only experience but also "class pride and maturity."[136] Notwithstanding, both Werner Scholem and Ruth Fischer could already look back on an impressive amount of experience in the workers' movement despite their youth. The only thing all four of them lacked—or had to acquire deliberately—was class pride, for they had been raised in Jewish middle-class families.

Ruth Fischer, who was born as Ruth Elfriede Eisler in Vienna the same year as Werner Scholem, was as colorful and multifaceted as the many

FIGURE 17. Arkadi Maslow, Heinz Neumann, and Ruth Fischer (from left to right), Ahlbeck, 1922. Private archive of Renee Goddard.

names and pseudonyms she used. As one of the founders of Austria's Communist Party, she arrived in Berlin in 1919 and soon assumed important functions within the local party. She was described as a charismatic young woman who became the only leading figure in the KPD who was usually addressed by her first name, as "Comrade Ruth." She was romantically involved with Arkadi Maslow, who, like her, had been raised in a bourgeois Jewish family and had come to Berlin as a child from the Ukrainian city of Elisavetgrad (later Kirovohrad, and as of 2016 Kropyvnytskyi). Starting in 1921, the couple headed the Berlin party organization, and Maslow was considered the ideological thinker of the Left Opposition within the KPD. Like the others, Arthur Rosenberg also belonged to the Berlin KPD, where he had been serving as a city councillor since 1921. The November revolution had inspired the academically trained historian and ancient philologist to join the workers' movement, to which he had fully dedicated himself from then on. In addition to these four, the group of the Left Opposition within the KPD included Ivan Katz in Hanover and Hugo Urbahns in Hamburg. Urbahns, who came from a farming family and had been trained to be a primary-school teacher, was the only non-Jew in the group.[137]

What Gershom Scholem described as "indigestible" was the degree to which Moscow and the Comintern intervened in the daily business of the KPD and imposed their directives upon the party. Representatives of the Comintern in Germany determined the political course the party would take; whoever grumbled about it was expelled, a practice that had already gained a foothold by the early 1920s.[138] At the same time, protocols from numerous meetings, conferences, and congresses proved that a lively culture of debate was still being nurtured in the KPD during the first half of the 1920s. Despite the heavy hand of Comintern, party members criticized each other and the leadership.[139]

Yet by early 1923, the conflicts within the party began to intensify, and Werner Scholem's group formed and called itself the "Left Opposition"; later this group would be pushed out of the party, derogatorily labeled the "Ultraleft." In the winter of 1923, the topic addressed in fierce confrontations between the party leadership and these leftists was none other than the event to which the KPD owed its existence: the German revolution. Werner Scholem and Arthur Rosenberg accused the party chairman, Heinrich Brandler, of misjudging the actual situation in the country. Germany, they believed, found itself wracked "by a terrible revolutionary crisis" sparked by hyperinflation, on the one hand, and the occupation of the Ruhr region by French and Belgian troops, on the other. Therefore, the task of the Communist movement at that moment was not to dillydally in parliamentary politics, as Heinrich Brandler was doing, but to use the enormous revolutionary potential of the working class and to man the barricades and form a soviet-style regime.[140]

At the Leipzig party congress, which took place shortly afterward, rather than addressing the issues raised by Werner Scholem and Arthur Rosenberg, Brandler castigated the intellectuals in the party, declaring that such "bloody radicals" would inevitably turn out to be opportunists: "In most radical movements . . . the only contribution intellectuals made was to cause unrest among the membership because they confuse the workers with wild phrases and irresponsible criticism." At the congress not one member of the Berlin district leadership—and thus the Left Opposition—was elected to the party's Central Committee, almost causing a split within the KPD.[141] Afterward, in early April, a face-to-face talk between the sides was held in which Werner Scholem vehemently demanded the right of free speech within the party. Consequently, he faced a party inquiry and arbitration panel regarding possible organizational irregularities on his part.[142]

The prevailing friend-or-foe attitude within the KPD created a general atmosphere of constant fear of expulsion. The accusation of betrayal had become commonplace ever since the disputes in the fall of 1920, which had led to the split with the USPD and the acceptance of Lenin's Twenty-One Conditions. Yet the roots of the internecine conflict went back to the events that had given rise to the KPD in the summer of 1914, when the SPD supported the war in violation of the call for international solidarity, and to the winter of 1918 when that same party shared responsibility for the bloody suppression of the Spartacist uprising. Constantly threatened with the accusation of betrayal, the professional revolutionaries cultivated a "ritualized culture of friendship," placing trust in small groups, whose loyalty could be assessed. As the conflicts within the Left Opposition would show, friendship, based on the shared belief in a utopian vision, and betrayal, because of ideological and personal differences, existed side by side in the Communist milieu.[143]

In addition to friendship, Werner Scholem counted upon the loyalty of party members of his age in creating his political networks.[144] Youth emerged from the war experience as a distinct and formerly neglected political and social factor, which found an ideological home in youth movements. Aware of this, Werner not only involved himself in matters concerning schools and universities but also supported—against party dictates—a revolutionary group in Neukölln, which called itself "Erwachende Jugend" (Awakening Youth), which had split off from the young Communists. Despite a reprimand from the highest party echelons for doing so, he declared publicly his support for the oppositionist spirit of the group. He defended them, saying that they had been vilified and expelled because they had protested against the aging leadership of the young Communists. In this case, as in the debate on the general direction of the party, he demanded the protection of freedom of speech and opposed the practice of expulsion and defamation.[145]

The question of loyalty also became acute for the Berliners of the Left Opposition in another, very controversial context, that of anti-Semitism. The group was not only vulnerable because its members were considered to be intellectuals without class consciousness, but also because they were Jews—or at least were perceived as such. In that regard they found themselves in the impossible situation that the Dutch historian and political scientist André Gerrits described for Jewish Communists in general: "Their social and political predicament not only stimulated their aversions to being associated with

Jews (their conscious or unconscious Jewish self-negation), it also forced them, as it were, to prove themselves; to be even more radical than were their non-Jewish comrades; to be more Catholic than the pope."[146] In the debate on anti-Semitism, both within the party and in the press, this conflict of loyalties would bear strange fruit, as the summer of 1923 showed.

In general, the KPD ignored the hostility toward Jews that had been influencing public debate and daily interactions in Germany since the end of the war. It neither fought anti-Semitism nor utilized it for political purposes—only anti-Semitic remarks from party leaders were frowned upon. In true Marxist tradition, the problem itself was considered a by-product of capitalism and would disappear on its own in the wake of the revolution. Since the KPD did not appeal to the Jewish constituency, which was primarily middle-class, party strategists saw no need to take action on this issue.[147]

All that changed in the early summer of 1923, when Karl Radek, the Comintern commissar in Berlin, urged the German Communists to make overtures to the rightist and nationalist electorate.[148] Ruth Fischer immediately responded to his directive by giving a notorious speech to a German nationalist student organization in which she asked her audience the following rhetorical question: "You decry Jewish capital, gentlemen? Whoever decries Jewish capital, gentlemen, is already a fighter in the class struggle, even if he doesn't realize it." As if that were not enough, she went on to express her support for the violence of anti-Semitic circles and incited the students—barely a year after the murder of Walter Rathenau—to lynch Jewish entrepreneurs: "Trample down the Jewish capitalists, hang them from the lampposts, crush them." Under the headline "Ruth Fischer as Anti-Semite," the Social Democratic newspaper *Vorwärts* published her speech verbatim, and the account must have been accurate since she did not subsequently issue a denial, as she had been known to do on other occasions.[149]

The editorial staff of the *Vorwärts* found the controversial topic too tempting to drop; the very next day it printed a poem entitled "Die neuen Antisemiten" (The new anti-Semites) mocking those Jewish Communists who now appeared to make common cause with known anti-Semites, such as the Reichstag deputy Richard Kunze and the politician Ernst Graf zu Reventlow:

> Hip, hip, hurrah, and out with Jews
> Pogrom is coming, that's Hitler's news?

What comes is tumbling down the street
Lots of burghers feel the heat.
But look, the Communists.

Hip, hip, hurrah! In front, all one,
  the staff of *Die Rote Fahne* [The Red Flag]." Sobelsohn
(Karl Radek) leads the dense swarm
  With Reventlow, arm-in-arm!
    And then comes Werner Scholem.
Scholem bears a great big sign:
  "Hang the kosher profiteer swine!"
One hears him say with good grace:
"Don't I already have an Aryan face?"
  And then follows Ruth Fischer.
Her hair bleached a poisonous blond
  Ruth Fischer marches not far beyond
Around her, brave and strong
  The student body comes along
    And then—Kunze the club.
Friend Kunze looks with satisfaction
  Smirks and says: "I like this action.
With Radek, Scholem, and Katz I go around
  And merrily find Jews to hound."
    Crack—the first glass window breaks

("Hep-hep, heilo und Juden raus!"
Rückt Hitler zum Pogrome aus?
Die Straße wälzt es sich entlang,
Und mancher Bürger drückt sich bang.
    Doch sieh—die Kommunisten.

"Hep-Hep!" Voran die Redaktion
Der "Roten Fahne." Sobelsohn
(Karl Radek) führt den dichten Schwarm,
Den Reventlow hat er am Arm!
    Und dann der Werner Scholem.
Der Scholem trägt ein großes Schild:
"Hängt auf die kosch're Schiebergild!"
Man hört, wie er befriedigt spricht:

"Hab ich nicht schon ein Arisch-Gesicht?"
    Und darauf die Ruth Fischer.
Die Haare giftblond oxydiert,
Ruth Fischer kommt dahermarschiert,
Um sie geschart voll Mut und Kraft
Die völkische Studentenschaft
    Und dann—der Knüppel-Kunze.
Freund Kunze schaut befriedigt aus.
Und grient: "Hier bin ich wie zu Haus'.
Ich geh mit Radek, Scholem, Katz
Auf fröhlich-frische Judenhatz."
    Klirr—kracht die erste Scheibe)[150]

Ruth Fischer and Karl Radek had indeed pandered to anti-Semitic populism, but Werner Scholem had not. Just before this incident, he had called on his party to distance itself from "racket-making Communism." He was one of the few Communist politicians, if not the only one, who responded to anti-Semitic remarks in parliament and defended himself against them.[151] In fact, he was mentioned in this satirical poem because of his looks, which had often been the case. In Werner Scholem's face, the anti-Semite recognized the typical physiognomy of a Jewish intellectual. For the *Vorwärts*, this made him an easy target: the public Jew, recognizable to all, who hoped that his ideological conversion might also make him look less Jewish.

Werner Scholem did not comment on this public insult, but his relatives were appalled. Although Werner and Emmy still had no contact with Arthur Scholem, whose sixtieth birthday had passed without any reconciliation with them, they did meet Betty and other relatives on a regular basis. One major reason for this was the new development within their own small family: in the winter of 1923, they had become parents to a second daughter, whom they named Renate. Shortly after Renate's birth, Emmy returned to her job as a secretary and stenographer for the Central Committee of the party, where she had been employed since 1921.[152]

Only two and a half weeks after Renate's birth, the grandmother from Hanover came to visit and brought the four-year-old Edith with her. While she was in Berlin, the children were switched: Emma Wiechelt took the infant back with her to Hanover, and Edith remained in Berlin with her parents. Decades later, Edith Capon remembered February 1923 as the moment in which she suddenly lost her early childhood home. From one day to the next, the little girl was forced to adapt to life with her rather unfamiliar parents, whose daily routine was filled with work, danger, and insecurity. The child soon learned the codes, protocols, and rhythms necessary to survive as professional revolutionaries—people who were willing "to dedicate their entire life to the victory of the revolution" as Lenin had demanded.[153]

Edith was compensated for the loss of her family in Hanover with the large Scholem family in Berlin. Werner, Emmy, and Edith kept in contact with Reinhold and Erich, their families, and Betty. For her part, Betty reported time and again in her letters to Gerhard/Gershom how the members of the small family were getting along, but she could not resist the temptation to joke about the tensions between politics and everyday family life. In the midst of the "German October" of 1923, when it briefly looked as if the German revolution had indeed arrived, Betty wrote to her son, who had left for Jerusalem not long before, reporting on Werner's family, whom she called the "Kommunistens": "My Commies made the weekly visit to Erich's on Sunday. Little Edith is adorable & full of gracefulness, she said she had been that morning to the coiffeur to have her hair washed & her pageboy trimmed, & Werner said she was now getting dancing lessons & etiquette instruction, & he is looking for a better apartment, but wants to wait for the revolution (announced for 10 November!) & then they had to go because they had a rabbit for lunch for 1³/₄ billion. Erich said to me that it was extremely amusing and yet very sad to hear this politician talk."[154] Werner Scholem was thoroughly convinced that the fall of 1923 would finally bring Germany the long-awaited revolution, and this hope for imminent change shaped the daily lives of his family. In hindsight, long after this moment had passed, he wrote that it had then been the best situation that "the German revolution ever gave us."[155]

However, the "German October"—the course and rhythm of which was dictated from Russia—proved to be a further catastrophic defeat in the history of the German revolution. Moscow had set great stakes in this victory, which it needed badly to escape from its difficult economic and political plight. When hunger drove German workers into the streets to demonstrate in the summer of 1923, and the government showed signs of increasing instability, the Soviets believed that all signs in Germany were pointing to revolution. Leon Trotsky planned the uprising for the fifth anniversary of the Weimar Republic, 9 November 1923. However, according to Comintern orders, the uprising was to begin in October, in central Germany, in a united front with the leftist Social Democrats. But when the SPD withdrew its

FIGURE 18. The five-year-old Edith Scholem, Berlin, 1923.
Israeli National Library, Archive Gershom Scholem.

support at the last minute, Moscow feared that a debacle like 1921 would again occur, and the uprising was postponed. Still, the feeling of revolution hovered in the air until early November, and at party headquarters the German Communists continued to anticipate a somewhat delayed October Revolution for Germany. Instead, it was the KPD's political opponents on the right who exploited this atmosphere of upheaval; on 8 and 9 November, Adolf Hitler and Erich Ludendorff attempted a putsch in Munich.[156]

Following the failure of the "German October" to materialize, the KPD was outlawed, the party newspaper was forced to cease publication, and the party lost a great majority of its paying members. The party leadership under Heinrich Brandler and August Thalheimer had to take responsibility for the failure of the revolution and resign. Many KPD voters were disappointed that the political opportunity had been missed and discouraged by the ensuing setbacks for the labor movement, such as the abolishment of the eight-hour workday. The most radicalized among them joined the Left Opposition in the KPD, which was revolutionary in spirit and categorically rejected the idea of making a common cause with the Social Democrats.[157] The SPD was discredited in the eyes of the radicals, because, to restore order in the country, along with the labor unions, it had collaborated with the established elite, namely, the military, large landowners, high-level officials, and industrialists, and it had been forced to make major compromises. Discontent among workers over the lack of social welfare and the dominant position of the military and the old economic elite continued to drive many to join the ranks of the radical and revolution-inclined KPD, even though it was outlawed.[158] Even so, Arthur Rosenberg wrote many years later that by then the Left Opposition had already realized that the actual evil did not lie with the dethroned party leadership and their willingness to compromise with the Social Democrats. The real problem was the growing and despotic influence of Moscow, and it was at this moment that the Left Opposition should have broken its ties to Moscow in order to create an independent party of its own.[159]

Precipitous Heights

Astonishingly, politics did not occupy Werner Scholem's life completely. He also found time to pursue another passion: mountain climbing. He regularly spent his vacations hiking and climbing in the high mountains, accompanied by fellow enthusiasts and sometimes also his wife or mother.[160] He was a member of the Deutscher und Österreichischer Alpenverein (German and Austrian Alpine Club) and witnessed a stormy political confrontation between 1921 and 1924, which split the group. As a reaction to the growing anti-Semitism in the club, both Jewish and non-Jewish opponents to these "Aryanization efforts" joined together to found the Sektion Donauland (Section Danube) in 1921 in Vienna. In 1924, the club decided by a large majority to expel this section from the organization; protests against this decision were voiced only in Berlin. When these were ignored, more than six hundred members of the Berlin section resigned and formed the independent club Deutscher Alpenverein Berlin.[161] At the inauguration of the new organization in April 1925, the chairman, a lawyer named Hans Kaufmann, declared the new club to be a politics-free zone for Christians, Jews, and not the least also for women, who had been denied membership in most alpine associations up to that point.[162] Kaufmann was a good friend and fellow alpinist of Werner Scholem, who was also a member of this new alpine club, which was commonly called the "Jewish alpine club" everywhere else.

To compare the "Aryanization" of the alpine association with the development in the KPD between 1924 and 1926 would be an oversimplification. Still, certain parallels cannot be overlooked. With the acceptance of the Twenty-One Conditions, required of all parties belonging to the Comintern, heads began to roll within the USPD and the KPD as early as 1920, and after Lenin's death in 1924, this situation was aggravated. Werner Scholem recognized the danger, and in 1924 he began to warn the party against the threat of factionalism.[163] The consequences were all too predictable: the fragmentation of the Communist movement into groups of dissidents and those who had been expelled.

During the last three years of the 1920s, the KPD was completely Stalinized (or, as it was then called, Bolshevized). The result was a centralized party, thoroughly obedient to the directives of Moscow, whose public image had not only been cleansed ideologically but also "Aryanized."[164] Toward the end of the Weimar Republic, no Jew held a publicly visible position in the leadership of the KPD. In the vain hope of winning the support of National Socialist voters, the Communist newspaper *Welt am Abend* proudly publicized this development in August 1931.[165] While anti-Semitism did not play a role in Communist ideology, it did in practical party work at the end of the 1920s, when the Communists vied with the extreme right for the votes of the proletarian masses.

FIGURE 19. Climbing trip,
1929. Private archive of
Renee Goddard.

Ironically, this process began just as Werner Scholem was reaching the pinnacle of his political career, jeopardizing his achievements. The power struggles in the Russian Communist movement following Lenin's death and their impact on Germany, as well as the increasing dependence of the German party on its Russian counterpart, made for a treacherous political landscape. In addition, the position of intellectuals and Jews in the Communist Party became increasingly insecure. Moreover, the political culture of the Weimar Republic favored utopian dreams, whose realization seemed possible, though it seldom if ever was.

The year 1924 was the most successful in Werner Scholem's short career. It began with a trip to Moscow, during which the Executive Committee of the Comintern decided that the Left Opposition should assume the leadership of the KPD following the debacle of the "German October."[166] Joseph Stalin called the members of this delegation a new type of leader, who would be more credible for workers than the older ones had been, including Heinrich Brandler with his deep Social Democratic roots: "The left in Germany—these are people like Comrades Scholem, Hesse, Ruth Fischer. . . . Perhaps they have little theoretical training, but as pragmatists and agitators, as people tied to the revolutionary masses they are great fellows."[167] During Werner Scholem's six-week stay in Moscow as a member of the German delegation, he wrote a sketch on the profile and the history of the group now leading the KPD. In it he claimed that the "Left Opposition" was the "only ideologically unified group in the KPD" at the time, a group that had always resolutely pursued the same goals since 1921 as the leadership of the Berlin district. Proudly he emphasized their unwillingness to compromise, which made them the true heirs of the old, radical Social Democrats. Their declared enemy was the revisionism of Heinrich Brandler and the so-called "middle group," who advocated a united front with the current SPD and thus stood ready to compromise on the grounds of bourgeois democracy. Under no circumstance should the actual aim of the struggle, namely, a dictatorship of the proletariat on German soil, be abandoned.[168]

Having arrived at the center of power, Comrade Scholem, once back in Berlin, seldom had time to meet his mother regularly as they had done before. Ironically Betty noted that Werner was now "a very busy parish-pump politician [Kirchturmkopf]," who only found time for her when one of his numerous meetings was unexpectedly canceled. Even though she did not share her son's political views, she was proud of his growing fame— particularly when his caricature appeared in the weekend supplement of the Vorwärts, showing him in a harmonious family portrait of Russian and German Communists. "Father brought two copies back so that I can send you one and you can express your opinion of it," wrote Betty to Gershom Scholem. "We find the portrayal of his characteristic ears splendid and the expression superb. I have to say that I am almost proud; to be caricaturized is part of being a politician!"[169] Arthur Scholem also appears to have enjoyed the success of his son a bit, even if Werner was being ridiculed as an immature offspring, dependent on and nourished by omnipotent Moscow.

The harmony between the Russian and German Communists depicted in the caricature did not reflect reality. On the contrary, a great deal of tension had developed by then between the Left Opposition and the leadership in

FIGURE 20. Ernst Thälmann (center), Werner Scholem (second from left),
Arkadi Maslow (fourth from right), and Ruth Fischer (third from right) in Moscow,
January 1924. Private archive of Renee Goddard.

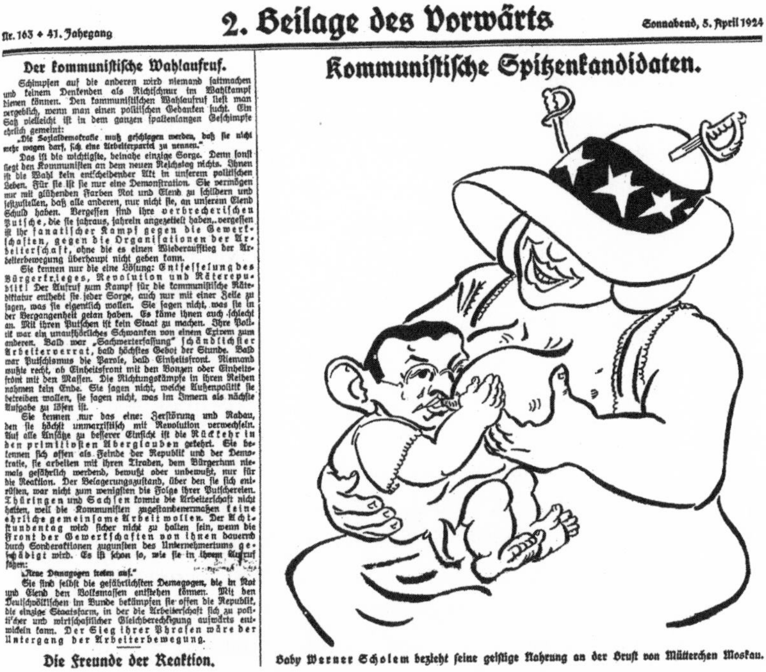

Nr. 163 • 41. Jahrgang

2. Beilage des Vorwärts

Sonnabend, 5. April 1924

Der kommunistische Wahlaufruf.

Schimpfen auf die anderen wird niemand sattmachen und keinem Denkenden als Richtschnur im Wahlkampf dienen können. Den kommunistischen Wahlaufruf liest man vergeblich, wenn man einen politischen Gedanken sucht. Ein Satz vielleicht ist in dem ganzen spaltenlangen Geschimpfe ehrlich gemeint:

„Die Sozialdemokratie muß geschlagen werden, daß sie nicht mehr wagen darf, sich eine Arbeiterpartei zu nennen."

Das ist die wichtigste, beinahe einzige Sorge. Denn sonst liegt den Kommunisten an dem neuen Reichstag nichts. Ihnen ist die Wahl kein entscheidender Akt in unserem politischen Leben. Für sie ist sie nur eine Demonstration. Sie vermögen nur mit glühenden Farben Not und Elend zu schildern und festzustellen, daß alle anderen, nur nicht sie, an unserem Elend Schuld haben. Vergessen sind ihre verbrecherischen Putsche, die sie jahraus, jahrein angezettelt haben, vergessen ist ihr fanatischer Kampf gegen die Gewerkschaften, gegen die Organisationen der Arbeiterschaft, ohne die es einen Wiederaufstieg der Arbeiterbewegung überhaupt nicht geben kann.

Sie kennen nur die eine Lösung: Entfesselung des Bürgerkrieges, Revolution und Räterepublik! Der Aufruf zum Kampf für die kommunistische Rätediktatur enthebt sie jeder Sorge, auch nur mit einer Zeile zu sagen, was sie eigentlich wollen. Sie sagen nicht, was sie in der Vergangenheit getan haben. Es käme ihnen auch schlecht an. Mit ihren Putschen ist kein Staat zu machen. Ihre Politik war ein unaufhörliches Schwanken von einem Extrem zum anderen. Bald war „Sachwerterfassung" schändlichster Arbeiterverrat, bald höchstes Gebot der Stunde. Bald war Putschismus die Parole, bald Einheitsfront. Niemand wußte recht, ob Einheitsfront mit den Bonzen oder Einheitsfront mit den Massen. Die Richtungskämpfe in ihren Reihen nahmen kein Ende. Sie sagen nicht, welche Außenpolitik sie betreiben wollen, sie sagen nicht, was im Innern als nächste Aufgabe zu lösen ist.

Sie kennen nur das eine: Zerstörung und Radau, den sie höchst unmarxistisch mit Revolution verwechseln. Auf alle Ansätze zu besserer Einsicht ist die Rückkehr in den primitivsten Aberglauben gekehrt. Sie bekennen sich offen als Feinde der Republik und der Demokratie, sie arbeiten mit ihren Tiraden, dem Bürgertum niemals gefährlich werdend, bewußt oder unbewußt, nur für die Reaktion. Der Belagerungszustand, über den sie sich entrüsten, war nicht zum wenigsten die Folge ihrer Putschereien. Thüringen und Sachsen konnte die Arbeiterschaft nicht halten, weil die Kommunisten zugestandenermaßen keine ehrliche gemeinsame Arbeit wollen. Der Achtstundentag wird sicher nicht zu halten sein, wenn die Front der Gewerkschaften von ihnen dauernd durch Sonderaktionen zugunsten des Unternehmertums geschädigt wird. Es ist schon so, wie sie in ihrem Aufruf sagen:

„Neue Demagogen treten auf."

Sie sind selbst die gefährlichsten Demagogen, die in Not und Elend den Volksmassen entstehen können. Mit den Deutschvölkischen im Bunde bekämpfen sie offen die Republik, die einzige Staatsform, in der die Arbeiterschaft sich zu politischer und wirtschaftlicher Gleichberechtigung aufwärts entwickeln kann. Der Sieg ihrer Phrasen wäre der Untergang der Arbeiterbewegung.

Die Freunde der Reaktion.

Kommunistische Spitzenkandidaten.

Baby Werner Scholem bezieht seine geistige Nahrung an der Brust von Mütterchen Moskau.

FIGURE 21. *Vorwärts*, 2nd supplement, Saturday, 5 April 1924: "Baby Werner Scholem gets his intellectual nourishment from the breast of Mother Moscow."

Moscow, as is illustrated by a letter received by the KPD headquarters at the end of March 1924. The letter came from Grigory Zinoviev, Comintern chairman and one of the most powerful politicians in the Soviet Union after Lenin's death, next to Joseph Stalin and Lev Kamenev. At the beginning of the year, he had supported the rise of the Left Opposition in the KPD, but meanwhile he feared that the party leadership would lose contact with the base very quickly. In his letter, he lamented that various political currents existed in the Left Opposition: namely, the truly revolutionary-minded worker and the intellectual leadership, to which extremely competent minds belonged, whereas, there were "also extremely immature elements, without Marxist training, without serious revolutionary tradition, with a tendency to empty revolutionary phraseology, who could greatly harm the German Communist movement." Among those belonging to the second group in Zinoviev's opinion were Werner Scholem and Arthur Rosenberg, whom he mentioned by name and accused of being "Ultraleft." This was a reference to their refusal to cooperate with the SPD, their return to Rosa Luxemburg's views on the matter of party organization, and, not least, their criticism of Moscow and the Comintern. Intuitively, Zinoviev knew how he could play the various groups within the Left Opposition against one another and thereby drive a wedge into the KPD leadership, splitting them into true proletarians, competent intellectuals, and immature elements.[170] In a personal letter to Ruth Fischer and Arkadi Maslow, he encouraged them to work very openly against these "Ultraleftist" dissenters.[171]

Meanwhile, Arkadi Maslow had established contact with Max Levien, who had been one of the leading minds of the KPD in the Bavarian Soviet Republic and now lived in Moscow. Maslow had written Levien that he and Ruth Fischer would give "the Scholomites and other varieties of this species 'a good whipping.'" In a highly confidential letter, Levien answered that he had no doubt that the two would soon take care of the "little 'ultra'-left academic tomfools." He and Ruth were "a hundred times smarter and more thoroughly trained politically than these academics." Moreover, they were of stronger character and had a much better link to the masses.[172] Levien's campaign against Werner Scholem and Arthur Rosenberg may indeed have made sense with regard to the latter, at least in a formal sense. However, unlike Arthur Rosenberg, Werner Scholem, who had by then only studied two half semesters of history, was no academic, unlike Levien himself, who had earned his doctorate at the University of Halle. Like Zinoviev, he condemned a type of "bad" intellectual, who rested on the laurels of his professed knowledge, detached from the masses, in contrast to "good" intellectuals, like Fischer, Maslow, or Levien and Zinoviev himself, who had abandoned their middle-class backgrounds to become part of the groundwork of the workers' movement. Furthermore, the label "Ultraleft" made it possible to vilify any deviation from Moscow's directives as dissident behavior.[173] In contrast to the label "Trotskyism," created later under similar circumstances, those who were called "Ultraleft" never used that term for themselves.

In April 1924, the still outlawed KPD held its ninth party congress in Frankfurt. Moscow's influence on the delegates attending the congress was not yet strong enough to determine their decisions. Against Zinoviev's wish, the delegates elected only members of the Left Opposition to head the party: Ruth Fischer, Arkadi Maslow, Werner Scholem, and Arthur Rosenberg—four (Jewish) intellectuals. They were joined only by one proletarian, Ernst Thälmann, who was loyal to the Comintern. However, at the very time of the party congress, Arkadi Maslow was unexpectedly arrested and charged with high treason for actions he was accused of committing during the "German October," and Ruth Fischer assumed the political leadership of the party and Werner Scholem, the organizational direction for the entire country.[174]

The decisions passed at the Frankfurt party congress were in the interest of the new leadership and placed the following points on the agenda: "Organization of the Revolution," the campaign against the German nationalists, and the restructuring of the KPD along the lines of the Soviet party. This course was based on the illusion that a revolutionary atmosphere still prevailed in Germany, although the country had entered a phase of relative stability as a result of the Dawes Plan and American loans.[175] The revolutionary impatience of the new KPD leadership reflected that of a great majority of the workers. At the same time, they maneuvered the party into a dead end, because they did not understand that the revolutionary spirit had faded away. Under the catchword "Bolshevization," the new party leadership did indeed plan to learn from the Soviet party, but no one except Ernst Thälmann wanted to subordinate the party to the influence of Moscow. Therefore, people in leadership positions, who were trusted by the Comintern, were marginalized within the KPD and replaced with activists whom the party leadership trusted.[176] Observing this, the SPD politician Kurt Schumacher claimed that Communists could no longer be found among the Communists, "just Scholemites."[177]

On 4 May 1924, Reichstag elections were held, and the KPD was allowed to participate. Prior to the election, the political satire magazine *Kladderadatsch* entertained its readers at the expense of the KPD's quite young party leadership in an article entitled "Career Counseling." In it, the following career "advice" was given: "If the lad can speak well or if he even has that which the Berliners call a 'große Schnauze' [big mouth], he should become a party leader, optimally a red one, naturally, because the prospects here are currently splendid." Furthermore, should he demonstrate a propensity for violence, continued the article, he would do best to run for office on the Communist ticket.[178] In fact, the KPD, whose campaign strategy was directed toward revolution and against parliamentary politics, did very well in the election, as did the extreme right. With 12.6 percent of the votes and sixty-two seats in the Reichstag, the KPD could assert itself for the first time as a proletarian mass party.[179] Werner Scholem entered the national

parliament (whereas previously he had been a member of a regional legislature) as the representative of the electoral district Potsdam I. Proudly his
mother related in her letters to Jerusalem that his name could be read daily
in the newspapers. Betty wanted to attend the opening day of the new
Reichstag, but her son feared that she would behave too well and not "make
the necessary noise, so his party had to give the tickets to people more
dependable than I am unfortunately! When the young Bismarck approached the podium to speak, Werner called out 'Woe betide you that you
are a grandson.' Every newspaper from every party noted the interjection,
which I do not find particularly witty since it is all too obvious."[180]

Betty was referring to the entry of Otto Fürst von Bismarck (grandson
of the legendary Otto von Bismarck), who entered the Reichstag as a representative of the right-wing DNVP party. At that time it was not unusual for
the first session of the parliament to be interrupted by the noise and uproar
of the Communists and the German nationalists. At this opening session in
May 1924, the Communists sang "The Internationale" and the rightists
sang the "Deutschlandlied." This musical battle caused the session to be
abruptly adjourned.[181]

Immediately in the first regular session of parliament, the new deputy
Werner Scholem rose to deliver his maiden speech. Once again he was one
of the youngest present but now no longer an unknown name. According
to the protocol, he was met with noisy protests from the right-wing parties.
In its story on the opening session, the *Manchester Guardian* reported that
Deputy Scholem was hated to an extraordinary degree by the right. Werner
Scholem did not disappoint his opponents, immediately lambasting "the
government of this republic of profiteers" for holding Communist deputies
illegally behind bars. As in the Prussian Landtag, his political opponents
made fun of his physical appearance with anti-Semitic remarks. In this first
session of the Reichstag, Josef Andre, a member of the Center Party,
declared his "long nose" an object of ridicule. Scholem retorted with a
remark about Andre's "big belly," but the rest of his speech was drowned
out by anti-Semitic hooting. Whether he liked it or not, the right perceived
him not as a KPD deputy in the Reichstag but as the representative of a
state vilified as the "Moses Republic." For them, he represented a new Jewish species, those " 'disguised' Jews who appeared in German political life
as individual Germans without a Jewish mission."[182]

Undeterred by the tumult, he continued his unrestrained attack. For
example, at one point he asserted that the German nationalists denied class

struggle and believed this to be "a Communist invention, an order from Moscow, a Jewish-Marxist trick." As rightist hecklers assured him that his assessment of their opinion was accurate, he went on to note that Communists per se were labeled traitors in many places. Again the right agreed and added that this was particularly the case if the Communists in question were Jews. "Of course, particularly if he is a Jew—that's self-evident!" answered Werner Scholem. "As we know, it's in the race that the swishiness comes out!" Filled with indignation, he then accused the Reichstag of what he said had been long known by all: namely, that the German justice system weighed crimes committed by the left differently than those committed by the right, that, for example, it was but a trivial matter to sentence an executive editor of the *Rote Fahne* to fifteen months' imprisonment for a frivolity. In a long statement, he lamented the four hundred—mostly unpunished—political murders committed by the right compared to only twenty assassinations by the left. In the preceding five months alone, there had been twenty thousand charges leveled against members of the Communist Party, and seven thousand comrades were currently sitting behind prison walls. All of this was due to the "shameful system of the sham democracy," he summed up.[183]

Werner Scholem's provocative performances were not only being closely watched in Berlin. From the Italian island of Capri Walter Benjamin kept a critical eye on his friend's brother. In a letter to his former teacher, the sociologist Gottfried Salomon-Delatour, Benjamin wrote in early June 1924: "Among the consequences of the conditions in Germany is also the horrible impression given by the Reichstag protocols, which occasionally fall into my hands. In full view of the country and abroad, the Germans have now happily yielded the rostrum to the riffraff of their people. A marauding soldiery, on the one side, and on the other such little rascals like 'Deputy Scholem,' whom I know. One has truly to be a good Kabbalist to purify oneself from the brotherly relations with this person." A few days later he expressed his disgust over the public shenanigans of Deputy Scholem with the great Kabbalist himself. In his letter to Gershom Scholem he wrote: "Europe is full of Deputy Scholem. Even the Pan-Germans sitting next to me in the café talk about him. Everywhere he stirs up—justifiably—strong storms of *rishes* [anti-Semitism]. His rise to fame and honor make me rather sad."[184]

Benjamin's remark about conversations that he had heard on Capri is evidence of the unusual vehemence of the anti-Semitic reactions to the public figure of Werner Scholem. However, did Benjamin, with all his irony, really believe that the anti-Semitic reactions triggered by Werner were "justified"? Such twisted logic can only be understood as a product of the political culture prevailing in the Weimar Republic, in which Jews themselves were held responsible for anti-Semitism. In part, Benjamin may have believed this, but at the same time his criticism of the most recent developments in the KPD also sprang from his own Marxist leanings during that early summer.

Meanwhile, other accounts of anti-Semitic reactions to his brother were reaching Gershom Scholem in Jerusalem. For example, Betty wrote about a grotesque incident, which had occurred among the relatives. Her brother-in-law, Georg Scholem, a physician, had complained that Christian patients no longer came into his practice anymore, and the only reason for this could be the public performances of his nephew. In Betty's words, she then "let loose a gale of scornful laughter and asked him whether he had ever heard something about anti-Semitism! No, he said, his clients were not anti, but the dumb *Gajes* [goy, non-Jew] did not know whether the Communist Scholem was his father or his son or even himself and so they didn't want to have anything more to do with him." Little to her surprise, Arthur agreed with his brother, continued Betty, and also entered the losses booked by "the diminishing business of Georg's practice to the sizable debit side of Werner's account." The famous and wayward Scholem discomfited the entire clan, and his mother regularly had to hear all sorts of horror stories about him, almost all of which proved to be untrue.[185]

In his memoirs, Gershom Scholem remembers that, as the youngest and most prominent member of the Reichstag, his brother also landed "at the head of the Nazis' blacklist."[186] Indeed, in the spring of 1924 he received a prominent place in their propaganda.

The twenty-six-year-old Joseph Goebbels, who was not yet a member of the banned National Socialist German Workers' Party (Nationalsozialistische Deutsche Arbeiterpartei, NSDAP) noted in his diary on 14 July 1924: "The internationalists in Communism are Marx, Liebknecht, Radek, Scholem, that is, the Jews. The real workers are actually nationalists to the core, regardless how international they act. It's shameful to them that the Jews are so intellectually superior and destroy them with their mush of platitudes. A worker would never come up with the idea of the International."[187]

On both the left and right sides of the political spectrum, anti-Jewish sentiments were as much in the air as anti-intellectual animus. Even the

FIGURE 22. Werner Scholem (bottom center) on an NSDAP poster, November 1924. Bundesarchiv Berlin, poster 002–039–007, artist anonymous.

election of the new KPD leadership had been accompanied by anti-Semitic undertones during the party congress, and the German Comintern commissar Josef Eisenberger hoped that the "brazen Jewish rascals [*die frechen Judenbengel*]" Ruth Fischer, Ivan Katz, and Werner Scholem would soon run themselves into the ground.[188] Even the veteran revolutionary Clara Zetkin expressed concern in July 1924 to the Comintern about the dominance of intellectuals in the German Communist Party. The KPD must not be flooded by these people, explained Zetkin, because they distorted the nature of the party and would "facilitate and strengthen tendencies toward embourgeoisement, toward opportunism." The intellectuals were the "wavering, unreliable allies of the proletariat and they had to be checked regularly to see if they had permanently abandoned their bourgeois nature.[189] Although Clara Zetkin had condemned the anti-Semitic remarks heard among party officials at other times, her criticism of intellectuals was essentially the same because, as Werner Scholem noted, in the KPD it was almost only Jews who were attacked as being intellectuals. Non-Jewish academics were not given this derogatory label.[190] Zetkin's demand was put into practice through a regimen of strict self-control that shaped the everyday life of all party members whose background was bourgeois, intellectual, and often also Jewish. Sometimes they sought to adapt their way of life, penchants, and interests to the proletarian ideal or relegated them exclusively to the private realm. For example, they concealed appreciation of classical music by purchasing a record player.[191]

In their rear apartment in the Moabit quarter of Berlin, Emmy and Werner Scholem attempted to live by Zetkin's standards and deliberately presented a modest appearance. After spending some time helping her son buy a new coat, Betty Scholem noted that the search for the correct one had been a difficult undertaking. The perfect item was not to be the "latest fashion statement" but "inconspicuous and suitable for a lawyer of the people." However, as a grandmother, she greatly enjoyed encouraging the bourgeois airs and graces of little Edith. She granted her granddaughter's every wish, even if it was as unusual as a doll in a suitcase. "Emmy always feels so embarrassed when the child comes up with such wishes," reported Betty following a family gathering. "But for me it is incredible fun to watch how neither Communism nor the rear courtyard apartment can repress the noble character of the child. Werner says she has incredible inner pride. But naturally, children very rarely turn out as their parents want."[192]

When it came to Edith, the father let the grandmother do what she wanted because, among other things, he had little time to think about the upbringing of his daughter. As the head of the organization department of the Central Committee, he was responsible for the party organization in the whole of Germany, a task he undertook with great energy and diligence. At internal party meetings, he complained about the party's extremely poor state of organization when he assumed the job. Following the events of 1923, he noted, the KPD had been dominated by a crazy atmosphere that he felt he could best describe "with an old Gothic word like 'meshuga.'"[193] This ironic remark was probably a retort to Heinrich Brandler, who had once described the Left Opposition derogatorily as "meshuga intellectuals," not accidentally using a Yiddish word.[194] Now, Werner Scholem was convinced, several of these former KPD leaders were creating cells of resistance in Moscow from which they wanted to influence German politics. During an internal party meeting, he noted that a bad influence was now emanating from Russia altogether, both from the Comintern and from Joseph Stalin himself, who was becoming increasingly powerful.[195]

His political work came to an abrupt halt in October 1924 because the Reichstag, which had been in a stalemate since the election, was dissolved prematurely, meaning that the immunity of the deputies was also lifted. Wanted posters for Werner Scholem and the other members of the party headquarters were issued: "1.67 meters tall, black hair, dark eyes, hooked nose, sometimes wears horn-rimmed glasses." Until his reelection in December, he went underground and waited for the moment he could return to parliament with what had become a significantly smaller Communist faction.[196]

Between Werner's election in the early summer of 1924 and the end of that year, his volatile political career again became a topic of Walter Benjamin's correspondence with Gershom Scholem. Actually, Benjamin wrote to his friend about his own leanings toward Communism, which were still unclear in many respects, except that the writings of the Marxist philosopher Georg Lukács played a major role for him. "This all has little to do, I hope, with the lively activity of your brother Werner," Benjamin was quick to add. "Regarding communism, the problem with 'theory and practice' seems to me in effect to be that, given the disparity that must be preserved between these two realms, any definitive insight into theory is precisely dependent on practice."[197] On Capri, Benjamin had begun an affair with the Latvian theater director, actress, and revolutionary Asja Lācis, whose work as the head of a proletarian children's theater had exposed him to the practice-oriented side of Communism.

After returning from Italy, Benjamin reflected on the changes that had occurred in him during his summer on the Mediterranean island in his letters to Gershom Scholem. His need to distance himself from Werner Scholem became more evident, though he still neglected to explain the precise difference that lay between him and Werner. His own interest in Communism was clearly individualistic and intellectual, far from party activity. However, through his acquaintance with Asja Lācis, he did attempt to approach the grassroots and practical application of Communism. Thus he found something in common with the movement that led him into that nadir where he would also find Werner Scholem, although Werner's lack of bourgeois manners and behavior were abhorrent to him.[198] He wrote to Gershom Scholem:

> I hope some day the Communist signals will come through to you more clearly than they did from Capri. At first they were indications of a change that awakened in me the will not to mask the actual and political elements of my ideas in the Old Franconian way I did before, but also to develop them by experimenting and taking extreme measures. . . . As long as I do not manage to approach texts of a totally different significance and magnitude from a stance that is appropriate to me, that of commentator, I will generate a "politics" from within myself. And in view of this, my surprise at the various points of contact I have with radical Bolshevist theory has of course been renewed. It is really a shame that I still do not anticipate producing a coherent written statement about these matters, and that, until I do, I may remain the object of your speculations on the elective affinity between Walter Benjamin and Werner Scholem.[199]

A while later Gershom Scholem observed how the paths of these two very different Marxists once again crossed.

In early February 1925, Arthur Scholem died, thoroughly unexpectedly, at his printing shop shortly before his sixty-second birthday. That afternoon, Werner had spontaneously decided to visit his mother and invite her to Bellevue Café on Potsdamer Platz, which is where they learned of the death of husband and father. When it came time to distribute the personal belongings of her husband, Betty offered his golden wristwatch to the wayward son. Since it held less emotional value for Werner than it did for the oldest son, Reinhold, the latter asked to have it as an heirloom. In turn, Reinhold gave his sister-in-law Emmy a watch that he himself had received from his mother-in-law at his engagement. At the time, Reinhold's marriage was in crisis, so he quite enjoyed knowing that the watch given to him by his upper-class mother-in-law now graced the arm of his proletarian sister-in-law. "If *Frau Commerzienrat*[200] only knew," noted Betty in great amusement over the inner-family gift swap, "that her present now ticks in the company of Communists, her highness would burst." On top of that, Emmy wore her new watch when she went to Moscow in the spring of 1925, where she made sure to buy souvenirs for Betty.[201]

In late March, the Enlarged Executive Committee of the Communist International held a two-week session in Moscow, which the KPD leadership also attended, including two secretaries who worked at party headquarters, Emmy Scholem and Irma Volkmann. Among the delegates from around the world was also Joseph Berger-Barzilai, who was secretary of the Communist Party of Palestine and a founding member of the Lebanese Communist party. During the meetings, Berger-Barzilai noticed the young leader from the German party, Werner Scholem, who greatly impressed him as an excellent speaker. About this time Grigory Zinoviev is also said to have described Comrade Scholem as the most influential man in the KPD and the dictator of the Organization Office.[202]

During these two weeks, relations between the German delegation and the Comintern were very discordant, leading to a de facto schism within the KPD. The conflict was sparked by controversy over the upcoming elections for the German Reich presidency, for which the German Communists had nominated Ernst Thälmann as their candidate. Since Thälmann had no real chance of winning the presidency, Grigory Zinoviev demanded that, in the second round of voting, the KPD should support the candidate of the "Weimar Coalition," the Center Party politician Wilhelm Marx, arguing that this was the only way to prevent the election of Paul von Hindenburg, the candidate of the rightist parties and the embodiment of imperial Germany and German militarism. Ruth Fischer agreed with Zinoviev, but Werner Scholem and Arthur Rosenberg opposed his proposal vehemently. Eventually, Fischer backed them up, but later, when Marx lost the election because of the Thälmann candidacy, she switched to Zinoviev's side.[203]

In view of the dwindling party membership, Ruth Fischer and—from his prison cell, where he was serving a sentence for treason—Arkadi Maslow came to the conclusion that no progress could be made without a "unified front from above," meaning cooperation between Communists and Social Democrats initiated by the party leaderships. The SPD warily took note of this change of direction, and the *Vorwärts* warned its readers that this was a tactical maneuver with which Moscow sought to capture the votes of SPD supporters.[204] Meanwhile, Ivan Katz, Arthur Rosenberg, and Werner Scholem maintained their vehement opposition against any such coalition staged from above. However, by then, if not earlier, their rejection of the united-front tactic was no longer compatible with the Bolshevization of the party, rapprochement between the German Communists and the Moscow leadership. As a result, the three men landed on the Comintern's blacklist.[205]

In early May this matter was discussed within the KPD, and during this discussion Werner Scholem appealed for party unity. He was of the opinion that one should be allowed to speak freely and express reservations even within a Bolshevized party. He explained that he rejected liaison with the Social Democrats because such cooperation would require the unconditional acceptance of a bourgeois government to represent the proletariat. Instead, he argued in favor of a tactic of a "united front from below," in which the grass roots of the parties were to work together in the common cause of opposing fascism. However, Chairwoman Ruth Fischer was not willing to listen to any of this. She and the KPD leadership chose to side with the Comintern and accused the three oppositionists of mutiny and splitting the party.[206]

Thus began the campaign against the so-called Ultraleft. The first step was to prevent the reelection of Werner Scholem and Arthur Rosenberg to leadership positions within the Berlin party district.[207] Shortly before the start of the Tenth Party Congress of the KPD in early July, Werner Scholem presented his standpoint on current developments in a special issue of the magazine *Die Internationale*, published by his friend Karl Korsch. In his piece, he criticized the party leadership of erroneously assuming "that the Prussian army before the war" has been "roughly the embodied ideal of a Leninist party." Again he called for a greater right of codetermination and spoke out in favor of decentralizing power, in which the authority and influence of party leadership was to be limited for the benefit of self-determined local and regional groups. Indirectly, he was thus challenging the Bolshevization of the KPD, which envisioned the concentration of power in the hands of a few. In forthright terms, he also demanded a reduction of the Comintern's influence, because it was less and less committed to serving the interests of all Communist parties and instead promoted Russian foreign policy.[208] Scholem, Katz, and Rosenberg were not alone in their criticism; other leading minds of the Communist movement, such as the Marxist philosopher Korsch, agreed. Subsequently, the talented organizer Scholem made it his task to consolidate the oppositional left.[209]

At the party congress, he was the chief speaker of the group, who called themselves the Left Communists, while everyone else called them the Ultraleft. The party congress condemned the dissident behavior of the Left Communists with slogans like "Hands off the party! Down with the faction makers!" They were told to fall in line behind the party leadership.[210] In confidential conversations outside the meeting, Ruth Fischer allegedly cursed her oppositionist friends and called them the true enemies of the Bolshevization of the party.[211] Despite this, a rapprochement between the two groups again took place during the congress, and both Werner Scholem and Arthur Rosenberg were reelected to the Central Committee of the party. From the standpoint of the Comintern, this headstrong behavior on the part of the KPD could only be perceived as an affront, and in response it began to turn away from Ruth Fischer and toward Ernst Thälmann. Thälmann, who had formerly worked as a stoker on a freighter and as a dockworker, was a far more reliable partner for the Comintern than the all too flexible Ruth Fischer.[212] During the summer, Werner Scholem, Ivan Katz, and Arthur Rosenberg increasingly came under fire despite the backing they received from the party's Central Committee, and more and more voices within the KPD called for disciplining them harshly.[213] Such a step proved to be unnecessary because the Comintern intervened and ordered a German delegation headed by Ruth Fischer to report to Moscow.

On 1 September 1925, an "Open Letter" was published in the *Rote Fahne* in which, to the surprise of many readers, the Comintern described its poor relations with the current KPD leadership. In addition to the Left Communists, who were labeled enemies of Bolshevism, harsh criticism was leveled particularly against Ruth Fischer and Arkadi Maslow. Because they did not resolutely fight the oppositionists but instead had made a pact with them, they were accused of exhibiting "anti-Muscovite" tendencies. Most of the bodies and representatives of the KPD were forced to accept the open letter, succumbing to pressure one after another. Even Ruth Fischer signed

FIGURE 23. Werner Scholem speaking on Antiwar Day in Potsdam, 1925, with his handwritten notation: "remarkably grotesque visage." Private archive of Renee Goddard.

it and thus—as she noted years later—her own political death sentence. From this point on, Ernst Thälmann headed the German Communists. The later hero of the German Democratic Republic restructured the party, making it subservient to Stalin's directives, as required by the Comintern.[214]

Werner Scholem and Arthur Rosenberg answered the open letter by openly rejecting its accusations. They distanced themselves from the directives of the Comintern and called for freedom of speech for every member of a Communist party worldwide. In a programmatic text with the title "For the Unity of the German Left," they expressed their conviction that the campaign against the Left Opposition was only the beginning and that eventually the entire left KPD—including Ruth Fischer and Arkadi Maslow—would be affected.[215] Werner Scholem saw his own future prospects and those of the party as bleak, as is shown in a short note that he added to a letter his mother was writing to Gershom Scholem in early October. He wrote that he was "currently out on a limb. The KPD is on the threshold of death, and before that happens they want to throw out everyone who does not go to Noske." This is a reference to the Social Democratic politician Gustav Noske, who had ordered the repression of the Spartacist uprising while he was the People's Commissar for Army and Navy. Since 1919, Werner had felt an almost personal feud with him, and, to his mind both in 1919 and 1925, this disaster proved that the SPD could not be trusted.[216]

Werner was correct in his prediction that his days in the party were numbered. Soon his fellow comrades were declaring him to be the central enemy in the struggle against Ultraleft sectarianism. In a highly confidential letter from the KPD Central Committee to the Comintern, Scholem was identified as the sole leader of the opposition and denounced fiercely.[217] As if this were not enough, his opponents attempted to implicate him in a corruption scandal from the previous year. In 1924, Werner Scholem and Ruth Fischer had hired a new treasurer, Arthur König, who lost great sums of party money through mismanagement and bad investments and had to defend himself against the charge of fraud. Although the case had been considered closed by this point, it was brought up again in the campaign against Werner Scholem so as to pin the blame for König's alleged corruption on him.[218] In the wake of this accusation, König was apparently persuaded to issue a false statement in which he claimed that Ruth Fischer, Werner Scholem, and Arkadi Maslow had told him to reserve secret funds for a campaign against the Comintern. In a circular issued by the Left

Communists, Werner Scholem defended himself against this accusation and pointed out that he had been one of the first to call for König's dismissal. He claimed to be a victim of an intrigue started by Arthur König and Ernst Thälmann, who wanted to get him in such trouble that he would be ordered to go to Moscow, detained there, put on trial, and subsequently convicted as the key culprit in the König case.[219]

From the very end of October to early November 1925, the first national congress of the KPD was held, during which this conflict was to be openly fought out. However, prior to the congress a resolution against the Left Communists was adopted, which actually decided the entire matter before it could be discussed.[220] Although in the past Ernst Thälmann had always differentiated between the two Ultraleft wings—the good one led by Ruth Fischer and the bad one by Werner Scholem—at the national conference he lashed out against both. In his speech, Thälmann called the oppositionists the "pests in the party" and Werner Scholem an "anti-Bolshevist" and Leon Trotsky's brother in spirit.[221]

Arthur Rosenberg supported and defended his friend, but Ruth Fischer joined those who signed the written attack against him—although she herself was coming under increasing criticism. Disappointed, Werner Scholem reacted to this betrayal, angrily calling Ruth a rat.[222] He defended himself by leveling sharp counterattacks against the accusations, which did not, however, prompt a reaction. Instead, a commission was set up to investigate his political methods and an arbitration court was to judge his case. In disgust, he refused to testify before this commission, which he claimed was nothing more than a political farce, and instead resigned from all of his offices and responsibilities in the party. Although several members of the Scholem Commission also resigned because they found the entire episode unfair, the arbitration court declared the accused guilty in absentia, and he was expelled from the Central Committee and thus from the KPD's party leadership.[223]

In Alliance with Trotsky

In the second half of the 1920s, Bertolt Brecht characterized the "intellectual revolutionary" as a type of whom "the proletarian revolutionary is suspicious: this is the type who expects a thoroughgoing improvement from the revolution. In no sense standing under unbearable pressure, but freely selecting and choosing what is better, he opts for revolution."[224] It is not by accident that this text was composed at the time when a number of Communist intellectuals were expelled from the leading bodies of the KPD and finally from the party itself: Werner Scholem, Ruth Fischer, Arkadi Maslow, Ivan Katz, Karl Korsch, Arthur Rosenberg, Hugo Urbahns, and many more. In Russia, Grigory Zinoviev and Leon Trotsky met with the same fate because they were blocking Stalin's seizure of power.[225]

The epithet "intellectual" proved to be a practical means with which to discredit established politicians from one day to the next, in order to justify their liquidation—the technical term used—from public life and to abruptly end their career. Werner Scholem's path toward expulsion was strewn with such attributes, especially since he had been caught in the crossfire of similar attacks in the past. He was fully aware of this negative image and therefore could not have been very surprised to learn that he was being vilified as the "bohemian" of the party and the "coffeehouse writer" of the German workers' movement.[226]

In the assault on the Left Opposition, which was actually an assault on the party leadership, the anonymous authors, presumably Comintern officials in Germany and Russia, deemed it necessary not just to level accusations against the people in question but to delegitimize them fully. For this purpose, the Comintern commissioned the writing of a "History of the Ultraleft" as a history of a group of intellectual petit bourgeois who had been misguided from the start. Yet the project did not remain merely a defamation of these people as petit bourgeois; the rhetoric became increasingly fierce. The history called the Ultraleft an illness, abscesses, and ulcers that needed to be cut out of body of the party.[227] The authors of this supposed history intentionally used language similar to that of anti-Semitic nationalism.

Every effort was made to describe the Left Opposition as a small group of individualistic, obscure outsiders. This was by no means true, because in reality they posed a real danger for the new course taken in the worldwide Communist movement, since the KPD was a particularly influential party. Joseph Stalin estimated that only 10 percent of the KPD members were his opponents, while others calculated that nearly half of the membership supported the Left Opposition. They were popular among the workers because they fit the image of the Communist fighter. At the same time, they did not comprise a homogeneous bloc but consisted of various groups who formed around headstrong leaders and got into ideological arguments among themselves. This also explains why the trust that many supporters placed in them would be squandered in the years to follow.[228]

It is unclear where and when Werner Scholem met Joseph Stalin for the first time. That they didn't like each other was confirmed by many sources. "The Secretary General disliked him [Scholem] heartily," recalled Ruth Fischer, "because he turned aside any appeal couched in hyper-Bolshevist terms with the crude cynicism of the Berliner."[229] In early 1926, Joseph Stalin declared his rival Werner Scholem to be the real problem in the conflict in Germany. In two speeches, the Russian party head attacked the Left Opposition in Germany and demanded that Ruth Fischer and Arkadi Maslow should cease to shield the "Scholem group." On the contrary, they should make every possible effort to overcome and obliterate the "Ultraleft" biases of the German Communist Party.[230]

From the end of February to the beginning of March, all of the individuals involved were ordered to Moscow where they were to defend their position before the Enlarged Executive Committee of the Comintern. Margarete Buber-Neumann, Martin Buber's daughter-in-law, recalled that the person who cut the worst figure in her eyes was Ruth Fischer. She was accused of keeping false accounts and called a liar. Buber-Neumann expressed a more sympathetic view of Werner Scholem when she noted: "Werner Scholem, who refused to sign the 'open letter' because he did not want to let himself be called an 'anti-Communist, anti-Bolshevist, or even a corrupt element who sold out to the bourgeoisie,' bravely worked to save his skin and was interrupted time and again by interjections." The mood was tense, the Left Oppositionists were increasingly put under pressure, and much was indeed at stake for the Comintern: should the German renegades join an international "Left Opposition," the result would be a second Communist International. Arthur Rosenberg bowed to this pressure and returned penitently to the KPD fold under the leadership of Ernst Thälmann.[231]

The stress of all the conflict and intrigue also began to leave its mark on Werner Scholem; increasingly he failed to attend meetings for health reasons. Tersely Betty Scholem noted that he had "liver & gallbladder dilation, & furthermore is in an appalling position." His absences were held against him in the party, and it was said that Comrade Scholem preferred to travel to Tyrol to go climbing than to answer to the charges brought against him. In the meantime, his brother sent him a request from Palestine for a subscription to the *Rote Fahne* so that he could better understand what was behind the conflicts.[232] Werner was quite happy not only to fulfill his brother's request but also to receive this offer to revive their political dialogue of earlier years. He provided Gershom Scholem with a subscription and a series of texts that he and Arthur Rosenberg had written in the previous months. Because no outsider could really understand the peculiar Marxist scholasticism involved in the controversy, he wrote his brother a very personal analysis of the entire matter and entreated him to handle the letter as highly confidential and under no circumstances to let it fall into the hands of the Communist Party of Palestine. The events in Germany, he explained to his brother, were closely linked to the power struggles taking place in Russia between Leon Trotsky and his followers, on the left, and Joseph Stalin and Nikolai Bukharin, on the right. He himself believed in an eventual victory of the Trotskyites and predicted the end of the Comintern and Bolshevism. What would emerge in Russia would be a democratic worker and peasant state. However, his predictions for his own political future were much darker because he was convinced that Moscow would manage to have him and all other oppositionists expelled from the party: "They attack us, the people who in reality want to uphold the old principles of the Communist International, as being the enemies of the Communist International, a maneuver that repeats itself with ridiculous similarity time and again in similar incidents throughout history." He also thought the end of the KPD was near and wished to see the bureaucratic apparatus financed by Russia land on the manure pile of history. The Left Opposition, he was certain, would become the core of a new Socialist revolutionary workers' party in Germany.[233]

In the summer of 1926, Werner took Emmy to a spa resort, where he hoped to recover from his illness and the exertions of the previous months. The resort he picked was Karlsbad of all places, the spa town visited by the Jewish middle class from all over Europe. But what difference did it make now? Since being stigmatized as a petit bourgeois intellectual—and a Jew on top of it—Werner no longer had a good reputation to lose. Besides, the fashionable spa resort was the place to find not only the eastern European Jewish proletariat strolling along the promenades and through the woods, their cures financed by Jewish welfare organizations, but also the memory of Karl Marx. Fifty years before, the master himself had undertaken the same liver and gallbladder cure in Karlsbad as his disciple now did.[234]

Upon his return to Berlin, Werner Scholem leaped back into the political arena with renewed vigor. As the leader of the Left Opposition, he organized a coalition of support from all oppositionist groups to publish the "Letter of the 700." This public manifesto, which was signed by no less than

FIGURE 24. Emmy and Werner Scholem with their friend Gerhard Fink in Karlsbad, summer 1926. Private archive of Renee Goddard.

seven hundred supporters of the opposition, was fiercely attacked by the KPD. Far more discouraging for those involved was the fact that, not long afterward, the Russian opposition led by Trotsky and Kamenev in the Comintern also distanced themselves from the German opposition.[235]

On 1 November 1926, Werner Scholem announced his resignation as an editor at the *Rote Fahne* because he was now being berated every day in the party organ and called a "party splitter" and "mortal enemy of the KPD." His resignation marked the beginning of the Stalinist restructuring of the paper, at the end of which there were almost no intellectually inclined writers left on the staff. Four days later, the KPD Central Committee decided to expel Werner Scholem and Hugo Urbahns from the party. This followed the expulsion of Ruth Fischer and Arkadi Maslow, who had been thrown out in August.[236] In his last speech before the party leadership, Werner Scholem took the offensive in countering all the attacks against him and again proclaiming his support for the Russian opposition despite the recent developments. The response of his former party friends was harsh: they accused him of having always been in the opposition, of being the eternal dissident. They called him a pitiful hero, one whose "entire objective was to prevent the turmoil within the party from coming to an end."[237]

The *Vorwärts* reported on the recent purges within the KPD and that the fifteen expelled Reichstag deputies had joined together to create their own parliamentary faction, the Left Communists. This coalition was born more out of practical necessity than ideological conviction. By refusing to resign their mandates and creating this new faction, they remained present in public political life, quite independent, with financial backing until the next elections, and they also did not have to fear criminal charges due to revocation of their immunity.[238]

Unlike her husband, Emmy Scholem lost her job when he was expelled from the party. She had already been forced to give up her long-held position as a stenographer at the party's Central Committee the year before. In the meantime, she had landed a well-paid job at the Soviet Trade Mission in Berlin, from which she was now dismissed. Since she continued to be a party member, she appealed emphatically in a letter to her fellow comrades not to fire her. She even went as far as distancing herself from all political activities of her husband. She still lost the job.[239]

In early December, the members of the Left Opposition were summoned to Moscow to present in person their objections to being expelled from the party. The invitation arrived by telegraph and read more like an order: the group was to arrive in Moscow within the next twenty-four, at most forty-eight, hours. Evasions or delays would not be tolerated. Within a day the German delegation did arrive in Moscow, where they were isolated in a hotel and made to wait, despite the urgency professed in the invitation, for several days. This is at least how the visit was described in a report written by Werner Scholem, Ruth Fischer, Hugo Urbahns, and Wilhelm Schwan upon their return to Germany. The internal report was conceived as a justification to be presented to the supporters of the Left Opposition, because naturally the party press had published another version of the events. As described in the report, the talks with the responsible commission in Moscow proved to be a farce. The questions were inquisitorial, the atmosphere disrespectful. To no one's surprise, at the end of the talks the commission upheld the party exclusions of all those involved.[240]

At the same time as these proceedings, which would seal the fate of the German opposition within the Communist movement, Gershom Scholem received a letter from Moscow—not from his brother but from his friend Walter Benjamin. In early December Benjamin had traveled to Moscow for a three-month visit that had as much to do with his relationship with the Latvian revolutionary Asja Lācis as it did with his interest in the Communist movement. For various reasons—not the least being his unsuccessful academic career up to that point—he was thinking about joining the KPD. On 10 December, he wrote Gershom Scholem that by "a rather curious coincidence, I believe that your brother is here in Moscow as well, from what I gathered yesterday, he has been invited to the extended session of the Comintern here as one of the representatives of the German 'opposition.' Let me immediately reassure you by making clear that I am not here on any official mission. But naturally I am finding out a great deal about things that are quite useful and interesting for me to know." As had happened before, Benjamin was most anxious to deny any similarities between him and his friend's brother, despite the fact or precisely because their ideological and political paths crossed more often than he liked. During his stay in Moscow, Benjamin heard reports and rumors about the struggle against the Ultraleft opposition within the German Communist Party, and in his journal he noted: "then the political news: members of the opposition removed from important positions. And in identical fashion: countless Jews removed from middle-level posts." Benjamin was able to observe the disciplinary measures of the Comintern directly. These observations most likely played a significant role in his later decision against joining the KPD.[241]

After returning from Moscow, Werner Scholem began to work closely with Hugo Urbahns and Ruth Fischer. Together they published the *Mitteilungsblatt Linke Opposition der KPD* under rather primitive conditions and distributed it from Werner and Emmy's apartment.[242] Starting in mid-1927, they published as a group of orthodox Marxist-Leninists the *Fahne des Kommunimus* with a much greater circulation. Although most of the articles were unsigned as a protective measure against the vigilant eyes of the Weimar censors, the tone of many of these is unmistakably that of Werner Scholem, as is evidenced by the stinging criticism of Stalin's politics or by the use of quotes by Rosa Luxemburg and Karl Liebknecht, a link to his own political—and oppositional—origins.[243] In addition to his publishing activities, he did what he had always done: he appeared as the main speaker at numerous evening events in Berlin and other major cities. Sometimes he encountered public altercations with representatives of the KPD, as in Freiburg, where he confronted Herbert Wehner, who had taken the offensive in order prevent the Trotskyites from gaining a foothold in Freiburg.[244]

In March 1928, the group associated with Hugo Urbahns and Werner Scholem founded the Leninbund, which was to run as the party of the Left Opposition in the next elections. The Leninbund also had its own newspaper, the *Volkswille*, and advocated a united workers' front and an offensive campaign against National Socialism. Its members were all young oppositionists and, as Werner Scholem announced at the founding meeting, numbered five to six thousand; he estimated the number of sympathizers and supporters to be much higher at eighty thousand to one hundred thousand workers. Although this unusually high number was questioned time and again, it might not be unrealistic, seeing how enormously attractive the Left Opposition was to the working class.[245]

In the Leninbund, Werner Scholem now returned to his own political roots more than he had ever done before and depicted himself and his fellow party members as the heirs of the Liebknechtian opposition to the world war. In this context, he organized a May Festival in 1928 featuring choirs, theater groups, and gymnasts on the Hasenheide in Neukölln, where the roots of the Spartacus League lay. Though his career as a student of history had been short, it was a matter of great concern to him to ensure his party its place in the historical chain of German social democracy. At the same time, the work in the Leninbund was also a sobering experience for Scholem, the ambitious organizer. Not only was there an extreme shortage of the funds for even the most basic party work, the organizers urgently needed information and networks. Since all links to the KPD had been thoroughly severed, the Leninbund found itself in a fairly isolated position and hamstrung by a lack of money. The stigma of being the outsider was reflected in incidents such as the tumult that broke out during an event when the Leninbund was called a "gang of Jews."[246]

While the members in the Left Opposition knew little about what was going on in the KPD, that party was well informed about what was going on in the Leninbund. The intelligence service of the KPD spied regularly on the renegades and, for instance, reported each of Ruth Fischer's criticisms of Stalin at various events and Werner Scholem's remark in a speech that "the course to reformism" was now being pursued in the Soviet Union "behind a jumble of flags, parades, and revolutionary emblems."[247]

When the leadership of the Leninbund decided that the group should run in the upcoming parliamentary elections, Werner Scholem resigned his membership. In a public statement, he announced that he was no longer able to pursue the aims of the group. As a second Communist party, the Leninbund would divide the workers' movement and would have to adapt to a future lingering on the sectarian sidelines. The French historian and biographer of Trotsky Pierre Broué argues that Werner Scholem's reasons for leaving the party show great similarity with Leon Trotsky's views. As a careful observer of politics, Werner Scholem probably had drawn some conclusions from the disastrous financial and organizational circumstances of the Leninbund. Together with sixteen other oppositionists, including Ruth Fischer and Arkadi Maslow, who resigned from the Leninbund on the following day, Werner Scholem made a last attempt to return to the KPD. The Russian opposition had taken the same step, and now the German opposition held false hopes that the Comintern and the party leadership in Moscow were taking a turn to the left.[248] This unsuccessful attempt earned Werner Scholem, Ruth Fischer, and Arkadi Maslow the reputation of being unreliable and vacillating. Indignant over the news, Erich Mühsam, a German Jewish anarchist and writer, quite well-known in his day, commented on the step they had taken in his magazine *Fanal*:

> Maslow, Ruth Fischer, Scholem were again for currying favor with the party and left the Leninbund, which they themselves had founded, at the last possible moment. They did this, following the fine example set by Zinoviev and Kamenev, not without once again buttering up in a very undignified way to those people who had

previously criticized them day in, day out; people who had suggested to their hate-ridden supporters—a crowd trained to attack only the left—that they [Scholem, Fischer, and Maslow] should be beaten as lumpen, traitors, and Menshevik herders.[249]

In the spring of 1930, the International Left Opposition was founded under the leadership of Leon Trotsky, who had been living in exile since 1929. The Trotskyite paper *Permanente Revolution* was printed in Germany, one of the most important countries for the oppositional left. In it appeared numerous programmatic texts written by Trotsky, which propagated cooperation among the workers' movement against National Socialism. Trotsky's son, Léon Sedov, who was often in Germany and had become his father's most important liaison there, sought out Werner Scholem in March 1931. He told Scholem that his father considered him an important man and wanted him to help him become the leader of the Trotskyite opposition in Germany. From that point on, Werner Scholem began to work with Trotsky, without ever being in direct contact with him. Erwin A. Ackerknecht, who worked as Trotsky's liaison under the pseudonym E. Bauer, visited him every week and listened to Scholem's oral reports. Occasionally Werner Scholem also handed him written elaborations, some of which appeared in the *Permanente Revolution* between 1931 and 1933.[250]

Ruth Fischer took a more critical view of Leon Trotsky at the time and only began to grow closer to him while working for him between 1933 and 1935 in Paris. She described the important role that Werner Scholem had played for the early years of the Trotskyite movement in Germany: "Scholem never stopped arguing about the necessity of cooperating with Trotsky in building up an international opposition." For this reason, Pierre Broué found it disconcerting that, after the Second World War, Trotskyites had been hesitant to commemorate the memory of Werner Scholem, even though he had clearly been one of them.[251]

In an interview given in the early 1970s, Gershom Scholem described the political demise of his brother with the following words: "They 'threw him out' six years later for being a Trotskyite, like a good many of the Jews in the Communist movement (actually, an overwhelming number of the leading Trotskyites were Jews, something one seeks to keep secret today, as is always done with things that are found to be irksome)."[252] As an attentive observer of the Communist movement in the twentieth century, Gershom Scholem knew all too well that a good number of his brother's former colleagues and political opponents had become influential men in the GDR. They made sure that any memory of this renegade in the early phase of the Communist Party went unmentioned in the publications of the Institute for Marxism-Leninism. If he or any other oppositionist was ever mentioned, it was only as sectarians or unbelievers who had been driven by abnormal ambition.[253] This image of the Left Opposition as "petit bourgeois gone wild" became so entrenched that it even found its way into West German historiography.[254]

Oh the Shark Has Pretty Teeth, Dear

As a former professional revolutionary, Werner Scholem had to find not only a new political home but also a new living. Thus the thirty-one-year-old began to study law at Berlin University in the summer semester of 1927 while he was still serving as a Reichstag deputy, which is how he financed his studies. However, he knew that he would lose this source of income after the next election. Should the Reichstag dissolve before the legislative period ended, which was certainly a possibility, he and his wife would find themselves in deep financial crisis. It was then that his brothers Reinhold and Erich Scholem promised that, should this scenario become reality, they would support him with funds from the family firm that represented his legally stipulated inheritance.[255]

Betty Scholem was concerned about her restless son and doubted that he could endure this new start and stick with his law studies. "With his pessimism, his little faith in himself & his famous name it is *not* beyond question that he will attain his goal. But what else should he do?" At first it looked as if her fears would be confirmed. In early 1928, Deputy Scholem could still be heard speaking frequently against the "Stalin Communists" in the Reichstag. In addition, he wrote regularly for the newspapers of the opposition. This left little time for his university studies until the spring of that year, when a new Reichstag was elected. Toward the end of his term, Werner Scholem became worried that the criminal charges from 1923 would be brought again once he was no longer protected by the immunity granted to Reichstag deputies. A month and a half after the 1928 elections, he found that he could breathe easily again because on 14 July 1928, a national amnesty law was passed under which he was given a clean record "with no previous convictions." Relieved, he now concentrated on his stud-ies, to which he devoted much time and intensive effort, if not always rewarded with great success.[256] The party expulsion had repercussions for the entire family. Edith was forced to leave the youth organization Rote Jungpioniere (Young Red Pioneers), and Emmy had to step down from all her functions, even though she remained a member of the party. She was dismissed from her job at the Soviet Trade Mission, and so in 1927 she took over the accounting of the Gewerka Verlag in Berlin-Wilmersdorf, a publishing house specializing in handbooks and journals on legal and taxa-tion matters.[257]

That same year, the family moved to the Hansaviertel near the Tiergar-ten, Berlin's central park. Gershom Scholem visited them there several times when he was in Berlin in 1927 and 1932. Later he would recall a rear apartment "on the elegant Klopstockstrasse, whose residents were, for the most part, wealthy Jews, including a few who were related to us by mar-riage." By moving to the Hansaviertel, the "Commies" had left the working-class neighborhood behind them and had arrived in a very traditional, middle-class, residential neighborhood, which happened to have been favored by leftist revolutionaries. At the end of the nineteenth century, Rosa Luxemburg had lived on the corner of Klopstock and Cuxhavener streets; in 1912, Lenin had spent some time living illegally at Klopstockstrasse 22; and Ernst Toller, a writer and leading politician of the short-lived Bavarian Soviet Republic, lived around the corner on Altonaer Strasse.[258]

Although the Communist Scholems did not lodge in the *bel étage* but in the less elegant rear courtyard, the daily life they now cultivated was primarily a bourgeois one. They lived in four large rooms with a kitchen, bath, and a servant's chamber. The furnishings were, if in part inherited, representative and elegant. The living room furniture had once belonged to Käthe Schiepan, Betty Scholem's sister, and consisted of everything that belonged to a bourgeois home, including a secretary, a desk, and book-shelves that covered two walls and housed Werner's library, chiefly of politi-cal literature, and his political archive, of which he was very proud. It was here that he spent his days, memorizing legislative texts and legal regu-lations.[259]

The dining room furniture was made of light birch wood and had been given to the family by Betty when she redecorated the dining room of the Neue Grünstrasse dwelling shortly after Arthur Scholem's death. Emmy and Werner themselves had furnished their bedroom with mahogany pieces

FIGURE 25. Werner
Scholem, 1930, at home in
Berlin "cramming" (with
Lenin's portrait in the
background). Private archive
of Renee Goddard.

and the children's room for their two daughters with simple but pretty
white furniture. Rugs, crystal glasses, vases, silver flatware, and a porcelain
piece from Rosenthal that had been a gift from Betty put the finishing
touches to the middle-class ambient. A maid ran the household and
ensured that Werner's shirts were meticulously starched, his suits brushed
and pressed, and his shoes polished. Emmy continued to prefer unpreten-
tious clothing, even though she could now afford a larger wardrobe and
frequently was dressed quite elegantly.[260]

With time it became clear that it would be difficult to maintain their
accustomed lifestyle. Emmy's income was less than it had been before and
not sufficient to support the family even with the added income from the
Scholem company. So it was left to Betty to support the family as much
as she could. Since the death of her husband, Betty had drawn closer to

Werner and his family. She found her daughter-in-law to be a nice and reasonable person, and sometimes pitied her for always having to put up with the political "gibberish" of her husband.[261]

Even though it was probably never openly talked about, Betty was aware that her son and his wife led a rather permissive sex life, and she did comment on it in her letters. The intellectual Communist milieu of the Weimar Republic rejected the bourgeois maxim of monogamy. As early as 1920, Ruth Fischer, like other authors at the time, had published a small pamphlet on the "sexual ethics of Communism" and promoted in it a new ideal of partner-like relationships beyond bourgeois conventions. This sexual freedom was made possible by new forms of contraception and gave rise to the demand for the right to abortion. "Your body belongs to you" was a popular slogan, and with the help of doctors in the leftist milieu women were also able to live what they preached.[262]

In March 1928, Emmy Scholem confided to her mother-in-law that she was now trying out a brand-new form of contraception, after having had several abortions. Rather indiscreetly, Betty wrote to Gershom in Jerusalem that her daughter-in-law had let "a doctor—(Comrade! And therefore the highest authority for her!)" implant "one of those contraception things" in her. Most likely, this "thing" was an intrauterine device. Betty's sister Käthe Schiepan, who was a medical doctor, had emphatically warned Emmy against having this implantation, and, months later, she was horrified by Emmy's condition. By the time Emmy appeared at Käthe's clinic, noted Betty, her daughter-in-law was half dead. Fortunately, Käthe was able to help her. During a long stay at a spa in the summer of 1928, Emmy recovered from the exertions, but she suffered increasingly from the long-term complications of the procedure.[263]

In a dialectical way, Emmy Scholem combined the two images of women, which were propagated by the Weimar KPD and in women's magazines associated with the party. On the one hand was the feminist, independent woman, who controlled her own body and her own life, and on the other hand, the ideal spouse, housewife, and mother, who gave her politically engaged husband free reign, ran the household efficiently, and raised the children according to the political ideology.[264] These two inconsistent ideals haunted the Scholem household as well and were constantly renegotiated, whether Emmy was responsible for supporting the family, or Werner played the part of the supportive husband and offered prospects for a tranquil future beyond working for a living. The new image of the woman was bound up with a new image of the mother, which reached both leftist and bourgeois circles. Less is more, it stated: women should spend dedicated time with their children and be more a good friend than an exemplary authority.[265]

Such a friendship did exist between Emmy and her older daughter, Edith, whereas at first she had little contact with her younger daughter, Renate, who rarely came from Hanover with her grandmother to visit the family in Berlin; her parents were strangers to her, as she later recalled: "I don't know when I first became aware that these funny smelling people were supposed to be my parents. My mother would come and visit, this woman who smelled of soap and perfume and was altogether strange, and it generally seemed embarrassing." Renate did not really know how to respond to this woman who, at bedtime, preferred to sing "The Ballad of Mack the Knife" or "Pirate Jenny" from Brecht's *Threepenny Opera* or the newest cabaret hits, rather than traditional lullabies.[266]

Renate had only been seventeen days old when her grandmother Emma Wiechelt brought her to Hanover. There everyone called her Reni Wiechelt since she grew up under her mother's maiden name. Reni helped her grandmother with the household chores and spent her free time on the streets of the proletarian community of Linden. There the children of the neighborhood played games that were not even interrupted at noon, when the mothers lowered baskets of sandwiches for them from the windows above. The apartment where Reni lived with her grandparents was tiny, her clothes were homemade, and meat rarely appeared on the table. Emmy and Werner probably paid for the upkeep of their daughter, but their support only sufficed for a very modest life. Despite this, Reni enjoyed a happy childhood with her grandmother Emma, Emma's husband August Wiechelt, and her aunt Linchen (Lina), Emmy's half sister. On their plot in the community garden, Reni and her grandfather gardened and puttered about together. He even built her a little summer hut of her own that was called "Renate's cottage."[267]

Shortly before Reni's fifth birthday, Werner and Emmy decided to move their daughter to Berlin, where their new apartment had enough room for her. In Berlin, the child spent a great deal of time alone or with the housemaid, since Emmy was seldom at home. To Renate she seemed more like a nice aunt than a mother. She related that when Emmy did spend time with her, she liked to think of something special for the two of them to do. She would take Renate to eat sausages or to one of the big Berlin department

FIGURE 26. Edith and Emmy Scholem, August 1924. Private archive of Renee Goddard.

stores. On one of these occasions, the little girl had the chance to see a replica of an entire African village, an experience that impressed her greatly. Most likely, the two of them had visited the Oriental Room at the Wertheim department store on Leipzigerstrasse, where an exhibit with living animals was being shown in the fall of 1932 under the title "Jungle Life and Negro Culture."[268]

Since Renate did not have any playmates in Berlin, she asked for a doll as large as herself instead of a friend. Her father bought one for her, and

FIGURE 27. Renate (in front) and Edith Scholem (on the lap of her mother Emmy's half sister Linchen [Lina] Wiechelt), with their grandparents Emma and August Wiechelt, in front of their garden house in Hanover. Private archive of Renee Goddard.

from then on she played under the living-room table with her new friend, while Werner Scholem sat at the table working or studying. In her memoirs, Renee Goddard noted that her father left his radicalism at the door when he came home. Within the family's apartment walls, he conformed to conventional, bourgeois ideas of raising children and was as distant and strict to his children as his father had been to him. When Renate piped up to tell something at the dinner table, she was told that "Kinder bei Tisch, stumm wie ein Fisch" (Children at the table should be as dumb as a fish [the German equivalent of "children are to be seen, not heard"]). As in many bourgeois families, the parents never vacationed with their children: Werner went to the Alps, sometimes accompanied by his wife, and Emmy left for a recuperating stay at a health spa. In the summer, the girls were taken to Zernsdorf in the Spreewald, where Arthur Scholem had purchased a simple vacation house shortly before his death. There Renate played with her cousin Irene, her uncle Erich's daughter, who was nearly the same age. In Zernsdorf the children were cared for by the elegant and always-a-bit-distant grandmother Betty, who called Renate "Goldschnäuzchen" (goldfinch).[269]

In fact, Renate never felt at home in Berlin, and her parents did not seem to know exactly what to do with this free-spirited child who spoke in the broad dialect of the Hanoverian proletariat. "I think I must have been as alien to my parents as they were to me," she noted as an adult. "Like so many revolutionaries, Emmy and Werner Scholem were too busy working to make the world a better place for all children to have much time for their own." Unlike her big sister, Renate was not willing to learn and accept the codes and manners of professional revolutionaries. She talked about everything that popped into her head and was therefore told less and less. In the fall of 1929, she started school, but after a year her parents decided to send her back to Hanover for another year. There she attended elementary school and was not called back to Berlin until the beginning of 1933.[270]

In contrast to the way Renate remembered it, Betty Scholem was critical of the way Werner and Emmy were bringing up their daughters and regarded it as far from bourgeois. She thought they were left alone far too much and at the same time had to suffer ideologically motivated pedagogical measures. In November 1932, she wrote to Jerusalem: "We were at Werner's on Sundays, which proved quite amusing. I thoroughly reject his educational principles for raising children, and his sex education craze is at least as repulsive as the earlier system of keeping everything hush-hush." She was convinced that Emmy and Werner were demanding too much of their children and confusing them politically. On her twelfth birthday, Edith was taken to the theater for the first time in her life, not to see a middle-class comedy, but to see a contemporary revolutionary and tendentious play, *Des Kaisers Kulis* (*The Kaiser's Coolies*) by Theodor Plievier. The play was based on Plievier's very successful novel of the same name, an antiwar drama about the grievances and abuses in the German navy during the final war years. Erwin Piscator directed the play at the Lessing Theater and had the actors, among them Plievier himself, read long passages from the novel, supplemented by a Communist review of the twelve years of the Weimar Republic. The premiere took place in late September 1930, and Edith attended either this performance or one immediately afterward.[271]

During 1928, this small and unconventional family bought their own camera, and the pictures they took document the far from uncomplicated constellations of their family relations and the relationship of a rather uncommon couple in the eleventh year of their marriage.

Werner Scholem started a photo album, which survived the war and was in Renee Goddard's possession. The first pages of the album contain a

FIGURE 28. "Emmy 'from
a sweet angle,' 9 Sept.
1928. Werbellin." Private
archive of Renee Goddard.

series of studio portraits of Emmy, dating back to the years of the First
World War. This carefully arranged collection was followed by photos taken
with their own camera of an older, happily smiling Emmy: Emmy at the
lake, in the woods, bathing, "from a sweet angle" or "in an attractive pose."
These photographs show the romantic and loving side of the couple's relationship. Betty once remarked that when she brought up the subject of
their extramarital affairs, Werner became terribly jealous. The sentimental
romance in the photo album was at odds with the ideal of the extramarital,
comradely sexual relations of Communist revolutionaries.[272]

Conspicuously absent in this album are family photos featuring father,
mother, and daughters together, although close friends, like Karl Korsch,
appear often in photos taken on hikes or excursions. The final pages of the

album are filled with many small-format photographs showing Werner and his fellow mountaineers on climbing excursions in the northern and southern Tyrolean Alps.

Early in 1932, Werner had a studio portrait made of himself, the first since he had been photographed wearing the uniform of the Imperial Army in 1915. A "photo comrade" had done him the favor, noted an amused Betty Scholem when she sent the photograph to his brother in Jerusalem, at Werner's request. The brothers had recently resumed sporadic contact. Betty had given Gershom Scholem an extensive account of the abrupt end of his brother's career, and Werner had been having the *Rote Fahne* sent to him in Palestine since 1926. In the summer of 1928, Gershom asked his mother, somewhat bewildered, why Werner was now being vilified in his own paper? Betty answered that it was linked to the party's shift to the left. "Yes, Werner just has a talent for getting caught in the middle," she summarized. "The party leadership is now pursuing the politics for which he was expelled back then." And, indeed, several of the demands called for in the past had now been adopted by both the German party leadership and the Comintern, though the KPD had by now become thoroughly Stalinized.[273]

Contact between the Scholem brothers remained sporadic and limited to a few succinct lines. Yet in the spring of 1931, Werner wrote his brother a long letter, thanking him for the congratulations Gershom had expressed on Werner's latest success: in early March, Werner had not only passed the first law exam for the Kammergericht, the Prussian high court, but had scored very well on it. As Werner wrote, he had found the preparation for the exam very difficult because he did not feel that he had a talent for civil law. He could pursue "the matter only as a way to earn a living, not as a passion." Following this, he planned to work three years as a law clerk, when he could be qualified as an assessor (an intermediate stage in the German legal profession), and finally as a full-fledged lawyer. "Then I will take up politics again, of course, because I have in no way gone over to the bourgeoisie," he emphasized to his brother. He was convinced that a new workers' movement would emerge in Germany within the next three to four years. With regard to his personal life, he said there was nothing new to report. "Edith is already a real *Backfisch*, unfortunately without any interest in the sciences, although she is not stupid. The little one, Renate, is a *Goite ohne Beimischung*. Don't yet know what will turn out there," he wrote succinctly about his children. "This, a portrait of a family of today. I feel

FIGURE 29. Werner Scholem, 1932, taken in the studio of Franz Pfemfert, Berlin-Wilmersdorf, with a dedication "to my brother Gerhard, W. Scholem, January 1932." Israeli National Library, Archive Gerhard Scholem.

alive in the summer when I go climbing. I hope someday, before I become an old man, I will take a plunge. I would also advise you to become a climber (big brother!) because there are also rock walls where you are. Then you could die in beauty before you become fat."[274]

Emmy was still stricken with health problems, but at least her position at the Gewerka Verlag had improved. The company had changed owners and was now equally divided between a Jewish and a non-Jewish owner. Emmy headed the commercial business of the publishing house, and since she had bought 20 percent of the company's shares from the new owners, her monthly income had increased considerably.[275] While she prospered, the year was turning out to be less profitable for the printing business of A. Scholem. Betty had traveled to Palestine in the summer, during which the first rumors about business difficulties reached her from Berlin. By the time she returned, it was clear that Erich and Reinhold Scholem would have to declare bankruptcy. Their business debacle had been caused by the German banking crisis, which in turn had been sparked by the failure of the Danat Bank in July 1931. Betty had to give up her apartment and move in with her son Erich, which she did not find difficult to do since she had once lived in that same building. However, Werner was upset by the move, because he had been used to visiting his mother's apartment once every week to eat and chat.[276]

The elections in April 1932 resulted in an enormous win for the National Socialists not only in the Prussian Landtag but throughout the entire country. Tension heightened between National Socialists and Communists, erupting in violence several times. The fear of civil war lingered in the air. That fall, Gershom Scholem visited Berlin and saw his brother for the first time in five years. Gershom reported:

> The major economic crisis that prevailed since 1929 led him to believe again in a leftist revolution in Germany, and he was anticipating it when I visited him in Berlin in October 1932. Either the revolution will come, he said to me, or barbarity will rule. Although he had a clear eye for the general situation, he remained blind to his own personal situation should the latter scenario occur. I couldn't believe my ears when he told me with a naïveté incomprehensible to me: "When it comes down to it, they won't do anything to me because I am a war veteran."

Did Werner Scholem still believe in a Communist revolution in the fall of 1932? In early November, around the time of the second Reichstag elections that year, a revolutionary atmosphere did indeed hang over Berlin. The employees of the Berlin public transportation company were on strike, Communists and National Socialists were fighting one another in the streets, and in the election the NSDAP suffered great losses across the entire country.[277]

At some point during the fall of 1932, Werner Scholem planned a trip to Turkey. Since his expulsion from the Soviet Union in 1929, Leon Trotsky had been living on Prinkipo, an island in the Sea of Marmara near Istanbul. Among the numerous visitors whom he welcomed there had been only a few German sympathizers, although Trotsky regarded them as the "only organized oppositionist power" outside of Russia. Now Werner Scholem announced his wish to visit, but Trotsky asked Léon Sedov to prevent him from coming. Trotsky was of the opinion that Werner Scholem, as the leader of the Left Opposition in Germany, "should not take the political risk of being in Turkey at precisely the time when the fate of the proletariat

and Communism might be decided."[278] So, he did not travel to the Mediterranean. Yet from a letter to his brother, it can be surmised that he saw little
reason for hope in the recent developments. The electoral losses of the
National Socialists did not appear to him to be reason to let down one's
guard. "The Night of the Long Knives has been postponed for a while, but
next year something will happen here. The Nazis will indeed come to
power. I hope I am off climbing when it happens." Prophetically with
respect to the situation of German Jews and naively with respect to his own
situation, he added: "You all will again get many visitors from Berlin, hee-
hee. You are now a hope and a contact. Not all too much can happen to
me because for the last twenty years I have been accustomed to abstaining
from the goods of the earth." Along with his own greetings he added those
of Emmy and—with a skewed glance—the "half-blood" Edith.[279]

Christmas 1932 was celebrated in the Scholem household on Klopstockstrasse with a big party and many friends, as it was every year. Late that
evening, Emmy, Werner, and Edith made their way to Alexandrinenstrasse
to celebrate further with the rest of the Scholem family. Close and distant
relatives arrived, laden with washing baskets full of gifts. On the following
day, Edith took a long walk with her parents around the lake Grunewaldsee,
and they talked about all sorts of things. On 29 December, Werner celebrated his thirty-seventh birthday at home with many friends, including
Karl Korsch and Arthur Rosenberg. The next day, Edith was allowed to
accompany her parents to a cabaret, where Ernst Busch was performing. As
1932 yielded to 1933, the mood on the streets of Berlin was quite exuberant;
people danced, drank, and, as the *Vossische Zeitung* reported, "regained
hope."[280]

3

EXILE IN GERMANY

[Job's] lament is infinite in all dimensions, it is of
a greater infinity than this life itself, for it even
reaches to realms beyond the worldly boundaries
of his life, the anarchy of which and its threatening
encroachment into his world terrify him.

—Gerhard Scholem, *Tagebücher*, Summer/Fall 1918

Ein neuer Frühling wird in die Heimat kommen
alles wird so wunderbar
Und man wird wieder das Lied der Arbeit singen
g'rade so, wie's einmal war

(A new spring will come to the homeland
everything will be so wonderful
and people will sing the song of labor again
exactly the way it once was)

—Comedian Harmonists, "A New Spring
Will Come Home," 1933

Unlawful Times

On 12 February 1933, less than two weeks after Hitler had been appointed chancellor, the family gathered at Werner and Emmy's home on Klopstockstrasse in Berlin's Hansaviertel to eat stuffed pigeon, which—according to Betty Scholem—was "delicate." She was visiting her son's family on this Sunday and was in such a good mood that even Werner's unremitting pessimism couldn't deflate her spirits, even though his "constant doomsday prophesies" were particularly bad that day. Current political developments were causing him great concern, and he drew "ruinous conclusions" about his future, especially since he had not been a member of the KPD since 1926, and his Reichstag mandate for the Left Communists had expired in May 1928.[1]

Thirteen days later, on the evening of 27 February, the Reichstag was set on fire, and at five o'clock the next morning, the doorbell rang in the Klopstockstrasse apartment. Since no one opened the door, the police constable and two auxiliary police officers broke into the apartment. For more than an hour, they searched the premises—even the children's room—without finding any incriminating evidence. Nevertheless, since the officers had a warrant for Werner Scholem's arrest, they took him back to the police station. His mother was terribly upset by the news, especially since, as it appeared to her, he was completely innocent this time. Fatalistically she noted: "his past haunts him & he is a marked man." Emmy, on the other hand, had been running around since the early morning, trying to find a lawyer for him. This turned out to be a nearly futile endeavor, because she could turn neither to Jewish nor to Communist lawyers if she wanted be of any use to Werner.[2]

Over the course of 28 February 1933, the Reich cabinet issued the "Notverordnung zum Schutz von Volk und Staat" (Emergency Decree for the Protection of the People and State), which suspended all civil rights and made it possible to arrest citizens for no stated reason.[3] Even if the National Socialists were not directly responsible for the Reichstag fire—a question that remains open—they were able to exploit the episode in order "to smash the political left, particularly the KPD."[4] As the *Vossische Zeitung* announced in its evening edition, the cabinet planned to propose to the Reich president another "Notverordnung zum Schutze des deutschen

Volkes vor der kommunistischen Gefahr" (Emergency Decree to Protect
the German People Against the Communist Danger), since it was said to
be "proven beyond a doubt that Communist leaders are directly involved
in the arson attack on the Reichstag and, moreover, Communists have prepared acts of terror, which make it necessary to immediately take action
against them with the strongest means."[5] This newspaper, which had not
yet been subjected to *Gleichschaltung*—literally "synchronization," but,
under the Nazis, it meant a system of totalitarian control and coordination
over all aspects of society—reported that 130 nightly arrests had been carried out on the orders of Hermann Göring, the Reich commissar at the
Prussian Ministry of the Interior. A number of Communist Reichstag deputies and oppositional lawyers were listed by name, including Hans Litten.
Others were the Berlin sex educator Max Hodann and the writers Egon
Erwin Kisch, Erich Mühsam, and Carl von Ossietzky. Werner Scholem was
named among the arrested KPD faction leaders, since he was still thought
of as a leading Communist figure, despite his years of absence from the
political stage.[6] His arrest did not go unnoticed outside Germany. In Palestine the daily newspaper *Davar* ran a headline publicizing his arrest, and
Leon Trotsky was informed by his son in a letter about the fate of the
German oppositionist leader.[7]

    In an atmosphere of tense uncertainty, during the days leading up to
the Reichstag election, more and more house searches were conducted. All
the while, Emmy Scholem had received no word at all about her husband's
whereabouts. Fearful, she spent the entire week with friends. However, on
the day of the election, 5 March, to everyone's great surprise, her husband
was released, thanks to the lawyer and Socialist Reichstag deputy Kurt
Rosenfeld. Rosenfeld had been the Prussian minister of justice briefly in
1918 and had been regarded as one of Berlin's prominent citizens since
then. For his concerned relatives, Werner played down the five days he
had spent in the Moabit prison as amounting to no more than a pathetic
incident—after all, he had experienced worse, he maintained.[8]

    In many middle-class Jewish families, the mass firings and suspensions
of officials, primarily on the left, sparked fears of pogroms, even if they
themselves were not immediately affected. In her regular reports to her son
in Jerusalem, Betty put the terrible news that appeared daily into perspective. For example, at the end of March she noted that everything was calm
in Berlin and that 99 percent of the "Tartar news" was no more than outright lies. The recipient of her letter had little tolerance for this attitude; on

the contrary, Gershom Scholem argued that it was urgently necessary for even the "most politically uninvolved Jewish families to leave Germany with kit and caboodle and abandon everything in order to convince the world outside Germany that at least the moral pressure under which Jews in Germany were suffering has now become unbearable."[9]

Despite his efforts, Gershom was not able to convince his own relatives in Berlin to leave. Following his release from prison, Werner returned to his position as a clerk in a Berlin law firm. The very first anti-Jewish decree was the "Gesetz über die Zulassung zur Rechtsanwaltschaft" (Law on Admittance to the Legal Profession), issued 7 April; it revoked as invalid the admission of all Jewish lawyers to the legal profession. However, this did not yet directly affect Werner because an exception was made for veterans who had fought on the front lines during the First World War.[10] In mid-April, he traveled to Prague to visit Ruth Fischer and Arkadi Maslow, who had avoided arrest on 27 February by going underground until they were able to cross the border into Czechoslovakia on their motorcycle with sidecar on 9 March. Werner had helped them organize their escape and now he was getting together with them before they left for Paris, via Austria and Switzerland. While in Prague, Werner also wanted to look into employment possibilities and prepare his own escape.[11] Why did he then return to Berlin, feeling confident that he was safe when other oppositionists had long since fled and hysteria and panic had broken out even among Jews who were not politically active? He probably felt that his status as a former frontline soldier protected him and that his retreat from politics insulated him. Furthermore, as will be shown, he had a steadfast faith in the German legal system as it had existed until then, a faith that his own history of former convictions and prison terms during his youth had nurtured and that he himself now embodied as a member of the legal profession. Above all else, of course, what caused him to return was his determination not to leave his wife and daughters alone in Germany.

Meanwhile, Betty Scholem continued to write regularly to Palestine on current events in Germany and her family. Since the emergency decree had suspended the privacy of correspondence, she had to assume that her letters, especially those headed abroad, might be read by censors. In the future, she would not always find it easy to describe events with sufficient caution. Her self-censored letters constitute the most important testimony on Werner Scholem's persecution, which was just about to start.

On 24 April 1933, she wrote the following lines to Gershom, reflecting her great bewilderment and uncertainty: "Something terrible has happened again. On Sunday night, the 23rd, W. again and, to our horror, also Emmy were arrested. Why, for what reason, no idea. He had begun to make promising plans for a future & when I was at his place on Saturday evening, he was, contrary to his usual pessimistic attitude, very hopeful." Werner had planned, she wrote, to complete his law studies by getting his doctorate, in order to have better chances at earning a living abroad. To this end he had contacted the physician Karl Meyer, a longtime friend of the Scholem family who lived in Switzerland. Werner planned to travel to Zurich on Sunday with an allegedly excellent recommendation from his Berlin professor in his pocket. There he intended to stay with Betty's cousin Arthur Hirsch, a professor for mathematics at the Swiss Federal Institute of Technology in Zurich, whom Gerhard had also visited once during his years in Bern. But five hours before his planned departure, Werner was arrested.[12]

At 5:30 Sunday morning, the doorbell rang at the Klopstockstrasse apartment, and at the door stood—not the Sturmabteilung (SA, the paramilitary units of the Nazi Party), as was to be expected—but the police. Not until months later, when a lawyer was finally allowed to see the prosecution's files on the case, did Werner's mother and brothers discover what had happened next in the apartment. This lawyer revealed details of the arrest to Erich Scholem in strictest confidence. Since Betty was spending the summer and fall of 1933 first in France and then in South Tyrol, where she did not have to fear censorship, she then related the events of that night to her son in Jerusalem.

It quickly became clear that morning that the police officers had come with an arrest warrant for Emmy, not Werner, since she had been denounced by a coworker at the publishing house where she was employed. Three days earlier, Werner had received a visa to travel abroad, without which he could not go to Zurich. Until then he had been very nervous and had said that he would flee immediately if his request for a visa was turned down. Still, he did not leave Germany the day he got his visa, a Thursday, but waited two more days until his wife returned home from a business trip. On the following morning, the Sunday in question, he had planned to take an early morning train to Zurich. "Now we hear," wrote Betty, "that the arrest warrant back then was only issued against Emmy; they simply decided in passing to take Werner, too, because he happened to be there, the stupid fool! 'Well, now,' said the policeman, 'we were thinking that you

were in Zurich; we gave you the visa.' Then he called the police station &
they said he should only bring Werner if he is there!! Isn't that just
ghastly?!"[13]

Years later, Werner's daughters Edith and Renate, who witnessed the
early morning arrest, described how it came about that Werner was arrested
"in passing": While the maid went to answer the door, Emmy explained to
her oldest daughter, Edith, that Werner was in the bedroom, the police did
not know that, and that was how it was to stay. She instructed the fourteen-
year-old to accompany her father in the early morning hours to the
train—it was imperative that Werner get on the train to Zurich. When the
police officers entered the room, Emmy learned the reason for the visit: she
was to be picked up for questioning about her marriage to the Jew Scholem
and thus possible abnormal sexual practices linked with it. This caused the
hotheaded husband to bolt from his hiding place in the bedroom in order
to defend his wife's honor. The surprised officers—and here the daughters'
story matches the version Betty learned from the indictment—did not
know what to do with him and contacted their police station by telephone.
Subsequently they took the couple with them to the police station at Alexanderplatz, now the headquarters of the Gestapo. Apparently Werner Scholem had considered fleeing for a moment, but he had decided against it on
the advice of his wife.[14]

As soon as she learned of the calamity that morning, Betty went to the
apartment to pick up the two girls, but Edith had gone to stay with her
grandmother in Hanover immediately after the arrests and remained there
for five days. When she returned to Berlin, Edith went directly to Emmy's
office in order to find out where her parents had been taken. At the police
headquarters she was given permission to speak with her mother, who told
her that there were no charges against either of them and that it could only
be a denunciation. The officers gave the girl hope that at least her mother
would soon be released. Then Edith picked her sister up from Betty and
brought her back to their apartment on Klopstockstrasse, where they ran
into their relative and neighbor Traude Zucker. The Zuckers had often
taken care of the children when they were at home alone. However, since
Werner and Emmy's arrest, they had broken off contact. When Traude
Zucker now met the girls on the street, she neither greeted them nor
inquired about their parents. Instead, she asked them in a hurried whisper
why they had not left days ago to stay with Emmy's relatives in Hanover.
Later, when relating this extremely disturbing incident, Betty remarked: "As

things now stand, even just the suspicion that you know a former Communist can be ruinous for the person involved."[15]

The girls started to go to school again and lived alone in their family's
large apartment until another solution was found. The maid ran the household for them and prepared meals and baked goods for Emmy and Werner,
which Edith brought to her parents in prison. On the weekend, their grandmother took the two of them to the small Scholem family vacation home
in Zernsdorf and enjoyed time with her granddaughters, whom she
described as pleasant and well-behaved. Not only did Betty look out for
Edith and Renate, she also went to the authorities every day requesting
information about Emmy and Werner. As Gershom later told Walter Benjamin, Betty wrote "most uninhibitedly and in detail" to her son in Jerusalem
"about all these conditions and her experiences with the new German
'mentality.'" At police headquarters on Alexanderplatz, she was treated surprisingly well. Although she received no permission to speak with either
Werner or Emmy, she was allowed to write them and send them food.
In his first letter from prison, Werner reported that he had not yet been
interrogated and therefore could not hire a lawyer. His request to speak
with Emmy about the children and other family matters had also been
denied. He did not write a word about the prison conditions at "Alex,"
which were imaginably bad in the spring of 1933, even if one was lucky
enough to be put in a single cell and not in the overcrowded mass cells. All
prisoners suffered from the terrible sanitary conditions, infestation of
insects, and poor provisions.[16]

News reached the family on 25 May that Werner had been transferred
to Spandau Prison. Shortly thereafter, Betty was permitted to speak with
her daughter-in-law for the first time, and she learned that Emmy had been
told during her interrogation that she had indeed been denounced by a
coworker. As Communists, she and her husband were accused of high treason. After this short visit, in which the two women had been permitted to
talk for just ten minutes, Betty spoke with the state prosecutor in charge.
He explained that Emmy and Werner had been imprisoned for "subversion" and added, much to Betty's ire, that "'even back at the Dorotheen-
städt. Realgymnasium [the secondary school that Werner had attended]
your son wrote offensive letters to my director!'(*My* director, he said. He is
a younger man, possibly a classmate of Werner!) You would think we lived
in a village and not in a city of four million! 'And is that still being pinned
on him *now*?!,' I couldn't refrain myself from asking."[17]

The situation in which Emmy and Werner found themselves was not unique. By the end of April, it is highly probable more than fifty thousand opponents of the regime had disappeared in German prisons and temporary concentration camps.[18] However, frequently groups of those arrested were suddenly and unexpectedly released. On 4 July 1933, the Scholem family received news that Werner would be released that very day from police headquarters at Alexanderplatz. Yet, he was not among those freed, and no explanation for his absence was given. At the same time, all mail sent to him at Spandau Prison was returned bearing the stamp "released." His mother suffered severely from this bluff and stated that she now only had the choice of being either "apathetic or enraged." Betty had long lost her early illusions about the regime and its treatment of the Jewish population. Yet she also found herself grumbling about the imprudence of her son, which had so impacted her own life: "Isn't it terrible how Werner has ruined his life with these damned politics! How right our father was when he said he [Werner] should *first* complete his studies & ensure a vocation, *then* he could toss as many bombs as he liked." It was not only her concern about the two prisoners that weighed on Betty, it had also become her responsibility to handle his family affairs and dismantle the Klopstockstrasse apartment. To her relief, her two granddaughters had found places to live. Renate returned to Hanover and Edith went to live with her uncle Reinhold Scholem and his wife Käthe. On the weekends, Betty retreated to Zernsdorf to recuperate in the "green tranquillity" there, where everything was simple with few amenities, where there was no running water or heat—but also no telephone to bring ever more terrible tidings. For financial reasons, the family had to sell half of this refuge, but the other half remained in their possession and was often frequented until 1938.[19]

Meanwhile Emmy and Werner had been transferred from protective custody and placed in pretrial detention—he in Moabit and she in the women's prison on Barnimstrasse. Now they could begin to look for a lawyer, but finding one proved to be very difficult. Evening after evening, Werner's brother Erich met lawyers, but they only turned him down. The matter was just too dangerous for all of them, and even those who had already agreed to work on similar cases refused to touch this one. Every once in a while, a lawyer would accept the assignment but then back down before a meeting with the accused could even be arranged. Even Werner's fellow mountain climber Hans Kaufmann, chairman of the the Jewish alpine club Deutscher Alpenverein Berlin, to which Werner belonged, refused to help and maintained that no lawyer would take on such a case in times like these. Werner raged over the cowardice of his friends and party comrades, all of whom let him down. However, several of them were themselves behind bars and others had fled. As long as Werner had no lawyer, he could not view the prosecution's case files and learn why he had been imprisoned. Erich tried desperately to make his brother understand how drastically the legal situation in Germany had changed over the course of the previous two months.[20]

Before he was arrested, Werner Scholem had only experienced the beginnings of what rapidly became a new legal system. The Nazi regime passed law after law, making the legal restrictions against Jews ever more numerous and harsher. At the same time, political opponents were completely stripped of their rights. By now everyone who was directly affected or was willing to listen knew that Germany was no longer a constitutional state based on the rule of law. What passed for justice was the worst form of injustice. "We live in a thoroughly unlawful time; there are laws enough, but no justice," complained Betty in a letter to Gershom. In prison, Emmy and Werner could not comprehend how dramatically the situation had worsened in just a few weeks. The propaganda fliers that they were allowed to read in their cells did nothing to change this. "Poor Emmy and W. himself are of the erroneous opinion that we live under lawful conditions," ascertained Betty.[21]

In early July 1933, a lawyer finally agreed to speak with the accused, although he did not promise to take the case. Since he was permitted to see the indictment, the thoroughly desperate couple finally learned what they were accused of. In Betty's letter to Jerusalem—written and posted during a summer trip to France—she says that Werner and Emmy had been arrested, along with about twenty others, for belonging to a "secret organization that aimed about three years ago to embed Communists into the German army and from there to bring about a coup. It was Emmy who had participated in this group—either with or without Werner's knowledge, they didn't know—in any case she had not been arrested because of his incriminatory past, instead it is he who was arrested because of hers." Indignant, she added that her daughter-in-law had remained a member of the party after it had expelled Werner. Even if they had made this decision together to have Emmy retain her party membership, why hadn't she immediately left Germany in February? "*If* Emmy had a guilty conscience, then in our opinion they should not have stayed here after Hitler's seizure of power! They were not at all ignorant of the seriousness of the situation and must have thought nothing could happen to them because she was no longer really politically active." Although nothing had yet been proven, continued Betty, such an accusation in itself was dangerous because "the hatred with which the government exterminates—one can really put it that way—every Communist is shocking." The entire Scholem family agreed that the two of them had been obtuse, incautious, and unfathomably reckless. The immediate relatives, especially Werner's brothers, felt that his imprisonment endangered and threatened them and their families. Moreover, they feared that Emmy had been involved in some sort of illegal currency dealings, which would have explained her frequent business trips abroad. If this suspicion were to be explored in the indictment, Werner's brothers feared the consequences for the entire family.[22]

Despite her anger and incomprehension, Betty Scholem was indefatigable in looking after the interests and concerns of her son and daughter-in-law. She brought packages of food to Moabit and looked for people to buy the contents of the eighteen boxes of books that she had had transported from the Klopstockstrasse apartment. As she noted, it was "nothing but junk"—political works and worthless editions by poets whose books had been burned by the Nazis and which could no longer be sold under the current conditions. Nothing but pulp material, claimed a consulted bookseller derogatorily. Although Betty was already overcommitted, she appointed herself as the archivist and conservator of Emmy's and Werner's violently interrupted lives. For this purpose, she collected the numerous letters that had been exchanged since April between the various prisons, her apartment on Alexandrinenstrasse, and Emmy's family in Hanover. After the couple was prohibited from corresponding with one another, Betty was forced to play the go-between and wrote more letters than ever. In early July 1933, after her first conversations with Werner and Emmy, she expressed her relief over their agreement on exchanging a weekly letter, since "the assigned censor expressly requested us to limit our correspondence; no inmate would have such an amount of mail. He said he had just needed $2^1/2$ hours to read the Scholem corr[espondence] & that didn't work. I do understand this, some days I have received three letters & Werner's scrawl 6 & 8 pages. In the end, one is just rehashing the same things."[23]

Still, the censor missed nothing, as Betty discovered one day when police detectives stood at her door and demanded Werner Scholem's "suitcase full of notes and writings." Not long before, he had asked his mother in a letter—an exceptionally imprudent thing to do—to take this suitcase out of the Klopstockstrasse apartment in order to avoid its seizure by the Gestapo. The suitcase no longer contained any incriminating documents since these had been removed in time, but it did hold Werner's past and future. In it were the journals he had written in 1916 while serving on the front. He had always guarded these zealously, because the experiences he described in them had formed the basis for his political views and his aversion to nationalism, which he considered to be the cause of the horrors of the war. In the hands of the Gestapo, these pacifist writings, which did not omit a single German crime he had witnessed on the front, could become a dangerous weapon against him. Did they play a role in his further persecution, and if so, to what degree? This is not known. In addition to the journals, the suitcase contained the passports that would have enabled the couple to flee to Switzerland and, to the total astonishment of his mother, Werner's completed dissertation. "The boy really has such incredibly bad luck," wrote Betty after having made this discovery, because Werner had always made a future in exile contingent on first completing his dissertation, which he had been working on until the spring of 1933.[24]

Werner also began to wonder why he had such bad luck.[25] Misfortune and bad luck are vague terms for what was actually a calamitous combination of interrelated factors. In Werner's case these would be political miscalculation resulting from a diehard idealism—belief that revolution was possible; fatal naïveté about the new political order and underestimating his own vulnerability as a prominent Jew in Germany; and, finally, sentimentality and loyalty to his wife uncommon for a professional revolutionary. While scrutinizing his decisions and asking himself why he was plagued by so much misfortune, Werner Scholem produced an important document, crucial to understanding his biography. On 5 October 1933, he sent the only letter he ever wrote from prison to his brother in Jerusalem. Betty had told him that Gershom, who had held a position as a lecturer at Hebrew University up to that point, had been offered a professorship in Jewish mysticism there. He wrote:

> Dear Gerhard! I learned from Mother that you have become a professor and therefore wish to send my congratulations and greetings to you. You have accomplished something because you abandoned the idea of wanting to become something or someone in Germany. If you had become a professor here, you could now begin to wander

the world like many of my acquaintances and my law instructors. I do hope for you that all of you can continue to live there in peace. As long as the Arabs are not allowed to murder you—and for the time being such a change does not appear likely, even if it can certainly be expected someday—you will do well, which pleases me.

In just a few words, Werner settled the score with both of their political utopias, and thereby also with the idealistic hopes they had shared in their youth. His attempt at a political career in Germany—and thus the attempt to realize his vision of another Germany—had failed miserably. He admitted that both Gerhard's personal and political utopias had proven far more successful, but he could not help but point out the expiration date of this good fortune: he was certain that it would not be long before the conflict between the Arab nationalist movement and Zionism, which had become openly evident since 1929, would fully escalate. Therefore, Palestine was neither a safe haven nor a realistic alternative for him: "Right now much is going on where you are. Whether those people who now discover their love of Palestine are exactly the cream of the crop, I venture to doubt. One has to wonder anyway at the emotional bearing of German Jews in this situation. The earlier strength of character, so often praised in similar situations in the Middle Ages, appears to have suffered considerably with faith." Despite his rejection of religion, it was obvious to the revolutionary, who had always been driven by a messianic-like conviction, that strength of character and faith went together. His archenemy was the same one that had fueled the fervor for the brothers' radical utopias twenty years earlier and one that Gershom Scholem still shared with his brother: the assimilated, accommodating, far too bourgeois and far too conformed German Jew.[26]

After the experiences of the preceding months, Werner admitted to his brother that he had reached the point where he could assess his own situation more realistically than he had been able to even in April 1933:

I am doubly affected, as a Jew and as a former politician. The six years of law school and law clerking were completely in vain. I thus frittered away the decisive years of my life, without even managing to be granted amnesty for my former political activity. You will remember our conversation during your last visit a year ago in

which I—decried by all as a "pessimist"!—predicted this development. Except that it turns out I was not a pessimist but a jolly rose-
red optimist because I did not believe that they would also make
mincemeat out of worn-out hackneys. After having left the KPD
already back in 1926, I could not have assumed that they could still
stick me and Emmy with a trial for high treason. *Nemini parcetur!*[27]

A witness—someone whom he did not know—had leveled an accusation
against him, and there was little hope that he or his wife would be released
soon. He did not know what Emmy was accused of, and he worried a great
deal about her. Imprisonment was hard on her, he wrote, and she was not
in good health, a consequence—for which he blamed himself—of her years
of employment. What would become of her and the girls? What of himself,
should he be released? Werner did not sign this last letter to his brother
with his name, as he commonly did, but instead with the words "Your
brother—Job." Was he aware that Gerhard had studied the figure of Job
years before in the final months of the First World War? Possibly. Back then
Gerhard had described Job in a way that now appeared to match Werner's
situation—caught in a Kafkaesque struggle: "The setting of the Book of Job
is comparable to a court, in which a constantly repeated charge is heard
before an infinitely growing number of witnesses, without the judge ever
appearing."[28]
     As one of the first victims of the National Socialist persecution of Jews,
Werner could not imagine what was going to happen; he had been forced
into the role of the accused, and the charges leveled against him were his
Jewish origins and his political convictions. By referring to Job, he anticipated an intellectual debate that began immediately after World War II, in
which Job came to represent the persecuted and annihilated Jewish people.
After 1945, Werner's Communist Jewish Job from the autumn of 1933 was
transformed into a symbol of the catastrophe of the Holocaust in the writings of Margarete Susman, Karl Wolfskehl, and Nelly Sachs.[29]
     However, was it actually his intention to compare himself to the biblical
Job? Job had been a fortunate man until God, in whom he believed, made
a kind of bet with Satan and subjected Job to trials, which exceeded any
conception of human suffering. Until the end, Job asserted his innocence
and nevertheless was abandoned by everyone, marked, and ostracized. Werner Scholem, too, had had to live with disillusion in the previous months,
feeling that he had been abandoned by his friends, with no legal support,

and, although he constantly proved his innocence, he remained in prison indefinitely. Like other Jewish Communists and Socialists, he had also believed it was possible to create a situation beyond the "Jewish question." However, this endeavor not only proved to be impossible to accomplish, but it also turned against him in barbaric fashion. The comparison to Job is also closely related to the question of how far Werner Scholem's Communist worldview can be seen as parallel to a traditional Jewish outlook, marked by biblical structures: a world in which good and evil govern at the same time, and in which it is occasionally difficult to separate the two— although the basic idealistic goal assigned to it is to identify the good and work for it.

This movement toward the most tragic figure in the Hebrew Bible, this turn toward Job, likewise appears as an allegory of the existence of a large number of non-Jewish revolutionary Jews: they gave themselves over to belief in their utopia beyond Judaism and there, contrary to their hopes, they fell into the force field of an ideology that was built on the same anti-Semitic structures as the reality they wished to leave behind. Thus they found themselves once again between two worlds, confronted with the rebuke, that they were to blame for their own fate, without having any actual guilt to assume. Their stubborn clinging to a utopia, coupled with an equally stubborn ignorance of political and social reality, enabled them to live in a kind of hubris: the belief that everything was possible and they themselves were untouchable.

Alfred Döblin also used the figure of Job in his Berlin novel, which describes the last years of the Weimar Republic. He does not explain Job's disaster in that he has lost everything, but rather in that he cannot give up his ideal, his opposition. Thus he has Job's inner voice say: "That's it, Job, that's what you suffer from most. You do not like to be weak, you would like to be able to resist, or rather be full of holes, your brain gone, your thoughts gone, and then become like a beast of the field. Make a wish." As Döblin depicts him, Job is not persecuted by fate, but rather a stiff-necked oppositionist, who found his reason for being in resistance.[30]

Through his persecution, Werner Scholem saw himself confronted by doubts as to whether he might have lost everything in the combat zone of his idealism: his life, his family, and his future. In the person of Job he debated with himself about his political beliefs, his bad luck, his guilt in his innocence, and despite it all, he could not abandon his utopian hopes, his Job-like opposition. Day after day he endured in the poor and narrow dwelling of his solitary cell: always well dressed in his blue suit, the suit of whose trousers he had to mend after a while because of so much sitting, in expectation that this day would put an end to his senseless imprisonment, and that he could leave prison behind on the way to a new life.[31] As in the past, his everyday life was marked by a utopian yearning—but no longer centered on world revolution, nor on the dream of a revolutionary career. Instead his yearning was now focused on a family, a wife, two daughters, and the dream of a comfortable life in exile.

Wayward Paths to Exile

Decades later, Renee Goddard née Scholem described the relationship between her mother and her sister by noting that Emmy could count on the discretion, silence, and loyalty of her older daughter. Indeed, it took only quickly whispered instructions early in the morning of 23 April 1933, just moments before she and Werner were taken away by police, for Edith to know what she had to do. By the time Betty Scholem had arrived at the apartment a few hours later, Edith had already packed a small suitcase and disappeared—to Hanover and Emmy's family, as Betty was told. However, Betty was not someone Edith trusted with her confidence. Betty's attitude toward both Communism and the family politics of her son and his wife was too critical. She did not make it a secret that she disapproved of the way they raised their daughters and that, in her opinion, the girls had to spend far too much time alone. Toward the end of her life, in the only interview she ever gave, Edith said that she had never really trusted her father's family; furthermore, she could never truly trust anyone except her parents.[32]

So that morning the fourteen-year-old disappeared without telling anyone, including her sister, where she was actually going, which was Switzerland. There she met a bank official who gave Edith her parents' savings. It can be assumed that Emmy, ever cautious, had long ago provided the necessary authorization and power of attorney for her underage daughter. With this money, apparently a substantial sum, she returned to Berlin and handed it over to family friends, as her mother had instructed her to do. Without any hesitation, she then proceeded to the police headquarters at Alexanderplatz and demanded to see her mother because she and her little sister were now left on their own. As she later explained, she knew she had to make as much fuss about her parents as possible in order to keep them from simply being killed. The prison officials showed kindness toward her—especially since she looked younger than she was—and led her to her mother. Emmy used the opportunity to give Edith further instructions: to find friends who had gone underground and to quickly secure the services of a lawyer. The fact that these tasks far exceeded the level of responsibility appropriate for a person of Edith's age—though she had been raised since early childhood to follow the rules of conspiracy—did not seem to bother Emmy.[33]

Emmy's decisiveness regarding the duties and opportunities of her older daughter is also shown in her reaction to the idea of enabling Edith to flee Germany. In June 1933, Gershom Scholem suggested to his mother to bring his niece to Palestine to the youth village Ben Shemen.[34] There was a boarding school at this agricultural cooperative near Lod in which young immigrants were prepared for a life in the Land of Israel; most of them were now coming from Germany. "She is in actuality a Jewess, isn't she?" asked the uncle, though he knew that Edith and Renate, as the children of a non-Jewish mother, were actually not Jews according to Jewish religious law.

Yet hadn't the year 1933 challenged this definition and turned many Germans into Jews who were not considered as such according to Jewish religious law? Although "half-Jews" in Germany were not yet persecuted, they were still considered half-*Jews*. Edith fell into this new category—so why not send her to Palestine? Betty's first reaction was to reject the idea: at the moment such a trip was out of the question because, for one, they lacked the money necessary for such travel. More important, they could not readily get the parents' consent under the current circumstances. Betty was still waiting to be granted permission to talk with Werner or Emmy. It wasn't until later that summer that she had the chance to tell her daughter-in-law about the idea during the short meetings at the prison. After that Emmy wrote a letter to her brother-in-law, which no longer exists, and another to her mother-in-law. In these letters she expressed her conviction that "this stay should be selected for Edith (I don't think that the emigrant atmosphere will have a beneficial effect on her), only if it would not be possible [to find] an apprenticeship for her in Switzerland, Italy or France." She did not think Palestine would be particularly suitable since Edith would have to settle there. Yet she, Emmy, hoped to be together with Edith once she was released; Emmy wanted to support her and at the same time would depend on her help. Consequently, Gershom Scholem gave up his plan. The school in Ben Shemen was only recommended for youths who intended to remain in the country and to this end wanted a Jewish-national education.[35] There is no evidence that Werner Scholem heard of this suggestion, and, if he had, he, too, probably would have rejected sending his daughter to Palestine.

The girls lived on their own with the housemaid from the end of April to the end of May, when Emmy's parents took Renate to live with them in Hanover, and Edith moved into the home of Werner's oldest brother, Reinhold, a former member of the national-liberal German People's Party. All seemed to be going well until one day Edith appeared at the prison to visit her parents "all done up" with makeup and polished nails. Upset with what they saw, Emmy and Werner wrote to the relatives, asking what was going on with the child and why they were not taking their responsibility seriously to look after her? Reinhold's wife, Käthe, was insulted and put all the blame on the girl: fourteen-year-old Edith was an extremely spoiled thing who let others serve her and must have learned her coquetry somewhere else. For two entire weeks, wrote Käthe, Edith had refused to have her hair combed, in order to force her aunt to permit her to cut off her braids. Only her mother's last-minute veto, issued from prison, prevented the abrupt transformation of the girl into a young lady. With makeup and bobbed hair, Edith would have looked like the new young woman of the Weimar years (like the flappers of the 1920s in America)—something both the bourgeois relatives and the Communist parents wanted to prevent. At the same time, Edith had been regularly given tasks during the preceding three months that went beyond what could be expected of someone her age. So it is not surprising that she wanted her outward appearance to reflect the age she subjectively felt she was. All the while, Reinhold and Käthe never tired of emphasizing that they had raised the child "simply and modestly" and rejected the idea that they could be blamed for Edith's behavior. Whatever had actually happened, the result was that they no longer wanted to have Edith living with them. Since it was the middle of summer, the girl was temporarily brought to the summerhouse in Zernsdorf, where Erich Scholem and his family were vacationing. From there she also disappeared time and again, sometimes overnight, sometimes for a few days. When she did, she was visiting Karl Korsch and other friends of her parents who had gone into hiding. Such a situation could not continue for long because Edith was increasingly evading all supervision and control. So, at the request of her parents, she was sent to Hanover-Linden. Since her grandparents were already housing Renate in their small apartment, Edith went to live with Emmy's half sister Lina Schädler, eleven years Emmy's junior, and her husband Eduard. In Hanover, Edith resumed a fairly regulated daily routine and began to attend school again, something she had not done for weeks in Berlin.[36]

This episode demonstrated to the imprisoned parents just how disoriented and overwhelmed their adolescent daughter had felt because of the responsibility placed on her shoulders. Within the limited realm of his possibilities, Werner now tried to be a father to the girl even from prison, and in his letters he reminded her what he expected from her and what her limitations were: she should regularly attend her after-school tutoring lessons and make up for what she missed at school during the spring. He reminded her that her misconduct had not yet been forgotten. "How is it going with the interesting utensils of 'beauty care,' which, by the way, were called 'ridiculous' and 'unfeminine' in a very reasonable government decree recently," he wrote, thereby citing, in his effort to give his daughter parental guidance, the questionable authority of the criminal regime that had incarcerated him for seven months without trial. Yet he also knew that, for her age, his daughter possessed and—in order to survive—*had* to possess a keen and rational understanding of the political situation. His remark on beauty care may appear rather absurd, but in the final years of the Weimar Republic the political left and the political right were in agreement in their opinion on "the use of powder, perfume, and lipstick": makeup was said to be "unnatural." However, with regard to female employment and sexual liberation, the two political camps held opposing views. The image of the "new woman"—young, employed, wearing makeup and often short hair—also implied a degree of sexual activity, which explains why Edith's parents were startled by their fifteen-year-old daughter's desire to alter her looks.[37]

On the same day that Werner wrote this letter to Edith from his cell, namely, 23 November 1933, his wife unexpectedly received the good news that the Reich court had ruled on her application for a writ of habeas corpus. Although her arrest warrant was upheld, she would be "spared further pretrial detention" on the condition that she report twice a week to the police station responsible for her. She was still under strong suspicion, but the court considered the chance of her absconding to be negligible. The thirty-seven-year-old woman had been worn out by seven months of imprisonment and harsh interrogations. She had also developed serious stomach and gall-bladder disorders and left Moabit prison, as her mother-in-law noted, "thin as a thread." During her imprisonment, Emmy had insisted that each month fifty reichsmarks be paid from their savings to her husband and only ten to her. She ate little, needed no newspapers, and could do her own wash, she once wrote Betty. "You can imagine that our misfortune hits him so terribly hard because we could not be prepared for it; he had believed to the last that, as a war veteran, he would indeed be able to become a lawyer. It is so hard for him to bury his hopes. Therefore I would like to make things now as easy as possible for him & that he receives what he needs."[38]

Werner was relieved to learn of Emmy's release. Not only would his wife be able "on the outside" to take care of her health and their two daughters, but it would finally be possible to communicate directly again. Since the family's apartment had been vacated, Emmy traveled to Hanover, where she planned to remain until new lodgings in Berlin were found. When her first letter arrived, Werner Scholem was irritated by its distant tone. This did not come out of the blue, since Emmy had repeatedly been pressured during imprisonment to divorce her husband. Although he did not learn about this until months later, he did fear that the regime wanted to drive a wedge between him and his family. Besides persecuting oppositionists, the National Socialist regime also imposed a new system of moral values meant to influence even the private and intimate realms of couples and families. The new government viewed the Scholems as enemies in a twofold sense: as active communists and as a couple who had broken social and religious taboos. The marriage of an Aryan woman to a Jewish man, particularly of a proletarian woman with a Communist party leader who came from the Jewish middle class in Berlin, contradicted all National Socialist principles.[39]

The estrangement between the partners grew when Emmy learned, shortly after her release, who her biological father had been. Up to that point, her mother had carefully guarded this secret, and Emmy had known nothing except that she was an illegitimate child. Now fear for her daughter's life impelled Emma Wiechelt to tell her daughter who her biological father was. At first it appeared as if Werner found it amusing that his wife, who had been known for her "big mouth" since her early youth in the workers' movement, turned out to be the granddaughter of a pastor. It was truly amazing, he wrote ironically, how strong the Protestant element was evident in her, even though she had never lived in this milieu and had known nothing about her origins. "How would it be if you would quickly challenge your marriage on the grounds that you have lived twenty years in the mistaken assumption about a significant characteristic of my . . . person." He was referring to the precedent of the first cases in which partners in "mixed-race marriages" were divorced because the Aryan partner claimed not to have known that the other was Jewish or had only come to understand through National Socialism that a "racial difference" existed. In this way, the heavy restrictions on divorce could be circumvented, and marriages between Jews and non-Jews could be ended quickly and with little bureaucracy. The National Socialist newspapers that Werner was given to read in prison reported on the first divorces of this kind. So he suggested to Emmy, with a good measure of irony but also a bit of concern, that she "marry into a parish farm in the Lüneburg Heath, especially since apparently you all have now become pious!"[40]

Werner had learned in letters from Hanover that his wife had been attending church since her release from prison and that Renate had sung in the choir on Reformation Day (31 October). The entire family was suddenly becoming all too Christian for his taste and he feared that he no longer fit in. "Although a pious saying hangs in my cell, I am stubborn and believe neither in the Jewish nor the Christian god!" Despite it all, he was a Jew, and he also identified as one. The girls' estrangement from him and his origins worried him. "I also do not like that our children, as I learned from the letters last month, deny their half-Jewish origins in school because such behavior creates a breach in character that is more dangerous than any eventual hurdles posed by anti-Semitic teachers or schoolmates. In this way, Reni in particular is being raised to be a little hypocrite." Although he was glad that the ten-year-old liked being in Hanover, he also hoped that she would not forget where she came from. Concerned that the child could slip away from him and become all too estranged, he requested that she write him often.[41]

For years, Werner Scholem had ignored his Jewish roots. This topic, he had said repeatedly, had no place in the workers' movement and would not play a role in a post-revolutionary society. Yet by now, if not earlier, it must have become clear that there would be no such society. In fact, his Jewishness now played a greater role than ever. Therefore, he began, in accordance with his inherent oppositional nature, to warm up to this new type of insurgency: a defiance that proudly paraded his roots. As he repeatedly stated in his letters, he also hoped and expected the same from his children, certainly no easy assignment.[42]

While sitting in his cell, as his letters show, he pondered not only ideological questions but also very practical matters concerning the immediate
future of his family: where should Emmy and the girls live, what should
happen with their rented Berlin apartment, which had been vacant for half
a year? He suggested that Emmy and Edith should lease a smaller apartment
in Berlin, while Renate remain temporarily in Hanover until it was certain
that Emmy would not be arrested again. He wrote that the idea of parting
with the Klopstockstrasse apartment left him with a heavy heart, because
losing it represented the loss of a life together. He found Emmy's proposal
to give away what furnishings still remained in the apartment outlandish:
why give up their "home" and their entire household in exchange for a
furnished apartment again? Feeling nostalgic and sentimental, he asked
Emmy to take a picture of herself and Edith with her camera, a picture
similar to the one they had taken in 1922 and sent to him when he was in
prison then.

As Christmas neared in 1933, Werner gloomily recalled all the festive
parties they had given in their home each year with friends. Since all packages for prisoners had suddenly been forbidden, he ordered a fir branch
with tinsel for twenty-five pfennig, a pound of *Spitzkuchen* (a gingerbread-
like Christmas cookie), and a quarter of a smoked goose breast from the
prison canteen. The smoked goose breast was denied him at the last
moment, so he spent the holidays in his cell looking at the decorated tree
branch, eating cookies, and reading a book that Emmy had recommended,
Kristin Lavransdatter. He wasn't very enthusiastic about the dramatic love
story set in the Middle Ages by the Swedish Nobel laureate Sigrid Undset:
too pious, he thought, and "the constant talk about 'sin'" got on his nerves.
His suspicion that Emmy and the girls had turned to Christianity only grew
stronger the more he read. "It is a distinctly Catholic book," wrote Werner
to his family via Betty. "Because she was so enthusiastic about it, I have
already asked myself whether Emmy has also become religious and if she
will regret the 'sins of her youth' for the rest of her life?"[43]

The holidays in prison were tedious in themselves, but Werner Scholem
had another reason to wish they were over. Shortly before Christmas, he
had contacted a new lawyer whose response he impatiently awaited. Wilhelm Braubach, who had accepted the case in August, had proved to be a
disappointment. He had not been in contact with Werner during the past
four months except to send the bill for his fees. So Werner turned to an old
acquaintance, Walther Neye, and asked him, "in view of the many years of

our legal affiliation as my former teacher," not to let him down. Neye had tutored law students facing state exams and knew Werner Scholem well. What Werner did not know was that Neye had joined the NSDAP back in May. Therefore, this preholiday petition remained unanswered, and Werner was once again disappointed.[44]

Emmy Scholem had also been reluctant to write her husband during these weeks and let his letters go unanswered for long periods of time. As Werner had suggested, she moved to a small apartment on Königsweg in Berlin-Charlottenburg with Edith in January.[45] However, from this moment on, she began to make her own plans, about which she neither could nor wanted to tell her husband. The only evidence of the adventure that was about to unfold is the interview given by Edith Capon née Scholem shortly before her death. Aware that she was the last person alive to have witnessed these events, she agreed to tell her story for the first time in several decades. When the conversation with an actor she had befriended took place, Edith Capon was already very ill and found it difficult to speak. Even though the memory of some aspects of her story may have become distorted or forgotten during the long intervening time, the following is based closely on her depiction of an extraordinary flight from Germany.[46]

It was at the end of January or the beginning of February 1934. A Berlin lawyer—as it later turned out, Werner's fellow mountaineer Hans Kaufmann—warned Emmy of her impending rearrest. At about the same time, the man whom Emmy had to thank for her early release found that his own situation had worsened: Heinz Wiegel-Hackebeil had been an apprentice at the publishing house where Emmy had worked until the previous spring. According to Betty Scholem, Hackebeil had been a "staunch Nazi for three years" but was still "colossally concerned" about her Communist daughter-in-law. The tall, blond youth had been so enamored of Emmy, who was many years older, that he willingly brought trouble on himself by helping her. Like Emmy, he had come from very humble beginnings but had been adopted by the well-to-do publisher from Berlin Alt-Tempelhof Eugen Hackebeil, who was an early supporter of the National Socialists and soon published the regime's new school books in his business, the Gipfel Verlag. Despite his youth, the adopted son Heinz quickly rose in the ranks of the Nazi organization to Obertruppführer of the Berlin SA and Standortführer of Greater Berlin. However, in January 1934 he was forced to hand over his pistol because his relationship to Emmy Scholem had prompted an investigation of him. Only the intervention of his longtime

acquaintance Karl Ernst, SA Gruppenführer of Berlin Brandenburg, prevented any further steps from being taken against him immediately. Still,
he was allegedly in danger of being shot. At Kaufmann's urging, Hackebeil
fled with Emmy over an unofficial crossing point along the natural border
to Czechoslovakia. Edith remained behind in Berlin and was told by her
mother to pack a few things and travel the same route alone to join them.
Not only did Emmy expect her adolescent daughter to make her way alone
to Prague, but she was to bring as much as possible from their apartment.
"I was fifteen at the time. It sounds odd but I swear I was about thirty-
nine," said Edith Capon in the interview.[47]

Not only was Edith left to fend for herself, but the sudden disappearance of her mother also put her in danger. Carefully and anxiously, she
moved along Berlin's streets back to Königsweg only to find the police
waiting in front of their apartment. Before she was spotted, she ran away
and hid in her old school, where the school director found her. Shaking his
head, he is supposed to have said: "Little Scholem, little Scholem, what's
going on?" Since Edith feared that he would turn her over to the police,
she ran away again and went to friends of her parents. There Karl Korsch's
secretary Hanna Kosterlitz closed the door in Edith's face out of the fear of
getting involved, and so the exhausted girl returned to the old apartment
on Klopstockstrasse, where she was arrested that very night. She was
brought to the police station on Kaiserdamm, and she feared the worst.
The year before, the then fifteen-year-old Gerhart Friedländer had found
himself in a similar situation, and things had not gone well for him. His
mother, Ruth Fischer, had gone into hiding with her partner Arkadi Maslow the night of the Reichstag fire. In early March, she had instructed Gerhart to return to the family apartment and pick up the items necessary for
his parents' flight out of the country. Then he was to travel on his own to
Vienna to stay with his grandfather, the lawyer Jakob Friedländer. Unfortunately the boy was arrested in the apartment by an SA squad, beaten and
tortured for days, then expelled to Vienna before the month's end thanks
to the intervention of his grandfather.[48]

This was known to Edith, who feared the same fate, but nothing happened to her. The officers brought her breakfast and kept her locked up for
two days and two nights. During this time she was interrogated repeatedly
and asked where Emmy had been since her prison release. Edith lied and
said that her mother was probably lying in some hospital unbeknownst to
her and therefore had not been able to make her twice-weekly appearance

to the police. After the police finally released Edith, she went directly to Hans Kaufmann, who supplied her with the information necessary for her flight through Silesia and the Giant Mountains to Prague. However, as Edith left his apartment, a welcoming committee was waiting for her on the street in the form of a limousine and an influential-looking man in civilian clothes: Eugen Hackebeil. Hackebeil hoped to learn the whereabouts of his stepson from Edith. If Emmy and Heinz were still in Berlin, they could be found and thereby a scandal avoided. He brought Edith to his home in a villa nestled in a large garden in Tempelhof. The exhausted girl was sent to Heinz's room to recuperate. Edith did not reveal how scared she was. Instead she behaved politely, yet she remained adamant that she knew nothing concerning her mother's whereabouts. On the fourth day, when the Hackebeils began to trust her and left her unsupervised, she ran away. All that Sunday afternoon, from two to six o'clock, she ran through Berlin, jumping hedges, riding buses, streetcars, and subway trains—whatever was available. Although she feared that she was being followed, she had no idea that Hackebeils were having a missing-person announcement broadcast all day long on the radio. Not until evening did Edith feel she could go unobserved to friends of her family—Austrian Jews who were not political comrades. They helped her get to Silesia, where she walked through deep snow to cross an unguarded point on the border to Czechoslovakia. Although Edith regretted not having said farewell to her father, she said that, back then, she never wanted to return to Germany.

She took the train to Prague, where she found her mother by way of a contact address and thus ended her twenty-four-hour journey. Edith had expected to see Heinz there, but she was surprised to find that Heinz was being addressed intimately as "Heinzche," and he had become her mother's lover. It took seven weeks in Prague before the three of them received their refugee passports and a visa for a month-long stay in Great Britain. They then set out immediately, traveling through Austria and Switzerland before reaching Paris in March 1934. There they were helped by Ruth Fischer and Arkadi Maslow, who housed them in an apartment in which a very nervous Leon Trotsky was also staying; he had arrived in Paris without the required permission to do so. Soon afterward, Edith, Emmy, and Heinz crossed the Channel and arrived in Newhaven in East Sussex, not knowing whether they would be allowed to enter the country. Emmy lied to the authorities, successfully convincing them that she wanted to bring Edith to an English school and then return to Germany. Once in England, they spent the first two weeks at the home of Werner's friend Arthur Rosenberg, who was living in exile in Liverpool and held a professorship there. Rosenberg referred them to the German Jewish Aid Committee, located in Woburn House in the London area of Bloomsbury. It was here that Emmy and Edith first made close contact with Jewish institutions. As the wife and daughter of a prominent Jewish prisoner in Germany, they were given help. From then on, they lived under the protection of the Jewish Refugee Committee and its financial support.[49]

All the while, Werner Scholem sat in his cell in Berlin with no idea what had happened to his wife and daughter. On 22 February 1934, a new warrant for Emmy's arrest was issued. Betty received his distraught letters and said, after she had spoken with him, that it could "break a person's heart how the boy sits there and cries, he wails like a child that he hears nothing from the wife, that *we* should find out where she is." The fact that Emmy had simply disappeared worsened both his legal situation as well as his emotional state. The only good news he received during these weeks was that Hans Kaufmann had agreed to take his case, despite all his concerns. As the only person privy to Emmy's and Edith's escape, Kaufmann now seemed to want to assume some responsibility for his friend.[50]

Finally, at the end of March, Betty learned from friends of her son that Emmy had escaped with Edith and wanted Werner to know that "she would never leave him & always take care of him." Betty was infuriated by this message from her daughter-in-law, who had simply disappeared for such a long time, leaving Betty to care for both her desperate son and their remaining household. At the beginning of April—ten weeks after Werner had last heard from his wife—Betty received four letters that Emmy had written in Paris and were sent by way of Switzerland: one to Werner, one to his lawyer, one to the judge, and, finally, one to Betty herself. Emmy had nothing but accusations for her mother-in-law. "Outrageous," found Betty. After she, Erich, and Reinhold had done all that was humanly possible for Werner's family, Emmy still did not trust them and preferred to turn to people alleged to be friends, people who had never lifted a finger for them. Betty reported that Emmy had written: "When Werner is free, he will *not* need you, that is a great comfort to me." Betty was distraught, because she knew how greatly her son had suffered from Emmy's disappearance. When she next visited Werner, the content of Emmy's letter was being reported to him by a guard, because Werner was not allowed to receive a letter from abroad without the permission of the examining magistrate, who was on vacation at the time. According to Betty, Werner made

> a wild scene, yelling at the officials that they were being inhuman to keep the letter from him. He ranted until he was completely hoarse; it was awful. . . . In the end, the officials were yelling, too; what an uproar! They repeatedly reasoned with him, and I have to say, I am surprised that they did not have him carried off! However, these people do know the case & they will know that he has skidded into this place innocently. He has now been sitting for a year; in the last nine months he has not been interrogated. The files are rotting away in Leipzig [at the Reich Court of Justice]. It is truly unconceivable. But his unsteadiness & his whimpering for the woman are such an unpleasant and undignified spectacle. . . . And why? She could be unfaithful to him! A tragedy.

Werner Scholem did not even know the whole truth and at the time had no idea that Emmy did not flee on her own but with "Heinzche." He only knew that, thanks to his wife's escape, to use Gershom Scholem's words, this made "his plight even worse, of course."[51]

During these unsettling and troubled times, one member of the Scholem family was happy and content: Renate. When her grandmother Emma Wiechelt brought the ten-year-old back to Hanover in May 1933, it was a homecoming for Renate, who again became Reni Wiechelt or "Renischen," as her grandmother called her. At the start of 1933, she had been living again with her parents and Edith, but Renate did not warm up to life in Berlin. She missed her playmates and her grandmother, whose place in her life no one could fill—neither her mother Emmy nor her friendly but aloof grandmother Betty, even though the latter lovingly called Renate her "Goldschnäuzchen," her little goldfinch. Therefore, Renate was anything but sorry when she was taken back to Hanover following the arrest of her parents.

However, much had also changed there over the course of the previous six months. Despite initial resistance and numerous arrests, the NSDAP had established itself in Red Linden, and Reni enthusiastically watched the marches of the New Order. When she came home one day wearing the brown jacket of the Bund Deutscher Mädel (BDM, League of German Girls in the Hitler youth movement), the grandparents did not say a word; nor did they protest when Reni asked her grandfather to attach small swastika flags to her bicycle. In Linden, everyone knew Renate Scholem only as Reni Wiechelt, and the Social Democratic grandparents did everything they could to deflect suspicion from the child. So Reni was allowed to hike, sing, and march with the others. She learned to abhor Communists and Jews and to forget her own origins and family. Reni was bursting with pride and happiness when she and a friend were the only ones in their school chosen to accompany other girls from Hanover to greet the Führer at the train station with braided blond hair, in white linen dress, and waving swastika flags.[52]

During this period, the Wiechelt grandparents managed to evade Nazi supervision and remained in close contact with Betty Scholem in Berlin, who forwarded news and letters between Berlin, Hanover, and London. In the summer of 1934, Renate went to Berlin at the request of her father. Betty met her there and took her shopping for new clothes—for the trip, as she later told Renate. The girl learned only then that her mother and sister were in England and that she herself would soon be taken there. Then Betty accompanied her granddaughter to the prison to see Werner and say farewell. In a small room in which two guards also stood, she met a very happy Werner. As usual, Betty read to him the most recent letter from Emmy, and then father and daughter talked about a photograph that showed Renate in her school in Hanover. Toward the end of the visit, Renate recalled, Werner said he should have become an actor and not a politician.[53] Following this meeting, Betty wrote to Gershom Scholem: "The visit went pleasantly well indeed. Werner was quite delighted to see the child & she was also very cheery and did not cry. She did not register the awfulness of the situation while sitting in the very comfortable office with two pleasantly smiling prison guards." Betty could not refrain from noting how pretty the little one was and how she resembled her sister more and more, "no longer so altogether 'Aryan'!" Werner also wrote to his mother that evening about Reni's visit, about how proud he was of the girl he described as cute, brave, intelligent, and lovable. He thought it was "quaint" that the many years she had spent in Hanover had manifested themselves not only in her language but also in her appearance—she now completely took after Emmy's mother, he wrote.[54]

Discussions about which side of the family Renate resembled were not new, but they took on another dimension in light of National Socialist legislation and propaganda. Everywhere observers were now confronted with stereotypes of what were typically Jewish or typically Aryan faces and bodies, which, in turn, were thought to reflect Jewish and Aryan character-istics. The chasm between the two stereotypes was not new, but it had become state doctrine since 1933 and unbridgeable for children from so-called mixed marriages. Since Renate was now on her way into exile, Betty pulled her instinctively to the Jewish side of the divide, not the least in the hope that the girl would be accepted in England as a Jewish refugee child. Werner, however, pushed his daughter onto the other side, the side of the nonpersecuted and nonstigmatized German population—a place where he himself could not be. As he well knew, his own facial features corresponded all too exactly to anti-Semitic caricatures.

Just before Renate left for England with Emma Wiechelt, Werner wrote his mother-in-law to thank her for the many years of loving care given his daughter. He also asked her to bring back as much information as possible from London for him about Emmy's health, whether she had help with the household, and how her business was doing. He asked for a sketch of their apartment, for photos of Emmy and Edith, and for letters from both daugh-ters. The letter to Emma Wiechelt, which was indirectly addressed to Emmy, also contained a series of questions and comments on the education of the girls and the selection of their schools. Reni was to learn only "good English" and not "London Cockney," he requested, probably in view of her Hanoverian accent and his own unmistakably Berlin accent, which he never unlearned, much like his younger brother. In his post to Emma, he included another letter addressed directly to Renate. In it he prepared her for her emigration and simultaneously stripped her of all illusions about a return to Germany in the near future. He reminded her to help her mother in these difficult times and to learn English quickly; then she could be his teacher when he arrived soon after her.[55]

On 12 August 1934, the day came when Renate and her grandmother started on their trip to England. Heinz Hackebeil risked his life in order to come back to Hanover and accompany them to London. Later Renate would recall how difficult it was for her to leave Germany, not the least due to the ideological indoctrination that she had undergone in the preceding months. She was leaving Germany, of which she was proud, to go to England, which, she had been taught, was a cultural desert. Furthermore, she was terrified at the news that her grandmother would not remain in England with her. After a few days together in London and on the Isle of Wight, Emma Wiechelt returned to Hanover to her husband, and Renate lost contact with the most important person of her childhood.[56]

FIGURE 30. Edith Scholem (in front) and, behind her (left to right), Emma Wiechelt and Emmy and Renate Scholem, Isle of Wight, 1934. Private archive of Renee Goddard.

Of the many Jewish children sent to England from Nazi Germany, the stories of Renate and Edith Scholem were more dramatic than most because of their father's prominence as an enemy of the regime. Each girl escaped under different circumstances, reflecting their respective places in the family. The elder girl had to shoulder the burden of conspiratorial knowledge, while her younger sister suffered the humiliation of being excluded from such knowledge, roles they maintained in exile.[57]

Imprisoned in the Tower of Berlin

"Of course England is the very best solution possible for the children. And there are said to be rocks to climb there, too, for there is a three-volume work on climbing in England!! However, right now I could hardly do anything since all the sitting has weakened me to the point that I already feel tired merely after visiting hours. And if they send me for a few extra years to the Bourtanger Moor,[58] then I am afraid that will be the end of it. But still, I can at least hope to be a human once again someday," wrote Werner Scholem in the summer of 1934 to his brother Reinhold, in a letter that was to be passed on to his family in London. Reinhold had agreed to take over the correspondence and the visits in prison while his mother recuperated for a while. The events of the past months had left her so exhausted that she spent some time recovering in Switzerland and the Black Forest. The uncertainty surrounding the disappearance of her daughter-in-law and granddaughter earlier that year had weighed heavily on her. Moreover, correspondence between the couple had been banned since Emmy's escape, and it fell to Betty to play the role of liaison between Berlin, London, and Hanover. Werner was allowed both to write and to receive three letters per month, and all letters went through the hands of both Betty and the censor. It was not uncommon for Werner's letters to turn into monologues, particularly when Emmy ignored uncomfortable questions, and he eventually gave up asking again. Therefore, Betty began to add commentary to Werner's letters for the benefit of her daughter-in-law, who, as Betty knew, was overwhelmed by the many challenges of her new life. Arrows and comments pointed out the important or repeated questions and requests for small favors, such as receiving the alpine association newspaper. The letters he wrote during this summer indicate a reawakened hope and vitality. Emmy, Edith, and Renate were getting settled into their London exile and he began to imagine new prospects. England was no longer just some abstract place abroad; it was an address, an apartment, full of pictures, places, and names. Werner asked his brother for an English-German dictionary in order to help him better understand the English literature that he read in his cell and to expand his vocabulary. As a person accustomed to being active and always moving, he suffered from the idleness forced upon him and the torturous boredom of solitary confinement. The regime newspapers given to him in his cell only angered him, so he was relieved to have found a meaningful activity. For several hours each day, he worked on improving the English he had learned in school. Even at night, when he lay awake until the early hours of the morning, unable to sleep, he memorized irregular verbs in the dark. But he lacked a partner with whom he could practice conversation. In his cell all he could do was "talk to the walls in English." Often that is exactly what he did, and in his lonely monologues he attempted to use a polished English straight from the book. Despite his positive efforts, he worried a great deal about whether he would ever be released from prison.[59]

Werner would have gladly sacrificed the biweekly visit of fifteen minutes with his mother in exchange for permission to correspond directly with

Emmy. Betty did not appear to him to be physically and psychologically capable of maintaining the regular visits. Yet for now, nothing could be done, and when Betty returned from her vacation, her son instructed her how best to organize the short visits they had. According to the former head of the Organization Office of the KPD, she was to do the best she could to avoid being distracted by the prison atmosphere of the visiting room, not to waste any time lamenting, and not to forget to put on her reading glasses before she entered the room. More important to him than any other news were the letters from London, which she was to read to him, if possible, in their entirety. Betty did as she was asked. She related all news concerning the children and read Emmy's letters, which now arrived regularly in her mailbox and were always so pleasant that Betty assumed they could only have been "tweaked" a bit to seem more "rosy."[60]

In her letters Emmy did indeed omit any mention of her difficulties in dealing with the new country and its language. Instead, she wrote about a successful new start: together with a business partner, she had founded an advertisement company with which she circumvented the hurdle of being denied a work permit as a foreigner. Her partner already ran successful branches in Switzerland, France, and Czechoslovakia, and with the financial help of an investor, Emmy was able to enter the business as a shareholder. In the summer of 1934, she moved into a two-room apartment near Edith's school in the London borough of Camden. With the financial support of the Jewish refugee welfare, Edith was placed in a boarding school with a good reputation; she came home to visit on the weekends and sometimes afternoons and was now living the normal life of a sixteen-year-old. She went camping in the summer and worked hard to get good grades. Renate had also quickly settled into her new life. With the help of an acquaintance, her mother had managed to have her toys and even her bicycle sent from Hanover. She lived with Emmy and attended a school run by Catholic nuns. Surprisingly, her father had no objection to this; on the contrary, he thought that Catholic schools had good reputations in education and nursing. Yet he was less enthusiastic about discovering that Renate attended the Jewish religious school of St. John's Wood Synagogue on Sundays. "My sympathies for the Jewish religion are not any greater than for every other superstition. On the contrary, if I were indeed religious, then I would be Catholic; they have at least 1,000 saints from among which a person can pick one to meet any situation. The Jewish religion is not really a religion at all because it lacks the idea of the afterlife; it is nothing more than *völkisch* rite. Asked to choose between Christmas and Hanukkah, I am for the former because we are German, despite anything said to the contrary."[61] Werner reversed himself. Just a year earlier, he had feared that Renate would completely forget her Jewish heritage while living in Hanover. What appeared to be important for him in National Socialist Germany seems to have been irrelevant for England. There the girls should have the chance to assimilate and, as English women, to leave behind their Jewish but not their German origins, he let it be understood. He was probably serious in calling the Jewish religion a *"völkisch* rite" against the background of National Socialism. His idea of a Jewish school was shaped by his personal experiences at the Samson School, where Judaism at the turn of the century was indeed cultivated as part of a nationalistic German popular culture. In the correspondence with his brother during the war, he had frequently expressed a positive view of Jewish culture and language, but that did not last for long. He had felt estranged from this Jewish world for years, and so he wrote to his family from his prison cell at the beginning of 1935: "Under no circumstance am I in favor of Reni learning Hebrew as well. What for? There are only two cases in which this language is needed, namely, to immigrate to Palestine or to actively participate in the Jewish religious service." Neither case would ever come under serious consideration for Renate. Instead, he recommended, she should improve her English, learn French, Spanish, or Italian, and, above all, not forget her German. But "don't come at me with Hebrew. Who put that bee in your bonnet?"[62]

Well, who? Did Werner Scholem suspect that his brother had a hand in it? Reni's Hebrew lessons were indeed linked to her uncle's influence, but Gershom Scholem didn't actually know about it. Emmy had no time during the day to care for the eleven-year-old girl and could not afford to hire someone to look after her. So, through a referral by the Jewish Refugee Committee, Renate was taken into a Jewish family as a child-refugee lodger. In the coming years, she lived during the week with the family of Jonas and Naomi Birnberg, who paid for her schooling and upkeep; in exchange, the girl took care of the couple's two young sons. Naomi Birnberg was the sister of Norman Bentwich, who had been attorney general for the British Mandate of Palestine and was now a professor of international relations at Hebrew University. Were it not for her famous uncle in Palestine, Renate would not have been taken in by the family, as Betty reported to her son. However, "when the name Scholem was mentioned, you came immediately into the picture & then they were willing to keep Renate at least until the end of her schooling!" The unconventional reform pedagogue Birnberg treated Renate like a daughter and raised her to become English and Jewish.[63]

Under the protection and welfare of Jewish refugee facilities, Emmy and her two daughters experienced Jewish culture for the first time, and it influenced them. A similar transformation was playing out among the Scholems who had remained in Berlin. Under the pressure of the Nazi regime, they had given up their secular identities. Erich and Reinhold Scholem studied Hebrew and hoped to be allowed to immigrate to Palestine and join their brother. Betty also sent money regularly to Jerusalem in preparation for her immigration there. The Scholem printing business had gone bankrupt and the private building on Alexandrinenstrasse had been sold to an NSDAP publishing business. In reaction to the increasingly hostile environment, the Scholems now attended synagogue regularly, and, in broken Hebrew, Erich recited the blessing over bread and wine every Friday evening.[64] Meanwhile, Werner sat in his cell, unaware of the changes that his family was undergoing and still harboring his long-held reservations against Jewish particularism.

Since September 1934, Werner had been allowed to receive mail directly from his daughters. The content of the correspondence dwelled nearly exclusively on family matters and innocuous details about his legal situation, yet entire letters were often randomly "not delivered on the grounds of partially impermissible content." Werner and Emmy were still not allowed to correspond directly with one another. Nevertheless, the parents and children did manage to create a kind of family life in their letters. Werner sent the girls heartfelt birthday letters and told them about his study of English literature. In exchange, he asked them to do small favors like sending him a description of "normal daily life" in the greatest possible detail. In the silence and immobility of his solitary confinement he would thus be able not only to participate in their everyday life but also to attach his own visions of the future in exile to concrete daily routines. With their future shared life in London in mind, he asked his wife to write a diary for him. He called Emmy his "person in the present," and, with this diary, she would then not have to tell him anything about these months later on. "By the way, I remind Reni, reliable girl that she is," he wrote sometime later, "to make sure every day that Mommy makes an entry in the famous notebook. I will be looking at it later day for day!" He attentively followed every change of which he was informed, especially the often occurring moves of the family. "Despite her actual Lower Saxon lineage, Mommy appears to have become a female wandering Jew, for she wanders from apartment to apartment," he wrote in amusement to Edith, and once again asked about the business, Emmy's fragile health, and what food appeared on her daily menu.[65]

Repeatedly he asked for photos of their life together and about the few memorabilia from his political career: "Were my photo album and my valuable prophetic caricature album saved?" Apparently the latter was lost, but Emmy had taken the photo album with her to England. She sent him photos from earlier times and, in order to feed his imagination, new photos depicting their life in exile as a bright and happy world. When he finally received the long-desired portrait photograph of his wife in December 1934, he studied it closely and with a power of deduction worthy of a Sherlock Holmes, he joked. The picture showed Emmy in a hat and winter coat in front of her new apartment in London's Highgate neighborhood. He recognized her old hat and coat, making her look familiar to him in the photograph. At the same time he also realized that her income as a businesswoman was modest, although she never failed to have the money he needed sent to him.[66]

Actually, Emmy's advertising business was doing so poorly that she had to look around frantically for additional sources of income. "Do I understand correctly that the articles of the new business are 'beauty items?'" asked Werner somewhat irritatedly. "Sounds a bit ridiculous, and from a business standpoint the question to ask would be whether, in a time when the world is being barbarized, these articles aren't a business flop." As it was later revealed, the business was not with beauty-care items but with lubricants. Fascinated by the extraordinary business acumen of his wife, Werner wanted to know who her partners were in this business and how the oil was produced. He never learned that this business was nothing more than another temporary measure in her struggle to survive. Emmy ran the advertising business from a room in her apartment, while renting another room to the son of the exiled Berlin playwright and intendant Hans José Rehfisch, for whom she also worked on the side. Heinz Hackebeil boiled down the soldering fat and lubrication oils by hand in a shack located in the back courtyard. As Betty Scholem noted during a visit to London, the "Heinz boy" worked untiringly—in the shack, at the advertising office, and doing household chores—and had become "very human" in his nature. Furthermore, the relationship between him and Emmy was strictly one of friendship. As Betty noted dryly, she herself was, from her very nature, "miles away from [passing] any 'relationship judgment,' finds it repulsive to always sense something going on behind the scenes—here I could not discover anything like that even if I had wanted to."[67]

Once, in a letter to her husband, Emmy mentioned on the side that Heinz Hackebeil was in London and relieved her of a good amount of work. "When I read that to him," related Betty, "Werner fell over backwards & asked me to find out more from Emmy about it." Until this moment, he had not known that the young Nazi had accompanied his wife to London. However, Emmy was able to convince Werner that she desperately needed Heinz's help but that she could not go into more detail because of the censors. Somewhat later, she had Werner's lawyer give him the following verbal message: "It is indeed true that it did not lie within our power to make a choice. After Heinz had stood up for us once because he knew that we were innocent, events ran their course and one thing led to another. We had no choice to stay or to go. It was certainly not easy for Heinz to part with his party, for which he had fought many years, and he is still today true to his ideals, but he did not part with the party at all, he was parted with." Emmy claimed that this had all only happened because he stood up for them and was a decent person, and therefore, for her, he now belonged to the family.[68] As a former Communist, Emmy could understand commitment to a political ideology, even if it be National Socialism. However, what she meant when she spoke of Heinz Hackebeil's ideals remains unclear.

In general, Emmy Scholem cultivated only a few contacts with old friends or political comrades. She kept her distance from Communist exile organizations and political meetings, for fear of being deported. Karl Korsch lived nearby and so they met regularly; in Liverpool, Arthur Rosenberg also remained a good friend. Other émigrés came to visit, including Bert Brecht, Dora Fabian, Willy Brandt, and Emmy's close friend Rosa Meyer-Leviné. Gerhart Friedländer lived with them for a short while for he had come to England to go to school, while his mother, Ruth Fischer, remained for the time being in Paris with her partner Maslow.[69]

With the censors in mind, Werner Scholem seldom complained about his own situation. In the summer of 1934, he was transferred to the facility at Plötzensee, where a pretrial detention prison had been temporarily set up next to the penitentiary. Prisoners who had earlier been placed under the jurisdiction of the Reich Court of Justice in Leipzig were now assigned

FIGURE 31. Emmy Scholem, London, November 1935. Private archive
of Renee Goddard.

to the recently established People's Court (Volksgerichtshof), leaving the
Berlin prisons desperately overcrowded. Emmy's regular money transfers
enabled Werner to have a relatively good life in prison. He could buy additional food in the canteen, have his clothes washed regularly, and visit a
doctor if it was necessary. Despite this, prison life was more "penitentiary-
like" than it had been in Moabit, he wrote, and he felt it a particular tor-
ment that the lights went off every evening at eight o'clock.[70]

He wrote to the girls about one of his most entertaining distractions,
hunting flies, "which has to be done constantly here because these germ-
carriers infest the prison cells in droves." In the previous week he had successfully wiped out eighty-one of the creatures. When Edith told him that
she had visited the Tower of London with her school and had learned about
the execution of Anne Boleyn and Catherine Howard, the parallels to his
own situation were just too strong for Werner not to point them out. He
remembered visiting Plötzensee in 1932 with a group of law clerks. They
were shown the old execution site of the jail, which had not been in use for
a very long time because, it was said, such practices were frowned upon.
Only two years had passed since that visit, but now there were more than a
few prisoners awaiting their execution.[71]

Routine and boredom were briefly interrupted in October 1934, when a group of foreign lawyers was given a tour of Plötzensee. In the days before the visit, the entire prison was cleaned and polished. "But they were only over by Ernst Torgler," reported Werner afterward, "then they took off, and for lunch we got excellent peas with bacon!" Christmas 1934 did not pass all too dismally because Werner's former buddies from the Jewish Deutscher Alpenverein Berlin pooled their money and sent him ten reichsmarks. With this he could afford a bit of luxury in the Plötzensee canteen, and the fir bough was free that year. Over the holidays he enjoyed receiving a new portrait photograph of his wife and read, with the help of his dictionary, Charles Dickens's *A Christmas Carol*. He was doing fine, he said, because he had a clear conscience and harbored no illusions.[72]

At the same time, he was sustained by Emmy's repeated efforts to preserve a spark of hope. She worked earnestly to project the image of a shared future in exile and allowed her husband to believe that she wanted to hear and listened to his opinions regarding work decisions and the children's upbringing. Without a trace of cynicism or mistrust, he responded to her desire to be freed from the hardship of earning money by assuring her that, as soon as he was in London, she could "finally once retire into housewifery." Twenty years of working had taken its toll on Emmy's health, and in the future Werner intended to fulfill the role of the traditional husband and family breadwinner as well as that of a strict but caring father. At the same time he knew, of course, how independent his wife had become and joked a little about both of their roles in this game. "Perhaps Emmy is glad that she no longer has to 'deal' with me. Back then she always swore she would—once she was rid of me—live 'in the lap of luxury' for the first half of the month and live off stale bread in the second half." Emmy did not comment on this and similar remarks; instead she frequently repeated that everything was ready for his arrival. "I am very happy about the new apartment," he answered following one of her many moves, "even if I don't know where it lies and what it looks like, at least I once again have a feeling of home, in as much as alien sons of the desert can possess such a thing."[73]

The General's Daughters

Each day, this dream of a life in British exile was confronted with the harsh reality of a life consisting only of waiting for an indictment and a trial. In

July 1934, it was announced that his case had been transferred to the newly established People's Court together with those of a number of other oppositionists. Despite its name, this special political court did not at all represent the interests of the "people"—typical of the Nazi distortion of language. Since its creation in the summer of 1934, the purpose of the court was to try those accused of high treason and *Landesverrat* (a charge of treason often involving espionage) against the Nazi state. Thus it became the authority implementing the persecution of voices critical of the regime. Before the war, legal persecution by means of the People's Court was undertaken primarily against the archenemies of the NSDAP, namely, members of the KPD and the organized left resistance. For the many people who had been arrested by the regime since the Reichstag fire, the summer of 1934 simply meant waiting, until at some point they were informed of the special humiliating conditions of the new court. Among these was the stipulation that a lawyer could not be freely chosen but first had to be confirmed by the court. Furthermore, the judges, all of whom were NSDAP members, usually informed the accused and their lawyers of the indictment's content only shortly before the main trial was to begin, making it extremely difficult to build a defense.[74]

Ironically, for the first few years, this political court held its sessions in the building of the former Prussian Diet, Werner Scholem's first place of work as a politician. How coincidental, he noted, comparing his fate with that of the French revolutionary Marie-Jean Hérault de Séchelles, who was guillotined at the age of thirty-five together with Georges Danton at the location of his former victory, the Place de la Révolution. Werner's image of the young revolutionary was shaped by Georg Büchner's play *Danton's Death*, in which Hérault de Séchelles is portrayed as a good-looking and easygoing character, an anarchist clown popular with women who rebels against the totalitarian revolution, whose maxim is unconditional individualism, and who defies group pressure. "We are all fools and no one has the right to impose his particular brand of folly on anyone else. Everyone must be able to enjoy himself in his own way—but not at others' expense, not if he interferes with other people's enjoyment." It is not surprising that Werner Scholem identified with this figure. When the culture of open and free debate within the early KPD increasingly gave way to totalitarian uniformity, he had refused to go along and armed himself instead with the weapons of irony and humor. In the end he failed, much like Hérault de Séchelles. "Ah, Danton, I can't so much as crack a joke. The time has

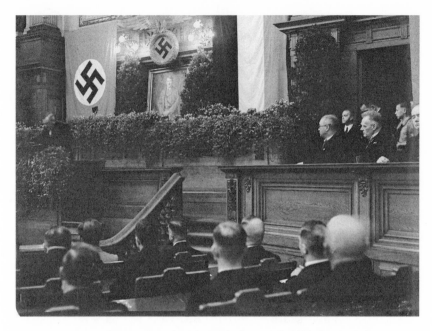

FIGURE 32. First session of the People's Court, July 1934. Bundesarchiv,
Sign. Bild 102–16037. Photographer: Georg Pahl.

come," Büchner has his young revolutionary cry out on the scaffold.[75] Werner had been reminded earlier of the French Revolution and of the horrors that accompanied it. Although the beheadings in the KPD were bloodless, the National Socialist counterrevolution now rebuilt the scaffold. But as it would soon be clear, this young revolutionary was betrayed by someone from his own revolutionary ranks.

On 23 June 1934, the court's preliminary investigation was completed in the case of Werner Scholem. However, by the end of July the accused still did not know what he was charged with. With mounting impatience he awaited the indictment "both as a person as well as a lawyer!!" His friend and lawyer Hans Kaufmann asked to be admitted by the People's Court as Werner's defense attorney, but, as a Jew, his chances were not good. Until that decision was made, he was not permitted to have either verbal or written contact with the accused. By mid-August it was certain that Kaufmann would not be confirmed because the examining magistrate responsible for the case learned that he had helped Emmy Scholem flee the country.[76]

However, with the help of Betty Scholem, Hans Kaufmann was able to forward to his client written information about the indictment, which he had received from the court. In this short summary of the indictment, reference was made to the "subversion work" in the Reichswehr and the *Schutzpolizei* (uniformed police), in which Werner and Emmy Scholem, together with the KPD Reichtstag deputy Wilhelm Koenen, were supposed to have been involved. They were accused of having been not only members but also the masterminds of the so-called "Hansa cell," which was said to have existed in the spring and summer of 1932 in Berlin for the purpose of infiltrating the Reichswehr and police in the interest of the KPD. When this became known, Betty was dumbstruck; it was truly "hair-raising and incomprehensible" that this "poor person" could be incarcerated for sixteen months on the basis of such an "idiotic & unfounded denunciation." In the meantime, Emmy contacted Wilhelm Koenen in his Paris exile and asked him for help. Koenen knew Werner from their time together at the *Hallesches Volksblatt*, yet they had not had much to say to one another since the factional infighting of 1925, at the latest. Notwithstanding, Koenen immediately agreed to write a letter meant to exonerate his former party comrade in every respect. His intervention had no effect, however, because he himself had been indicted in absentia.[77]

Emmy Scholem, convinced of her husband's innocence, undertook another effort to gain his release. In a written statement, she presented her position on her escape and the accusations against them both. The document was forwarded by the German embassy in London to the examining magistrate in charge. In her statement, Emmy claimed that she did not learn the real reasons for the arrests of herself and her husband until after her release in November 1933:

> The reason I was interrogated for the first time after 25 days imprisonment was because no other grounds for our arrest existed except the statement of Marie Luise, daughter of the Reichswehr General Freiherr von Hammerstein-Equord, in which it was claimed that she came into contact with the Communist Party through my husband and me. Neither I nor my husband was confronted with this statement that prompted our arrest. . . . Because no one told us about the statement but it was deemed better to keep us in jail, probably to protect General von Hammerstein and his daughter, my first statement was scrutinized for points to be used against us and the

necessary "witnesses" were found, whose testimony was presented to me during the second interrogation after 28 days in jail, and to my husband at his first questioning on the same day.

Werner had had an affair with the general's daughter, but in her statement Emmy did not say how furious she was upon learning that they had landed in prison because of that affair. She was accusing the court of leveling two different charges against her and her husband: one was the denunciation by the general's daughter; the other was a case of high treason, which was built on the testimony of paid witnesses in order to avoid bringing the Hammerstein family into the case. Emmy declared herself and her husband innocent in the matter of the general's daughter, which offered no grounds whatsoever for legal action against them. "I myself never mentioned the daughter of Freiherr von Hammerstein in my statements so as to spare her any trouble. Now that I know that you also must have known she was a member of the Hansa cell, I ask you to question her as a witness on the matter of me and my husband. I am quite willing to testify on this matter." Emmy offered utter silence to the examining magistrate in exchange for her husband's release. Otherwise, she threatened, she would publicly expose the general's daughter and her family.[78]

The "Hansa cell" played a major role in Werner Scholem's case before the People's Court. Described as a gathering of KPD activists, primarily intellectuals, the group (which probably never existed) was accused of having created Red cells within the Reichswehr in order to win the support of soldiers for the Rote Einheitsfront (United Red Front). Indicatively this Hansa cell appears only in the case of high treason against Werner Scholem and in Emmy Scholem's statement pertaining to Marie Luise von Hammerstein.[79] Because the intelligence service of the KPD had been involved since 1924 in so-called "subversion work" in the Reichswehr, the accusations against the Scholems seem plausible at first glance. However, despite all that is known about the intelligence activities of the KPD, the existence of such a cell has not yet been confirmed.[80]

Why would Emmy Scholem herself then talk about this cell, whose name, probably invented, recalled the Hansa quarter of Berlin, where the Scholems had lived, on Klopstockstrasse? Had Emmy merely invented the group in order to discredit the general's daughter and force the release of her husband? Certainly it would be no easy matter for Marie Luise von Hammerstein to prove that she had never belonged to a Communist cell that possibly never existed. If it is true that the Hansa cell never existed, as we assume, then Emmy Scholem had unwillingly created a golem that could now also be used against her husband and was included in the indictment.

Emmy's written statement aroused the interest of the examining magistrate, and, in answer to his request, she described in detail the acquaintanceship between Marie Luise and Werner in a second statement:

> In 1927–28, as a student of law, my husband met Miss Marie Luise von Hammerstein, who was then also studying law in Berlin. In this way, I also made her acquaintance. At the time, she was already accustomed to attending Communist and other left Socialist public meetings often. So, she had held this interest for quite a while before she met us. During the course of 1928, she expressed the wish to become a member of the KPD. I advised her against it, but she would not be deterred. So I suggested to her to be particularly cautious in the KPD.[81]

Neither Emmy nor her husband had had any further contact with the general's daughter after July or August 1928. Werner Scholem had then retired from active politics, and she herself had remained a party member only on paper. Emmy repeated her request to the examining magistrate that the general's daughter be questioned again. This implies that Emmy was convinced that Marie Luise von Hammerstein was unable to make any tenable accusations against Werner, so that no danger threatened from this direction. Never, emphasized Emmy at the end of her letter to the examining magistrate, were the "professional affairs of her father" mentioned in the conversations between them and the general's daughter. "My husband and I were extremely and most unpleasantly surprised when the now well-known publication of documents belonging to General von Hammerstein occurred. If a proper and public trial about this document theft were initiated, it would immediately show that we have nothing to do with it."[82]

At this point espionage comes into play, most likely connected to the Gestapo's interrogation of Marie Luise von Hammerstein. In their article on the political career of Werner Scholem, the political scientists Michael Buckmiller and Pascal Nafe were the first to conjecture that Werner Scholem and Marie Luise von Hammerstein might have been involved in espionage activities for the illegal intelligence service of the KPD.[83] However, no evidence of this exists, contrary to the case of another Jewish Communist, the true key figure in this story, Leo Roth. The eighteen-year-old Roth probably attempted to establish contact with Marie Luise von Hammerstein. As a youth, he had joined the workers' Zionist party, Poale Zion, and he had also been a member of the Jewish Communist youth group "Schwarzer Haufen."[84] As a supporter of the oppositionist Karl Korsch, he was expelled from the Communist youth organization in 1926 and subsequently switched to the Leninbund. A short time later he returned repentantly to the KPD and became a full-time activist in its illegal intelligence and espionage service and the secretary of its head, Hans Kippenberger. Roth found Marie Luise von Hammerstein to be a cooperative party comrade. She secured access to her father's study in the Hammerstein home for him and his immediate superior, Gustav König, and over two days Roth and Kippenberger copied documents from the general's desk, perhaps including the correspondence between the general and leading members of the Landbund (the National Rural League, the political organization of the rural population and the Prussian landed aristocracy), which fell into the hands of the KPD at this time and was published.[85] Since Marie Luise did not prove to be a good informant in the long run, in 1930 Leo Roth turned to her younger sister, the seventeen-year-old Helga, who was already a supporter of the KPD, and she began to rummage through her father's papers for Roth. After a while, the general became suspicious that someone was compromising the security of his study by tampering with his documents, and he informed the espionage department at the Reichswehr ministry. By 1932, Helga von Hammerstein was living with Leo Roth and probably married him. Roth was denounced and arrested on spurious charges of espionage in Moscow in 1936 and executed a year later, a victim of Stalin's purges. Until then Helga von Hammerstein had continued to work for the KPD intelligence service but ended this activity after her husband was murdered.[86]

Among the papers that the general's daughters had procured from him was the indictment of Marinus van der Lubbe for setting the Reichstag fire. However, Helga von Hammerstein was probably not involved in divulging Hitler's first speech to the military leadership, which he gave on 3 February 1933, in the home of General Hammerstein. One name repeatedly mentioned in the context of the Hammerstein daughters' espionage activities, besides those of the intelligence service operators, was that of the editor in chief of the *Rote Fahne*, Werner Hirsch. However, unlike Hirsch and Leo Roth, Werner Scholem's name is not mentioned even once in this context, and it would indeed have been strange to find any reference to him in view of his expulsion from the party and his many years of Trotskyite activities.[87]

There has been much speculation about why Werner Scholem was arrested. Michael Buckmiller and Pascal Nafe assume that he was used to put pressure on the general, a critic of the regime, by way of his daughter. Hans Magnus Enzensberger has Werner Scholem say in a fictional conversation that he was being held hostage to blackmail the general. Alexander Kluge, in a fictitious biography of Scholem by his fictitious biographer, explains that the aim was to protect the general's daughter and simultaneously "interrupt the flow of information to the KPD" by keeping the informant Scholem locked up.[88] All this speculation about why the National Socialists were so interested in Werner Scholem is closely linked to the tragic conclusion of the story. His arrest undoubtedly had something to do with Marie Luise von Hammerstein, but the National Socialists had other reasons for their interest in him, as explained below.

"What has happened to me and Werner is nothing more than bad luck, from which we are not the only ones to have suffered and suffer," wrote Emmy to her brother-in-law in the summer of 1934. "Not one word of the accusations against us is true. It is true that Werner has not been interrogated in more than a year, because there is nothing to question him about, because in reality there is nothing to hold against him, just as there was nothing to hold against me." When the ban on correspondence between Emmy and Werner was lifted shortly thereafter, in December 1934, there was a short exchange between the two, primarily on the "point of difference" concerning extramarital relationships. In view of the calamitous affair with Marie Luise von Hammerstein, they agreed to remain true to one another in the future. "In the end, our entire calamity can be traced ultimately to such a thing," noted Emmy. "But apart from this, it is a particular misfortune, and I blame myself for not having put up serious resistance to these things earlier. Only now do I know, since being in jail, how deeply that had eaten into me, even though I often predicted to you that it would."[89]

When her mother-in-law learned of Werner's affair with the Hammerstein daughter, Betty Scholem felt little sympathy for her son and his "bad luck." Instead, she became very angry at him for, in a way, having made every blunder possible. "With downright profound cunning, Werner recruited the daughter of General von H. to Communism. When this Marie Luise von H. was arrested in April '33, she toppled, of course, & sought to whitewash herself by accusing Werner of seducing her. (Hopefully only to Communism!) I had only heard about this girl once, when Werner boasted that an aristocrat belonged among them. He is truly an ass of fantastic proportions!" Since Betty had already heard about her son's connection with the general's daughter in the 1920s, it is extremely unlikely that he was involved in espionage. Had he indeed been a member of the illegal intelligence service of the KPD, he certainly would not have revealed the identity of his informant, let alone boasted about it—especially not to his mother, whom he did not trust when it came to politics. Werner's distrust of his mother's "big Berlin mouth" supports the argument that there is nothing to the story except its potential for sensation.[90]

A Kafkaesque Trial

For months Werner Scholem waited for his indictment and trial without knowing whether they would ever take place. The more time passed, the more probable it became that he would be placed in "protective custody," meaning prison or concentration camp without any conviction or justification. This form of administrative detention was used to protect the regime and the "national revolution," or, as it was explained to the public, to protect society from the prisoners while simultaneously protecting the prisoners from public anger and reprisals. Regime critics and oppositionists against whom no legal charges were found could be taken into custody this way and locked up in penitentiaries, police jails, or concentration camps. For example, the KPD politician Ernst Torgler, who was imprisoned in the Plötzensee facility, like Werner, was exonerated from any guilt in the Reichstag fire at his trial, but he was still taken into protective custody.[91]

By the end of September 1934, it became likely that charges would be leveled against him and also against Emmy in absentia. Acidly, Werner commented on what Kaufmann had conveyed to him about the indictment: "Apparently we are viewed as 'accomplices' in all these crimes unknown to me that were committed by dozens of people unknown to me. So one can be glad that none of these people were in possession of potassium cyanide or cholera bacillus in preparation for high treason or stored dynamite in child coffins, for we would otherwise end up being considered 'accomplices' for all that. I am particularly curious about the justifications for the charge of complicity. Just think what I could have still learned from this for the bar examinations!"[92] After the People's Court rejected Hans Kaufmann as a lawyer, a new one had to be found quickly before the court appointed a defense counsel itself. With Kaufmann's help, a young lawyer from Tempelhof, Heinrich Reinefeld, was contacted. In June 1933, Reinefeld himself had been detained and mishandled by the SA because of his work for the Social Democrats during the "Köpenicker Blutwoche"—a series of attacks by the SA on civilians, primarily oppositionists, in the Berlin district of Köpenick from 21 to 26 June 1933. Now he acted as a dedicated lawyer on behalf of those persecuted by the regime and in this capacity had already become experienced in dealing with the People's Court. In October, Emmy received a letter from him, saying he was willing to take their case. Furthermore, he reported that charges were finally being brought against them. In Reinefeld's estimation, Werner's prospects were not particularly rosy, an opinion Emmy could not understand. What crime was he supposed to be guilty of? Even Werner himself, who was still not allowed to have any contact with his lawyer, began slowly to despair. "I don't understand anything anymore and am starting to give up hope that I will ever be free again," he wrote in October. Not until November was the lawyer allowed to see the indictment in which, as Betty Scholem noted, "new, outrageous & bogus accusations" had been added. The lawyer shared Werner's fears of a long prison sentence, Betty continued, "because lies that have been confirmed by oath are difficult to refute. At the last visiting hour, Werner was prepared for the worst—& it is precisely from that I derive hope, for when he sees things *so* blackly, then the sentence will hopefully not throw him. A horrible perspective!"[93]

When Werner was finally allowed to see the indictment during a visit by Reinefeld shortly thereafter, he was stunned. As Betty reported: "A number of those who had been arrested at the same time were released, reworked into witnesses for the prosecution, & they are said to have sworn that W. & E. were to 'subvert' the Reichswehr! Have you ever heard such nonsense?" Betty was not very far off the mark. An attentive reading of the various versions of the indictment reveals clearly that the accusations were invented out of thin air in order to pin a crime on them. The charges were intentionally drafted to involve the Reichswehr and the uniformed police, because the amnesty law of 20 December 1932 did not apply to such cases.[94]

Werner's case was associated with the charges, brought in the name of the German people, against a twenty-two-year-old woman named Frida

Hüffner, an unskilled and unemployed metalworker who had been social-
ized in the KPD environment. She was accused of planning high treason
with the intent of establishing a dictatorship of the proletariat along the
lines of the Russian model. Twenty factory and office workers, all of whom
were unemployed at the time, were charged with her and, like her, were
accused of trying to convince soldiers to join the Communist cause. On 21
June 1933, it was decided to extend the investigation to include eight more
people, including Emmy and Werner Scholem, who had been incarcerated
for two months at that point. As Emmy wrote in her letter to the examining
magistrate, she was interrogated in May and shortly after that presented
with a number of witnesses who could testify against her. The original
charges against Werner and Emmy, which had also included Wilhelm
Koenen, were expanded over the course of the summer into a fat dossier in
which a number of formerly accused persons were now named as witnesses.
The trials against Emmy Scholem and Wilhelm Koenen were temporarily
postponed due to their absence, leaving only Werner Scholem to be the
primary focus of the charges.[95]

Werner's dossier reaches far back into his past and begins with his criminal record arising from the repeated banning of the KPD during the early
1920s. Mention is made of rowdiness in the Reichstag, of previous convictions of resistance and defamation, and of an "investigation into the planning
of high treason" from 1924, which was not pursued because of the amnesty
law. According to the dossier, the accused claimed that he had not been active
in the KPD since May 1928 "and, in particular, not to have belonged any
longer to the Hansa cell." Most likely, this sentence was intentionally worded
imprecisely, because elsewhere in the dossier it is noted that the accused had
claimed *never* to have been a member of this cell. His statement was challenged by three witnesses, all of whom maintained that they had known
Werner Scholem as a member of this cell: the Berlin workers Willi Walter
and Wilhelm Thöns, and a butcher named Theobald Mann from Bad Kis-
singen in southern Germany. As far as Mann is concerned, it still remains
thoroughly unclear what possible connection he could have had to this trial.[96]

The witnesses testified that Werner had continued to work for the KPD,
primarily because Emmy was a member of the Hansa cell until 1932. They
said they had observed Werner when he picked up his wife at "Schlüter's
Communist hangout on Stromstrasse in Berlin-Moabit, called 'Dreckige
Schürze' [Filthy Apron] where the Hansa cell met." The preposterous name
of the pub, making this testimony sound like a third-rate parody, was

mentioned repeatedly in the pretrial investigation reports but not in the final trial, in which reference is made just to the "Gastwirtschaft Schlüter" (Schlüter's Inn). While the pretrial investigations only established Werner Scholem's presence there, he is described in nine points of the indictment as being the main agitator and instructor of the cell, together with Wilhelm Koenen. One of the witnesses testified that in the summer or fall of 1932 he had observed Werner Scholem and Koenen conducting "individual sub-version work among members of the Reichswehr" in said pub: attempting to indoctrinate soldiers with propaganda. Moreover, Scholem and Koenen were said to have devised guidelines for subversion of the Reichswehr and the uniformed police and to have disseminated these to others only ver-bally, since one of the most important rules of the "Hansa cell" forbid anything in written form, testified the witnesses. Thus the lack of documen-tary evidence was explained.[97]

Two of the witnesses against Werner had themselves been accused in the case of Frida Hüffner. The first, the unemployed baker's assistant Ernst Wernicke, retracted his testimony against Werner Scholem shortly after submitting it, only to then retract his retraction. A second witness, also previously accused, was Walter Mildenberg, a Jewish merchant and the hus-band of Grete Mildenberg, who had once been a KPD city councillor and Reichstag deputy. Allegedly, Grete Mildenberg had still been active in the Communist Party in 1933 and had therefore been in prison since then. Her husband, who had never been politically active but was supposed to have joined the KPD in 1932, was arrested with her and now sat in preliminary detention in Plötzensee. He was accused of having been the agitprop head and instructor of the "Hansa cell." Ernst Wernicke was also the witness here, and he later retracted the claim that he knew Mildenberg. Evidently Mildenberg also retracted his incriminating testimony against Werner Scholem, and it stands to reason that he had been pressured to testify because of the precariousness of his own situation and that of his wife.[98]

The key prosecution witness was Willi Walter, an unemployed twenty-eight-year-old factory hand who was said to have been a KPD member for a short time in 1931 and 1932. Despite his brief membership, he was incredibly well informed about the illegal activities of the "newly discovered yet long-existing Hansa cell, designated to carry out illegal assignments." Although Walter presented himself as an insider in this Red underground cell, he himself was apparently under no suspicion of wrongdoing. His testi-mony of 18 April 1933 became the basis for the indictment and the reason given for the arrest of Werner and Emmy Scholem. In it, Walter described the "Hansa cell" as a group of intellectuals centered around Wilhelm Koenen and the Scholems, a group intending to do "subversion work" among the ranks of the uniformed police and the Reichswehr.[99] A report dated 19 April 1933 included with the testimony, stated that, besides Koenen and the Scholems, the former deputy Hans Jendretski and the editor Walter Wenzel had also been involved. The report went on to note that only Werner Scholem and Wenzel were in protective custody; all the others had fled.[100] This proves that the two documents had to have been fabricated, since in April 1933 Emmy had not yet fled the country and Werner was not being held in protective custody. Both documents must have been created after Emmy's escape, that is, in the spring of 1934. Their purpose was to establish the reason for the arrest and to cover up the involvement of Marie Luise von Hammerstein. Besides the witnesses' testimony, the actual evidence against Werner Scholem comprised nothing more than his notebook, in which he had meticulously noted all professional and private appointments, papers on the investigation held in 1924 against him and other members of the new KPD leadership, as well as a two-volume report by the Berlin attorney general's office from 1923 on Werner's activities as a politician and journalist.[101]

Finally, early in 1935, things began to move in the case, and the trial date was set for the end of January. Heinrich Reinefeld was the first lawyer to actively defend Werner; even his friend Hans Kaufmann had done nothing for him. Furthermore, Kaufmann kept putting off giving his testimony, although he was the most important defense witness. Despite everything his lawyer was doing on his behalf, Werner became more and more certain that the Gestapo would not let him go and that he could land in a penitentiary, namely, in Luckau or Brandenburg. His fears were confirmed when the trial was postponed for no given reason shortly before the court date. This gave Reinefeld enough time to build a stronger defense, time that he had lacked following the sudden announcement in January. The new trial date was set for 4 March, and the verdict was expected to be handed down five days later on 9 March.[102]

Just then, Werner's prison conditions worsened. Although he had often complained about solitary confinement, he also feared sharing a cell. Since Plötzensee was now filled beyond capacity, he was placed for a short time with a young thief, who was very nice and even gave Werner the bed, while he slept on the floor. But after twenty-two months of solitary confinement,

Werner had—by his own assessment—become "very strange" and therefore suffered from having a cellmate. Fortunately, he had the cell to himself again after only a week. "Hardly was he gone, I began an incredible major cleaning, and afterward I arranged everything just as I have been accustomed for years. I have become a really odd chap: if the toothbrush, comb, dusting cloth or any other item is not found in the same place day in and day out, then I feel unhappy, have less of an appetite and poor digestion."[103]

The trial took place in the former Prussian Diet, the building between Prinz-Albrecht and Leipziger streets, and as it turned out, in a room familiar to him. The school committee, to which Werner had belonged, had always convened in Room 8; at the same time it had also been the room in which the KPD faction had met and the place where he had made his political debut. The office of the KPD faction had been right next door. In October 1925, in reaction to the open letter, it had been decided to expel him from the party in this room; and in 1927 the Left Opposition, to which he belonged, had held their meetings there. "Actually it would suffice for my acquittal if the walls in Room 8 were suddenly given tongues and would repeat to Senate 1 of the People's Court everything that they had heard in roughly the last ten years about the name Scholem, but walls are unfortunately silent and therefore not suitable as witnesses," wrote Werner to Emmy. One way or another he would enter this room on 4 March "not without being emotionally moved."[104]

To Emmy's distress, no word was heard from Hans Kaufmann, even two days before the start of the trial. Werner wrote his last letter to Emmy from his pretrial detention cell and told her that a prankster from the library had sent a book about the Reichswehr to him in his cell. It was quite apparent that the events involving the former Reichstag deputy were being closely watched in Plötzensee. Werner's lawyer displayed confidence and cheerful spirits. Still, as his client knew, this only meant that Reinefeld was following one of the golden rules for lawyers. Even though Werner did not feel guilty on any count, he prepared himself for a shorter or longer period in prison. He adjured Emmy never again to let him go without news for a long time, and the idea of leaving the protective environs of his cell and mingling with people, of giving up his daily life and routine, made him nervous and insecure. This was a letter of farewell prompted by his fear of protective custody, which would place him somewhere beyond the realm of legality and thus even farther away from his family.[105]

The mass trial of twenty-three people, including Werner, started on 4 March 1935 and lasted for more than five days. Since Hans Kaufmann remained silent, Betty Scholem was summoned to testify that she had been in Tyrol with her son in the summer of 1932, precisely when the informer claimed to have seen him in the Moabit pub. As evidence, Betty brought her travel journal with her. In the end, her testimony was not necessary because Kaufmann himself suddenly appeared. He testified that he had been with Werner at the time in question, attending the dedication of a mountain lodge in the Tyrolean Alps. On 3 July 1932, the Friesenberghaus was opened, the first and only lodge of the Jewish German Alpine Association of Berlin and the Austrian Jewish Sektion Donauland. The building, located at an altitude of 2,500 meters in the Zillertal Alps, was consecrated by a priest with a short "sermon on the mount," which had been worded to fit the occasion: "The Lord handed down the Ten Commandments on Mount Sinai. Therefore, may honesty, justice, and human kindness prevail in this new abode." Among those attending were fellow mountaineers from Berlin, who confirmed Kaufmann's testimony.[106]

It was asserted during the trial that Werner Scholem had picked up his wife from the pub in Moabit several times. However, this was also false because, as Reinefeld could prove, the main witness was serving a prison term at the time in question and could not have been freely roaming the streets of Berlin. Just as this witness was being released from prison, the accused was preparing for his trip to Tyrol and had left the city the very next day. Therefore, it was in fact impossible for the witness to have seen either Werner or Emmy Scholem several times in this pub. In addition, during the testimony it was established that "at the time neither the witness Walter nor the accused Wernicke even knew the defendant Scholem and the defendant Koenen. Instead, both did not identify Scholem and Koenen as the people in question until photographs were presented to them in the course of the investigation. Under these circumstances the possibility of mistaken identity cannot be excluded, especially when it is taken into consideration that the defendant Scholem, as he irrefutably maintained, has lived in enmity with Deputy Koenen for years and has never come to terms with him." During a break in the trial proceedings, Betty and Erich were able to talk briefly with Werner, who stood in the large group of defendants. "He looked like a pheasant among crows, he doesn't even know any of these people!" his mother reported.[107]

On 9 March, the verdict was handed down in a court session open to the public. Seven defendants received prison sentences ranging from one to three years, which was not uncommon in similar trials before the People's Court. The charges against twelve of the accused, including Walter Mildenberg, were dropped because the amnesty law was applicable in their cases, and it could not be proven that they had committed any acts of high treason after December 1932. Defendant Werner Scholem and three others were acquitted. The evidence presented to prove his guilt had not even appeared sufficiently convincing to the National Socialist People's Court.[108]

Elated by this news, Emmy telephoned Betty from London and said Werner should come to England as quickly as possible; she ruled out any chance that he would again be placed in protective custody. All of the defendants were sent back to the Plötzensee prison following the pronouncement of the verdicts, and only one of the acquitted was released that very day. Reinefeld hoped they would let his client go after the weekend; at worst he feared Werner would remain in protective custody for two to three months before he was finally released. Yet three weeks later, there was still no news of him. Betty went to the Gestapo, where she was put off and told she should submit a written petition—which she did. However, Betty was so exhausted as a result of the trial and a bad case of the flu that she accepted the invitation of one of her daughters-in-law to travel to Meran in South Tyrol to recuperate, despite all that was still going on.[109]

In Goebbels's Hands

At the beginning of this month, my brother Werner came before the "People's Court," in a large trial with about 25 defendants, after he had been in detention for almost two years. After four days of sequestered proceedings, he was one of 4 to be acquitted, but he was promptly taken into protective custody and there has been no trace of him since. He has undoubtedly been taken to some concentration camp or other. We are all very upset. I feel even more sorry for my poor mother, who has already suffered through so very many and much too dramatic incidents in this case, than for my brother himself, whose behavior in those crucial days [when he might have escaped] I will be unable to comprehend until the end of my days.

Nobody knows yet whether he will be held ad infinitum as a special object of the Gestapo's hatred, as is Torgler, for example, or if he can be successfully gotten out.

Gershom Scholem sent this depiction of the outcome of Werner's trial to his friend Walter Benjamin in Paris at the end of March 1935. Many émigrés had similar stories to tell in the early years of the Nazi dictatorship about friends or relatives who were in a prison or concentration camp because of their opposition to the regime. This was also true of Walter Benjamin, whose brother Georg was still in Germany with his wife, Hilde, in the spring of 1934. Georg Benjamin was about the same age as Werner Scholem and, like Werner, a veteran of the First World War. He joined the KPD in 1922 and had lived since then as a socially committed doctor in Berlin-Wedding. In 1926, he married Hilde Lange, a non-Jewish Communist and law student. In the correspondence between Walter Benjamin and Gershom Scholem, the fate of both their brothers in Germany since 1933 was a major recurring topic.[110]

In May 1933, Walter Benjamin had written from Ibiza about a horrible rumor he had heard: "I have learned, from a serious but not necessarily infallible source, that my brother Georg, who practices medicine in Berlin N[orth] Brunnenstraße, fell into the hands of the SA, was severely brutalized, and lost an eye. He is presumed to be in the state hospital, either as a prisoner or in preventative detention, and is most likely cut off from the outside world." Later he learned that Georg had not lost an eye, but that he was indeed being held in protective custody and would remain detained in Plötzensee. Like Gershom, Walter Benjamin could not understand why Werner hadn't tried to flee Germany and avoid arrest. Twice during the spring of 1933, after Georg's release, it was rumored that he was dead. Still he and Hilde remained in Berlin because he secretly worked for the KPD. He was arrested again and placed in Sonnenburg concentration camp in August 1933 and remained in protective custody until the end of the year. After he was released, he stayed in Berlin, as did his wife and their young son Michael. Hilde Benjamin was now employed at the Soviet Union's trade commission, where Emmy Scholem had worked previously. The family only traveled abroad for rest and relaxation, though they could have left Nazi Germany for good. In 1936, Georg Benjamin was arrested yet again, deported to Brandenburg concentration camp, and murdered in Mauthausen in 1943.[111]

Just as Georg Benjamin had disappeared without a trace in May 1933, there was also no way to find out what had happened to Werner Scholem. For two months, his family received no news about his whereabouts. When prisoners were taken into protective custody and deported to a concentration camp, they entered a nebulous counterworld in which all traces of them were erased. This emergency state existed parallel to the supposed state of law and was not accessible to the rest of the population. Rather than an exterritorial place, it was more like a dystopian place of exile on German soil.

Finally, in the first week of May, Betty Scholem received news from her son that he was in the Lichtenburg concentration camp in Saxony. He was not allowed to tell her that he had already been there for a month and had previously been imprisoned in the concentration camps Columbia-Haus and Oranienburg. This first letter from Werner Scholem documents his entry into the concentration camp system with all of the rules and prohibitions of this alternative world, on which a person's survival depended. Several of these rules had to be explained to family members on the outside: from this point on, every month he was permitted to receive no more than two letters of at most four pages and to write no more than two letters of that length. All correspondence would pass through the hands of a strict censor. The letters were to arrive "with the most meticulous punctuality and regularity" by a certain date, otherwise they would not be delivered. Werner let Betty know that she was allowed to write him about his lawyer's further efforts on his behalf. He also asked her to have thirty reichsmarks sent to him each month because he had developed a healthy appetite here. He was not allowed to say anything about the insufficient provisions and the transition from inactive waiting in solitary confinement to the daily grind in a labor detail. Instead, his letter included stiff, positively worded sentences, uncommon for his style of writing: "I am doing well. You need not worry about my personal welfare. I have already adjusted completely. If I receive news from you regularly and can also count on that money, then everything is in good order." He emphatically requested detailed news about the previous two months and especially letters from the girls, their school grades, and photographs. Since London had moved to the edge of his horizon, news from the family was now essential for him.[112]

Two weeks after this first letter, another one followed in which the language was less stiff but the tone was desperate. His first letter had not been answered; instead, Betty Scholem had written the camp administration and

FIGURE 33. Prisoners in the courtyard of Lichtenburg Castle, around 1935.
Sammlung Gedenkstätte KZ Lichtenburg Prettin.

asked for permission to speak with him. Although her initiative was well
meant, she had only caused him more hardship. Visits were only possible
with the written permission of the Gestapo, and Werner asked his family
"only to come when really very serious family or economic matters are to
be addressed, which I hope is not the case. Your long silence & the fact that
I hear nothing from Emmy, however, cause me again to fear the worst. . . .
The commandant is of course not to be approached. I ask that you strictly
refrain from submitting such petitions! You all have truly naive ideas!"
Emmy's soothing and gentle answer was not long in coming. She assured
him that she would continue to write regularly and to send the money
punctually. The lawyer was still on retainer, working for his release in the
near future. Emmy remained steadfastly hopeful: Werner would soon arrive
in London, take over the advertising business, and eat his favorite dishes,
which she would cook for him. With all the rumors and stories circulating
around London about concentration camps, Emmy was probably quite

capable of filling in the blanks about his life, of imagining the things he left unmentioned. Despite this, she asked him to tell her, cautiously, about his world in Lichtenburg.[113]

What was life like during these years in one of the first concentration camps? When Werner Scholem arrived in Lichtenburg in the spring of 1935, the camp had already been in existence for two years. Like the Sonnenburg and Brandenburg concentration camps, the "Lichte," as the camp was called, was a former prison that had closed a few years earlier, housed in a Renaissance castle in Prettin, a town on the Elbe River. The sanitary and structural conditions in the palace were exceptionally bad and became catastrophic through overcrowding. In addition to political prisoners, the men sent here were primarily homosexuals, later also professional criminals and so-called "race defilers" (*Rassenschänder*). The "disciplinary and penal code" (*Lagerordnung*) established in Dachau was also used here, thus integrating torture, flogging, and painful physical exercise into daily life. Prisoners were housed in huge, unheated sleeping rooms under the palace roof or four to a cell that previously been occupied by a single prisoner in solitary confinement. The provisions were poor, and visitors were only permitted in exceptional cases. The prisoners' situation was essentially dependent on the camp commandant, who—as in the case of Otto Reich at Lichtenburg—could make an effort if not to improve conditions then at least not to let them worsen. But Reich could also be extraordinarily brutal, like Hermann Baranowski, who was the camp commandant at Sachsenhausen later.[114]

After his release, Ludwig Bendix, a Berlin lawyer who was transferred to the "Lichte" in the fall of 1935 at the age of fifty-eight, wrote an extensive report about his experiences and the laws, rituals, and practices in this concentration camp. According to him, the same procedure was repeated whenever a person was committed to the camp. "The third door had barely shut behind us when we found ourselves standing across from a large number of black coats, armed with guns, who were meant to intimidate us and—in my case but certainly also for most of the others, as our fearful behavior proved—did indeed intimidate us." Following this, the SS assigned the newcomers to separate units: homosexuals, race defilers, political oppositionists, and, once the Nuremberg Laws went into effect, Jews as well. As Bendix describes it, military drill, an aggressive hatred of intellectuals, and anti-Semitism were predominant everywhere in the camp. While their heads were being shorn, soon after their arrival, the prisoners were left among themselves, and it was then that the barbers gave the newcomers the most important information about the camp, such as the names of the prominent prisoners, including the Communist politician Walther Stöcker, the SPD politician and social scientist Carlo Mierendorff, the lawyer Hans Litten, and the Reichstag deputy Werner Scholem. As the prisoners quickly learned, the Communists kept to themselves and were the strongest group with the greatest say in the "Lichte."[115]

In answer to Emmy's request to tell her about his daily life, Werner wrote in June 1935 that he had been working in the camp laundry for the past month and was slowly turning into a specialist in operating the mangle. The more than two years of imprisonment and the isolating effect of the camp had left their marks on him; as he wrote: "The longer I sit, the more everything that belonged earlier to my life falls away. Only you and the children remain. I think day and night of the children; you cannot imagine how much I miss them & how happy I am over every piece of good news."[116]

On 18 September 1935, Betty and Reinhold Scholem traveled to Prettin for the first time and were on the road for more than ten hours to make a thirty-minute visit. "I am glad to have seen him," Betty reported afterward, "but now, following it, the hopelessness makes the matter even more distressing. He is fearfully depressed, which one can indeed understand! His appearance is healthy and good, the treatment humane and benign—but no end to it." Not long after that, Betty traveled to London to talk alone with her daughter-in-law about Werner's situation and prospects. As a guest in the new apartment in Evelyn Court in the north of London, Betty could say things that she had not been allowed to in Germany: "In a Nuremberg speech in which he 'debunked bolshevism' (!!), that swine Goebbels called Werner 'Ruler of the Red Flag,' referred to him by name; after 16 years they still dig out his stupidities. How can a person then hope that they will let him go! . . . Werner asked us immediately when we visited if we had heard the speech; the camp heard the entire rally in Nuremberg on the radio & when Werner's name was mentioned, all those who knew him turned around to look at him. What celebrity."[117] The night of the Reichstag fire, when Werner Scholem figured prominently on the list of those arrested, had already demonstrated that he had not been forgotten as a public figure in Germany. In September 1935 during the party rally in Nuremberg, Joseph Goebbels referred to Scholem as a prominent representative of Bolshevism in Germany, and Goebbels regarded Bolshevism as a devilish and murderous ideology sponsored solely by international

Judaism. In his celebrated speech of 13 September, the Reich propaganda minister spoke extensively about the German left, which he claimed was dominated by Jews. In this context he declared: "The Berlin Communist press was dominated by the Jews Thalheimer, Meyer, Scholem, Friedländer, and others." Of the four names mentioned only Werner Scholem was still on German soil and at the mercy of German power holders. August Thalheimer and Paul Friedländer, Ruth Fischer's first husband, were in French exile; Ernst Meyer, Rosa Meyer-Leviné's husband, had a Jewish-sounding name and a Jewish wife, but was himself not Jewish and had died in 1930. So the only available enemy was Werner Scholem, whom Goebbels had already noticed in 1924 at the high point of Werner's career in the KPD. At that time, Goebbels wrote in his diary that the international idea in Communism was supported exclusively by Jews, and he compiled a list that included the name Scholem along with Marx, Liebknecht, and Radek. The fact that Goebbels grouped the young politician and journalist together with Karl Marx, Karl Liebknecht, and the Comintern commissar Karl Radek indicates that the young Nazi was observing Werner Scholem closely. Personal animosity might even have developed between the two, because, as an editor at the *Rote Fahne*, Werner Scholem had been among the harshest critics of National Socialism in its early days.[118]

Two days after his appearance at the Nuremberg rally, Goebbels gave a second speech before an internal group of trusted party activists. While speaking at the Sondertagung der Gau- und Propagandaleiter (Special Conference of Gau and Propaganda Leaders), the minister analyzed the importance of what he had asserted two days earlier regarding Bolshevism and its representatives in Germany. He was convinced, he said, that his Nuremberg speech offered the basis for "very effective anti-Semitic propaganda" because in it he had associated Bolshevism with a circle of people who were almost exclusively Jewish. "If we avail ourselves of this material, I believe that we will have a more resounding impact than if we only make do with general locutions."[119] To avail themselves of this material meant nothing other than to exploit public figures in Germany. Werner Scholem was a good candidate for this not only because of his well-known—and unmistakably Jewish—name, but also because he was still remembered as the Communist Jew par excellence, the target of rightist parties, an intellectual, a dissident, and an individualist.

Goebbels's speech significantly increased Werner Scholem's prominence at Lichtenburg—and thus worsened his situation. In a concentration camp, prominence attracted greater attention from the SS, and that was far from a good thing. From London, Betty wrote that her son was now thoroughly discouraged. "The prisoners are not allowed to make any requests, and his lawyer can do nothing more for him because he is asked at each visit to the Geh.Staatspol. [Gestapo] why he defends a Jew. In the lawyer's opinion, Werner is now in prison mainly because he is a Jew. Since everyone at home and abroad has just heard Werner called a Jewish Bolshevist in Goebbels's speech, the Geh.St.Pol. will no longer ever let him go." And that is precisely what happened: a petition for release, which Betty had submitted almost concurrently with the Nuremberg speech, was turned down with no explanation by the Gestapo.[120]

Were it not for uncertainty about the future and seeing his "mental powers disappear," Werner would have said that things had gone relatively well for him at Lichtenburg up to this point. The overcrowded, narrow cells and the many hours of physical work offered little opportunity to read or think about anything for any length of time. He had been lucky when it came to his work crew. As he wrote Emmy, he was now the "foreman of a detail of sock darners, a work that I do very gladly. When I finally get to live with you again, I will artistically darn all of the family's stockings. You see, I am now learning things that are far more valuable than, for example, the entirely pointless study of law that I completed." However, he soon found a way to put his formal legal training to good use, although he dared not tell his family about it because of the censors. Together with Hans Litten and Ludwig Bendix, he offered legal aid to his fellow prisoners. On their own initiative, the three lawyers started to advise other prisoners— originally for free, later for a small fee.[121]

With the adoption of the Nuremberg Laws, the situation for Jewish prisoners, who were increasingly isolated, worsened immediately. Beginning in September 1935, they were kept in cells with other Jews and assigned to work crews made up exclusively of Jews. At this time, for six weeks, Ludwig Bendix lived in one of these Jewish cells with Werner Scholem and four others. As Bendix recalled, the former politician greeted him with a speech on the need for mutual consideration in the narrow cell that indicated "an extremely embarrassing pedantry of the most extreme degree." Werner Scholem insisted that, after the noon meal, he and his fellow prisoners would quietly read and not have any conversation. Bendix saw little reason to oblige him, though he realized that his behavior was the result of years of solitary confinement. They eventually got into a fight over a minor issue, after which they no longer spoke to one another. Ludwig Bendix first met Scholem when he was assigned to Scholem's sock-darning detail. Scholem had instructed Bendix, as he recounted: "With what appeared to me to be an unjustified zeal for the thing, he explained the basic rules about sock darning to me, greenhorn that I was, without me understanding in the least what he was talking about and without him being in the least concerned that I understand." Bendix thought that the former Reichstag deputy was trying to make himself important. However, Bendix did have to admit that there was a sense of solidarity in his work crew. The men worked together to darn the number of socks assigned to the whole group, so that the fast workers made life easier for the slower ones.[122]

During these months, Emmy Scholem from England tried to find ways to get her husband released and, at the same time, to improve her own situation. She was thinking of moving to Vancouver and hoped that the naturalization laws in Canada would be less strict than they were in England and that Werner could follow her and the girls. He thought it was an excellent idea "to make the jump over there, which would forever separate us and particularly our children from the European atmosphere. Not only the need for quiet and alpine romanticism, but our own interests and the future of the children make the place a serious consideration." Werner assumed that the Nazis would more likely let him go to Canada than to London, so he began to prepare for their "future home" by studying books on British Columbia from the camp library. However, after Emmy submitted the application for naturalization in Canada, she was informed that the same conditions as those in Great Britain applied to her there: first her husband had to be naturalized, only then could she follow—or she would have to get divorced. The fact that her husband was locked away in a concentration camp was of no interest to the bureaucrats. When Emmy suggested to her husband that they divorce so that she could become naturalized, he rejected the idea. He trusted that she only made this suggestion, he wrote, because she was struggling with great difficulties in London. Yet, even at the risk of disappointing her, he refused to give his consent to a divorce: "It really isn't acceptable that, in addition to all the other terrible and totally pointless sacrifice that I have had to make the past three years, I should now also have to give up correspondence with you!" For Werner, the practical and immediate consequence of a divorce, according to the rules of the concentration camp, would be the severance of all connections to his wife and children. He asked her to leave him in the illusion that there was still hope for a common future—even if she would not want him after his release.[123]

Back in the spring of 1935, Emmy had contacted the Quakers with the help of the Jewish Refugee Committee. The Quakers were interested in Werner's case, but in order for them to help him Werner had to be not only innocent but also unwell. "That W. is innocent, they are convinced, but he also had to be sick & not able to endure prison," noted Betty Scholem. "And unfortunately, for that is W. too dumb. He has not taken a single hint; Emmy has mentioned his gallbladder to him 100 times, & it is so easy with the gallbladder; he could simulate it easily but he still prides himself on being healthy!" In March of that year, a Quaker representative visited him but found that he looked healthy and, thanks to Emmy's financial support, was not seriously undernourished. For that reason, they did not think they could help have him released. As Emmy later learned, the Quakers also had another reservation about his case because "his former political life reveals such an unconditional Com[munist] mind set that they rule out the possibility he will change his views, and therefore thoroughly expect him to renew his activity in a subversive sense if released!" However, given that a number of KPD politicians who had been active until 1933 were indeed released, this justification sounded unconvincing. Betty also could not believe that anyone could see her son as a serious threat and therefore, incensed, noted: "In my opinion, as a politician, all he did was commit stupidities and dumb tricks, write inflammatory articles, and tooted his horn in the Reichstag—a member of p[arliament]!!—& he is supposed to be so dangerous!"[124]

Meanwhile, in Palestine, Gershom Scholem was pursuing the idea of applying for a visa for Werner and bringing him to Jerusalem. Officially, Gershom stated that, as a professor for Jewish mysticism, he urgently required the collaboration of his brother for his work. In order to convince Werner to pursue this idea, Emmy told him that she and the girls were also applying for a visa and would go to Jerusalem. In December 1935, Gershom Scholem wrote Walter Benjamin about a "final attempt on my part (still in the works) to rescue my unfortunate brother from the concentration camp by means of a special form of intervention; I still have no idea what the outcome will be (I must ask you not to mention this to anyone at all, no matter who), and this difficult matter tends to strain my nerves to their limit—the chances of success have now become quite slim."[125] His efforts to save Werner coincided with his efforts also to bring Benjamin to Palestine, meaning that the latter project was somewhat neglected in the face of the urgency of the steps undertaken to liberate Werner from the concentration camp.

At first it appeared that Gershom's plan would be successful. At the end of March 1936, Werner was notified that the mandate government of Palestine had granted him and his family an entry permit valid until the end of June. For the immigration he would need a certificate of health and a vaccination record, both of which the camp doctor could provide him. However, he also needed a valid passport, so he asked either to be given back the passport that had been confiscated in 1933 or to be allowed to apply for a new passport. Soon the process was well under way: Werner was vaccinated by the camp doctor and certified as healthy; the application for a passport was submitted. What he still lacked was official permission from the Gestapo to emigrate. By mid-April it was clear that this permission would not be granted, although no official notification or explanation was issued. Outraged, Gershom wrote to Walter Benjamin that his initially very promising rescue attempt had been

> thwarted at the last moment, when all concerned, especially the British [meaning Werner's family in London] and my poor brother himself, believed everything had been properly arranged. Goebbels needs a couple of Jews on hand in order to demonstrate that he has stamped out Bolshevism, and my brother is apparently among those selected to play the part. I only learned the dismal news a week ago, and we have now lost hope entirely. On April 20 he will have been in custody for three whole years. There is no other course of action left to take. The brutes had already told my brother he would be released, and he had already been allowed to send a letter with the news to his wife. So now the reaction will be horrible, since that represented his last shred of hope. The affair has also taken a severe toll on my mother.

Betty was so devastated by this setback that, weeks later, her son Erich still had to take care of Werner's affairs and correspondence instead of their mother.[126]

Werner did not let his disappointment show because he knew how difficult the situation already was for Emmy, the girls, and his mother. Correspondence with the family became all the more important for him. He sent loving birthday letters, involved himself in selecting an occupation for his daughters, and announced that he would be a better father to his children following his release than his own father had been. Lovingly he let his wife know how much he thought of her, yet wondered if she was the same Emmy whom he knew four years ago. For a short time during the summer of 1936, her business had done well enough that she could afford to purchase a used car, and she wanted to take the girls on a trip through the Tyrolean Alps in it. Werner's imagination was so inspired by this possibility that he retreated into the memories of his own mountain hikes. "I could now compile for you the most beautiful itinerary, even from the perspective of an automobile, which I, as a backpacker, approved little of earlier. Will you send me your itinerary before departing? I will be with you when you visit Landeck, Innsbruck, Rattenberg, Reschen-Scheideck, Achensee and the Brenner Pass, explore the rose garden on Walterplatz in Bozen, and drive up to Lake Karer."[127]

In October 1936, during one of her rarely permitted visits to Prettin, Betty found that her son was suddenly doing considerably worse. During their thirty-minute conversation in the presence of five SS men, his lips quivered incessantly; he repeatedly requested yet was denied permission to tell his mother certain things. Betty feared he might have been assigned to a penal detail. Furthermore, a one-sided correspondence ban was imposed on him that forbade him from writing a single letter for two months. He was allowed to take only toiletries and a notepad from his mother, but none of the food she had brought—neither the cough drops nor the two apples. Betty was so shaken by his appearance that she cried all the way back to Berlin. "He implores you to write punctually and extensively," she informed her daughter-in-law, "it is the only thing that keeps him going."[128]

In his report on his experiences in concentration camp, Ludwig Bendix describes the incident that must have led to this change. The two central figures were Werner Scholem and SS-Obersturmführer Edmund Bräuning. One day, Bräuning, a relatively well-educated guard, had

> the entire company marched out of the cells and held a political speech about the equality of all workers, particularly also in the camp itself. The highpoint of the speech was when he read an excerpt from a letter in which the activity in the sock-darners' detail was described as particularly pleasant and was praised over that of the outdoor work detail, leaving the listener with the impression that the author of the letter was thanking his Creator for being

spared from this other work, which he so disdained. Bräuning closed by identifying the author as Scholem, against whom general indignation was loudly voiced, which switched to satisfaction when Bräuning announced that he would give Scholem the opportunity to review his opinion in the latrine detail. Scholem, who accurately assessed his enemies and anticipated their moves, had always retained a copy of his letters, also in this case; he maintained convincingly that Bräuning had torn the excerpt out of context and in doing so had given it an incorrect meaning. He even tried—and as a camp "elder" could—to take the liberty of pointing out Bräuning's mistake to him. But Bräuning refused to respond and asked instead whether Scholem wanted to make a complaint and have his comprehensive written depiction of events forwarded to the next official level. Scholem declined because he assumed that he would not win against the company leader, even if he was indeed in the right and assumed deep down that Bräuning had acted maliciously.

Werner Scholem knew all too well that filing a complaint would not help him; on the contrary, it would worsen his situation. Therefore, according to Bendix, he swallowed "the injustice committed against him silently." The latrine crew was a penal detail, to which more Jews and especially intellectuals were assigned once the Nuremberg Laws were in place. The men had to scoop the excrement out of the prisoner latrines, transport it in rickety barrel-shaped wagons, and spread it on the garden fields as fertilizer. The tools were so bad that the men frequently could not avoid working with their bare hands. They could wash their clothes only occasionally, even though they were soiled with excrement again every day. Moreover, they were forced to sing while working, as were other outdoor work crews. They often sang "The Lorelei" or the song of the latrine detail:

Ihr seid jetzt Jauchkolonne
Und Schiebt die Tonn' um Tonne
Gleich einem Leichenwagen
Ihr werdet bald verzagen!

(You are now the latrine detail
and push ton after ton
like on a hearse
you're soon woebegone!)[129]

It is not certain how long Werner Scholem kept this foul job, and this was not the only source of his troubles. He was increasingly isolated at Lichtenburg, because the Communist prisoners had the say there. Ludwig Bendix witnessed a confrontation between Werner and a Communist foreman, which took place in the only unsupervised place in the camp—the latrines. The foreman, a man named Schulz, and his henchmen maintained that

> it was a fairy tale that Scholem deliberately tried to spread, that he had ever turned his back on politics, that instead he had stayed in the party press to oppose the Stalinist-oriented party from a Trotskyite standpoint. And Scholem complained with a certain resigned contempt that his old party friends no longer knew him in the camp and continued to treat him as an enemy and wrecker of the party. . . . Scholem, who was amazing in the way he kept himself under control, walked up to Schulz, wildly agitated but fully restrained, and hissed at him: "I have been done with politics since the end of the 1920s and will never return to it! But this I tell you, if I would ever do that, then I would write a book with the title *In the Clutches of National Socialists and Stalinists*."[130]

Like a Dead Man in His Grave

One morning in early February 1937, the doors of all the "Jew cells" at Lichtenburg were opened, and the men were ordered to pack their belongings with lightning speed. In the clothes storehouse all the prisoners were given civilian clothing and forced to turn over even the tiniest scrap of paper in their possession. No one knew what was about to happen. The prisoners were taken by train from Prettin to Herzberg, where they transferred to the third-class cars of a slow local train. There were "always two SS men guarding four prisoners. The windows of each train compartment were covered. Bräuning stood in the aisle and waved away travelers who wanted to board by saying: 'Reserved for Strength Through Joy!' "[131]

On 4 February 1937, the prisoners and their guards arrived in Dachau, where the sadistic Hermann Baranowski was waiting for them. Baranowski had himself been transferred from Prettin to Dachau earlier. According to the report of the Berlin lawyer Friedrich Kaul, Baranowski first had the

Jewish prisoners from Prettin beaten for an entire day. Dachau was more despotic and brutal than Lichtenburg. The newcomers were assigned to the so-called "Jew company" (*Judendkompanie*) and greeted in a friendly manner there by the *Blockältester* (block or barracks leader) Heinz Eschen, the only Jewish kapo in the camp. As Bendix recalled, the friendliness of the Bavarian Communist was not extended to all: "No sooner had he heard the name 'Scholem,' of which he probably was made aware by those 300% Communist party strategists . . . than he ran up to him and shouted in a harsh commanding tone: 'Here you do not have the opportunity to confuse people and forge your old schemes! Remember that! Here you will keep your place like everyone else! Don't you dare act as if you deserve special treatment. . . . I demand the same from you that I demand from each person! But from you I demand it twice as diligently!'" Werner Scholem remained quiet in the face of this harsh greeting, and the violence that dominated the place discouraged anyone from standing up for him. Ludwig Bendix reported that he was the only one who went up to Eschen afterward and told him that, if it ever got to that point, he would later testify against Eschen.[132]

Despite a certain degree of solidarity among the prisoners of the "Jewish barracks," the conditions in Dachau were much worse than in Prettin; hunger, cold, and emaciation plagued the men. After his release in the summer of 1939, Gerhard Pintus reported that Werner Scholem had to do heavy labor in a work detail, known as the moor express, "that transported cement, stones, sand, etc. in a wagon." As Pintus writes, the harassment of the SS men was usually directed at Jewish prisoners, and he himself found it particularly terrible that a person's life was constantly at the mercy of their capriciousness.[133]

As difficult as his role as a KPD dissident was, Werner Scholem was also admired as an intellectual maverick who had remained true to his political convictions. Emil Carlebach, a member of the Communist elite in Dachau, who was not at all sympathetic toward dissidents and Trotskyites, wrote that Werner played a major political role in Dachau "because, even though most rejected him, they still listened closely to him." Among other activities, Werner participated in an educational program for political prisoners that had been organized by Heinz Eschen. Benedikt Kautsky, the son of the Marxist theoretician Karl Kautsky and also a prisoner, described Werner Scholem as one of the "cleverest and at the same time most pessimistic members of the Communist opposition." Furthermore, he was someone about whom stories were told in Dachau, especially ones in which he, having been imprisoned for a long time, did not let himself be quickly intimidated by the SS. With admiration, Ernst Federn, a young Austrian Trotskyite, told the following story about the man, twenty years his senior, who had befriended him:

> One day Scholem was assigned to a work crew that was working on the square surrounded by the dwellings of the SS troops. A young SS guard wanted to have some fun and ordered Scholem to say "I am a Jew with a crooked nose!" Scholem obeyed in a quiet voice. "Louder!" Then Scholem let loose the voice that had made him famous in the Reichstag: "I am a Jew . . ." All the windows opened and the women looked out. "Quiet, quiet," bellowed the guard. That was Scholem, not one to be humiliated and not one to be broken, because today's reader cannot know how much courage and inner strength were necessary to stand up to the SS.

Federn described himself later as the loyal camp assistant of the prominent yet isolated Scholem, a man whose manner rubbed people everywhere the wrong way. He recalled that Werner Scholem had been respected "but not loved, above all he was known as the blackest of the prophets of doom. It was said: 'The superlative of pessimism was Scholemism.'" His fatalism and his refusal to adapt politically irritated people and earned him no friends, something that could endanger a person's survival in camp. Moreover, he had apparently become an obsessional neurotic who planned his daily schedule in detail and became "nervous, fearful, even sick" when things went other than planned. Most prisoners could muster little understanding for this type of weakness.[134]

It can be gathered from the letters he wrote in Dachau that, after four years of imprisonment, Werner Scholem no longer harbored any illusions that he might ever be released. His letters, written on the camp's lined stationery, were noticeably shorter than those from Lichtenburg, and he wrote less often. His main topic was now the request for money: "Don't hold it against me that I only write about money in every letter like the blessed Hieronymus Jobs, but it's the only thing that you can do for me. You help me incredibly that way!" he informed his family. The only—and therefore all the more important—advantage of being in Dachau was that he was allowed to receive mail once a week. After his arrival, he received a

letter from Emmy in the second half of February 1937, but then he suddenly heard no more from her for a long time. He asked about his wife
again and again, but he only received mail from his mother and a single
letter from Edith, which included no mention of Emmy. Werner could not
understand what kept her from writing. Since the urgently needed transfers
of money from England no longer arrived, the Berlin Scholems had to
provide them, although they themselves no longer had any income.[135]

Werner Scholem would never learn that his wife had traveled to Paris
in February 1937 and met a former acquaintance from Berlin there. Isak
Isidor Aufseher came from eastern Galicia, where he had been raised in a
religious Jewish family. As a supporter of Poland's Communist Party, he
had been forced to leave the country in 1928 and had moved to Berlin
where he joined the KPD. After a few months, he was expelled from the
party because of alleged oppositional activity and joined the Leninbund,
which had been established that same year. As one of the leading figures in
the Leninbund, Werner had probably befriended Isak Aufseher, and, in fact,
his photograph is included in Werner's album. In the winter of 1933, Aufseher fled the Nazis to Paris and, by the end of that year, had moved on to
Barcelona, where a left-liberal government was currently in power. Aufseher dedicated himself to the cause of the anarchists in Spain and com-
muted back and forth between Paris and Barcelona. He probably met
Emmy during one of his stays in Paris. The two fell in love and began a
passionate affair. In April 1937, she followed him as an English correspondent to Barcelona in order to report on the civil war. By late 1936, however,
Trotskyites and anarchists were already being purged from Spain at the
behest of Moscow. Once open fighting broke out in early May in Barcelona,
the situation became dangerous for all anti-Stalinists. Therefore, Emmy and
Isak Aufseher left the country on 17 July 1937, and headed back to Paris.
Until winter she traveled regularly to London but continued to live with
him in France for long stretches of time.[136]

In early June, in an insistent letter to her granddaughter Edith, Betty
Scholem demanded to hear from her daughter-in-law while at the same
time assuring her: "Tell your mother that I will be understanding about any
decision she makes, she can do what she wants without ever losing my
sympathy, but she should say what it is!!" Finally, in early August, Betty
received an answer from Emmy, who wrote that she had just returned from
a long business trip but would soon have to leave again. Betty already knew
that Emmy had been in Spain, but she was surprised to learn that another

man was involved. She feared that Emmy would abandon her son's cause, and she herself would no longer be able to transfer money to Dachau. Then Gershom Scholem agreed to provide most of the necessary sum for the time being. According to a letter from the Jewish Refugee Committee, Emmy Scholem was having health problems that fall and her business, which she had turned over to Heinz Hackebeil during her absence, was ruined. Now she planned to immigrate to Ecuador with Renate because she supposedly felt chances there would be better for herself and for Werner's release. However, she did not tell a soul that this plan to leave Europe included Isak Aufseher. The Jewish Refugee Committee agreed to support her plans, but only on the condition that Emmy and Renate would be able to manage in Ecuador. The financial support paid to the family in England for years was about end in any event. Emmy's plan failed, as Renee Goddard relates, because the Ecuadorian consul put one condition on his willingness to issue the necessary visa: to spend a night with the nineteen-year-old Edith. Disgusted and outraged, Emmy refused.[137]

In September 1937, a letter from Hans Behrend in Buenos Aires arrived in the mailbox at Emmy's London address. Behrend had been a prisoner in Dachau with her husband and had been released in mid-July. He wrote that Werner was "very concerned and bitter at having been left with no news for weeks." Werner did not know whether something was preventing Emmy from writing him or whether a secret postal ban had been placed on him. Behrend emphasized how dependent Werner was on his wife or his mother to submit further petitions for his release to the Gestapo, since he himself could do nothing. Release would now only be thinkable in combination with a visa for overseas or Palestine—he would no longer be allowed to go to London, wrote Behrend. Meanwhile, in Berlin, Betty, Erich, and Reinhold Scholem were attempting to secure help for Werner by way of the Reichsvertretung der Deutschen Juden (Reich Representation of German Jews). They turned also to the Palestine office of the Jewish agency, which had enabled thousands of refugees to immigrate legally and illegally to the British mandate. Since Werner was subjected to a postal ban between November 1937 and February 1938, they could neither inform him of their plans nor get any word from him. Only later would they learn that he had been suffering from a serious case of diphtheria at the time.[138]

In the spring of 1938, after the postal ban was lifted, Werner received letters from London again on a regular basis. For an entire year, Emmy had fled from the drama of her husband's fate, but now she was back again and assumed responsibility for him. He was grateful that she had returned to him, although he did not know what had happened during this period. That summer he learned that his brothers Reinhold and Erich were planning to escape to Australia, so he urged his mother to go with them; he saw no reason for her to hesitate any longer. Yet Betty wanted to remain in Berlin and take care of his affairs, even though she was having health problems and would celebrate her seventy-second birthday at the end of the year.[139]

In September 1938, a group of 2,200 Jewish prisoners were deported from Dachau to Buchenwald, filling that camp to capacity. Among the newcomers was Werner Scholem, who arrived at the Ettersberg on 17 September wearing his own civilian clothing, carrying a briefcase, a fountain pen, and a pocket watch with chain and given the prisoner number 1980. Everything that he brought with him had to be handed over upon his arrival and was apparently stolen shortly afterward. While Dachau had been a change for the worse compared to Lichtenberg, Buchenwald represented an even farther descent into hell. Food provisions were deplorable and the prisoners worked thirteen hours a day. Werner was housed in Block 23, where many political prisoners and, for a short time, professional criminals were put. However, by December 1938, the only prisoners there were Jews. As in Dachau, he was assigned to a "cart gang" (*Fuhrkolonne*), of which there were five, with about twenty Jewish prisoners in each one. The men had to load sand rocks, some large and some split, into large carts, sometimes with their bare hands. Then the carts were pulled by the men at a speed set by an SS guard on a motorcycle. While pulling, the men were forced to sing and to carry out physical exercises, often hurting themselves. As Ernst Federn relates, Werner Scholem was privileged to have the best possible task in this very strenuous work detail, for he pushed the cart from the rear. "This position allowed him to control how much strength he exerted, whereas the job of pulling could, of course, be judged by the tenseness of the straps. That was the only privilege that Scholem, Reichstag deputy and leader of the Left Opposition of the KPD, could achieve in the camp." He was sick for a long time in the fall of 1938, most likely as a result of a work accident: he suffered from a phlegmon on his hand, a purulent inflammation of the connective tissue usually caused by streptococci.[140]

Among the prisoners in Buchenwald, as in other camps, the kapos who who had been in charge since 1939 were all Communists. In his memoirs, the Austrian Social Democrat Benedikt Kautsky describes them as either young functionaries or veteran Stalinists, whose worst enemy were Communist dissidents of all "shades of deviation to the right or left." Most of these oppositional mavericks were "intelligent if also nonconformist people, on average good comrades who strove to keep their intellectual individuality, yet were indeed agreeable people, as well they had to be because no one would have dared to go it alone in the camp. . . . Of course, they could not become camp functionaries, but if they were Aryan, they found a safer place working in the factories—just like the Social Democrats; for the Jews among them, even if they were long-serving prisoners, it was difficult to find a halfway decent work detail." Werner Scholem, who was known in Buchenwald as the leader of the Trotskyite Left Opposition in Germany, could count on little help, as had also been the case in Dachau. After two years in prison and three and a half years in concentration camps, he had by now "the reputation of an extremely tough and brave prisoner, if also an intellectual maverick. He was admired because he survived the terrible punishing drills like no other. Like a ballet dancer, as one says, he bounced across the roll-call grounds with his chin up." At this camp as well he did not hide his political convictions, his "reverence for Trotsky and his contempt of Stalin and his politics." However, in Buchenwald, the German and Austrian Trotskyites formed a type of countersociety. Bound to solidarity through their political stance, they discussed their exposed and weak position in the camp among themselves. Their precarious situation was the reason why the group did not leave behind any written notes.[141]

After arriving in Buchenwald in the fall of 1938, Werner wrote to Emmy that in the coming October it would be exactly twenty-five years since they had met in Hanover. He promised that he would think about her and their life together even more than usual on that day. Just how important it was for a prisoner to leave the camp at least in his or her imagination is emphasized by Benedikt Kautsky in his memoirs: "Nothing was more erroneous than the idea that the memories of the 'outside' weakened a person and were harmful. Granted, every person had a few aspects in his relationship to the outside world that were better off left alone. But, in general, thinking about family, art, and science, and especially the political cause to which one was committed, offered the greatest support." For this reason, the SS tried insistently to persuade the wives of prisoners to divorce them. For intellectuals and loners in particular, another major problem of camp was that a person was never alone and every activity took place in full view of others. As Kautsky put it, "What is but a seeming contradiction to this feeling of never being alone was that of being isolated from the world. The camp was not perceived as a collective that could be placed adjacent to the normal societal environment. It was precisely the best of us who clearly felt that the outside world had no idea of the conditions in the camps. And as important as the thin threads of correspondence were that connected a person to family and friends, they were not enough to banish the feeling of deathly solitude."[142] Despite frequent bouts of despair, Werner Scholem was not resigned to being forgotten; hence he asked his family time and again to work for his release with every possible means. He learned of only a few of the numerous attempts to free him. After Kristallnacht, his mother worked feverishly in Berlin on her own escape. She planned to emigrate to Australia with her daughter-in-law Edith, Erich's wife. When Emmy heard in London about the violent anti-Jewish riots in all of Germany, she wanted to have her mother-in-law brought to London by a relative from Hanover. But Betty had no passport; besides, while still planning her emigration to Australia, she continued to work for Werner's release. Tirelessly, she hurried from one office to another, addressed the Jewish community, and asked for advice from the Hilfsverein der deutschen Juden (Aid Association of German Jews), an organization that assisted Jews in their escape from the country. Werner Scholem's history of persecution made a big impression on the organization, which then promised to do everything humanly possible on his behalf. However, in the end, the Hilfsverein also let the family down, leaving the Scholems empty-handed and the sole advocates for Werner's release.[143]

In London, Emmy mobilized friends and her husband's former party comrades, who had shown little concern about his situation until then. The few initiatives undertaken had all started with Ruth Fischer, who had prompted the *Manchester Guardian* to report on Werner's trial in late 1934. Early in 1937, she had approached the British member of Parliament Morgan Philips Price, asking him to take up the banner in this "scandalous affair." She told him about Werner Scholem's career in the Communist movement and noted further: "He has been in prison since 1933. In itself, that would be nothing special—who isn't imprisoned under Hitler? But there are two particularities about this case that make it outrageous: namely, first, Scholem is a man expelled from the KPD, is not even mentioned by any political organization, least of all from those dependent on the KPD (Rote Hilfe, etc.). He is sitting like a dead man in his grave, without any sense of purpose, without even knowing that someone cares about

him, to no political avail, and with the personal feeling that the entire world
has let him down. Furthermore—and this is the second particularity—he
is imprisoned *for no reason.*" Even if it made little sense to talk about justice
and rights in connection with Hitler, she pointed out that Werner had been
acquitted by a National Socialist court. In her opinion, the pressure of
public opinion in Great Britain could still have an impact. Yet her intervention on Werner's behalf was unsuccessful. Most likely she also headed the
publication by the Groupe International that appeared later that year in
Paris. In it, an appeal was made to protest the injustice of the case, and
Werner Scholem was described as a victim of the joint efforts of National
Socialists and Stalinists.[144]

In November 1938, after all these initiatives failed, Emmy Scholem
turned to two of her husband's best friends: Karl Korsch, who was living in
Boston by then, and Arthur Rosenberg, who had moved to New York the
year before. She implored them both to help her by procuring two or three
affidavits each for her husband; by then, these were necessary for a visa.
Rosenberg, who was teaching at Brooklyn College, answered her immediately, expressing great doubt that Werner would now be freed to come to
America. After Kristallnacht, the United States had recalled its ambassador
from Berlin; diplomatic relations with Germany, although not broken, were
indeed very tense. Werner Scholem had been in five concentration camps,
and Rosenberg assumed he would have a great deal to tell expatriate circles
and the American left. Therefore, the only rescue Rosenberg could envision
was immigration to Palestine. Later Werner could be brought to the United
States from there. Rosenberg knew that his friend, like many other Jews of
the Left Opposition, was critical of the Zionist project, but at the moment
the main point was "to rescue him from the hands of the Nazis." He went
on to say that England had a bad conscience after the recent events in
Germany due to the strict British immigration regulations for Jewish emi-
grants. This bad conscience was responsible for the *Kindertransport* (children's transport) that began immediately after Kristallnacht as operations
to rescue Jewish children and youths from Germany and Austria. Rosenberg hoped that the British government would now also help a known
opponent of the regime like Werner Scholem and issue him a visa for the
Mandate of Palestine. He expected help in this endeavor from Israel Mat-
tuck, the rabbi of the Liberal Jewish community in London and, naturally,
from Gershom Scholem in Jerusalem. Whether and how Karl Korsch
reacted to Emmy's letter is not known. In any case, she did receive two

affidavits, one of which was drawn up by the American theologian Reinhold Niebuhr. It is also not known whether Niebuhr's support was the result of the efforts of Gershom Scholem, of the circle of exiles in New York centered around Paul Tillich, or of Karl Korsch, Arthur Rosenberg, and other "renegade" Communists. In any case, Edith Scholem, Werner's sister-in-law, attended to the matter in Berlin and, early in 1939, directed an inquiry to Raymond H. Geist, the U.S. consul general in Berlin. She pleaded with him to notarize the two affidavits and to issue her brother-in-law a visa. Certainly Werner Scholem would then be released at last. However, Geist refused and, once again, the rescue attempt came to naught.[145]

Meanwhile, the possibility of bringing Werner to Shanghai had arisen. Although Betty was sick and preparing for her own escape to Australia, she made the arduous effort to assemble all the necessary papers. Against all expectations, the camp administration in Buchenwald proved cooperative and issued permission to have passport photos taken and to submit a passport application. In March 1939, Betty set out on her flight via London to Australia, accompanied by her daughter-in-law Edith. In Berlin, her brother Hans Hirsch and her sister-in-law Sophie Scholem were to continue looking after Werner's affairs. The camp administration promptly notarized all papers for his immigration to China. With the help of the Zentralstelle für jüdische Auswanderung (National Office for Jewish Emigration), all the necessary documents were finally in the family's possession by April 1939: a tax clearance certificate, a character reference, and the new passport, which was ready to be picked up at Berlin police headquarters. With the passport, it was possible to apply for a Chinese visa through contacts in France and to book passage on a ship to Shanghai. The departure was scheduled for 16 August 1939. However, the prisoner had to pick up his passport from police headquarters in person, and, in order to do so, petition was lodged for his temporary release to make this trip to Berlin. From her new home in Sidney, Betty wrote that what was missing, "unfortunately as always so far," was the final permission, "the icing on the cake of his release by this monstrous Gestapo." Gershom Scholem also feared that the entire matter was no more than another "bluff by the Gestapo."[146]

Whereas the official request was for Werner Scholem's emigration to Shanghai, in reality he was to be taken to the Kitchener Camp in Britain. At this former military camp in Kent, the Central British Fund for German Jewry had taken in over four thousand refugees from Germany between February and September 1939. The idea of sending Werner there came

from Kurt Grossmann, who had headed the Deutsche Liga für Menschen-
rechte (German League for Human Rights) until 1933 and now presided
over the Paris office of the Demokratische Flüchtlingsfürsorge (Democratic
Refugee Relief). In May 1939, Grossmann contacted Otto Wollenberg on
the matter of Werner Scholem. Wollenberg was an expelled KPD function-
ary who ran the sister office of the same refugee relief organization in London. Grossmann asked him to intervene with Bertha Bracy on Werner's
behalf. She was the secretary general of the German Emergency Committee
run by the Quakers. Although the first request to the Quakers in 1935 had
failed, Werner Scholem had now been incarcerated for more than six years,
and it was hoped that the Quakers would show a greater interest in his
case. Grossmann suggested that a formal application for an overseas visa to
Shanghai be submitted. Since, however, the physically weakened man could
not be expected to undertake such a long and strenuous journey, a permit
for England and a limited residency permit were to be simultaneously
issued for him. Scholem could first recuperate for a while in Kent and
then calmly plan his journey elsewhere. Officially the money for the trip to
Shanghai would have to be made available so as to lend credence to the
emigration story. Later, the passage would be canceled, and the fare would
be refunded to the Quakers. Above all, Grossmann requested that action be
taken immediately in light of the urgency of the situation.[147]

Otto Wollenberg answered quickly and promised to help. "I myself was
incarcerated with Scholem for about three weeks in a hallway at the Berlin
police headquarters. He behaved then just as bravely and impeccably as is
stated in the report you sent me." The Quakers did indeed agree to help;
however, the funds for the ship passage overseas had to be provided by a
third party. This response disappointed Wollenberg. After all, the Quakers
were only being asked to lend the funds. Apparently, Gershom Scholem
assumed the responsibility of paying for the ship passage to Shanghai, but
at the end of June Emmy received a short message from Berlin: "Werner's
release has been turned down without any explanation and we have been
instructed to cancel the passage." Thus the last shimmer of hope had been
extinguished, wrote Hans Hirsch, Betty's brother.[148]

Yet Emmy Scholem still refused to give up. Instead, she attempted to
enlist the help of the Colombian consulate in Marseilles by way of a French
lawyer, but this application was also thwarted by the Gestapo. At the end
of August 1939, she received in the mail Gerhard Pintus's report on the
situation of his former fellow prisoners in Buchenwald. Pintus, who did not

know that yet another petition for release had been turned down shortly before, encouraged Emmy to try again. "We have the impression that now every Jew in protective custody will be released when his emigration papers are complete. This is confirmed by recent news that four heavily incriminated political prisoners, who in part have been in prison for just as long as Werner, were recently set free." Pintus also suggested the Kitchener Camp to her, but action had to be taken quickly, because Jewish prisoners in Buchenwald were now in great danger. Then the Second World War broke out, thereby obliterating forever any chance, however slight, for Werner's release.[149]

In December 1939, Gershom Scholem wrote his friend Walter Benjamin in Paris that no word had been heard from or about his brother since the summer. "I've had no news at all about my brother so far, not even indirectly. I'm afraid his situation remains unchanged. It has become very difficult to communicate with Paris from here nowadays and to say what one really thinks, so you can imagine how things are in his case." Indeed, news from Buchenwald rarely even reached Berlin. After Hans Hirsch and Sophie Scholem managed to flee the country at the last possible moment, the only person left behind was Betty's sister Käthe Schiepan, whose "Aryan husband" had divorced her. She was the last person to be in contact with Werner Scholem and was herself cut off from the world.[150]

The Masks of Job

With this final turn of events, this story nears its conclusion. But before this point is reached, we should look back to 28 November 1937, Werner Scholem's last public appearance in Germany, when, in the library of the German Museum in Munich, "Europe's greatest exhibition" was opened: *Der ewige Jude: Grosse politische Schau* (The Eternal Jew: Major Political Show). In twenty halls covering a space of 3,500 square meters, the National Socialists theatrically exhibited their propaganda of racial anti-Semitism. The Nazi newspaper *Völkische Beobachter* publicized the show as a scientific event, a claim that was underscored by the authoritative reputation of the location at which it was held: "Thus, the purpose of this thoroughly objective, almost dispassionate exhibition is to open the eyes of everyone on the basis of irrefutable documentation." One of the main objectives of the exhibition was to display the allegedly close intermingling between Judaism and Bolshevism. To this end, one of the halls featured a world map of Bolshevism, which was superimposed with the picture of a bearded Jew, the embodiment of the anti-Semitic stereotype. The Reich's propaganda minister Goebbels attended the opening of the exhibition and found the show to be quite "exquisite."[151]

Among the items displayed was the likeness of what was considered the ideal type of a Jewish Bolshevist of German descent, a life mask of Werner Scholem made in Dachau. In Germany, life masks had a tradition reaching back to the late nineteenth century when plaster casts were made of the indigenous population in Germany's colony Papua–New Guinea. The masks were brought back to Germany, colored, and exhibited in a wax museum in Berlin. This technique of transforming "faces into scientific objects" was soon replaced by photography.[152] The return to this archaic, colonial practice reflects the attitude of the National Socialists toward their victims and political enemies: in a humiliating and defamatory way, they transformed people's faces into objects of their propaganda. Both the material and technique used—plaster casts instead of photography—were meant to turn "civilized" people into "uncivilized" brutes.

His face was unmistakable: the prominent nose, the protruding ears, the high forehead—a typical Jewish intellectual as had been depicted since 1933 in every Nazi textbook on race. In the mid-1920s, the portrait of the politician Scholem had already appeared on National Socialist election posters. Back then he could laugh it off, but now his features and bearing had become the epitome of the enemy within: the internationalist German Jew. For the visitors to the exhibition who did not recognize the prominent face or were too young to know the politician who had left the political stage eleven years earlier, a plaque with his name was placed under the mask. A distant cousin of Emmy's, who had worked briefly for the family as a domestic servant when they lived on Klopstockstrasse, was horrified to discover the item. Not only did the mask show a face she knew, it also revealed the changes that the past four years had caused: it was a face etched with deep lines and aged by decades.[153]

Back in October 1935, during a relatively bearable period of imprisonment in the Lichtenburg concentration camp, Werner sent his family a drawing of himself, which apparently had upset Emmy, since in his next letter he wrote: "As far as the drawing you criticized goes, you are very much in the wrong. You forget that I no longer look like I did in December 1931! The drawing is completely true to life. If you don't like it, then it is

FIGURE 34. A display in the public exhibition *Der ewige Jude*, Munich, 1937.
Stadtarchiv München.

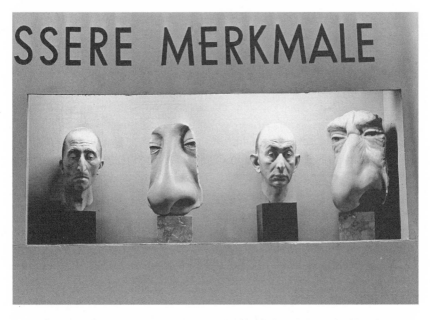

FIGURE 35. Plaster-cast mask of Werner Scholem's face. Stadtarchiv München.

to be feared that the original will someday please all of you even far less." In his report, Ludwig Bendix described Werner Scholem rather derogatorily as "the type of Jewish intellectual" whose outward appearance was marked by "unusually large ears" that "through exposure to the cold had taken on this ugly and immediately noticeable form" and who had "a certain furtive nature, always on the defensive. His behavior reminded a person of bad actors whose performance on stage revealed that they could not sufficiently tell their own private existence from the made-up reality of their role." Bendix said that he always acted the way "he wanted the guard posts to view him if they were watching him; in doing so he noticeably ignored these higher-ups whom he considered omnipresent. In any case, his busyness had a fabricated, artificial trait about it." Evidently the prominent prisoner felt exposed and closely watched, and, of course, insecure. The young SS guard in Dachau who had forced Werner to chant an anti-Semitic poem was probably not the only one who came up with that kind of idea.[154] In addition to his plaster mask, which was touring through Germany and Austria as part of the exhibition *Der ewige Jude*, Werner Scholem had made two further appearances as a media and literary figure. These, however, were less prominent and he probably never knew of them. In both cases his outward appearance, his character, and his political willfulness were causally bound up with the Job-like drama of his persecution. The result was an unrealistically distorted picture of his person and biography, which were employed for various kinds of propaganda.

The first misuse of his alleged likeness can be seen as the subtext of the plaster mask displayed in Munich, though it predated the exhibition by several years. In October 1933, the evening edition of the weekly newspaper *Berliner Illustrirte Nachtausgabe* featured a sensationalist series with the headline "16 Tage Moabit: Erlebnisse in Untersuchungshaft von Nr. 1621" (16 days in Moabit: Experiences in pretrial detention by no. 1621). This was a travesty of investigative journalism, which purported to have discovered, through a journalist's diligent research, what were claimed to be defamations by regime opponents. Borrowing from Karl May, the journalist portrayed himself as a lone adventurer who voluntarily spent two weeks in pretrial detention at Moabit prison and conducted his investigations undercover there. Afterward he reported to the German people the supposed truth about its enemies.[155]

With a group of recently arrested men, the author had himself brought to Moabit in a *Grüne Minna* (the nickname for the green buses used by police to transport prisoners), where new prisoners were to spend the night in a large cell with old prisoners. Such an arrangement was entirely unlikely, showing that the entire business was fabricated by the journalist, who describes at length the types of criminals with whom he supposedly spent the night talking. Eventually he comes to his last conversation with a "small, hectic Jew," whom he portrayed in particular detail: "A gaunt, unspeakably ugly person. Sly, innerly torn, constantly shifting eyes, large protruding ears. A real live specimen of Ahasver, the wandering Jew. Eternally at odds with the laws of a moral world order. It is not necessary to ask: on his narrow, sloping forehead it is written in invisible lettering that he belongs to the 'Politicals.'" The account remains improbable, for now the wandering Jew tells this newly arrived prisoner and complete stranger about his life, his worries, and even his secrets. "He was a Communist deputy in the Reichstag and the Prussian Diet. Three years ago they expelled him from the party following a major parting of the minds. Since then, he has studied law, prepared himself for the exams, and supposedly been no longer involved in politics. His wife, however, remained in the party. Yes, his wife! Tall, blond, pretty, Aryan from good Friesian blood, who became a passionate Communist through him. As always, I could not fathom that a German mother's child can mate with such a piece of wandering Jew." It becomes quite obvious that all the previous, shorter stories served only as subplots to frame this essentially true one. The article goes on to present information that was unavailable to Werner Scholem at the time, accusations that would only appear in his indictment, a year or so later:

> He emphasized repeatedly that he had not been politically active for the last three years. He only picked up his wife from time to time, late in the evening at a pub patronized by party members. Since he had been expelled, he was not allowed to enter, although now it is being said that the expulsions then were merely a sham. And now they had gotten him for high treason and subversion. At the time, soldiers from the national army also frequented the pub. He is said to have influenced them. And now it is all coming out in the Reich court and he, as a lawyer, knows what he can expect.

In this article the journalist has him confess to charges that had not yet been brought. Who profited from the article and where did the journalist get his information?

The "wandering Jew's" confession ends with him admitting his failure and accepting both his fate and the almightiness of the Third Reich. "He is convinced of the enduring power of National Socialism. Much to his great concern. 'Here I am hopeless that the National Socialist movement will ever be destroyed and that I can thereby be freed. A person clutches at all available straws, but I am too experienced, too schooled in such matters to see a chance for me." Although the name Scholem is never mentioned in this perfidious drama, the article reveals so much about his biography that it was easy for his contemporaries to recognize him: the failed German Jew, Communist politician, and eternal dissident. Thus, the article also found its way into Gershom Scholem's archive in Jerusalem.

Werner Scholem's second public appearance was in an unsuccessful novel by his friend and comrade Arkadi Maslow, the guiding spirit of the left wing of the KPD in the early 1920s and Ruth Fischer's husband. The novel, entitled *Die Tochter des Generals* (The General's Daughter), was intended for a sensation-hungry mass public. Maslow wrote it in the years 1935 to 1938 during his exile in Paris, supposedly out of financial need and in hope that someone might make a film based on it.[156]

At the novel's heart is Werner Scholem, depicted as a tragicomic figure whose story is linked to the events involving the daughters of General Kurt von Hammerstein and the peddling of a rumor, which would eventually be proven false—namely, that the general, together with the Reich chancellor Kurt von Schleicher, had planned to block the rise of Adolf Hitler. Maslow himself described his manuscript as a report on the "sinking or sunken classes in Germany," which is why he deliberately avoided writing about the working class: "The novel is actually not a roman à clef. Naturally, some real episodes from this Germany were used for the rather complicated cases in the book. But that in itself may be considered an incidental matter precisely because the selection of the untypical 'heroes' of the book—whether borrowed from reality or not—help represent several phenomena absolutely typical of Germany."[157]

For this purpose he did not hesitate to exploit the biography of his friend Werner Scholem and to make use of even the most intimate details of his life. Maslow made Werner seem ridiculous in the way he exaggerated and unfailingly placed his mannerisms, his physiognomy, and his habits in a negative light. Superficial, volatile, driven by sexual needs, both Werner and Emmy appeared in an ostensibly fictional plot, which actually stuck to real events, placing them in real time. In fact, a biographer might be tempted to use this material to fill in what is not known about the couple's lives, were the work not so polemic. None of this seemed to bother Maslow, however, because he pressed for quick publication of the book even though all protagonists were still alive. His efforts were fruitless; the novel was only published decades after Maslow's death.[158]

Arkadi Maslow, born Isaak Yefimowich Chemerinsky in 1891, had moved to Berlin as a child with his mother from the Ukrainian town of Elisavetgrad. In Berlin, he trained to become a concert pianist. In December 1918, he joined the Spartacus League and changed his name to Arkadi Maximowich Maslow. This name changed marked his transformation from a son of a good bourgeois Jewish family to a professional revolutionary. In the novel, the character Berger is his alter ego. Berger and his girlfriend (modeled on Ruth Fischer) are the only positive characters and represent all things good, meaning the working class, which otherwise went unmentioned. This down-to-earth labor leader is presented as a counterweight to the main character of the book, the Jewish intellectual who stemmed from the German bourgeoisie and who symbolizes a degenerate world and its demise. It order to establish this dichotomy, Maslow resorts to crass anti-Semitism, which he also expressed privately whenever the topic involved Jews, Judaism, or Zionism. When his stepson Gerhart Friedländer was forced to accept the help of Jewish refugee organizations in 1934, Maslow instructed him how to handle Jews who had not become reasonable, as he or Ruth Fischer had: "Jews blab a lot about God, Palestine, and their Jewishness; it is all watered-down and sometimes not so watered-down nationalism, just like Hitler practices, with the ludicrous ideology of the chosen nation upholding culture."[159]

 Maslow's depiction of the main protagonist, based on Werner Scholem in *Die Tochter des Generals* can only be understood against this backdrop: Gerhard Alkan—originally Maslow had selected the name Gerhard Chaim as Werner's pseudonym—is depicted as studying law somewhat late in life, and, when he makes his first appearance in the book, he is described as follows: "Slightly built, cleanly dressed, this man wore glasses on a large, Jewish nose. His complexion revealed distant Sephardic origins. Incredibly large, protruding ears and a nervous fidgetiness let the man appear slightly comical. But his eyes were not at all dumb; the black hairs on his head had already begun, mockingly, to thin out." This was followed by a detailed biographical sketch of Werner Scholem's youth and his acquaintanceship with Emmy—or Elly as she was named in the book. Despite Alkan's political success as an agitprop speaker, expert on school policy issues, and a representative of the Left Opposition, the author attributed great ignorance in theoretical questions to this character. Unlike the serious, solid Berger, Alkan was said to have only a superficial knowledge of Lenin's work and instead read Karl Kautsky's popular presentation of Marxist teachings. Since Kautsky was considered as a representative of the Second International and as a dissident in the Communist movement, the assertion that he was the source of Alkan's knowledge of Marxism came across as sharp criticism. On another level, Maslow also described the characters of Alkan and Berger as direct opposites: whereas Berger was depicted as a rational and sagacious professional revolutionary, Alkan appeared as a sentimental husband and the father of two daughters.[160]

At the heart of the plot are Gerhard Alkan's affair with Marieluise von Bimmelburg, the daughter of a general, and espionage, in which the couple inadvertently find themselves involved. However, the espionage turns out to be a farce; the real theft of documents goes through other hands. Although the rather dim-witted Marieluise swipes several files from her father's desk as proof of her affection for Gerhard, these files turn out to be worthless for him, and he doesn't care a bit about her failed attempt at spying. In fact, he laughs at her. However, Marieluise's stupidity triggers Alkan's tragic fate, for he is arrested soon afterward and sent to Moabit prison. The real blame, says the author, lies solely with the accused himself because he had recklessly passed up on his chance to flee in the spring of 1933. Arguing that he did not want to leave his wife and children behind, Alkan had returned to Berlin from a stay in Prague. As Maslow puts it, such sentimentality has no place in the life of a revolutionary: "The greatest and most unforgiveable mistake a revolutionary can make is to consider personal matters, personal *happiness*—what an idiotic expression—more important than the pursuit."[161]

In *Die Tochter des Generals*, Gerhard Alkan's trial is linked to the spectacular trial on the Reichstag fire and the historical figure of the judge Paul Vogt. This perfidious and cruel judge accuses the general's daughters of engaging in both espionage and sexual relations with Alkan. In order to protect their father and themselves, the young women confess to everything they are accused of and call their lover a conspirator on Moscow's payroll. Only after their interrogation do both young women realize that they have sacrificed an innocent man to the Gestapo. However, unlike the real-life figures, Marie Luise and Helga von Hammerstein, Maslow's women do not get off scot-free. They suffer the same tragic fate as Benita von Falkenhayn and Renate von Natzmer, who were exposed as Polish spies in 1935 and executed. From this point on, the fate of Gerhard Alkan becomes a sideshow in the story, though one about which Maslow was well informed. His interest in his protagonist ends with the detailed description of the work in the Lichtenburg latrine detail, for Gerhard Alkan, as the representative of a degenerate society, is doomed to destruction, even though he is innocent.[162]

Arkadi Maslow was shot to death in 1941 in Havana before he could publish his novel. Twenty years later and shortly before her own death, Ruth Fischer took it upon herself to get the novel published. Since she did not feel confident in the literary world, she secured the collaboration of the author Franz Jung, who had just returned to Germany from his American exile. The original manuscript was expanded and heavily revised, probably by both of them. Jung noted that what especially required revision were "the chapters on Scholem, which in today's style and atmosphere have to seem simply anti-Semitic." After Ruth Fischer's death in 1961, Franz Jung continued to work on the project alone and contacted the publishing house Verlag Cotta'sche Buchhandlung in Stuttgart. When informing the publishing house about who the historical model had been for the protagonist, Jung claimed that the topic "is rather cohesive and sufficiently documented due to the fact that Scholem had been one of Maslow's closest friends for years." He pointed out that the material was suitable for a radio play or film. Jung was also penniless and therefore pinned hopes on the novel similar to those of Maslow; after all, the plot was sensational and based in part on historical fact, although the degree of historical accuracy still had to be determined. For this purpose, Jung wrote his own exposé entitled "Betr. Hammerstein."[163]

In his exposé, Jung tried to bring the story more in line with historical fact and gave the characters their real names. With the distance of twenty-five years, this change seemed particularly important in order to arouse public interest in the story. Remarkably, he created a new figure out of Werner Scholem, namely, an enthusiast of above-average intelligence: "Outwardly Scholem was not very attractive with his stocky stature, very protruding ears, thick eyeglass lenses, and bulging lips. However this picture changed immediately when he began to show interest in a thing or topic—he suddenly seemed to become a totally different person, fascinating. Everything he said came across as precisely as clockwork, as a functioning and dynamic mechanism, very clear, very critical, without drifting into cynicism." Like his predecessors, Jung describes Werner's appearance by referring to the same, stereotyped facial features, but at the same time he removes the rigid mask that the theoretician Maslow created and turns him into a living, versatile, and not least, touching figure. Jung said that he was drawn to the topic out of an interest in the historical moment captured by the story: "What remains from a present long gone are not people and names but only the accent, the projection of an insect in flight, the slight shivering in the last drawn breath. To let this take shape while aspiring to remain generally valid is the task of the epic story about this present now past." In the end, *Die Tochter des Generals* did not bring Franz Jung the financial relief he sought; he died in 1963 and the project was forgotten.[164]

The manuscript, as revised by Jung and Ruth Fischer, was finally published in 2011 by a small Berlin publisher. It is indicative of Werner Scholem's anonymity that the editor did not identify him positively as Gerhard Alkan. She conjectured that the protagonist of the book reflected characteristics of the author himself, although Arkadi Maslow had done everything possible to distance himself from his tragic protagonist—from Alkan, this sentimental caricature of a revolutionary.[165]

In a letter to Ernst Jünger, Gershom Scholem had once described his brother Werner as having, like himself, "a small, angular Jewish face." In 1975 it may have been anachronistic to use such terms, but Scholem was harking back to the world of imperial Germany and the Weimar Republic, when Jews were routinely identified by their looks.[166] Although Werner Scholem had seen himself as beyond the categories of Jew/non-Jew, he always remained a Jew in the eyes of others. When it came to identifying a Jew, it was his name that was mentioned, as well as the ideology for which he stood and—most of all—his facial features. The way others viewed him ossified into a mask, which is now superimposed upon the wholeness of his being.

THE IDEA OF *HEIMAT*

This, a portrait of a family of today. I feel alive in the
summer when I go climbing. I hope someday, before I
become an old man, I will take a plunge.

—Werner Scholem to Gershom Scholem,
23 March 1931

Graves

In early November 1940, amid a most beautiful Australian spring, Betty
Scholem wrote a letter to her son Gershom in Jerusalem. Along with other
news, she told him that she had spent an afternoon with the publisher
Salman Schocken, who had recently been visiting from Palestine. "I had, to
a great extent, the joy of hearing about you in more detail at tea with Mr.
Schocken. He was in Sydney for only two days and devoted an afternoon
to me; he had to decline the invitation to lunch because he himself had to
lunch with 40 menfolk and shake their hands and also give a lecture exclusively about you and your research! . . . Had I not ruined my life with
Austräliä here, I could now at least be warming my old head in the reflected
glory of your fame, but as it is, I sit here and have some new mishap every
day."[1] Betty had been living with her oldest son, Reinhold, and his family
since her arrival in Sydney in April 1939. Despite the idyllic environment
of Como, a suburban community located on the water just south of Sydney,
Betty was unhappy. The city and language were too foreign for her, and she
missed friends, many of whom had ended up in Palestine. Therefore,

shortly after her arrival, she said she also wanted to move to Palestine. However, the war and the strict British immigration policy for Palestine stranded her in Sydney, where her sons Reinhold and Erich battled to survive the great difficulties experienced by refugees from Germany all over the world.

Betty wrote this letter while making sandwiches for hungry customers in Reinhold's general store. She had brought the stationery she used from Germany: "Betty Scholem, Berlin, Alexandrinenstraße" was printed at the top of the letter paper, followed by fifteen blank lines—the required format for letters to concentration camp prisoners. Betty had originally had the stationery printed for her correspondence with Werner.[2] But she no longer needed it for that purpose. At the end of September she had received the news from her cousin Arthur Hirsch that Werner had died. She had learned of his death but no other details. "I am numb & thoroughly beside myself," she noted then. "I had always firmly believed that he would still be freed, & now this is how 7.5 years of unspeakable misery ends. I cannot find any comfort or solace!"[3]

In Jerusalem, Gershom Scholem learned sometime later what his aunt Käthe Schiepan had reported from Berlin. In his diary he noted: "My brother Werner died in K-C [concentration camp] after 7 years sometime between 8 July, when he wrote a letter to Käthe Schiepan, and 17 July 1940, the day on which she was officially informed in Berlin of his death. More we don't know."[4] Many rumors circulated over the course of the years that followed. Betty once heard that, at the end, her son had held a post as an overseer in the concentration camp and had died in a typhus epidemic. She was relieved to hear this and hoped that his remains had been taken to Berlin and buried in the Scholem family plot.[5]

As in the case of many concentration camp prisoners, the exact circumstances of Werner Scholem's death are still not known. His death certificate states only that "Law Clerk Werner Israel Scholem" died on 17 July 1940 at 11:00 a.m. in Weimar. His personal property card, issued upon arrival at Buchenwald concentration camp, reveals a bit more about the story leading to his death. It mentions that, after having worked nearly two years in the labor group "Fuhrkolonne I" (wagon detail), he was transferred on 5 July 1940, several days before his death, to the "Kolonne Steineträger II" (stone carrier detail) and thus into the infamous quarry. Immediately after the war, the camp community of Buchenwald compiled a "list of the deceased comrades from the district of Berlin-Brandenburg." Werner's name is included in this list followed by the notation "shot while escaping." In post-war Germany, the rumor circulated that he had been shot at the quarry by the SS guards. However, no evidence to support this claim existed.[6]

Since the start of the Second World War, the Buchenwald concentration camp had been considered vital to the war effort, and the work at the Travertin quarry on the southern slope of Etter Mountain was carried out at an exhausting pace. Very few stone carriers in the unit to which Werner had been transferred survived for long. The SS also retaliated against prisoners, often the Jewish ones, in the quarry. Even conflicts within the prisoner community could be fought out there. "Feuds and intrigues within cliques and groups in the camp were settled by sending undesirable persons to the quarry and mistreating them there so long that they ran 'to the guard cordon,' meaning let themselves be shot," recalled Benedikt Kautsky. Purportedly, the camp administration encouraged kapos and prisoners to denounce others from time to time. Furthermore, in the summer of 1940, quite a large number of individual liquidations were also said to have occurred, particularly of prominent political prisoners, usually Jewish.[7]

Many of the murders were committed by two particularly brutal SS men who served in the quarry. One was Eduard Hinkelmann, a man who was always drunk and had fun torturing and mistreating prisoners. He knew Werner Scholem from the Lichtenberg concentration camp.[8] The other, Johann Blank, had been transferred in September 1939 from Dachau to Buchenwald and was the detail commander in the quarry. Kautsky described Blank as a man less interested in torturing prisoners than in shooting them straightaway. Among the numerous murders for which he was responsible was also that of Werner Scholem.[9]

Neither Kautsky nor Eugen Kogon, who wrote another account of Werner's murder, witnessed the incident. According to Kogon's account, Johann Blank, who knew Werner Scholem from Dachau, went with him "on a friendly walk for about ten minutes" and then shot him from the side with a revolver.[10] This version does not make any sense, countered Werner's friend and coprisoner Ernst Federn. Why would a *Hauptscharführer* go walking with a prisoner? Federn had heard another version of the story and was convinced that it was no coincidence that Werner Scholem's liquidation occurred in the same summer in which Leon Trotsky was murdered in Mexico by a Soviet agent. He cited the eyewitness account of a Social Democratic prisoner named Müller, who claimed that "members of the Stalinist prisoner organization in the camp [had] incited the two" guards.[11]

According to Federn, it became clear that something was going on when a long-serving prisoner like Werner Scholem was suddenly assigned to work in the quarry. This was indeed strange, because Scholem had long held the same, relatively privileged spot in the wagon work gang. Apparently, one day a new foreman, another prisoner, was assigned to the detail, a man who did not know Scholem, and he assigned him the much harder task of pulling the wagon. Federn recalled: "As he told me himself, Scholem became so angry that he said: 'One of the political commissars surely got you to do that.' To say this was a terrible mistake, because this foreman had no idea what Scholem meant but reported it immediately to his kapo . . . who was indeed a Stalinist. At any rate, Scholem was ordered to work in the quarry the next day. The assignment of jobs in Buchenwald was in the hands of the Stalinists and served as a decisive instrument of their power in the camp." Supposedly Eduard Hinkelmann arranged to have Werner, a prisoner whom he knew, work at a relatively good spot, which was not only on the periphery of the quarry but also on the periphery of the SS guard cordon. Werner Scholem had been working there a few days when Blank and Hinkelmann "came to him and ordered him to do a job beyond the cordon. Scholem trusted these two, whom he had known so many years. As soon as he was outside the SS guard cordon, Blank shot him. Since he was outside of the cordon, it was therefore said that he was 'shot while attempting to flee.' "[12]

Gershom Scholem expressed doubt about Ernst Federn's story. Emmy had told him back then that she knew from a trusted source that her husband maintained relatively good contact with the activists who had remained in the KPD.[13] This statement contradicts the numerous accounts from Lichtenburg, Dachau, and Buchenwald, in which Werner Scholem was described as an intellectual outsider and loner. Even though the complex mechanisms and structures of camp society have not been fully explained or understood to date, it goes without saying that outsiders had a more difficult time than others.[14] As a prominent figure, Werner Scholem also found himself always in the crosshairs of the SS, which would have made a denunciation from the prisoner ranks unnecessary. Yet there is another possible explanation of his murder. In addition to the Communists with their party fanaticism, Benedikt Kautsky describes criminal prisoners as another group in Buchenwald who had great influence, and he stated that they often denounced people after the war started.[15] In the final analysis, the circumstances that actually led to

Werner Scholem's shooting on that July morning on Etter Mountain remain a mystery.

Like all prisoners murdered in German concentration camps, Werner Scholem has no grave, but he has a tombstone, thanks to his brother Erich.[16] In the early 1960s, Erich had Werner's name inscribed on the stone of the Scholem family grave in the Jewish cemetery at Berlin-Weißensee: "Werner Scholem, born 1895 in Berlin, killed 1942 in Buchenwald." Despite the incorrect date of death, this gesture brought Werner back into the family fold. They are all inscribed there with Werner, on a headstone located at the edge of this oasis of old trees and ivy in the heart of Berlin: Arthur, Betty, Erich, and Gershom Scholem. Just Reinhold's name is missing, as are those of the four Scholem sons' wives. However, the grave itself is nearly empty. Only the remains of Arthur Scholem have rested here since 1925. Like Reinhold, Betty and Erich were buried in Australia. Gershom Scholem also has two tombstones, the second one, under which he is actually buried, is in the Sanhedria Cemetery in what is now an ultra-Orthodox quarter of Jerusalem.

Would Werner have picked this place—the cemetery of Berlin's assimilated Jewish middle class—as the location for his grave? He would probably have preferred to have his name inscribed on the same gravestone as that of his wife. But at which cemetery? A Christian or a Jewish one? In Berlin or Hanover? Emmy Scholem survived her husband by almost exactly thirty years; she died on 14 June 1970. Her grave lies neither in London nor in a Christian cemetery. She was buried at the Jewish cemetery in Bothfeld, a rural neighborhood on the edge of Hanover. She had expressed the wish to have Werner's name also engraved on her tombstone,[17] but only one name marks the small grave: Emmy Scholem.

Names

The night before his death, Werner Scholem appeared to his wife in a dream. Emmy suddenly saw him standing in front of her, then he vanished into thin air. As Gershom Scholem remembers, his sister-in-law could not explain this incident, nor could she forget it. The news of Werner's death probably did not reach Emmy until she received the letter written by her mother-in-law in September 1940. Since mail from Australia sometimes took two months to arrive, Emmy most likely received the news only in October or November.[18]

Seventeen-year-old Renate learned of her father's death by way of the Red Cross while she was in a detention camp on the Isle of Man. Later she described how she experienced that moment: "I felt it as a physical shock, but I couldn't feel emotion. I hardly knew him. Yet for most of my adult life I have felt anger, not just at those who killed him, but almost anger at him for having been killed. Anger because I never had the chance to know him, but perhaps most of all anger that he never knew me."[19] Despite her youth, Renate was detained as an enemy alien in Holloway, a women's prison in London, at the start of the war. With the help of her friend and mentor Naomi Birnberg, she was relocated from there to the Isle of Man in a detention camp containing four thousand women. For eighteen months, she lived in this camp with other Germans, some Nazis, but mainly Jewish refugees from Germany and Austria. Renate, who had grown up under Naomi Birnberg's wing to become a young Jewish Englishwoman, suddenly found herself living among Germans again.[20]

Unlike her sister, Renate had never had any contact with leftist youth organizations. However, on the Isle of Man she encountered the group Freideutsche Jugend. Founded as the compilation of Socialist and Communist youth groups in Prague and Paris, the group in England was popular particularly among the many Jewish children and adolescents who had arrived from Germany with the *Kindertransport*.[21] It was here that Renate again ran into Gebhardt Goldschmidt, a young refugee from Germany whom she had met at the home of the Birnbergs years before. They married in 1941 and, symbolically for their new lives in exile, created a new surname for themselves, Goddard. Thus, the child who had been known as Renate Scholem and Reni Wiechelt became the woman named Renee Goddard, whose identity comprised a complex mixture of German, English, and Jewish elements.[22]

Renee Goddard turned the art of adapting to her situation, which she had developed throughout her childhood when she slipped out of the skin of Reni in Hanover to become Renate in Berlin or vice versa, into her profession: she became an actress.[23] Certainly talent existed in the family. Not only had her father been a great speaker, her uncle was also famous for his theatrical performances at the lectern.[24] Renee turned down an offer to work under the direction of Gustav Gründgens in the devastated Germany of the immediate postwar period. Instead, she started to work in England with a very young and talented director who had been a refugee from Germany like herself, Peter Zadek, who was five years her junior.

FIGURE 36. Renee Goddard, 1955,
in London. Israeli National Library,
Archive Gerhard Scholem.

Renee, whose marriage did not last long, became Zadek's first love. He later described their life together as his *éducation sentimentale*, for Renee elicited awareness in him of his Germanness, his Jewishness, and especially his anarchist nature. She played her greatest roles with him, such as Portia in *The Merchant of Venice*, and toured with him all over Great Britain.[25]

In 1954 she played the role of the Jewish Fräulein Landauer in a London production of John Van Druten's play *I Am a Camera*, adapted from Christopher Isherwood's *Berlin Stories*. In order to speak with a Berlin accent, she imitated the English of her uncle Gerhard. Over the course of her life, Renee was married four times and had two children, whom she raised in part on her own. She lived in Berlin and Munich and spent some time in Israel, where she helped to set up national television at the end of the 1960s. From acting she switched to theater management and finally to the scriptwriting department for British television.[26]

Werner Scholem was informed of the marriage of his oldest daughter Edith in September 1939. Edith also lived in the world of theater: her husband, Eric Capon, taught acting and directing and later became the director of the prep school of the Royal Academy of Dramatic Art in London. Edith had two children and ran a summer school for young actors together with her husband. She also spent several years of her life in Berlin.[27] The fiftieth

FIGURE 37. Edith Capon (left)
with her two children and Emmy
Scholem, ca, 1946, in England.
Israeli National Library, Archive
Gerhard Scholem.

anniversary of the year 1933 stirred many memories for Edith Capon, and
for the first time she truly mourned the loss of her father. Throughout their
lives, both Edith and her mother had felt guilty about Werner Scholem's
death. In 1983, a few years before her death, Edith agreed to be interviewed
about her childhood and her adventurous escape to England.[28]

Edith and Renee maintained a good relationship with their uncle Gershom Scholem and his second wife, Fania. They would meet in Switzerland
(in Ascona or Sils Maria), London, Munich, or Israel. He was the Jewish
authority of the family, and when Renee's daughter began to take an interest in the topic as a teenager, he gave her literature that he hoped would
"fill in several nooks and corners of [her] missing Jewish education." When
Gershom Scholem published his autobiography in 1978 and dedicated it to
his brother Werner, he meant this also as a gesture to his nieces, who
learned about their father's youth from it. Gershom's correspondence and
diaries, published posthumously since the 1980s, revealed a great deal of
information about the family's history to Renee Goddard, things she had
not known about.[29]

Little is known about Emmy Scholem during the period immediately
following her husband's death. She had been unemployed since the beginning of the war and lived with Edith and her family. Before Betty Scholem
fled from Germany, she sent a suitcase full of linens and another with the
Scholem family silver to Emmy's mother in Hanover. The Wiechelts hid

the valuables in their garden plot and brought it all to England after the war.[30] Besides Werner's photo album and his letters from the concentration camp, the contents of these suitcases were the only mementos that remained of Emmy's life in Germany. After Werner died, Emmy continued to receive letters from her now nearly blind mother-in-law in Australia. Betty asked her to write and send news about herself and the girls, but Emmy was a sporadic correspondent. In May 1946, Betty died at the age of eighty in Australian exile, where she had never been happy.[31]

In August 1949, Emmy Scholem finally received her long-awaited British citizenship and thus official permission to run a business of her own.[32] Together with a friend, she took over a London restaurant in 1952, which she later had to give up because of a long-term illness. She then visited the health resort in the German town of Bad Mergentheim and, following other visits to Hanover, decided to return to Germany.[33] In the autumn of 1958, she moved to Bad Wimpfen on the Neckar River, where she could afford a large apartment in a nice part of town. She found this to be an excellent solution, because the rent was low and the small spa town offered everything that she appeared to need for her poor health. When her family predicted she would not last long there, the sixty-year-old dismissed their skepticism: she was looking for peace and quiet and felt too old for relatives and friends.[34]

However, she did enjoy visitors in quiet Bad Wimpfen, among whom were old comrades like Rosa Meyer-Leviné and Alexandra Ramm-Pfemfert. The latter, who was the translator of Trotsky's writings, considered moving to Bad Wimpfen with her sister Maria during the Berlin Crisis of 1958. In the end they decided against it because the small resort town was simply too tranquil and remote for them.[35]

Emmy Scholem decided to return to Germany primarily for practical reasons. Her business undertakings in England had never been very successful. She had no pension, nor could she expect any comparable support from the British government. Back in Germany she applied for restitution from the German government both for herself and her murdered husband. She claimed to be penniless and—as a result of her imprisonment in 1933, her escape to England, and her life there in exile—occupationally disabled. After a twelve-year-long legal process, she finally reached an agreement with the government of Lower Saxony. In addition to several one-time payments, she received a pension from which she could more or less live well.[36]

Emmy held out for five years in Bad Wimpfen, then she moved to Hanover—not to Linden but to Bult, on the east side of the city. There she lived in a Jewish retirement home, for which she did the bookkeeping and even took on administrative duties for a while. The home had been established by Holocaust survivors and is still located on property adjacent to the community center and the synagogue. At the time, the Jewish community in Hanover consisted of only a few Germans, a couple of Israelis, and primarily Polish Jews. Many community members had non-Jewish spouses who were integrated into community life and even buried in the Jewish cemetery. As a co-opted member of the community, Emmy Scholem was respected and reported that she led a happy life. In the winter of 1967, she told her family that she had moved in with her neighbor Ernst Hanff. The widower was several years younger than she, and the two of them shared an apartment in which they each had a space of their own. "I do not want to marry (at 70!); I am fused with the name Scholem, I will remain Scholem." However, as a matter of respectability, she asked that letters be addressed from that point on to Emmy Scholem-Hanff.[37]

Emmy Scholem lived in an almost exclusively Jewish world. Her only major non-Jewish contact was with her half sister, who still lived in Hanover. Emmy frequently made plans to visit her brother-in-law and his wife, Fania, in Jerusalem, trips that never materialized because of her poor health. She told Gershom that she was convinced she could "only live in a Jewish community" in "present-day Germany."[38] She did not find it necessary to explain why she thought so, but it was obviously due to anti-Semitism and signs of German nationalism, both old and new.[39]

Nevertheless, Gershom Scholem expressed surprise upon receiving a letter from Emmy in April 1968, in which she wrote that she had converted to Judaism with the help of Zvi Asaria, the chief rabbi of Lower Saxony. She said that she had prepared herself extensively and had been tested and "accepted with full ceremony." The only requirement from which the rabbi had exempted her, as an old woman, was to learn Hebrew. As is tradition in such cases, Emmy was to adopt a Jewish name, and she decided on Miriam, the name of the prophetess and sister of Moses, who returned with the Israelites from Egyptian exile.[40] The years of British exile and the persecution and murder of her husband had brought Emmy Scholem closer to Judaism. She had returned to Germany, but she only felt at home in a Jewish-Polish-Israeli Germany.

FIGURE 38. Emmy Scholem with her brother-in-law Gershom Scholem, Pforzheim, 1969, at the ceremony awarding him the Reuchlin Prize. Stadtarchiv Pforzheim, Sign. S1-17-1-1969-10g. Photographer: E. Bischoff.

In his memoirs, Gershom Scholem recalled a conversation with his sister-in-law on the topic of conversion: "Who could describe my astonishment when many years later, in the 1960s, she asked me: 'Why didn't Werner bring me into the Jewish fold?' I replied: 'But the two of you were Communists, and he left the Jewish fold just as you left the Church!' 'No matter,' she said with a naiveté that I never understood but that protected her all her life. 'It would have been the right thing to do.' One year before her death she converted to Judaism because she wanted at least to be buried among Jews."[41] Actually, back in the summer of 1916, the young Emmy Wiechelt had announced her willingness to convert to Judaism, a step she did not view as contradicting the ideology she and Werner embraced. This might testify to naïveté, but it also points to the potential for political and personal utopias that existed for a short time during the Great War.

Emmy remained in close contact with Gershom and Fania Scholem until her death. Though they were extremely different, she and Gershom had always held each other in high esteem. Their friendship dated back to

1918, and they shared not only memories of Werner but also of their youth and the dreams and goals that had united or divided them. In response to the student revolts of the late 1960s, Emmy reflected on the past visions of Communism and Zionism and summed up their youth in what was both a nostalgic and hopeful letter to her brother-in-law:

> How devoutly and courageously we set out to achieve our ideals, you, yours and we, ours. It would have been so much easier to accept the sacrifice if we had been successful. Oh, great successes were achieved, however not those that we wanted or expected. These already seemed to us to be strange and unwelcome successes when Werner was still alive, when we could see the beginning of these successes. A new youth appears to be developing. Perhaps one day this youth will pursue the path that we followed and perhaps our grandchildren and great-grandchildren will then continue to fight where we were defeated.[42]

Who Is a Jew?

"Who is a Jew?" In 1958, Israeli prime minister David Ben-Gurion posed this question to fifty Jewish intellectuals (not including Gershom Scholem). On the tenth anniversary of the founding of the state of Israel, the Israeli parliament debated the subject in connection with the Law of Return: Should children of non-Jewish mothers receive the right to immigrate to the state of Israel even if they were not Jews according to religious law? Since this political question included religious, social, and philosophical aspects, Ben-Gurion directed it to "Jewish sages" inside and outside of the country.[43]

One morning in August 1959, Gershom Scholem read about the answers given by his colleagues in the Israeli daily newspaper *Ha-Boker*, and the very same day he sent a dissenting letter to the editor. The question reminded him of Leopold Bloom, the protagonist in James Joyce's novel *Ulysses*; he wrote: "This character is, in fact, Jewish 'only' in the eyes of the author, in the eyes of his Irish surroundings—and in the eyes of all the readers (the undersigned included). In the eyes of the 'Jewish sages' . . . however, he is not a Jew at all as [he], the son of a Jewish father and a non-Jewish mother, was raised entirely as a non-Jew, and lives entirely as a non-Jew. Nevertheless, everyone considers him a Jew."[44] Referring to this letter several years ago, the Israeli historian Joseph Gorny proposed the model of the "historical Jew" as an alternative, scholarly concept. Borrowing from Scholem's remarks on Leopold Bloom, he argued that anyone should be considered a "historical Jew" who, on the basis of collective historical experience and memory, could be assigned to a Jewish realm of experience.[45]

Gorny's model has been used here insofar as this book presents the protagonists within the networks of their families, friends, comrades, and political opponents. Some of these "historical Jews" did not feel like Jews at all, while others, who were not Jewish according to Jewish religious law, still considered themselves part of the Jewish people as a community of experience. Like many other Communists of Jewish background, Werner Scholem replaced his self-image as a German Jew with a universalistic identity as utopian political revolutionary. However, the more he purged his self-image of Jewish elements, the more he was regarded as Jewish by others. Meanwhile, his wife and daughters, who had lived in a primarily non-Jewish environment while in Germany, drew closer to the Jewish world during their British exile and integrated elements of its culture in their own complex identities. What role Communism, Socialism, and Judaism played in the various phases of the protagonists' lives is therefore a key question, which runs like a common thread throughout this book.[46]

For quite a long time, no systematic study has existed on the often highly tragic connection between Judaism and Communism. Neither Jewish Communists nor historians of Jewish history were willing to tackle this politically and emotionally explosive subject,[47] contaminated to no small degree by National Socialist propaganda about the threat of a "Jewish-Bolshevik global conspiracy." The fact that Jews were disproportionately represented among Communists continues to preoccupy historians,[48] although other ethnic minorities were also overrepresented in the Communist movement, and the number of Jewish Communists decreased after a Communist party and regime were established. Notwithstanding, many Jewish Communists have been singled out as scapegoats and described as self-hating renegades against their origins.[49]

Isaac Deutscher, the British historian and biographer of Trotsky, confronted the problematic subject of Communist Jews back in 1958, the same year Ben-Gurion asked his question about Jewish identity after the Holocaust and in the state of Israel. Deutscher presented the concept of the "non-Jewish Jew" to the World Jewish Congress. He refused to accept the view then widely accepted in Jewish historiography that Communist Jews had removed themselves from the Jewish world and therefore should not be the subject of research in the field of Jewish studies.[50] Deutscher, a Jewish Jew who became, in his terms, a non-Jewish Jew, was fascinated by this exposed and vulnerable movement, motivated by longing for universal solidarity, toward change in a society in motion, in which anything seemed possible. Close examination shows that the path of each non-Jewish Jew was highly individual, making it virtually impossible to generalize about them as a group.[51] Consequently, most studies of non-Jewish Jews take the form of biography, which is the only way to do justice to their complex paths in life, their identities, and their fates.

Gershom Scholem undertook a project similar to that of Isaac Deutscher, although the two scholars could not have been more different. In 1973, the English translation of Scholem's major work on the Jewish heretic Sabbatai Zevi, the false messiah of the seventeenth century, was published, with a new preface by the author.[52] In this short text, he declared, as he had done previously, that he did not adhere to the school of thought that assumed the existence of "a well-defined and unvarying 'essence' of Judaism," particularly not in cases "where the evaluation of historical events is concerned."[53] In his opinion, the essence of Judaism could only be addressed in historical context and therefore had to be interrogated time and again. At the same time, Scholem pointed out the high price that the Jewish people had paid for the messianic ideology—and he did not mean this just in reference to the followers of Sabbatai Zevi: "Anyone who can appreciate the gravity of this problem will also understand why I have refrained from expressing opinions or drawing conclusions with respect to any contemporary issues bound to arise out of the subject matter with which this book deals."[54] At the time, he watched with some concern the student movement and the American New Left, in which Jews were conspicuously present. However, his observations were directed less to this group, whose future was still not known, than to the fateful sympathy that young Jews had felt for radical leftist utopias in the first half of the twentieth century.[55] He compared the numerous young Jewish Communists with the followers of Sabbatai Zevi and noted that even his brother and his friend Walter Benjamin had been victims of a "secular messianism," which, he admitted, had also fascinated him for a while. Messianism in the political context could only end disastrously, argued Scholem, but no one had wanted to heed this warning.[56] Gershom Scholem had redirected his own political interest in this topic into scholarly research on messianic currents and heresies, which he understood as also being a warning against the appeal of the messianic.[57] He used the concept of secular messianism to draw his friend and his brother back into the Jewish world. In other words, he extended the boundaries of the Jewish realm of experience through his research so far as, ultimately, to include the fate of Jewish Communists as well.

At first glance the term "secular messianism" does not appear to be very applicable to Werner Scholem, unlike Walter Benjamin. Werner did not demonstrate an interest in contemporary debates on the topic, nor had he been raised in Jewish religion and tradition, as had many Jewish Communists in eastern Europe. On the contrary, his Jewish education was limited to the highly rudimentary and very patriotically imbued German education of the Samson School. In the context of Jewish tradition and religion, Golo Mann notes that there was "nothing typically Jewish in revolutionary attitudes and practices."[58] However, if it is argued as Yuri Slezkine does, that the Jews embodied the characteristics, social practices, and horizons of experience of modernism in twentieth-century Europe, then Jewish revolutionaries must also be placed in this context.[59] Being alert to what they saw as a historical moment offering unprecedented political possibilities, they would have to have asked, as Gershom Scholem wrote in 1946: "Do we now face a unique opportunity to change the history of a people which has consisted entirely of failures, of possibility, of the problem of the future—into one of making a life in the present?!" This is the thinking that Gershom Scholem attributed to his brother and his friend, when they made their life choices.[60]

Werner Scholem's biography is a tale that is equally Jewish and German. He could not have known, of course, how tragically the story would end when he decided to devote his life to the German revolution. Paradoxically, both despite and as a result of the traumatic experience of the First World War, he was convinced that he had to find a way where others before him—particularly his father—had failed. Tragically, Werner was very similar to his father. What assimilation had been for the elder, rebellion was for the younger man. What they shared was faith in and loyalty to Germany, despite everything. Was the ideology of the Jewish revolutionaries, as the historian Werner E. Mosse wrote, "the extreme form of Jewish assimilation made possible by progressive liberal ideology"?[61] Gershom Scholem, who rejected this ideology, analyzed the self-deception in which the German Jewish middle class lived in a manner that can be applied astonishingly well

FIGURE 39. Gershom Scholem in Ascona, 1970s. Israeli National Library,
Archive Gerhard Scholem.

to his brother: "Looking back today, I am more firmly convinced than I
could have been in my youth, when I was swept away by the passions of
protest, that for many people illusion merged with utopia, and the anticipa-
tion of feeling at home gave them a happiness which was genuine to the
extent that every utopia must be credited with genuineness. . . . The more
enchanting the dream, the more shocking the awakening."[62]

In April 1981, Gershom Scholem received what can be seen as a final
obituary for his brother. The sociologist Alfred Laurence wrote him a letter
saying that he had long known and valued Gershom Scholem's work, but
that he had only recently learned that Gershom was Werner Scholem's
brother. In 1936 and 1937, he and Laurence had been friends in the Lichtenburg and Dachau concentration camps. He recalled "long conversations
with him" and had been mourning "him and many other common friends

for more than forty years now. So today I write to you in my melancholy and conviction that you also often think about this clever, dear, and steadfast man, who had to die far too young."[63] A few months later, Gershom Scholem himself died on 21 February 1982 in Jerusalem. In his obituary, the German literary critic Walter Boehlich also mentioned the German Jewish politician Scholem: "His brother Werner took another path and became a Communist; what was for him a social problem was for Gershom a religious one; he was murdered. As embodied by these two men, the two types of Jew, the 'non-Jewish' and the Jewish, confronted each other unreconciled."[64] Did—do—the non-Jewish and Jewish Jews continue to confront one another unreconciled? The biography of Werner Scholem contradicts this idea in every respect, as does this book.

NOTES

Prologue

1. Copy of the marriage certificate, IPW, Nachlass Scholem.

2. On Emmy Wiechelt's revocation of church membership, see field postcard from Werner Scholem to Gerhard Scholem, 12 Aug. 1917, INL, Archive G. Scholem.

3. Emmy Scholem to Gerhard Scholem, 5 Feb. 1918, INL, Archive G. Scholem. According to Renee Goddard, Emmy's parents were also not happy about their son-in-law because he was Jewish, middle class, and had been previously convicted. Goddard, "Erinnerungen," chap. 1, version 3, PRG.

4. Gershom Scholem, *From Berlin to Jerusalem*, 31; Werner Scholem to Gerhard Scholem, 22 Aug. 1917, INL, Archive G. Scholem.

5. Werner so quotes his uncle in a letter to Gerhard Scholem, 23 Oct. 1918, INL, Archive G. Scholem.

6. Testament of Arthur Scholem, 24 Sept. 1921, IPW, Nachlass Scholem.

7. Werner Scholem to Gerhard Scholem, 22 Aug. 1917, INL, Archive G. Scholem.

8. Gerhard Scholem began in 1917 to sign his letters occasionally as "Gerschom" or "Gershom"; see, for example, Gershom Scholem, *Briefe*, 1:68. He did not take the final step of legally changing his name until he immigrated to Palestine, which is the point used in this book to distinguish between the use of the names "Gerhard" and "Gershom."

9. Scholem, *From Berlin to Jerusalem*, 6, 16–20; Betty Scholem, in Scholem and Scholem, *Mutter und Sohn im Briefwechsel*, 529.

10. See Kerr, *Mein Berlin*.

11. Scholem, *From Berlin to Jerusalem*, 9; Gershom Scholem, *"Es gibt ein Geheimnis in der Welt,"* 55.

12. Betty Scholem, in Scholem and Scholem, *Mutter und Sohn im Briefwechsel*, 527–531.

13. Wreschner, *Die Reproduktion und Assoziation von Vorstellungen*, 29–30.

14. Scholem, "Es gibt ein Geheimnis in der Welt," 52; Scholem, *From Berlin to Jerusalem*, 3.

15. Scholem, *From Berlin to Jerusalem*, 36, 45; *Reichstagshandbuch, 2. Wahlperiode 1924*, 516.

16. Lässig, *Jüdische Wege ins Bürgertum*, 607–608, 621–622; Berg, *Jüdische Schulen in Niedersachsen*, 79–82, 123, 257–258.

17. Berg, *Jüdische Schulen in Niedersachsen*, 231; *Die Samsonschule in Wolfenbüttel. Realschule und Erziehungsanstalt mit Berechtigung für den einjährig-freiwilligen Militärdienst*, 13.

18. Scholem, *From Berlin to Jerusalem*, 32.

19. Samsonschule (Realschule) zu Wolfenbüttel, *Berichte . . . 1907–1908 bis 1910–1911*.

20. Scholem, *From Berlin to Jerusalem*, 6, 9, 31.

21. Ibid., 21–22.

22. For example, Walter Hasenclever's play *Der Sohn* (The Son) had already been published in 1914. Gay, *Die Republik der Außenseiter*, 152–153; Hans Mommsen, "Generationenkonflikt und politische Entwicklung," 116.

23. On 29 Dec. 1910, Arthur Scholem donated a sum to the "Witwen- und Waisenkasse" (Widow and Orphans Fund) of the Samsonschule. Samsonschule (Realschule) zu Wolfenbüttel, *Bericht . . . 1907–1908 bis 1910–1911*.

24. Shavit, "On the Hebrew Cultural Center in Berlin in the Twenties," 372.

25. Scholem, *From Berlin to Jerusalem*, 41; on the Jung Juda, see also Weiner, "Gershom Scholem and the Jung Juda Youth Group in Berlin."

26. Scholem, *From Berlin to Jerusalem*, 43–44; Scholem, "Es gibt ein Geheimnis in der Welt," 58, 61.

27. Scholem, *From Berlin to Jerusalem*, 41. He remained a member of the Young Social Democrats until 1916. *Reichstagshandbuch, 3. Wahlperiode 1924*, 351.

28. Scholem, *From Berlin to Jerusalem*, 41.

29. Scholem, "Es gibt ein Geheimnis in der Welt," 52, 58–60; Gerhard Scholem to the executive board of the Agudat Israel, 19 Oct. 1914, in Scholem, *Briefe*, 1:3.

30. Scholem, *From Berlin to Jerusalem*, 42; Betty Scholem to Gershom Scholem, 27 March 1933, in Scholem and Scholem, *Mutter und Sohn im Briefwechsel*, 287.

31. Gerhard Scholem, diary entry from 18 Feb. 1913, in Scholem, *Tagebücher*, 1:11.

32. Werner Scholem to Betty Scholem, 24 Nov. 1914, INL, Archive G. Scholem; the street name of the former Leopoldstrasse today is Johannssenstrasse.

33. Baedeker, *Hannover und die deutsche Nordseeküste*, 45.

34. Rabe, *Linden*, 32.

35. Ibid., 27, 34; see also the film *Linden: Ein Arbeiterlied*.

36. Werner Scholem to Gerhard Scholem, 14 Nov. 1914, INL, Archive G. Scholem; Werner Scholem to Betty Scholem, 2 Oct. 1938, IPW, Nachlass Scholem.

37. Emil Voigt, who was a bank director in Hildesheim and later in Berlin, had a small payment sent to Emma Rock every month. Yet when her daughter wanted to contact her biological father in 1914 and ask him to financially support her training, Emma Rock refused to give her daughter his address. Werner to Gerhard Scholem, 14 Nov. 1914, INL, Archive G. Scholem.

38. Stadtarchiv Braunschweig, birth register entry for Emma Johanne Wilhelmine Rock; Goddard and Glendinnig, *Reni and the Brownshirts* [radio play transcript], 9; Goddard, "Erinnerungen," chap. "Missionaries," PRG.

39. Goddard, "Erinnerungen," chap. "Missionaries," PRG; Werner Scholem to Gerhard Scholem, 14 Nov. 1914, INL, Archive G. Scholem, and 22 Sept. 1914, in Scholem, *Briefe*, 1:15; Antrag auf Grund des Bundesergänzungsgesetzes Emmy Scholem, NLA, vol. 1, appendix 1, "Schilderung des Verfolgungsvorganges," 7 Apr. 1954, p. 1; *Reichstagshandbuch, 3. Wahlperiode 1924*, 351.

40. Werner Scholem to Gerhard Scholem, 14 Nov. 1914, INL, Archive G. Scholem, and 22 Sept.1914, in Scholem, *Briefe*, 1:15.

41. Werner Scholem to Gerhard Scholem, 14 Nov. 1914, INL, Archive G. Scholem, Beuthstrasse was the Berlin address for the printing business of A. Scholem.

42. Scholem, *From Berlin to Jerusalem*, 30–31.

43. Werner Scholem to Gerhard Scholem, 14 Nov. 1914, INL, Archive G. Scholem. "Wir brauchen keine Schwiegermama" (We need no mama-in-law) was a popular tune in Berlin around 1900.

44. Goddard and Glendinnig, *Reni and the Brownshirts*, 9.

45. Gerhard Scholem, diary entry from 18 Feb. 1913, in Scholem, *Tagebücher*, 1:11.

46. Werner Scholem to Gershom Scholem, 23 Mar. 1931, INL, Archive G. Scholem.

47. Atina Grossmann, *Reforming Sex*, 4–6.

48. Enzensberger, *The Silences of Hammerstein*, 161.

49. Weißgerber, *Giftige Worte der SED-Diktatur*, 335.

50. Broszat, introduction to a lecture given by Gershom Scholem on 15 Mar. 1973, IfZ.

51. Hortzschansky et al., *Ernst Thälmann*, 200, 231, 239, 245, 266, 280–281.

52. Zilkenat, "Das Schicksal von Werner Scholem."

53. Zadoff and Zadoff, "From Mission to Memory."

54. Scholem and Scholem, *Mutter und Sohn im Briefwechsel*; Shedletzky, "Einleitung," 10.

55. Woolf, "The Art of Biography," 125.

56. Braun, *Stille Post*, 51.

57. IPW, Nachlass Scholem.

58. Interview with Edith Capon, PRG; Goddard, "Erinnerungen," chap. "Edith's Story," PRG.

59. Interview with Renee Goddard, 18 June 2006, PMZ; Goddard, "Erinnerungen," chaps. "Prologue" and "My Father," PRG; Renee Goddard to Gershom Scholem, undated [1976], INL, Archive G. Scholem; Völter, *Judentum und Kommunismus*, 34.

60. The album is located in the private archive of Renee Goddard.

61. Robert Louis Stevenson to Edmund Gosse, 10 June 1893, in Stevenson, *The Letters*, 8:104; Seymour, "Shaping the Truth," 253.

62. Seymour, "Shaping the Truth," 253; Bourdieu, "Die biographische Illusion."

63. Kinkead-Weekes, "Writing Lives Forwards," 235, 251–252.

64. For example by Maurois, "Die Biographie als Kunstwerk"; and Woolf, "The Art of Biography."

65. Lässig, "Biography in Modern History"; Tuchman, "Biography as a Prism of History"; Kershaw, "Biography and the Historian"; Berghahn, "Structuralism and Biography."

66. Scholem and Tsur, "An Interview," 25–26.

1. Two Utopias Seated at One Table

1. Scholem, *From Berlin to Jerusalem*, 17–18; Shedletzky, "Einleitung," 10; Scholem and Scholem, *Mutter und Sohn im Briefwechsel*, 528.

2. Scholem, *From Berlin to Jerusalem*, 22–24.

3. *Bekoved* (*bekowed*), Yiddish, meaning "honorably, with honor."

4. Yiddish, Magen David, Star of David.

5. *Schekelblätter*: contributions to the Jewish National Fund. Scholem, "Ex Oriente Lux," 114.

6. What is actually being said is "tefillin."

7. Scholem, "Ex Oriente Lux," 115–116.

8. Theobald and Hedwig Scholem did not arrive in Palestine until 1938, and then as refugees fleeing the Nazi regime. Gershom Scholem, *Von Berlin nach Jerusalem*, 29; the

reference is only found in the extended Hebrew and German editions, not in the English translation of this book, *From Berlin to Jerusalem*.

9. Scholem, *Von Berlin nach Jerusalem*, 201.

10. Ernst Jünger to Gershom Scholem, 16 Feb. 1975, INL, Archive G. Scholem; published in *Sinn und Form* 61, no. 3 (2009): 293–302; Triendl and Zadoff, "Ob mein Bruder Werner gemeint ist?"; Triendl-Zadoff, "Der unsichtbare Bruder."

11. *Scharfjüdisch* can roughly be translated here as "angular Jewish" (face). It was a word tinged with anti-Semitism and used in Jünger and Scholem's youth. Therefore it is an interesting choice of words that Scholem makes in his letter to Jünger, a writer known in his early years for his right-wing nationalist views and glorification of the First World War. Jünger was not, however, a supporter of the Nazis. Gershom Scholem to Ernst Jünger, 8 Apr. 1975, INL, Archive G. Scholem.

12. Ernst Jünger to Gershom Scholem, 20 Apr. 1975, INL, Archive G. Scholem.

13. Gershom Scholem to Ernst Jünger, 28 Apr. 1975, INL, Archive G. Scholem.

14. Ernst Jünger to Gershom Scholem, 21 June 1976, INL, Archive G. Scholem.

15. Gershom Scholem to Ernst Jünger, 3 July 1976, INL, Archive G. Scholem.

16. Gershom Scholem to Ernst Jünger, 17 May 1981, INL, Archive G. Scholem.

17. Ernst Jünger to Gershom Scholem, 1 June 1981, INL, Archive G. Scholem.

18. Scholem, *Von Berlin nach Jerusalem*, 46–47.

19. Jünger, "Siebzig verweht V," 181.

20. Ibid., 182–183.

21. Ibid., 181.

22. Jünger, "SP.R. Drei Schulwege," 747.

23. Jünger, "Siebzig verweht V," 181–182.

24. Schwilk, *Ernst Jünger*, 86–90.

25. Jünger, "Siebzig verweht V," 182.

26. Ernst Jünger to Gershom Scholem, 20 Apr. 1975, INL, Archive G. Scholem.

27. Miller, *Burgfrieden und Klassenkampf*, 45.

28. Nettl, *Rosa Luxemburg*, 574–575.

29. Laschitza, *Im Lebensrausch, trotz allem*, 464–466; Laschitza, *Die Liebknechts*, 231–232.

30. Laschitza, *Die Liebknechts*, 235–238.

31. Grotjahn, *Erlebtes und Erstrebtes*, 154.

32. Scholem, *From Berlin to Jerusalem*, 19, 51.

33. Betty Scholem, in Scholem and Scholem, *Mutter und Sohn im Briefwechsel*, 530; Gerhard Scholem, diary entry from 17 Aug. 1914, in Scholem, *Tagebücher*, vol. 1, 29.

34. Scholem, *Walter Benjamin*, 6.

35. Rosenthal, *"Die Ehre des jüdischen Soldaten,"* 40–46.

36. Seventy-eight percent of the Jewish soldiers fought on the front. Duker, *Jews in World War I*, 4; Mendes-Flohr, "Im Schatten des Weltkrieges," 17; Löwe, "Feinde ringsum!," 343.

37. Scholem, *Von Berlin nach Jerusalem*, 65.

38. The letters by Werner Scholem are probably not extant, and we possess only Gerhard Scholem's answer, dated 7 Sept. 1914, in Scholem, *Briefe*, 1:3–6; Scholem, *"Es gibt ein Geheimnis in der Welt,"* 64.

39. Gerhard Scholem, "Jüdische Jugendbewegung," in Scholem, *Tagebücher*, 2:101–106.

40. Brenner, "From Self-Declared Messiah to Scholar of Messianism."

41. Gerhard Scholem to Werner Scholem, 7 Sept. 1914, in Scholem, *Briefe*, 1:3.

42. Scholem, *From Berlin to Jerusalem*, 50–56.

43. The Erfurt Program was the party program of the SPD adopted in 1891 and valid until 1921; Gerhard Scholem to Werner Scholem, 7 Sept. 1914, in Scholem, *Briefe*, 1:3–6.

44. Jacobson, *Metaphysics of the Profane*, 54–55; Scholem, *Von Berlin nach Jerusalem*, 60; Zadoff, *Gershom Scholem*, chap. 3.

45. Gerhard Scholem to Werner Scholem, 7 Sept. 1914, in Scholem, *Briefe*, 1:5–6. Hasidism became known in Germany through the renarrations of Martin Buber: *Die Geschichten des Rabbi Nachman* (1906; *The Tales of Rabbi Nachman*) and *Die Legende des Baalschem* (1908; *The Legend of Baal-Schem*); see also Mendes-Flohr: *Divided Passions*, 85–86, 88–107.

46. Werner Scholem to Gerhard Scholem, 8 Sept. 1914, in Scholem, *Briefe*, 1:6–7.

47. Ibid., 7–10.

48. Ibid., 10.

49. Gerhard Scholem to Werner Scholem, 13 Sept. 1914, in Scholem, *Briefe*, 1:10–13; Zadoff, *Gershom Scholem*, chap. 1.

50. *Rachmonus* (Yiddish): compassion, deserving pity; Marxist-Zionist party: Poale Zion. Gerhard Scholem to Werner Scholem, 13 Sept. 1914, in Scholem, *Briefe*, 1:13.

51. Werner Scholem to Gerhard Scholem, 22 Sept. 1914, in Scholem, *Briefe*, 1:14–15.

52. Werner Scholem to Gerhard Scholem, 14 Nov. 1914, INL, Archive G. Scholem.

53. Gerhard Scholem, diary entry from 15 Nov. 1914, in Scholem, *Tagebücher*, 1:44–45.

54. Aschheim, "German Jews Beyond 'Bildung' and Liberalism," 31–44.

55. This religious holiday, known in Germany as Buß- und Bettag, is a day of repentance and prayer celebrated by some Protestant churches in November.

56. Werner Scholem to Betty Scholem, 24 Nov. 1914, INL, Archive G. Scholem.

57. Ibid.; Gerhard Scholem, diary entry from 21 Nov. 1914, in Scholem, *Tagebücher*, 1:58.

58. Werner Scholem to Gerhard Scholem, 2 Dec. 1914, INL, Archive G. Scholem.

59. Ibid.

60. Laschitza, *Im Lebensrausch, trotz allem*, 250–259.

61. Gerhard Scholem, diary entry from 4 Dec. 1914, in Scholem, *Tagebücher*, 1:70–71.

62. Gerhard Scholem, diary entry from 9 Dec. 1914, in Scholem, *Tagebücher*, 1:75; on the bookseller Rogon, see Werner Scholem to Gerhard Scholem, 8 Sept. 1914, in Scholem, *Briefe*, 1:10.

63. *Rishes*, a Yiddish term for anti-Semitism, from the Hebrew *rish'ut*, malice or wickedness. Werner Scholem to Gerhard Scholem, 2 Jan. 1915, INL, Archive G. Scholem.

64. Ibid.

65. Gerhard Scholem to Werner Scholem, 5 and 17 Jan. 1915, INL, Archive G. Scholem.

66. Luisenstädtisches Realgymnasium in Berlin, *Bericht über das Schuljahr 1914–1915*, 21; on the fact that this school had been attended by the Scholem brothers, their father, and their three uncles, see Betty Scholem, in Scholem and Scholem, *Mutter und Sohn im Briefwechsel*, 529.

67. Scholem, *Tagebücher*, 1:79 n. 18 and 133 n. 46; Scholem, *From Berlin to Jerusalem*, 52; Scholem, *Walter Benjamin*, 15; Falkenberg, *Geschichte der deutschen Arbeiterjugendbewegung*, 104; Scholze, "Karl Liebknecht," 1019, 1024; Luban, "Die Auswirkungen der Jenaer Jugendkonferenz 1916," 218; Kerff, *Karl Liebknecht*, 210; Wünsch, *Neukölln*, 17; *Die Internationale: Eine Zeitschrift für Praxis und Theorie des Marxismus* (1915). At the Hasenheide the brothers met the young poet and active oppositionist Bruno Schönlank, whose father had

turned the *Leipziger Volksblatt* into a major SPD publication and named his earlier protégée Rosa Luxemburg to be his successor there. The grandfather had been both cantor and teacher at the Jewish school. Nettl, *Rosa Luxemburg*, 187–188.

68. Gerhard Scholem, diary entries from 20, 23, 27, and 31 Jan. 1915, in Scholem, *Tagebücher*, 1:79–85, 88; Scholem, *Von Berlin nach Jerusalem*, 76; quote from Treml, "Between Utopia and Redemption," 85. On Orientalism, see Mendes-Flohr, *Divided Passions*, 81–132.

69. Gerhard Scholem, diary entry from 2 Feb. 1915, in Scholem, *Tagebücher*, 1:88.

70. It appeared on 5 Feb. 1915 in the *Jüdische Rundschau: Allgemeine Jüdische Zeitung* 20 (1915): 6, 46–47. Heinrich Margulies (1890–1989) immigrated in 1925 to Israel and became the director of the Anglo-Palestine Bank.

71. Scholem, *Tagebücher*, 1:89–90; facsimile of the letter in *Gershom Scholem (1897– 1982)*, 16; Scholem, *From Berlin to Jerusalem*, 60–61; Gerhard Scholem to Harry Heymann, 28 Dec. 1917, in Scholem, *Briefe*, 1:133; Gerhard Scholem to Martin Buber, 10 July 1916, in Buber, *Briefwechsel aus sieben Jahrzehnten*, 446.

72. Gerhard Scholem to Martin Buber, 10 July 1916, in Buber, *Briefwechsel aus sieben Jahrzehnten*, 446–447; Luisenstädtisches Realgymnasium in Berlin, *Bericht über das Schuljahr 1914–1915*, 20; The file on the disciplinary proceedings for the case of Gerhard Scholem could not be found in the inventory of the Provinzialschulkollegium (Landeshauptarchiv Brandenburg).

73. Scholem, *From Berlin to Jerusalem*, 62–63; Betty Scholem, in Scholem and Scholem, *Mutter und Sohn im Briefwechsel*, 531; Scholem, *Walter Benjamin*, 15.

74. Gerhard Scholem, diary entry from 27 Mar. 1915, in Scholem, *Tagebücher*, 1:96.

75. Brenner, *Jüdische Kultur in der Weimarer Republik*, 58–61; Biale, *Gershom Scholem*, 13; Weidner, *Gershom Scholem*, 63–65.

76. Luisenstädtisches Realgymnasium in Berlin, *Bericht über das Schuljahr 1914– 1915*, 20.

77. Gerhard Scholem, diary entries from 24 and 27 Mar. 1915, in Scholem, *Tagebücher*, 1:93, 95.

78. Gerhard Scholem, diary entry from 24 Mar. 1915, in Scholem, *Tagebücher*, 1:93; Matrikelschein [registration record] Werner Scholem, 21 Apr.1915, Universitätsarchiv Göttingen.

79. Gerhard Scholem, diary entry from 30 Nov. 1915, in Scholem, *Tagebücher*, 1:190; Werner to Gerhard Scholem, 19 June 1916, INL, Archive G. Scholem.

80. Gerhard Scholem, diary entries from 23 and 24 July 1915, in Scholem, *Tagebücher*, 1:132–134; Scholem, *Walter Benjamin*, 13–15; Scholem, *From Berlin to Jerusalem*, 70–71.

81. Soon afterward Benjamin broke off his engagement to Grete Radt. Gerhard Scholem, diary entries from 15 Aug. 1915, and 18 and 24 Aug. 1916, in Scholem, *Tagebücher*, 1:147, 313, 392; Scholem, *Walter Benjamin*, 18, 21; Zadoff and Zadoff, "From Mission to Memory."

82. Gerhard Scholem, diary entries from 13 and 16 July 1915, in Scholem, *Tagebücher*, 1:130–131; Scholem, *Walter Benjamin*, 19; Scholem, *From Berlin to Jerusalem*, 71; *Die Blau- Weiße Brille*, nos. 1 and 2, INL, G. Scholem Library; Erich Brauer (1895–1942) later worked as a graphic artist and ethnologist.

83. *Golus* (Yiddish): Diaspora, dispersion. Scholem, *Tagebücher*, 1:291, 298; Gerhard to Werner Scholem, 13 Sept. 1914, in Scholem, *Briefe*, 1:11.

84. Abiturzeugnis [*Abitur* diploma], reprinted in *Gershom Scholem (1897–1982)*, 14; Gerhard Scholem, diary entries from 7 Feb. and 23 Sept. 1915, as well as a report on the trip to Verden, after 20 Nov. 1915, in Scholem, *Tagebücher*, 1:185–188.

85. Gerhard Scholem, diary entries from 15 and 26 Dec. 1915, in Scholem, *Tagebücher*, 1:200–201, 216; Scholem, *Von Berlin nach Jerusalem*, 78; Breithaupt, *Volksvergiftung*, 51

86. *Die Blau-Weiße Brille*, no. 3, 1–2, reprinted in Scholem, *Tagebücher*, 1:299–301; Gerhard Scholem, diary entries from 15, 17, and 31 Dec. 1915, 4 and 6 Jan. 1916, and 1 Mar. 1916, in *Tagebücher*, 1:200–201, 204, 222, 226, 231, 257.

87. Contrary to the finding by Biale, *Gershom Scholem*, 17.

88. Gerhard Scholem, diary entries from 21 and 25 Dec. 1915, in Scholem, *Tagebücher*, 1:211, 214–215.

89. Gerhard Scholem, diary entries from 12 and 18 Dec. 1915, 5 Jan. 1916, and 6 Mar. 1916, in Scholem, *Tagebücher*, 1:198, 207, 229–230, 279; Scholem, *From Berlin to Jerusalem*, 52–53.

90. Gerhard Scholem, diary entries from 30 Jan., 1 and 3 Mar. 1916, in Scholem, *Tagebücher*, 1:251, 257, 260, 273; Gerhard Scholem to Harry Heymann, 1 Apr. 1916, in Scholem, *Briefe*, 1:28–29; Scholem, *From Berlin to Jerusalem*, 73; Scholem, *Tagebücher*, 1:311 n. 16; Scholem, *Briefe*, 1:480.

91. Werner Scholem to Gerhard Scholem, Berlin, 19 June 1916, INL, Archive G. Scholem.

92. Graudenz was a city on the Vistula River, then a part of West Prussia. Today the city is known as Grudziadz and is located in Poland. Before that, Werner Scholem was stationed in Serbia.

93. The Lake Naroch offensive took place in March 1916 in what is today Belarus; it was a dramatic defeat for the Russian army, which launched the attack with a force that far outnumbered the Germans.

94. Werner Scholem to Gerhard Scholem, Berlin, 19 June 1916, INL, Archive G. Scholem.

95. Ibid.

96. See also Werner Scholem to Gerhard Scholem, 23 June 1916, INL, Archive G. Scholem.

97. *Boches* was a derogatory name for Germans, derived from French and originating during the period of the Franco-Prussian War of 1870–1871. It then became very popular again during the First World War. Werner Scholem to Gerhard Scholem, 19 June 1916, INL, Archive G. Scholem.

98. Ibid. and 23 June 1916, INL, Archive G. Scholem. Later the rumor about Kalischer was proven to be false. Emmy Scholem to Gerhard Scholem, 5 Feb. 1918, INL, Archive G. Scholem.

99. *Mishpokhe* (Yiddish): family, relatives; *nebikh* (Yiddish): too bad, alas. Werner Scholem to Gerhard Scholem, Berlin, 19 June 1916, INL, Archive G. Scholem.

100. The sons of Arthur Scholem learned Yiddish expressions from Arthur's Zionist brother Theobald or from Betty's relatives, members of the Hirsch family. For his military service, Reinhold Scholem was awarded the Iron Cross. Scholem, *From Berlin to Jerusalem*, 10.

101. Gerhard Scholem to Erich Brauer, 21 June 1916, in Scholem, *Briefe*, 1:35–37; Scholem, diary entry from 18 June 1916, in Scholem, *Tagebücher*, 1:313.

102. Werner Scholem to Gerhard Scholem, 23 June 1916, INL, Archive G. Scholem.

103. Gerhard Scholem to Erich Brauer, 17 July 1916, in Scholem, *Briefe*, 1:38; Scholem, diary entries from 18 to 28 June 1916, in Scholem, *Tagebücher*, 1:313–328; Kerr, "Bleibt unverwirrt," 41–42.

104. Gerhard Scholem, diary entries from 28 June and 1 Aug. 1916, in Scholem, *Tagebücher*, 1:327–328, 345; Gerhard Scholem to Harry Heymann, 1 Apr. 1916, in Scholem, *Briefe*, 1:29.

105. Werner Scholem to Gerhard Scholem, 7 July 1916, INL, Archive G. Scholem.

106. Gerhard Scholem to Erich Brauer, 7 June 1916, in Scholem, *Briefe*, 1:30–31.

107. Werner Scholem to Gerhard Scholem, 7 July 1916, INL, Archive G. Scholem.

108. Ibid.

109. See also Sieg, *Jüdische Intellektuelle im Ersten Weltkrieg*, 112–132; George L. Mosse, *The Jews and the German War Experience, 1914–1918*.

110. Werner Scholem to Gerhard Scholem, 7 July 1916, INL, Archive G. Scholem.

111. Werner Scholem to Gerhard Scholem, 20 July [1916], INL, Archive G. Scholem; Gerhard Scholem to Werner Scholem, 15 July 1916, in Scholem, *Tagebücher*, 1:336; see also Lessing, *Der jüdische Selbsthaß*; Gilman, *Jewish Self-Hatred*.

112. Gerhard Scholem to Werner Scholem, 7 Sept. 1914, in Scholem, *Briefe*, 1:5–6; Buber, *Die Legende des Baalschem*, 30; Werner Scholem to Gerhard Scholem, 20 July [1916], INL, Archive G. Scholem.

113. Gerhard Scholem, diary entry from 13 July 1916, in Scholem, *Tagebücher*, 1:333–335; Werner Scholem to Gerhard Scholem, 7 July 1916, INL, Archive G. Scholem; Erich Brauer to Gerhard Scholem, 15 July 1916, in Scholem, *Briefe*, 1:349.

114. Words underlined in the original are in italics here. Gerhard Scholem to Erich Brauer, 17 July 1916, in Scholem, *Briefe*, 1:40–42.

115. Werner Scholem to Gershom Scholem, 20 July [1916], INL, Archive G. Scholem; Gerhard Scholem, diary entry from 29 July 1916, in Scholem, *Tagebücher*, 1:343.

116. Werner Scholem to Gerhard Scholem, 23 June 1916, INL, Archive G. Scholem.

117. Werner Scholem to Gerhard Scholem, 7 July 1916, INL, Archive G. Scholem. The article appeared in the fall of 1917 in *Der Jude* 1 (1916/1917): 12, 822–825, reprinted in Scholem, *Tagebücher*, 1:511–517.

118. Gerhard Scholem, "Jüdische Jugendbewegung," 822–825.

119. Gerhard Scholem, diary entry from 26 June 1916, in Scholem, *Tagebücher*, 1:325; Scholem, *"Es gibt ein Geheimnis in der Welt,"* 62.

120. Werner Scholem to Gershom Scholem, 13 July 1916, INL, Archive G. Scholem; scriptural quote taken from Genesis 12:1 of the Jewish Publication Society Bible of 1917; Blüher, "Die Untaten des bürgerlichen Typus," 18.

121. Gerhard Scholem, diary entry from 2 Mar. 1916, in Scholem, *Tagebücher*, 1:273; Scholem, *Walter Benjamin*, 26.

122. Werner Scholem to Gerhard Scholem, 31 Aug. 1916, INL, Archive G. Scholem.

123. Werner Scholem to Gerhard Scholem, 7 and 20 July 1916, INL, Archive G. Scholem. The diary was confiscated by the Gestapo in 1933 and has never been recovered.

124. *Politische Briefe*, no. 21 (28 May 1916), republished in *Spartakusbriefe*, vol. 1 (Berlin, 1921).

125. Gerhard Scholem, diary entry from 14 Aug. 1916, in Scholem, *Tagebücher*, 1:358–359.

126. Werner Scholem to Gerhard Scholem, 19 June 1916, INL, Archive G. Scholem; Mendes-Flohr, "Im Schatten des Weltkrieges," 20–21.

127. Gerhard Scholem, diary entry from 14 Aug. 1916, in Scholem, *Tagebücher*, 1:358–359.

128. Gerhard Scholem, diary entry from 15 Aug. 1916, in Scholem, *Tagebücher*, 1:373.

129. Werner Scholem to Gerhard Scholem, 22 Aug. 1916, INL, Archive G. Scholem.

130. Pulzer, "Der Erste Weltkrieg," 367–370; Rosenthal, *"Die Ehre des jüdischen Solda-ten,"* 50–53, 63.

131. Werner Scholem to Gerhard Scholem, 20 July 1916, INL, Archive G. Scholem; Scholem, *Tagebücher*, 1:340.

132. Werner Scholem to Gerhard Scholem, 2 Aug. 1916, INL, Archive G. Scholem.

133. Werner Scholem to Gerhard Scholem, 22 and 23 Aug. 1916, INL, Archive G. Scholem; Gerhard Scholem, diary entries from 17, 23, and 24 Aug. and 5 Sept. 1916, in Scholem, *Tagebücher*, 1:379, 382, 394–395.

134. Werner Scholem to Gerhard Scholem, 20 July, 22 and 31 Aug., and 13 Oct. 1916, INL, Archive G. Scholem.

135. Werner Scholem to Gerhard Scholem, 2 Aug. 1916, INL, Archive G. Scholem.

136. All of the quotes that follow are in Werner Scholem to Gerhard Scholem, 19 and 23 June, 7, 13, and 20 July, and 2 and 22 Aug. 1916, INL, Archive G. Scholem.

137. The Zohar is a foundational work of Jewish mysticism.

138. Werner Scholem to Gerhard Scholem, 11 and 13 Oct. and 26 Dec. 1916, INL, Archive G. Scholem. On 1 December 1916 he was deregistered at the University of Göttingen and a week later, on 8 December, he registered at the University of Halle. Matrikelschein [registration record] Werner Scholem, Universitätsarchiv Göttingen; Matrikelschein [registration record] Werner Scholem, Universitätsarchiv Halle.

139. Gerhard Scholem, diary entries from 27 Oct., 6, 21, and 22 Nov., and 18 Dec. 1916, in Scholem, *Tagebücher*, 1:410–412, 415–416, 423–430, 448. On the occasion of his son's nineteenth birthday, Arthur Scholem printed his Hebrew translation of the Song of Songs. Gerhard Scholem, diary entry from 3 Dec. 1916, in Scholem, *Tagebücher*, 1:444.

140. Shavit, "On the Hebrew Cultural Center in Berlin in the Twenties," 372; Dohrn and Pickhan, *Transit und Transformation*.

141. Werner Scholem to Gerhard Scholem, 26 Dec. 1916, INL, Archive G. Scholem; Gerhard Scholem, diary entry from 28 Dec. 1916, in Scholem, *Tagebücher*, 1:455.

142. Gerhard Scholem, diary entry from 4 Jan. 1917, in Scholem, *Tagebücher*, 1:464.

143. Gerhard Scholem to Harry Heymann, 27 Jan. 1917, and to Aharon Heller, 9 July and 17 July 1917, in Scholem, *Briefe*, 1:66, 81–82; Gerhard Scholem, diary entry from 27 Sept. 1917, in Scholem, *Tagebücher*, 2:42–43; Scholem, *"Es gibt ein Geheimnis in der Welt,"* 68; Landauer, "Sind das Ketzergedanken?," 122.

144. Werner Scholem to Gershom Scholem, 5 Feb. 1917, INL, Archive G. Scholem.

145. *Geschichte der deutschen Arbeiterjugendbewegung*, 140; Werner Scholem to Gershom Scholem, 22 Aug. 1917, INL, Archive G. Scholem.

146. Samsonschule (Realschule) zu Wolfenbüttel, *Berichte 1907–1908 bis 1910–1911*.

147. Laschitza, *Die Liebknechts*, 301–323.

148. Scholem, *From Berlin to Jerusalem*, 84.

149. One hundred marks in 1917 equals around 290 dollars in 2017. Arthur Scholem to Gerhard Scholem, 15 Feb. 1917, in Scholem and Scholem, *Mutter und Sohn im Briefwechsel*, 13.

150. Scholem, *From Berlin to Jerusalem*, 84.

151. Message communicated verbally from Meta Flanter-Jahr, in Scholem, *Briefe*, 1:367 n. 7.

152. Zalman Rubashov-Shazar (1889–1974), historian and third president of Israel (1963–1973). Scholem, *Briefe*, 1:480; Scholem, *From Berlin to Jerusalem*, 85–90. The book was *Jiskor: Ein Buch des Gedenkens an gefallene Wächter und Arbeiter im Lande Israel* [Yizkor: A memorial volume for fallen watchmen and workers in Erez Israel] (Berlin, 1918); but Gerhard Scholem did not want to be named as the translator.

153. Scholem and Scholem, *Mutter und Sohn im Briefwechsel*, 13–14 (Arthur Scholem to Gerhard Scholem, 12 May 1917), 531 (Betty Scholem), and 14–15 (Gerhard Scholem to Käthe Schiepan, 6 June 1917); Scholem, *Von Berlin nach Jerusalem*, 71.

154. Gerhard Scholem, diary entry from 15 May 1917, in Scholem, *Tagebücher*, 1:472; Scholem, *From Berlin to Jerusalem*, 84–85.

155. Gerhard Scholem, diary entry from 19 May 1917, in Scholem, *Tagebücher*, 2:18.

156. Werner Scholem to Gerhard Scholem, 3 June 1917, INL, Archive G. Scholem.

157. Gerhard Scholem, diary entry from 2 Sept. 1917, in Scholem, *Tagebücher*, 2:34. The idea of suicide played a major role for this generation. A public debate about the topic had been sparked by the publication of Émile Durkheim's book *Le suicide: Étude de sociologie* (Paris, 1897).

158. Miller, *Burgfrieden und Klassenkampf*, 156–166; *Reichstagshandbuch, 3. Wahlperiode 1924*, 351; Werner Scholem to Gerhard Scholem, 3 June 1917, INL, Archive G. Scholem.

159. Werner Scholem to Gerhard Scholem, 3 June and 22 Aug. 1917, INL, Archive G. Scholem.

160. Gerhard Scholem, diary entry from 15 May 1917, in Scholem, *Tagebücher*, 1:472; Scholem, *Briefe*, 1:480.

161. Gerhard's letter is considered lost. Werner Scholem to Gerhard Scholem, 17 June 1917, INL, Archive G. Scholem.

162. Ibid.

163. Scholem, *From Berlin to Jerusalem*, 90; Gerhard Scholem, diary entry from 9 June 1917, in Scholem, *Tagebücher*, 2:27; Werner Scholem, field postcard from pretrial detention in Halle, to Gerhard Scholem, Allenstein/Pr., 9 July 1917, INL, Archive G. Scholem.

164. Gerhard Scholem to Erich Brauer, 15 July 1917, in Scholem, *Briefe*, 1:77.

165. Gerhard Scholem to Aharon Heller, 17 July 1917, in Scholem, *Briefe*, 1:82; Scholem, *Von Berlin nach Jerusalem*, 108.

166. Scholem, *Von Berlin nach Jerusalem*, 108–109; Scholem, *Tagebücher*, 2:27; Gerhard Scholem to Aharon Heller, 25 July 1917, to Gerda Goldberg, 6 Aug. 1917, and to Werner Kraft, 3 Aug. 1917, in Scholem, *Briefe*, 1:83–84, 88–89.

167. Gerhard Scholem to Werner Kraft, 8 Apr. 1918, in Scholem, *Briefe*, 1:151.

168. Gerhard Scholem to Werner Kraft, 11 Aug. and 19 Aug. 1917, and to Harry Heymann, 14 Aug. 1917, in Scholem, *Briefe*, 1:93, 96, 101.

169. Kurt Singer, "Allgemeines zur Frage der Simulation," quoted in Eckart and Gradmann, "Medizin," 216; Brock, "Confinement of Conscientious Objectors," 247–264.

170. At the start of the century, Abraham had worked intensively with Eugen Bleuler at the Burghölzli in Zurich on this "narcissistic neurosis," which was described originally as a type of early dementia. Rüger, "Anfänge der psychoanalytischen Therapie in Berlin," 241, 245; Abraham, *Psychoanalytische Studien II*, 125–145; Brock, "Confinement of Conscientious Objectors," 247–264; Gerhard Scholem to Gerda Goldberg, 6 Aug. 1917, and to Harry Heymann, 14 Aug. 1917, in Scholem, *Briefe*, 1:88, 96; Scholem, *Von Berlin nach Jerusalem*, 108.

171. Emmy Wiechelt's letter is considered lost; Werner Scholem to Gerhard Scholem, 12 Aug. and 22 Aug. 1917, INL, Archive G. Scholem; Gerhard Scholem to Harry Heymann, 14 Aug. 1917, in Scholem, *Briefe*, 1:96.

172. *Zoppen* (Berlin slang): evade, shirk from, duck out, back out of/reverse a decision. Scholem, *From Berlin to Jerusalem*, 30–31; Gershom Scholem, "Zur Sozialpsychologie der Juden in Deutschland, 1900–1930," 246; Werner Scholem to Gerhard Scholem, 12 Aug. 1917, INL, Archive G. Scholem.

173. With his use of the phrase "weeping and gnashing of teeth," Werner is borrowing a turn of phrase used often in the New Testament to describe hell, such as in Matthew 8:12 of the King James Version. Werner Scholem to Gerhard Scholem, 22 Aug. 1917, INL, Archive G. Scholem.

174. Werner Scholem to Gerhard Scholem, 22 Aug. 1917, INL, Archive G. Scholem.

175. Ibid.

176. Ibid.

177. Scholem, *From Berlin to Jerusalem*, 100; Scholem, *Walter Benjamin*, 53; Betty Scholem to Gerhard Scholem, 16 Nov. 1917, and Arthur Scholem to Gerhard Scholem, 21 Jan. 1918, in Scholem and Scholem, *Mutter und Sohn im Briefwechsel*, 18, 19; Gerhard Scholem to Werner Kraft, 6 Oct. 1917, in Scholem, *Briefe*, 1:112.

178. Gerhard Scholem to Werner Kraft, 6 Oct. 1917, Scholem, *Briefe*, 1:110–112; Gerhard Scholem, "Dem Andenken Hermann Cohens," 189–190; Gerhard Scholem, diary entry from 5 Apr. 1918, in Scholem, *Tagebücher*, 2:166–167; Dathe, "Jena—eine Episode aus Gershom Scholems Leben," 76; Scholem, *From Berlin to Jerusalem*, 95–195.

179. Gerhard Scholem to Harry Heymann, 4 Dec. and 28 Dec 1917, and to Werner Kraft, 30 Nov. 1917, in Scholem, *Briefe*, 1:125, 128, and 132–133; Gerhard Scholem, diary entry from 13 Nov. and 1 Dec. 1917, in Scholem, *Tagebücher*, 2:79, 86.

180. "Hatschi" in German means "achoo" (sneeze).

181. Gerhard Scholem, diary entry from 1 Dec. and 3 Dec. 1917, in Scholem, *Tagebücher*, 2:87–88; Shedletzky, "Auf der Suche nach dem verlorenen Judentum," 36; Barouch, "Sprache zwischen Klage und Rache," 48–49.

182. Betty Scholem to Gerhard Scholem, 21 Sept. 1917, in Scholem and Scholem, *Mutter und Sohn im Briefwechsel*, 18; Werner Scholem to Gerhard Scholem, 9 Dec. 1917, INL, Archive G. Scholem; Emmy Wiechelt to Gerhard Scholem, 18 Sept. 1917, INL, Archive G. Scholem; Scholem, *From Berlin to Jerusalem*, 95–96.

183. Rosa Luxemburg to Sophie Liebknecht, mid-November 1917, in Luxemburg, *Letters from Prison*, 49. The last part of this quote can also be translated to read: "that it can be transformed into something tremendously great and heroic; and—should the war still continue a few more years—*has to* transform."

184. Werner Scholem to Gerhard Scholem, 9 Dec. 1917, INL, Archive G. Scholem. The translation of the Schiller quote was taken from Friedrich Schiller, *Don Carlos*, trans. R. D. Boylan, accessed 17 Dec. 2015, http://www.gutenberg.org/files/6789/6789-h/6789-h.htm.

185. Werner Scholem to Gerhard Scholem, 9 Dec., 18 Dec., and 25 Dec. 1917, INL, Archive G. Scholem.

186. Werner Scholem to Gerhard Scholem, 25 Dec. 1917, INL, Archive G. Scholem.

187. Gerhard Scholem to Werner Kraft, 28 Dec. 1917, and to Harry Heymann, 28 Dec. 1917, in Scholem, *Briefe*, 1:133, 135. Jung-Juda Zentrum was the group in Berlin-Mitte—the district in central Berlin—to which Werner and Gerhard belonged.

188. Werner Scholem to Gerhard Scholem, 25 Dec. 1917, INL, Archive G. Scholem; Emmy Scholem to Gerhard Scholem, 5 Feb. 1918, INL, Archive G. Scholem; Scholem, *From Berlin to Jerusalem*, 96; Gerhard Scholem to Reinhold Scholem, 8 Sept. 1976, in Scholem, *Briefe*, 3:145; Matrikelschein [registration record] Werner Scholem, Universitätsarchiv Halle.

189. Gerhard Scholem to Harry Heymann, 15 Jan. 1918, and to Aharon Heller, 2 Oct. 1917, in Scholem, *Briefe*, 1:105–106, 136; Scholem, *Briefe*, 1:480; Gerhard Scholem, diary entry from 22 Oct. 1917, in Scholem, *Tagebücher*, 2:69.

190. Emmy Scholem to Gerhard Scholem, 5 Feb. 1918, INL, Archive G. Scholem.

191. Werner Scholem to Gerhard Scholem, 10, 20, and 25 Feb. 1918, INL, Archive G. Scholem; Betty Scholem to Gerhard Scholem, 25 Feb. 1918, in Scholem and Scholem, *Mutter und Sohn im Briefwechsel*, 20.

192. Gerhard Scholem, diary entries from 1 and 4 Mar. 1918, in Scholem, *Tagebücher*, 2:145, 147; Werner Scholem to Gerhard Scholem, 20 Feb. 1918, INL, Archive G. Scholem.

193. Werner Scholem to Gerhard Scholem, 11 and 26 Mar. 1918, INL, Archive G. Scholem.

194. Gerhard Scholem, diary entry from 31 Mar. 1918, in Scholem, *Tagebücher*, 2:164; Gerhard Scholem to Escha Burchhardt, 24 Mar. 1918, and Arthur Scholem to Gerhard Scholem, 15 Mar. 1918, in Scholem, *Briefe*, 1:147, 376; Werner Scholem to Gerhard Scholem, 11 Apr. 1918, INL, Archive G. Scholem.

195. Scholem, *Von Berlin nach Jerusalem*, 109–110, 123; Gerhard Scholem to Escha Burchhardt, 21 and 23 June 1918, in Scholem, *Briefe*, 1:159, 167.

196. He probably wrote to Emmy as often as he could, but these letters have not survived. Werner Scholem to Gerhard Scholem, 13, 15, and 21 Apr. 1918, INL, Archive G. Scholem; Pietzsch, *Die Fronterfahrungen der deutschen Soldaten im Ersten Weltkrieg*, 32; Sieg, *Jüdische Intellektuelle im Ersten Weltkrieg*, 118; Molthagen, *Das Ende der Bürgerlichkeit?*, 73.

197. Gerhard Scholem to Harry Heymann, 28 Dec. 1917 and 1 Mar. 1918, in Scholem, *Briefe*, 1:142.

198. Werner Scholem to Gerhard Scholem, 15 May, 29 June, and 23 Oct. 1918, INL, Archive G. Scholem; see also Molthagen, *Das Ende der Bürgerlichkeit?*, 97–98.

199. *Geheimrat* was an honorary title for German public servants or state officals.

200. Werner Scholem to Gerhard Scholem, 29 July 1918, INL, Archive G. Scholem. The town of Kleinschingelsheim mentioned by Werner is purely one of his own invention, meant to represent some remote provincial place.

201. The offensive of French Marshal Ferdinand Foch, commander of the Entente on the entire western front, began on 21 August 1918 and was part of the final phase of the war. Werner Scholem to Gerhard Scholem, 1 Sept. 1918, INL, Archive G. Scholem.

202. Werner Scholem to Gerhard Scholem, 23 Oct. 1918, INL, Archive G. Scholem; Sieg, *Jüdische Intellektuelle im Ersten Weltkrieg*, esp. 116, 124; Molthagen, *Das Ende der Bürgerlichkeit?*, 97–99, 104.

203. Werner actually wanted to write "Unabhängige" (USPD), but out of fear of being censored, he used the English equivalent "Independents." In fact, he would leave the USPD only in December 1920 to join the KPD. *Reichstagshandbuch, 3. Wahlperiode 1924*, 351; Werner Scholem to Gerhard Scholem, 23 Oct. 1918, INL, Archive G. Scholem. The Spartacus Group was founded as Spartacus League on November 11, 1918.

204. Werner Scholem to Gerhard Scholem, 26 Dec. 1918, INL, Archive G. Scholem.

205. Werner Scholem to Gerhard Scholem, 20 Feb. and 26 Mar. 1918, and Emmy Scholem to Gerhard Scholem, 14 Oct. 1918, INL, Archive G. Scholem.

206. Werner Scholem to Gerhard Scholem, 26 Dec. 1918, INL, Archive G. Scholem.

207. Gerhard Scholem to Werner Kraft, 25 Oct. 1918, in Gershom Scholem, *Briefe an Werner Kraft*, 95; Gerhard Scholem, diary entry for 26 Oct. 1918, in Scholem, *Tagebücher*, 2:400; *Shidduch* is the Hebrew/Yiddish word for the traditional Jewish culture of arranging marriages.

208. Remarque, *All Quiet on the Western Front*, 213–214. Remarque (born 1898) also belonged to this generation.

209. Scholem, *From Berlin to Jerusalem*, 20.

210. Ibid., 42–43; Scholem, *"Es gibt ein Geheimnis in der Welt,"* 51. Not until both men were well advanced in years did Reinhold and Gershom Scholem start a correspondence between Australia and Israel about this period.

211. Scholem, *Von Berlin nach Jerusalem*, 42; Scholem, "Zur Sozialpsychologie der Juden in Deutschland," 250–251; see also Brenner, "A Tale of Two Families," 349–351; Brenner, *Jüdische Kultur in der Weimarer Republik*, 12–13; Geller, "The Scholem Brothers and the Paths of German Jewry."

212. Shore, "Children of the Revolution," 64.

213. Such as the children of the psychologist William Stern and his wife, Clara, or the siblings of Gustav Steinschneider; see Wobick-Segev, "Praying to Goethe and Other Misadventures"; Scholem, *Walter Benjamin*, 116; Gillerman, "The Crisis of the Jewish Family in Weimar Germany."

214. Georg Benjamin (1895–1942) fought in the First World War, became a member first of the USPD and later of the KPD, married the (non-Jewish) party comrade Hilde Lange, and was murdered in a concentration camp.

215. Gershom Scholem to Reinhold Scholem, 29 May 1972, in Scholem, *Briefe*, 3:29; Scholem, *From Berlin to Jerusalem*, 11, 29–31; Scholem, "Zur Sozialpsychologie der Juden in Deutschland," 242.

216. Brenner, *Jüdische Kultur in der Weimarer Republik*, 47.

217. Kafka, "Brief an den Vater" [1919]; Deleuze and Guattari, *Kafka*, 15.

218. There were two hundred Jewish organizations in Berlin already around 1900. Shavit, "On the Hebrew Cultural Center in Berlin in the Twenties," 372; Dohrn and Pickhan, *Transit und Transformation*; Scholem and Drews, *". . . und alles ist Kabbala,"* 16; Rebiger, "'Das Wesentliche.'"

219. Gershom Scholem to Salman Schocken, 29 Oct. 1937, in Scholem, *Briefe*, 1:471.

220. Mosse, "Gershom Scholem as a German Jew," 119.

221. Scholem, *"Es gibt ein Geheimnis in der Welt,"* 50–51.

222. Gerhard Scholem, diary entry from 23 July and 25 Nov. 1916, in Scholem, *Tagebücher*, 1:339–340, 437; Scholem, *Von Berlin nach Jerusalem*, 74; Betty Scholem, in Scholem and Scholem, *Mutter und Sohn im Briefwechsel*, 530–531.

223. Luxemburg, "Diskussion," 149.

224. He referred to an article by Max Hildebert Boehm, who in turn was reacting to Hermann Cohen and rejected the idea of a national Judaism in favor of assimilation into "Europism." Gerhard Scholem, diary entry from 29 Dec. 1915, in Scholem, *Tagebücher*, 1:222; Boehm, "Vom jüdisch-deutschen Geist."

225. As has been generally assumed until now; see Biale, *Gershom Scholem*, 10; Weidner, *Gershom Scholem*, 56–57.

226. Scholem, "Zur Sozialpsychologie der Juden in Deutschland, 246; Testament Arthur Scholems, 24 Sept. 1921, IPW, Nachlass Scholem.

2. In the Shadow of Revolution

1. Betty Scholem to Gerhard Scholem, 26 and 31 Oct., 9 Nov. 1918, in Scholem and Scholem, *Mutter und Sohn im Briefwechsel*, 20–23; Materna, "9. November 1918—der erste Tag der Republik," 144. Königgrätzer Strasse is now named Ebert Strasse.

2. Betty Scholem to Gerhard Scholem, 11 Nov. 1918, in Scholem and Scholem, *Mutter und Sohn im Briefwechsel*, 23–24.

3. A year later, in the fall of 1919, Reinhold and Erich Scholem became co-owners of their father's business. Betty Scholem to Gerhard Scholem, 18 and 29 Nov. and 23 Dec. 1918, as well as 22 Jan. 1919, in Scholem and Scholem, *Mutter und Sohn im Briefwechsel*, 25–26, 29, 34–35.

4. Betty Scholem to Gerhard Scholem, 18 Nov., 11 Dec. 1918, and 7, 13, 22, and 25 Jan. 1919, in Scholem and Scholem, *Mutter und Sohn im Briefwechsel*, 25, 27–28, 30–35; Liepach, *Das Wahlverhalten der jüdischen Bevölkerung in der Weimarer Republik*, 119.

5. Betty Scholem to Gerhard Scholem, 11 Dec.1918, in Scholem and Scholem, *Mutter und Sohn im Briefwechsel*, 28; see also "Umschau."

6. Fritsch, *Handbuch der Judenfrage*, 529; Zimmermann, "Zukunftserwartungen deutscher Juden im ersten Jahr der Weimarer Republik," 69–71; Angress, "Juden im politischen Leben der Revolutionszeit," 143–146.

7. Reichmann, "Der Bewußtseinswandel der deutschen Juden," 551–552.

8. Mann, speech given at the Jewish World Congress in Brussels on 4 August 1966, 49; Moshe Zimmermann, "Zukunftserwartungen deutscher Juden im ersten Jahr der Weimarer Republik," 70.

9. Quoted in *Im deutschen Reich* 25, no. 4 (1919): 188–189.

10. Berger, "Deutschland," 1443.

11. Weissenberg, "Der Anteil der Juden an der Revolutionsbewegung in Rußland," 1–7.

12. Kayser, "Der jüdische Revolutionär," 96.

13. Mendes-Flohr, "Im Schatten des Weltkrieges," 29–35.

14. Wassermann, *Mein Weg als Deutscher und Jude*, 117–118.

15. Angress, "Juden im politischen Leben der Revolutionszeit," 148–150.

16. Such an argument was used, e.g., by Wilhelm Stapel, editor of the publication *Deutsches Volkstum*. Stapel, *Über das seelische Problem der Symbiose des deutschen und des jüdischen Volkes*, 99.

17. Zweig, "Der heutige deutsche Antisemitismus," 456.

18. Ludendorff, *Kriegführung und Politik*, 133.

19. There are numerous reports and articles in the CV organ *Im deutschen Reich* on this, such as in issues 24, no. 12 (1918): 479; 25, no. 2 (1919): 75–76; and no. 6 (1919): 283.

20. Angress, "Juden im politischen Leben der Revolutionszeit," 146.

21. Buber, "Die Revolution und wir," 346.

22. See also Graf, *Die Zukunft der Weimarer Republik*, 61, 183–185, 308–316.

23. Werner Scholem to Gerhard Scholem, 26 Dec. 1918 and 2 Dec. 1914, INL, Archive G. Scholem.

24. Werner Scholem to Gerhard Scholem, 26 Dec. 1918, INL, Archive G. Scholem.

25. Werner Scholem to Gerhard Scholem, 26 Dec. 1918 and 7 Feb. 1919, INL, Archive G. Scholem.

26. Werner Scholem to Gerhard Scholem, 29 July 1918 and 7 Feb. 1919, INL, Archive G. Scholem.

27. Werner Scholem to Gerhard Scholem, 7 Feb. 1919, INL, Archive G. Scholem; Mlynek, "Hannover in der Weimarer Republik und im Nationalsozialismus, 1918–1945," 424.

28. Reinhold Scholem confirmed that he was a member of the DVP in a letter he wrote to Gerhard, congratulating him on his birthday, 25 Nov. 1919, in Scholem and Scholem,

Mutter und Sohn im Briefwechsel, 58; Werner Scholem to Gerhard Scholem, 7 Feb. 1919, INL, Archive G. Scholem.

29. Werner Scholem to Gerhard Scholem, 26 Dec. 1918, INL, Archive G. Scholem.

30. Gerhard Scholem, diary entry from 29 Dec. 1918, in Scholem, *Tagebücher*, 2:427.

31. Gerhard Scholem, diary entry from 28 June 1918, in Scholem, *Tagebücher*, 2:260.

32. Gerhard Scholem, diary entries from 25 July and 10 Sept. 1918 and 28 July 1919, in Scholem, *Tagebücher*, 2:275, 405, 500. The reason he turned away from politics probably also had something to do with Walter Benjamin, with whom, maintained Gershom Scholem years later, one could not talk about the war and its consequences at the time. Scholem, *Walter Benjamin*, 34–35.

33. Gerhard Scholem, diary entries from 13 and 18 Nov. and 25 Dec. 1918, in Scholem, *Tagebücher*, 2:406, 423–424; Scholem, *Walter Benjamin*, 100.

34. Gerhard Scholem, "Der Bolschewismus" (following the translation of Eric Jacobson, *Metaphysics of the Profane*, 195–196); Scholem, diary entry from 25 Dec. 1918, in *Tagebücher*, 2:423–424; Scholem and Drews, ". . . *und alles ist Kabbala*," 20; Jacobson, "Theories of Justice, Profane and Prophetic."

35. Werner Scholem to Gerhard Scholem, 7 Feb. 1919, INL, Archive G. Scholem.

36. Werner Scholem to Gerhard Scholem, 30 Mar. 1919, INL, Archive G. Scholem.

37. Betty Scholem to Gerhard Scholem, 5 Apr. 1919, and Gerhard Scholem to his parents, 26 Apr. 1919, in Scholem and Scholem, *Mutter und Sohn im Briefwechsel*, 41, 46.

38. The USPD had a rapidly growing electorate in Linden. Rabe, *Linden*, 38; Weber, *Die Wandlung des deutschen Kommunismus*, 2:286; Werner Scholem to Gerhard Scholem, 30 Mar. 1919, INL, Archive G. Scholem.

39. Werner Scholem to Gerhard Scholem, 30 Mar. 1919, INL, Archive G. Scholem.

40. Zweig, "Der heutige deutsche Antisemitismus," 456.

41. By 1922, Emil Julius Gumbel had counted a total of 354 political murders committed by the right, as opposed to 22 murders committed by the left. After his book *Vier Jahre politischer Mord* appeared, treason, high treason, and other disciplinary proceedings were initiated against him. The investigation into the charges proved inconclusive and was closed. Gumbel, *Vier Jahre politischer Mord*, 144–149; "Der 'Fall Gumbel,'" 54; Merkl, "The Corruption of Public Life in Weimar Germany," 66.

42. Gerhard Scholem, diary entries from 7 Oct., 3 Nov., 5 Nov., 21 Dec. 1918, and 14 June 1919, in Scholem, *Tagebücher*, 2:395–396, 402–403, 452–453, 464.

43. Gerhard Scholem to Werner Kraft, 10 Apr. 1919, in Scholem, *Briefe* 1:202–203.

44. Ibid.; the newspaper in question was the *Volksfreund*, not the *Volksstimme*.

45. Werner Scholem to Gerhard Scholem, 4 June 1919, INL, Archive G. Scholem.

46. Ibid.

47. Hirschinger, "*Gestapoagenten, Trotzkisten, Verräter*," 21.

48. Flechtheim, *Die KPD in der Weimarer Republik*, 154–156; Hirschinger, "*Gestapoagenten, Trotzkisten, Verräter*," 24; Werner Scholem to Gerhard Scholem, 22 Aug. 1917, INL, Archive G. Scholem.

49. Werner Scholem to Gerhard Scholem, 6 Aug. 1919, INL, Archive G. Scholem.

50. *Volksblatt: Sozialdemokratisches Organ für Halle und den Bezirk Merseburg (hereafter Hallesches Volksblatt)* 30, no. 171 (1919): 4; on the rumors about the murders of Luxemburg and Liebknecht, see also Geyer, "Korruptionsdebatten in der Zeit der Revolution 1918/19," 345–346.

51. *Hallesches Volksblatt* 31, no. 183 (1920): supplement 1; Hirschinger, *"Gestapoagenten, Trotzkisten, Verräter,"* 22–23.

52. Werner Scholem to Gerhard Scholem, 4 June and 6 Aug. 1919, INL, Archive G. Scholem; Gerhard Scholem, diary entry from 9 July 1919, in Scholem, *Tagebücher*, 2:476.

53. Gerhard Scholem, diary entry from 9 July 1919, in Scholem, *Tagebücher*, 2:476. Antrag auf Grund des Bundesergänzungsgesetzes Emmy Scholem, NLA, vol. 1, appendix 1, "Schilderung des Verfolgungsvorganges," 7 Apr. 1954, p. 1.

54. The apartment was located at Eichendorffstrasse 22; Adreßbuch des Saalkreises, 1920, Stadtarchiv Halle.

55. Werner Scholem to Gerhard Scholem, 6 Aug. 1919, INL, Archive G. Scholem.

56. Gerhard Scholem to Werner Scholem, 10 Aug. 1919, in Scholem, *Tagebücher*, 2:507–509. *Partei der Niemals Umgefallen* translates literally into Party of the Never Fallen, meaning the party of the unwavering, steadfast social democrats who never conceded to approving the war.

57. Ibid.

58. Gerhard Scholem to Werner Kraft, 24 Sept. 1919, in Scholem, *Briefe an Werner Kraft*, 119; Werner Scholem to Gerhard Scholem, 15 Sept. 1919, INL, Archive G. Scholem.

59. Scholem, *From Berlin to Jerusalem*, 144.

60. Scholem, *"Es gibt ein Geheimnis in der Welt,"* 52.

61. Emmy Scholem to Gerhard Scholem, 3 Dec. 1919, INL, Archive G. Scholem; Weber, *Die Wandlung des deutschen Kommunismus*, 2:286.

62. Scholem, *Walter Benjamin*, 65 (quote); Scholem, *Von Berlin nach Jerusalem*, 181.

63. Hirschinger, *"Gestapoagenten, Trotzkisten, Verräter,"* 28–29.

64. Ibid., 30–33; *Hallesches Volksblatt* 31, no. 189 (1920): 2.

65. Kautsky, *Die soziale Revolution.*

66. *Hallesches Volksblatt* 31, no. 189 (1920): 2.

67. Hirschinger, *"Gestapoagenten, Trotzkisten, Verräter,"* 33; Wheeler, "Die '21 Bedingungen' und die Spaltung der USPD im Herbst 1920," 120–122.

68. Wheeler, "Die '21 Bedingungen,'" 125–126.

69. *Hallesches Volksblatt* 31, no. 202 (1920): 7; Prager, "Die erfreuliche Spaltung," 28. According to Robert Wheeler, he was not yet on the staff responsible for the political section of the newspaper: Wheeler, "Die '21 Bedingungen,'" 135–136.

70. He is referring to the MSPD, the USPD, the KPD, and the Kommunistische Arbeiter Partei Deutschlands (KAPD), founded in the spring of 1920.

71. Werner Scholem, "Die Zukunft der Unabhängigen Sozialdemokratie," 5.

72. *Hallesches Volksblatt* 31, no. 208 (1920): 2.

73. On this, see Shylock's monologue in *The Merchant from Venice*, act 3, scene 1.

74. *Hallesches Volksblatt* 31, no. 208 (1920): 2.

75. Wheeler, "German Labor and the Comintern," 304–321; Wheeler, "Die '21 Bedingungen' und die Spaltung der USPD im Herbst 1920," 131–132.

76. *Hallesches Volksblatt* 31, no. 205 (1920): 1; no. 207 (1920): supplement 1; and no. 209 (1920): 2.

77. Dittmann, "Deutsche Arbeiter in Russland"; Dittmann, "Wahrheit über Russland."

78. Werner Scholem, "Solidarität mit Sowjet-Rußland?," 2.

79. Wheeler, "Die '21 Bedingungen' und die Spaltung der USPD im Herbst 1920," 129–130.

80. Werner Scholem, "Für die kommunistische Internationale"; see also *Hallesches Volksblatt* 31, no. 213 (1920): supplement 1; and no. 244 (1920): 3.

81. Werner Scholem, "In eigener Sache."

82. Wheeler, "Die '21 Bedingungen' und die Spaltung der USPD im Herbst 1920," 135–136, 139–142.

83. Werner Scholem, "Das rote Herz Deutschlands"; Scholem, "Versammlungsberichte," in *Hallesches Volksblatt* 31, no. 238 (1920: 15.

84. *Hallesches Volksblatt* 31, no. 240 (1920): 2; Hirschinger, *"Gestapoagenten, Trotzkisten, Verräter,"* 34–36; Weber, *Die Wandlung des deutschen Kommunismus*, 2:286; Angress, *Die Kampfzeit der KPD*, 105.

85. *Hallesches Volksblatt* 31, no. 244 (1920): supplement 1; Hirschinger, *"Gestapoagenten, Trotzkisten, Verräter,"* 34–36; Wheeler, "Die '21 Bedingungen' und die Spaltung der USPD im Herbst 1920," 149.

86. *Hallesches Volksblatt* 31, no. 294 (1920): 1; no. 295 (1920): 1; and no. 306 (1920): 1.

87. *Reichstagshandbuch, 2. Wahlperiode 1924*, 516; Antrag auf Grund des Bundesergänzungsgesetzes Emmy Scholem, NLA, vol. 1, appendix 1, "Schilderung des Verfolgungsvorganges," 7 Apr. 1954, p. 1; Hirschinger, *"Gestapoagenten, Trotzkisten, Verräter,"* 36; Weber, *Die Wandlung des deutschen Kommunismus*, 2:286.

88. Interview with Edith Capon, PRG.

89. *Reichstagshandbuch, 2. Wahlperiode 1924*, 516.

90. Foitzik, "Das kommunistische Intellektuellenmilieu in der Weimarer Republik," 229.

91. Ibid., 239, 244; Brauneck, *Die Rote Fahne*, 21, 48.

92. Martin Schumacher, *M.d.R.: Die Reichstagsabgeordneten der Weimarer Republik in der Zeit des Nationalsozialismus*, 506.

93. Gemeinsame Sitzung des Reichskabinetts mit dem Preußischen Staatsministerium vom 28. März und 29. März 1921, BAB Akten der Reichskanzlei, Weimarer Republik, nos. 221, 222.

94. Hirschinger, *"Gestapoagenten, Trotzkisten, Verräter,"* 38–46; Winkler, *Weimar, 1918–1933*, 150–154; Keßler, *Heroische Illusion und Stalin-Terror*, 64; Flechtheim, *Die KPD in der Weimarer Republik*, 127–129.

95. Winkler, *Weimar, 1918–1933*, 152.

96. *Sitzungsberichte des Preußischen Landtags*, vol. 1, 24th Session, 2 June 1921, 1437–1506.

97. Winkler, *Von der Revolution zur Stabilisierung*, 517.

98. *Sitzungsberichte des Preußischen Landtags*, vol. 1, 24th Session, 2 June 1921, 1444–1486.

99. Ibid., 1457–1461.

100. Ibid., 1469.

101. Ibid.,1476–1478.

102. Ibid., 1493, 1498.

103. *Die Rote Fahne* 3 (1921) 256 and 438: 1; Brauneck, *Die Rote Fahne*, 21, 48; Weber, *Die Wandlung des deutschen Kommunismus*, vol. 2, 285–286.

104. *Die Rote Fahne* 5, no. 103 (1922): 2.

105. *Sitzungsberichte des Preußischen Landtags*, vol. 10, 189th Session, 30 Nov. 1922, 13658.

106. Ibid., vol. 5, 104th Session, 22 Feb. 1922, 7386–7388.

107. Ibid., vol. 10, 202th Session, 23 Jan. 1923, 14342.

108. Bebel, *Antisemitismus und Sozialdemokratie.*

109. *Sitzungsberichte des Preußischen Landtags,* vol. 5, 104th Session, 22 Feb. 1922, 7391–7393; see also article in *Die Rote Fahne* 5, no. 91 (1922): 2.

110. *Sitzungsberichte des Preußischen Landtags,* vol. 5, 105th Session, 23 Feb. 1922, 7522–7525, and 107th Session, 25 Feb. 1922, 7641–7643; vol. 10, 199th Session, 20 Jan. 1923, 14249.

111. Ibid., vol. 5, 105th Session, 23 Feb. 1922, 7522–7525; vol. 10, 199th and 202th Sessions, 20 and 23 Jan. 1923, 1437–1438, 14343; vol.. 13, 261th Session, 22 June 1923, 18824–18825.

112. Ibid.; vol. 10, 190th Session, 1 Dec. 1922, 13770–13771; vol. 11, 210th Session, 23 Feb. 1923, 14926; vol. 12, 248th Session, 7 June 1923, 17695.

113. Geyer, *Verkehrte Welt,* 280.

114. The debate dated back to the so-called *Ostjudenerlass* (Eastern European Jew Decree), in which the Prussian minister of the interior, Wolfgang Heine (SPD), ordered "the temporary suspension of deportation of Jews from eastern, east-central, and southeastern Europe who have come, sometimes forced, to Germany as a result of the First World War." This decree affected between 70,000 and 100,000 people. Saß, "Ostenjudendebatte," 261–262, and "Ostjuden-Erlass," 262–263; Heid, *Oskar Cohn,* 112–125; *Sitzungsberichte des Preußischen Landtags,* vol. 10, 188th Session, 29 Nov. 1922, 13556–13622.

115. *Sitzungsberichte des Preußischen Landtags,* vol. 10, 188th Session, 29 Nov. 1922, 13556.

116. Ibid., 13557–13568; Bernstein, "Die Ostjuden in Deutschland," 36–37, IISG.

117. On the stance of German Jews with regard to the immigrants, see Niewyk, *The Jews in Weimar Germany,* 114–121; *Sitzungsberichte des Preußischen Landtags,* vol. 10, 188th Session, 29 Nov. 1922, 13580–13588.

118. *Sitzungsberichte des Preußischen Landtags,* vol. 10, 188th Session, 29 Nov. 1922, 13581–13582.

119. Schuster, *Zwischen allen Fronten,* 236–239.

120. *Sitzungsberichte des Preußischen Landtags,* vol. 10, 188th Session, 29 Nov. 1922, 13583–13586; Heid, *Oskar Cohn,* 113–115; Heid, *Maloche—nicht Mildtätigkeit,* 129.

121. Heid, *Maloche—nicht Mildtätigkeit,* 129; *Sitzungsberichte des Preußischen Landtags,* vol. 10, 188th Session, 29 Nov. 1922, 13587.

122. *Sitzungsberichte des Preußischen Landtags,* vol. 10, 188th Session, 29 Nov. 1922, 13582–13583.

123. Winkler, *Der Schein der Normalität,* 462; Merkl, "Corruption of Public Life," 63–64; Gay, "Der berlinisch-jüdische Geist," 190.

124. Of the delegates attending the Frankfurt Party Congress in 1924, 86 percent were under the age of forty and 35 percent were under thirty. Weber, *Die Wandlung des deutschen Kommunismus,* 2:26–27.

125. Weber and Herbst, *Deutsche Kommunisten,* 360–362; *Sitzungsberichte des Preußischen Landtags,* vol. 11, 237th Session, 4 May 1923, 16918–16922; 239th Session, 7 May 1923, 17020–17022; see also the reporting on this in *Die Rote Fahne* 6, nos. 99–102, 4–8 May 1923, esp. "Die Polizeiaktion im Landtag," 2.

126. "Die widerrechtliche Verhaftung der Genossen Scholem, Sobottka und Rosi Wolfstein," 9; Ernst Reuter, *Schriften, Reden,* 703–704.

127. Weitz, "Communism and the Public Spheres of Weimar Germany," 281; Raithel, *Das schwierige Spiel des Parlamentarismus,* 73.

128. Betty Scholem to Gershom Scholem, 2 Nov. 1923, in Scholem and Scholem, *Mutter und Sohn im Briefwechsel*, 94; Anträge an das Orbüro, BAB SAPMO, 24 Mar. 1925, p. 215; *Verhandlungen des Reichstags*, vol. 385, 46th Session, 3 Apr. 1925, 1345.

129. Politbüro-Sitzungen II, BAB SAPMO, 15 Sept. 1922, p. 3; *Bericht über die Verhandlungen des III. (8.) Parteitages*, 110.

130. Scholem, *Walter Benjamin*, 76–77, 143; Zadoff, *Von Berlin nach Jerusalem und zurück*.

131. He was registered from 24 October 1922 to 24 January 1924 under the number 835/113. Rektorat, Universitätsarchiv der Humboldt Universität Berlin.

132. Weber, *Die Wandlung des deutschen Kommunismus*, 2:286; *Bericht über die Verhandlungen des III. (8.) Parteitages*; Buber-Neumann, *Kriegsschauplätze der Weltrevolution*, 68.

133. Karl Radek (1885–1939?) and August Guralsky (1890–1960?), pseudonym Kleine, were representatives of the EKKI in Germany. Scholem, *From Berlin to Jerusalem*, 145.

134. Scholem, *Walter Benjamin*, 140.

135. Arthur Rosenberg to Ruth Fischer, 28 Nov. 1941, in Fischer and Maslow, *Abtrünnig wider Willen*, 144.

136. Angress, *Die Kampfzeit der KPD*, 288–290.

137. Weber and Herbst, *Deutsche Kommunisten*, 205, 484–486, 624–626, 811–812; Keßler, *Arthur Rosenberg*, 69; Keßler, *Ruth Fischer*.

138. Scholem, *Von Berlin nach Jerusalem*, 180–181; Weber, *Die Wandlung des deutschen Kommunismus*, 1:47 and n. 94, 173–175; Wirsching, *Vom Weltkrieg zum Bürgerkrieg?*, 198.

139. Bois, "Im Kampf gegen Stalinismus und Faschismus," 87.

140. Protokoll des KPD-Bezirksparteitages, 20 and 21 Jan. 1923, BAB SAPMO, pp. 35–40, 50; Rosenberg, *Entstehung und Geschichte der Weimarer Republik*, 400–404; Keßler, *Arthur Rosenberg*, 91.

141. Ruth Fischer and Arkadi Maslow backed down, but Arthur Rosenberg and Werner Scholem refused to do so. Angress, *Die Kampfzeit der KPD*, 305–309; *Bericht über die Verhandlungen des III. (8.) Parteitages*, 325–326; Protokoll der Sitzung der Zentrale mit den Vertretern der Berliner Bezirksleitung, 5 Apr. 1923, BAB SAPMO, p. 103.

142. Protokoll der Sitzung der Zentrale mit den Vertretern der Berliner Bezirksleitung, 5 Apr. 1923, BAB SAPMO, pp. 23, 189; Berlin-Brandenburg-Lausitz II, BAB SAPMO, 4.4.1923, pp. 88–90; *Bericht über die Verhandlungen des III. (8.) Parteitages*, 418–20.

143. Werner Scholem to Gershom Scholem, 6 Aug. 1919, INL, Archive G. Scholem; Danzer, *Zwischen Vertrauen und Verrat*, 17–21; Kroll, *Kommunistische Intellektuelle in Westeuropa*, 10–11.

144. On the concept of friendship and loyalty, see Danzer, *Zwischen Vertrauen und Verrat*, 17; Schulze Wessel, "'Loyalität' als geschichtlicher Grundbegriff und Forschungskonzept."

145. Politbüro-Sitzungen, BAB SAPMO, 29 June 1922, 3; Schreiben an die Parteizentrale, 24 June 1922, BAB SAPMO, 1–2; Werner Scholem an die "Erwachende Jugend," 1922, BAB SAPMO.

146. Gerrits, *Myth of Jewish Communism*, 186.

147. Silberner, *Kommunisten zur Judenfrage*, 266–267; Jay, "Anti-Semitism and the Weimar Left," 47; Liepach, *Das Wahlverhalten der jüdischen Bevölkerung in der Weimarer Republik*, 144; Barkai, "Politische Orientierung und Krisenbewußtsein," 106.

148. Since Radek praised the National Socialist Albert Schlageter in his speech, the period after that became known as the Schlageter Campaign. *Protokoll der Konferenz der Erweiterten Exekutive der Kommunistischen Internationale, Moskau vom 12. bis 23.6.1923*, 240–241.

149. "'Hängt die Judenkapitalisten auf': Ruth Fischer als Antisemitin." She did not deny saying this until decades later: see Silberner, *Kommunisten zur Judenfrage*, 269.

150. "Die neuen Antisemiten," 5; Kistenmacher, "Vom 'Judas' zum 'Judenkapital,'" 69–73.

151. Berlin-Brandenburg-Lausitz, Bezirksparteitag, 20 June 1923, BAB SAPMO, pp. 56–59. This was handled differently in the SPD, where the topic was brought up primarily by Jewish functionaries. Jay, "Anti-Semitism and the Weimar Left," 48–50.

152. Weber, *Die Wandlung des deutschen Kommunismus*, 2:286; Antrag auf Grund des Bundesergänzungsgesetzes Emmy Scholem, NLA, vol. 1, appendix1, "Schilderung des Verfolgungsvorganges," 7 Apr. 1954, p. 2.

153. Interview with Edith Capon, PRG; Buber-Neumann, *Kriegsschauplätze der Weltrevolution*, 67.

154. Betty Scholem to Gershom Scholem, 15 Oct. 1923, in Scholem and Scholem, *Mutter und Sohn im Briefwechsel*, 86.

155. Werner Scholem, "Skizze über die Entwicklung der Opposition in der KPD," 133.

156. Winkler, *Weimar, 1918–1933*, 214–215; Schüle, *Trotzkismus in Deutschland bis 1933*, 41–45; Bayerlein et al., *Deutscher Oktober 1923*; Hirschinger, *"Gestapoagenten, Trotzkisten, Verräter,"* 48–53.

157. Hirschinger, *"Gestapoagenten, Trotzkisten, Verräter,"* 52–53; *Klassenkampf*, 14 and 18 March 1924, cited in ibid., 53; Wirsching, *Vom Weltkrieg zum Bürgerkrieg?*, 238; Langels, *Die ultralinke Opposition der KPD in der Weimarer Republik*, 15; Gerd Reuter, *KPD-Politik in der Weimarer Republik*, 84–85.

158. Weitz, "Communism and the Public Spheres of Weimar Germany," 280–281; Weitz, *Creating German Communism*, 100–131.

159. Rosenberg, *Entstehung und Geschichte der Weimarer Republik*, 438.

160. Betty Scholem to Gershom Scholem, 12 Mar. 1930, in Scholem and Scholem, *Mutter und Sohn im Briefwechsel*, 217.

161. Kundt, "Juden und Mitglieder der Sektion Donauland unerwünscht," 19–28.

162. Kaufmann, "Gründung des Deutschen Alpenvereins Berlin," 51–52.

163. 3. [Dritte] Tagung des Zentralausschusses der KPD, 18–19 Oct. 1924, BAB SAPMO, pp. 97–113.

164. As Klaus-Michael Mallmann argues, the Stalinization of the party affected the party's grass roots far less than it did the KPD leadership: Mallmann, "Gehorsame Parteisoldaten oder eigensinnige Akteure?," 401–415, esp. 411; Mallmann, *Kommunisten in der Weimarer Republik*.

165. *Welt am Abend* 9 (1931): 179; Mosse, "German Socialists and the Jewish Question in the Weimar Republic," 137; Silberner, *Kommunisten zur Judenfrage*, 265; Barkai, "Politische Orientierung und Krisenbewußtsein," 106.

166. Weber and Herbst, *Deutsche Kommunisten*, 693.

167. Stalin, "Die deutsche Revolution und die Fehler des Genossen Radek," 448–449.

168. Scholem, "Skizze über die Entwicklung der Opposition in der KPD," 124–134.

169. Betty Scholem to Gershom Scholem, 8 Apr. 1924, in Scholem and Scholem, *Mutter und Sohn im Briefwechsel*, 102.

170. Sinowjew, "Zur Lage in der KPD," 239; Zinoviev, letter dated 26 Apr. 1924, in *Bericht über die Verhandlungen des IX. Parteitages*, 189–191; Winkler, *Weimar, 1918–1933*, 253–254; Weber, *Die Wandlung des deutschen Kommunismus*, 1:64; Langels, *Die ultralinke Opposition der KPD*, 260 n. 21.

171. This letter, dated 31 March 1924, was intercepted by the police and was not received by the person to whom it was addressed; reprinted in Weber, "Zu den Beziehungen zwischen der KPD und der Kommunistischen Internationale," 191–192.

172. The letter from Levien, written in late March, was also intercepted; reprinted in ibid., 192–194.

173. Bahne, "Zwischen 'Luxemburgismus' und 'Stalinismus,'" 360.

174. Tätigkeitsbericht des Orbüro, 10 Apr.–1 Oct. 1924, BAB SAPMO, p. 9; Weber, *Die Wandlung des deutschen Kommunismus*, 1:62–75 and 2:285–286; Winkler, *Weimar, 1918–1933*, 254.

175. Winkler, *Weimar, 1918–1933*, 254; *Bericht über die Verhandlungen des IX. Parteitages*, 381–387; Wirsching *Vom Weltkrieg zum Bürgerkrieg?*, 238–243.

176. Kaufmann et al., *Der Nachrichtendienst der KPD*, 94–96; letter from Karl Radek, cited by Maslow in Fischer and Maslow, *Abtrünnig wider Willen*, 361; Buber-Neumann, *Kriegsschauplätze der Weltrevolution*, 117.

177. Schumacher, "Nachklänge zum Parteitag," 147.

178. "Berufsberatung," 215.

179. "Bisher 448 Abgeordnete gewählt"; Winkler, *Weimar 1918–1933*, 261; Buber-Neumann, *Kriegsschauplätze der Weltrevolution*, 147.

180. M. d. R., *Die Reichstagsabgeordneten der Weimarer Republik in der Zeit des National-sozialismus*, 506; Betty to Gershom Scholem, 5 May and 3 June 1924, in Scholem and Scholem, *Mutter und Sohn im Briefwechsel*, 106, 108–109.

181. Mergel, *Parlamentarische Kultur in der Weimarer Republik*, 141–142.

182. "Reichstag Dispersed with Jeers," 9; *Verhandlungen des Reichstags*, vol. 381, 1st, 2nd, and 3rd Sessions, 27 May, 28 May 1924, 4, 22; Angress, "Juden im politischen Leben der Revolutionszeit," 148–150.

183. He referred to the statistics compiled by Emil Julius Gumbel, who spoke in 1922 of 354 political murders committed by the right and 20 murders committed by the left. Gumbel, *Vier Jahre politischer Mord*, 144–149; *Verhandlungen des Reichstags*, vol. 381, 10th Session, 24 June 1924, 240–246.

184. Walter Benjamin to Gottfried Salomon-Delatour, 10 June 1924, and to Gershom Scholem, 13 June 1924, in Benjamin, *Gesammelte Briefe*, 2:460, 468; see also, *Kladderadatsch* 77, nos. 24, 30, 31, and 32 (1924): 379–380, 478, 490, 507; "Zum Gruß!," 362.

185. Betty Scholem to Gershom Scholem, 3 June and 2 Sept. 1924, in Scholem and Scholem, *Mutter und Sohn im Briefwechsel*, 108–110.

186. Scholem, *From Berlin to Jerusalem*, 145.

187. Goebbels, diary entry from 14 July 1924, in Goebbels, *Tagebücher*, 1:102–103.

188. *Bericht über die Verhandlungen des IX. Parteitages*, 93, 289; Weber and Herbst, *Deutsche Kommunisten*, 180.

189. Zetkin, "Die Intellektuellenfrage," 45–46; Danzer, *Zwischen Vertrauen und Verrat*, 88–90.

190. Werner Scholem, quoted in Weber, *Die Wandlung des deutschen Kommunismus*, 2:327 n. 40; Silberner, *Kommunisten zur Judenfrage*, 267; *Bericht über die Verhandlungen des IX. Parteitages*, 93, 289; Keßler, *Die SED und die Juden*, 20.

191. Hilde Benjamin, *Georg Benjamin*, 178–182.

192. Betty Scholem to Gershom Scholem, 8 Apr. and 2 Sept. 1924, in Scholem and Scholem, *Mutter und Sohn im Briefwechsel*, 102, 109–110.

193. Orbüro unter Scholem, 1924, BAB SAPMO; Rede Scholems in der Sitzung der Zentrale mit Bezirkssekretären, 4 Sept. 1924, BAB SAPMO, 5.

194. Protokoll des KPD-Bezirksparteitages, 20 and 21 Jan. 1923, BAB SAPMO, 33–34.

195. 3. [Dritte] Tagung des Zentralausschusses der KPD, 18–19 Oct. 1924, BAB SAPMO, fiche 1, p. 1, and fiche 4, pp. 97–113; Bezirkskonferenzen Schlesien, Sitzung des Bezirksausschusses, 6 May 1924, BAB SAPMO, 1–8.

196. Now there were only forty-five deputies instead of the previous sixty-two. Weber, *Die Wandlung des deutschen Kommunismus*, 2:285–286; Anträge an das Orbüro, BAB SAPMO, 206.

197. He dwelt particularly on Lukács's book *History and Class Consciousness*; Walter Benjamin to Gershom Scholem, 16 Sept. 1924, in Benjamin, *Gesammelte Briefe*, 2:483; and Benjamin, *Correspondence*, 248.

198. Scholem and Drews, ". . . und alles ist Kabbala," 19–20.

199. Walter Benjamin to Gershom Scholem, 22 Dec. 1924, in Benjamin, *Correspondence*, 257–258.

200. Honorary title for a businessman, here purely ironic.

201. Betty Scholem to Gershom Scholem, 9 Feb. and 19 Apr. 1925, as well as 7 Feb. 1933, in Scholem and Scholem, *Mutter und Sohn im Briefwechsel*, 119–120, 128, 273; Weber and Herbst, *Deutsche Kommunisten*, 822.

202. Berger-Barzilai, *Ha-Tragedyah shel ha-mahpekhah ha-Sovyetit*, 22; Zinoviev quoted in Bahne, "Zwischen 'Luxemburgismus' und 'Stalinismus,' " 362.

203. "Kommunisten und Hindenburgwahl."

204. "Achtung Manöver!"

205. *Protokoll der Konferenz der Erweiterten Exekutive der Kommunistischen Internationale, Moskau vom 21.3. bis 6.4.1925*, 331; Rundschreiben von Scholem und Rosenberg, 15 Apr. 1925, BAB SAPMO, 1–4; Schreiben von Scholem, Katz, und Rosenberg an die Zentrale, 3 May 1925, BAB SAPMO, 5–8; *Dokumente und Materialien zur Geschichte der Arbeiterbewegung*, 8:132–133; Keßler, *Arthur Rosenberg*, 115–117; Fischer, *Stalin and German Communism*, 451–453; Langels, *Die ultralinke Opposition der KPD*, 50–59; Weber, *Die Wandlung des deutschen Kommunismus*, 1:106–111; Hirschinger, "Gestapoagenten, Trotzkisten, Verräter," 59.

206. Rede Scholems, Zentralausschuss der KPD, 5. Tagung, 9–10 May 1925, BAB SAPMO, fiche 5, pp. 78–82; Erklärung von Scholem, Katz, und Rosenberg, 5. Tagung, 9–10 May 1925, BAB SAPMO, fiche 9, pp. 229–229b; Beschluss des ZK, 237; Rede Scholems beim Jugendkongress in Leipzig, 15 May 1924, BAB SAPMO.

207. On this topic, see the articles that appeared in *Die Rote Fahne*, 9 and 10 June 1925.

208. Werner Scholem, "Zur Organisationsfrage," 65.

209. As part of his efforts to fulfill this aim, he published a circular for the faction, which he signed with "*semper idem.*" Weber, *Die Wandlung des deutschen Kommunismus*, vol. 2, 285–286.

210. 10. [Zehnter] Parteitag, Berlin, 12–17 July 1925, BAB SAPMO, fiche 3, pp. 73–74.

211. Meyer-Leviné, *Im inneren Kreis*, 138–140; see also Ruth Fischer's closing remarks at the party congress, in *Bericht über die Verhandlungen des X. Parteitages*, 637–646.

212. Weber, *Die Wandlung des deutschen Kommunismus*, 2:285–286; Langels, *Die ultralinke Opposition der KPD*, 64; Kaufmann et al., *Der Nachrichtendienst der KPD*, 96–97.

213. Plenartagung des ZK, 6–7 Aug. 1925, BAB SAPMO, 17–18; and 23–24 Aug. 1925, BAB SAPMO, 11–12.

214. Open letter, *Die Rote Fahne* 8 (1925): 200, quoted in Weber, *Der deutsche Kommunismus*, 218–242, esp. 226, 228; Winkler, *Der Schein der Normalität*, 422–433; Fischer, *Stalin und der deutsche Kommunismus*, 2:545; see also her article, in which she considered anyone who saw a major difference between Moscow and the KPD to be among the "worst enemies of the proletariat": *Die Rote Fahne* 8 (1925): 207.

215. *Die Rote Fahne* 8 (1925): 218; Material über Ultralinke, BAB SAPMO, fiche 2, pp. 62–69; Langels, *Die ultralinke Opposition der KPD*, 75.

216. Betty Scholem to Gershom Scholem, 4 Oct. 1925, in Scholem and Scholem, *Mutter und Sohn im Briefwechsel*, 132; Werner Scholem to Gerhard Scholem, 30 Mar. 1919, INL, Archive G. Scholem.

217. Bericht an EKKI, 19 Oct. 1925, BAB SAPMO; Parteikonferenzen Pommern, BAB SAPMO, 1–2.

218. Weber, *Die Wandlung des deutschen Kommunismus*, 2:285–286.; Weber and Herbst, *Deutsche Kommunisten*, 389–390.

219. Rundschreiben der Linken Kommunisten (Ruhrgebiet) 1925, BAB SAPMO, 97–100.

220. Plenartagung des ZK, 29 Oct. 1925, BAB SAPMO, 1, 2, 5.

221. Parteikonferenz der KPD, 31 Oct.–1 Nov. 1925, BAB SAPMO, fiche 2, pp. 81–103, and fiche 7, p. 305.

222. Ibid., fiche 1, p. 60.

223. Ibid., fiche 7, p. 266; fiche 10, p. 60; fiche 11, pp. 71–81; fiche 14, p. 203; Material über Ultralinke, BAB SAPMO, fiche 1, pp. 44–45; Langels, *Die ultralinke Opposition der KPD*, 79–81.

224. Stokes, *Paradigm Lost*, 228 (citing the translation offered here of the original German quote found in Brecht, "Typus des intellektuellen Revolutionärs," 64).

225. Bahne, "Zwischen 'Luxemburgismus' und 'Stalinismus,'" 361.

226. Parteikonferenz der KPD, 31 Oct.–1 Nov. 1925, BAB SAPMO, fiche 2, pp. 115–130, and fiche 5, p. 137.

227. Langels, *Die ultralinke Opposition der KPD*, 235–236; Politbüro-Dokumente zur Ultralinken, BAB SAPMO.

228. Bahne, "Zwischen 'Luxemburgismus' und 'Stalinismus,'" 363 (quoting Hans Pfemfert, in *Aktion* 16 [1926]: 148) and 364; Reuter, *KPD-Politik in der Weimarer Republik*, 87–91; Schüle, *Trotzkismus in Deutschland bis 1933*, 53–55; Langels, *Die ultralinke Opposition der KPD*, 79, 97–98.

229. Fischer, *Stalin and German Communism*, 440; Gershom Scholem also wrote that his brother "was not at all appreciated in his [Stalin's] eyes," Gershom Scholem to Reinhold Scholem, 8 Sept. 1976, in Scholem, *Briefe*, 3:144–145.

230. Stalin, "Über den Kampf gegen die Rechten und 'Ultralinken' Abweichungen," 1–9.

231. Buber-Neumann, *Kriegsschauplätze der Weltrevolution*, 163–166; *Die Rote Fahne* 9, no. 46 (1926): supplement 1; *Protokoll der Konferenz der Erweiterten Exekutive der Kommunistischen Internationale, Moskau vom 17.2. bis 15.3.1926*, 71–72, 181–187, 247–248, 594–595; Winkler, *Der Schein der Normalität*, 429; Keßler, *Arthur Rosenberg*, 125.

232. Betty Scholem to Gershom Scholem, 2 Feb. 1926, in Scholem and Scholem, *Mutter und Sohn im Briefwechsel*, 136.

233. Werner Scholem to Gershom Scholem [no date, probably early 1926], in Scholem and Scholem, *Mutter und Sohn im Briefwechsel*, 137–139.

234. Betty Scholem to Gershom Scholem, 29 June 1926, in Scholem and Scholem, *Mutter und Sohn im Briefwechsel*, 144; Zadoff, *Next Year in Marienbad*, 54–57.

235. The Russian opposition formed after the German opposition did, in the summer of 1926. In addition to Trotsky, its members also included Grigory Zinoviev and Lev Kamenev, the two men who formerly had been part of a troika with Joseph Stalin. Broué, *Trotzki*, 1:527–536; 543–544; Broué, *Die deutsche Linke und die russische Opposition*, 12; Weber, *Die Wandlung des deutschen Kommunismus*, 1:161–164 and 2:285–286.

236. A day earlier Scholem and Urbahns had publically protested against the party leadership. Bois, *Kommunisten gegen Hitler und Stalin*, 231; Material über Ultralinke, BAB SAPMO, fiche 3, p. 239; Foitzik, "Das kommunistische Intellektuellenmilieu in der Weimarer Republik," 233–234; Weber and Herbst, *Deutsche Kommunisten*, 206.

237. Plenartagung des ZK, 5 Nov. 1926, BAB SAPMO, fiche 1, pp. 31–56, 100, and fiche 2, p. 188.

238. "Ausgeschlossene Reichstagsabgeordnete"; "Die kommunistische Verlustliste"; see also article in *Die Rote Fahne* 9, no. 256 (1926): 3; Betty Scholem to Gershom Scholem, 7 Dec. 1926, in Scholem and Scholem, *Mutter und Sohn im Briefwechsel*, 151.

239. Material über Ultralinke, BAB SAPMO, fiche 3, pp. 240–241.

240. Werner Scholem et al., *Die Wahrheit über die Verhandlungen mit der deutschen Opposition in Moskau*; Weber, *Die Wandlung des deutschen Kommunismus*, 1:166–168.

241. Walter Benjamin to Gershom Scholem, 10 Dec. 1926, and diary entry for 9 Dec. 1926, both in *Moscow Diary*, 125 and 11; Scholem, "Vorwort," 10–11; Scholem, *Walter Benjamin*, 161, 170, 199, 239; Smith, "Afterword," 143–144.

242. *Mitteilungsblatt Linke Opposition der KPD* 1 (1927): 1; Broué, *Die deutsche Linke und die russische Opposition*, 16.

243. *Die Fahne des Kommunismus* 2 (1928): 2.

244. Announcements of his evening lectures, in *Die Fahne des Kommunismus* 1, no. 15 (1927): 1; no. 32 (1927): 170; no. 34 (1927): 182; no. 39 (1927): 227; and vol. 2, no. 4 (1928) : 1; and no. 13 (1928): 1; Müller, *Die Akte Wehner*, 48–49.

245. Lagebericht des Polizeipräsidiums Berlin, BAB SAPMO, p. 247a; Bois, "Im Kampf gegen Stalinismus und Faschismus," 93; Rüdiger Zimmermann, *Der Leninbund*, 98; Weber, *Die Wandlung des deutschen Kommunismus*, 1:183–184; Schüle, *Trotzkismus in Deutschland bis 1933*, 56–58; Broué, *Die deutsche Linke und die russische Opposition*, 8.

246. Berichte zur innerparteilichen Lage 1926, BAB SAPMO, pp. 167, 212–218; *Die Fahne des Kommunismus* 2, no. 17 (1928): 163.

247. Spitzelbericht einer Versammlung der Linken Kommunisten, 27 Oct. 1927, Berlin-Brandenburg Lausitz VI, innerparteiliche Auseinandersetzungen, BAB SAPMO, pp. 131–133; Kaufmann et al., *Der Nachrichtendienst der KPD*, 140–142.

248. *Die Fahne des Kommunismus* 2, no. 20 (1928): 107–108, 201–202; Material über Ultralinke, BAB SAPMO, fiche 4, pp. 271–281; Zimmermann, *Der Leninbund*, 77–79, 112, 115–116; Broué, *Die deutsche Linke und die russische Opposition*, 30; Bois, "Im Kampf gegen Stalinismus und Faschismus," 94–95; Schüle, *Trotzkismus in Deutschland bis 1933*, 53–55; Bois, *Kommunisten gegen Hitler und Stalin*, 267–268.

249. Erich Mühsam quoted in Buber-Neumann, *Kriegsschauplätze der Weltrevolution*, 168–169.

250. According to Pierre Broué, as cited in Peter Lübbe's introduction to Fischer and Maslow, *Abtrünnig wider Willen*, 518; Broué, *Die deutsche Linke und die russische Opposition*, 30–31; Broué, *Léon Sedov*, 95, 102; Schüle, *Trotzkismus in Deutschland bis 1933*, 144, 154.

251. Fischer, "Trotsky in Paris," 499; Peter Lübbe, "Einleitung," in Fischer and Maslow, *Abtrünnig wider Willen*, 7; Broué, *Die deutsche Linke und die russische Opposition*, 31. Even

today doubts are still raised whether Scholem was indeed a Trotskyite; see Peters, *Wer die Hoffnung verliert*, 172–173.

252. Scholem, *"Es gibt ein Geheimnis in der Welt,"* 51–52.

253. Reuter, *KPD-Politik in der Weimarer Republik*, 87; Langels, *Die ultralinke Opposition der KPD*, 236–237.

254. Hortzschansky et al., *Ernst Thälmann*, 200; Grebing, "Der Typus des linken Intellektuellen in der Weimarer Republik," 19.

255. He was registered on 26 April 1927 under the number 4010/117 and deregistered on 4 March 1931, Universitätsarchiv der Humboldt Universität Berlin; Testament Arthur Scholem, 24 Sept. 1921, IPW, Nachlass Scholem.

256. Betty Scholem to Gershom Scholem, 7 Dec. 1926, 27 Mar. 1928, 17 July 1928, and 31 Jan. 1928, in Scholem and Scholem, *Mutter und Sohn im Briefwechsel*, 151, 154–155, 160–161, 174; Werner Scholem to Gershom Scholem, 23 Mar. 1931, INL, Archive G. Scholem; *Verhandlungen des Reichstags*, vol. 394, Berlin 1928, session on 28 Jan. 1928, 12466–12469.

257. Goddard and Glendinning, *Edith's Story*, BBC, 25 February 2010; Antrag auf Grund des Bundesergänzungsgesetzes Emmy Scholem, NLA, vol. 1, appendix 1, "Schilderung des Verfolgungsvorganges," 7 Apr. 1954, p. 2; Betty Scholem to Gershom Scholem, 18 June 1928, in Scholem and Scholem, *Mutter und Sohn im Briefwechsel*, 169.

258. The house at Klopstockstrasse 7 in which the Scholems lived was destroyed in the war. Today there is a *Stolperstein* in the sidewalk in front of their former residence in memory of Werner Scholem. Scholem, *Von Berlin nach Jerusalem*, 180; Janiszewski, *Das alte Hansa-Viertel in Berlin*, 95–96, 111–119.

259. All of the information on the living conditions and household items is taken from Emmy Scholem's restitution application, Antrag auf Grund des Bundesergänzungsgesetzes Emmy Scholem, NLA, vol. 1, appendix 1, "Schilderung des Verfolgungsvorganges," 7 Apr. 1954, 2; as well as from a statement made by Eduard Schädler, 17 July 1962, ibid., vol. 2; Antrag auf Grund des Bundesergänzungsgesetzes Werner Scholem, NLA, appendix 1, and Schreiben Emmy Scholems an den Regierungspräsidenten, 2 Feb. 1955.

260. Goddard, "Erinnerungen," chap. 2, version 3, PRG.

261. Betty Scholem to Gershom Scholem, 25 June 1928 and 31 Jan. 1928, in Scholem and Scholem, *Mutter und Sohn im Briefwechsel*, 154–155, 171.

262. Friedländer, *Zur Sexualethik des Kommunismus*; Rühle, *Die Sozialisierung der Frau*; Kollontaj, *Die neue Moral und die Arbeiterklasse*; Grossmann, *Reforming Sex*, 78–106; Usborne, "The New Woman and Generational Conflict," 141; Weitz, *Weimar Germany*, 302–305.

263. Betty Scholem to Gershom Scholem, 27 Mar., 17 July, 18 Sept. 1928, in Scholem and Scholem, *Mutter und Sohn im Briefwechsel*, 160–161, 174, 178; Werner Scholem to Gershom Scholem, 23 Mar. 1931, INL, Archive G. Scholem; Jütte, *Lust ohne Last*, 309.

264. Such publications included *Die Kämpferin, Die Kommunistin, Die Arbeiterin,* and *Der Weg der Frau*; Danzer, *Zwischen Vertrauen und Verrat*, 97.

265. Prestel, "The 'New Jewish Woman' in Weimar Germany," 138.

266. Goddard, "Erinnerungen," chap. 2, version 3, PRG.

267. Goddard and Glendinning, *Reni and the Brownshirts*, 26–27; Goddard, "Erinnerungen," chap. 2, version 3, PRG.

268. Goddard, "Erinnerungen," chap. 2, version 3, PRG; Goddard and Glendinning, *Reni and the Brownshirts*, 22–28; Betty Scholem to Gershom Scholem, 31 Jan. 1928, in Scholem and Scholem, *Mutter und Sohn im Briefwechsel*, 155; Flachowsky and Stoecker, *Vom Amazonas an die Ostfront*, 33–34.

269. Goddard, "Erinnerungen," chap. 2, version 3, and chap. "Renate Scholem," PRG; Goddard and Glendinning, *Reni and the Brownshirts*, 10–11; Betty Scholem to Gershom Scholem, 22 Sept. 1924, 26 Apr. 1925, 18 Sept. 1928, and 12 Mar. 1930, in Scholem and Scholem, *Mutter und Sohn im Briefwechsel*, 114, 129, 178, 216–217; Emmy Scholem to Gershom Scholem, 20 Feb. 1954 and 21 Aug. 1962, INL, Archive G. Scholem.

270. Goddard, "Erinnerungen," chap. 2, version 3, PRG; Goddard and Glendinning, *Reni and the Brownshirts*, 2, 5–7, 21–24; interview with Renee Goddard, 10 Jan. 2008, PMZ; Völter, *Judentum und Kommunismus*, 100, 303–304; Betty Scholem to Gershom Scholem, 9 Oct. 1929 and 6 Oct. 1930, in Scholem and Scholem, *Mutter und Sohn im Briefwechsel*, 207, 221–223.

271. Goddard, "Erinnerungen," chap. 2, version 3, PRG; Betty Scholem to Gershom Scholem, 6 Oct. 1930 and 15 Nov. 1932, in Scholem and Scholem, *Mutter und Sohn im Briefwechsel*, 221–223, 269; Eloesser, "Zweimal: Die meuternden Matrosen."

272. Betty Scholem to Gershom Scholem, 25 June 1928, in Scholem and Scholem, *Mutter und Sohn im Briefwechsel*, 171; Friedländer, *Zur Sexualethik des Kommunismus*; Walter, "'Meine Frau hat keine Zeit!,'" 99; Engels, *Der Ursprung der Familie*, 170.

273. The "photo comrade" in question was Franz Pfemfert, who had been running a studio since 1927, in which he made numerous portraits of artists, publicists, and politicians. Betty Scholem to Gershom Scholem, 6 June 1928 and 9 Feb. 1932, and Gershom Scholem to Betty Scholem, 6 June 1928, in Scholem and Scholem, *Mutter und Sohn im Briefwechsel*, 169, 256, and 167; Bahne, "Zwischen 'Luxemburgismus' und 'Stalinismus,'" 383.

274. Certification dated 2 March 1931, grade "fully satisfactory," IPW, Nachlass Scholem; Werner Scholem to Gershom Scholem, 23 Mar. 1930, INL, Archive G. Scholem; Betty Scholem to Gershom Scholem, 21 Jan. 1930, and Gershom Scholem to Betty Scholem, 30 Jan. 1930, in Scholem and Scholem, *Mutter und Sohn im Briefwechsel*, 216 n. 3, and 215–216.

275. The owners were Dr. Salo Turnheim and Dr. C. Wurm. Antrag auf Grund des Bundesergänzungsgesetzes Emmy Scholem, NLA, vol. 1, appendix 1, "Schilderung des Verfolgungsvorganges," 7 Apr. 1954, p. 2, appendix 1; Emmy Scholem to the Regierungspräsidenten, 2 Nov. 1955, ibid.

276. Betty Scholem to Gershom Scholem, 19 July, 11 Aug., and 15 Sept. 1931, in Scholem and Scholem, *Mutter und Sohn im Briefwechsel*, 230–231, 239, 245, 252; Gershom Scholem to Betty Scholem, 5 Aug. 1931, in ibid., 244.

277. Scholem, *Von Berlin nach Jerusalem*, 181; Betty Scholem to Gershom Scholem, 28 Apr. 1932, in Scholem and Scholem, *Mutter und Sohn im Briefwechsel*, 264–265; Winkler, *Weimar, 1918–1933*, 457, 477–520, 532–538.

278. Broué, *Trotzki*, 2:759. Today the Turkish name for the island is Büyükada.

279. Werner Scholem to Gershom Scholem, 14 Nov. 1932, INL, Archive G. Scholem.

280. Interview with Edith Capon, PRG; "Die Nacht der Papierschlangen," 4.

3. Exile in Germany

Note to epigraphs: Scholem, *Tagebücher*, 2:378: "[Hiobs] Klage ist unendlich in allen Dimensionen, sie ist von einer höheren Unendlichkeit als dieses Leben selbst, denn sie erstreckt sich ja eben auch auf jene Länder hinter den Grenzen seines Lebens, deren Gesetzlosigkeit ihn schreckt und ihr drohendes Hereinragen in seine Welt."

The song "Ein neuer Frühling wird in die Heimat kommen" (A new spring will come home), performed for the first time on 29 September 1933, was a concession by the Comedian Harmonists to the "New Order" existing in the country and an attempt to deflect attention away from the Jewish members of the group. After the group was, in 1935, prohibited from performing with all of its original members, "Ein neuer Frühling" was understood as a song of resistance and is supposed to have been recorded abroad. On this, see Schoeps, *Ungeflügelte Worte*, 135; Brüninghaus, *Unterhaltungsmusik im Dritten Reich*, 19.

1. Betty Scholem to Gershom Scholem, 14 Feb. 1933, in Scholem and Scholem, *Mutter und Sohn im Briefwechsel*, 275; Schumacher, *M.d.R.: Die Reichstagsabgeordneten der Weimarer Republik in der Zeit des Nationalsozialismus*, 506.

2. Betty Scholem to Gershom Scholem, 28 Feb. 1933, in Scholem and Scholem, *Mutter und Sohn im Briefwechsel*, 278.

3. *Reichsgesetzblatt*, part 1, 28 Feb. 1933, no. 17, 1; Winkler, *Der Weg in die Katastrophe*, 881–883.

4. Longerich, *Joseph Goebbels*, 214, 750 n. 31.

5. "Neue Notverordnung in Sicht," *Vossische Zeitung*, 28 Mar. 1933, 1.

6. The figures often quoted in the secondary literature of up to 5,000 arrests made during this night on the basis of lists prepared well in advance are probably erroneous; estimates for Berlin speak of 1,500 arrests. Among those taken into custody was the sixteen-year-old son of Ruth Fischer, Gerhart Friedländer. *Vossische Zeitung*, evening edition, 28 Feb. 1933; Tuchel, *Konzentrationslager*, 96–99, n. 209; Pikarski, *Geschichte der revolutionären Berliner Arbeiterbewegung*, 30.

7. "Hitlerisatsia shel germania," *Davar*, 10 Mar. 1933, 1; Broué, *Léon Sedov*, 110.

8. Antrag auf Grund des Bundesergänzungsgesetztes Werner Scholem, NLA, Anlage 1; Betty Scholem to Gershom Scholem, 5 Mar. 1933, in Scholem and Scholem, *Mutter und Sohn im Briefwechsel*, 281.

9. Betty Scholem to Gershom Scholem, 27 Mar. 1933, and the reply by Gershom Scholem, 5 Apr. 1933, in Scholem and Scholem, *Mutter und Sohn im Briefwechsel*, 286–287, 289–291.

10. On the basis of this law, he was officially suspended from judicial service on 31 Aug. 1933 and received a certificate for his legal clerkship period from the president of the court of appeal (Kammergericht). Antrag auf Grund des Bundesergänzungsgesetztes Werner Scholem, NLA, Anlage 1, 20 Sept. 1933.

11. Peter Lübbe, "Einleitung," and Ruth Fischer, "Erinnerungen an die Jahre 1932–1933," in Fischer and Maslow, *Abtrünnig wider Willen*, 6–7, 531; Betty Scholem to Gershom Scholem, 9 and 18 April 1933, in Scholem and Scholem, *Mutter und Sohn im Briefwechsel*, 292–293.

12. Betty Scholem to Gershom Scholem, 25 Apr. 1933, in Scholem and Scholem, *Mutter und Sohn im Briefwechsel*, 295–296.

13. Betty Scholem to Gershom Scholem, 25 Apr., 1 Aug., and 23 Oct. 1933, as well as 10 Jan. 1935, in Scholem and Scholem, *Mutter und Sohn im Briefwechsel*, 292–293, 295–296, 320–323, 339–341, 398.

14. Interview with Edith Capon, PRG; Goddard, "Erinnerungen," chap. 2, version 3, PRG; Goddard and Glendinning, *Reni and the Brownshirts*.

15. Goddard and Glendinning, *Reni and the Brownshirts*, 18; Betty Scholem to Gershom Scholem, 1 May 1933, in Scholem and Scholem, *Mutter und Sohn im Briefwechsel*, 298–300.

16. Betty Scholem to Gershom Scholem, 1 and 10 May 1933, in Scholem and Scholem, *Mutter und Sohn im Briefwechsel*, 298–300, 300–301; Gershom Scholem to Walter Benjamin, 15 June 1933, in Benjamin and Scholem, *Correspondence*, 56; König and König, *Das Polizeipräsidium Berlin-Alexanderplatz*, 84–89.

17. Betty Scholem to Gershom Scholem, 28 May1933, in Scholem and Scholem, *Mutter und Sohn im Briefwechsel*, 304.

18. Drobisch and Wieland, *System der NS Konzentrationslager*, 37–38.

19. Betty Scholem to Gershom Scholem, 10 and 28 May, and 7 and 11 June 1933, and 25 Mar. 1939, and Gershom Scholem to Betty Scholem, 19 Oct. 1933, in Scholem and Scholem, *Mutter und Sohn im Briefwechsel*, 300–308, 465, and 338.

20. Betty Scholem to Gershom Scholem, 7, 18, and 27 June, 1 Aug. 1933, in Scholem and Scholem, *Mutter und Sohn im Briefwechsel*, 305–307, 309, 311–314, 322; [Erich Scholem] to Werner Scholem, 20 June 1933, IPW, Nachlass Scholem; Antrag auf Grund des Bundesergänzungsgesetztes Emmy Scholem, NLA, vol. 1, appendix 1, "Schilderung des Verfolgungsvorganges," 7 Apr. 1954, p. 2; and Entlassungs-Schein, 24 Nov. 1933; Häusler et al., "Die Eröffnung des Friesenberghauses."

21. Betty Scholem to Gershom Scholem, 18 and 27 June, 4 July, 1 and 19 Aug. 1933, in Scholem and Scholem, *Mutter und Sohn im Briefwechsel*, 309, 313, 316, 322, 324.

22. Betty Scholem to Gershom Scholem, 1 May, 4 July, 9/10 July, 1 and 19 Aug. 1933 in Scholem and Scholem, *Mutter und Sohn im Briefwechsel*, 322, 324–325; Gershom Scholem to Walter Benjamin, 4 Sept. 1933, in Benjamin and Scholem, *Correspondence*, 75.

23. Betty Scholem to Gershom Scholem, 12 June and 18 July 1933, 6 Mar. and 18 Sept. 1934, in Scholem and Scholem, *Mutter und Sohn im Briefwechsel*, 308, 319, 328, 329, 352.

24. Betty Scholem to Gershom Scholem, 27 June and 1 Aug. 1933, in Scholem and Scholem, *Mutter und Sohn im Briefwechsel*, 314, 322.

25. Werner Scholem to Emmy Scholem, 20 Dec. 1933, IPW, Nachlass Scholem.

26. Quotes taken from a letter from Werner Scholem to Gershom Scholem, 5 Oct. 1933, in Scholem and Scholem, *Mutter und Sohn im Briefwechsel*, 334–336; Scholem, "Zur Sozialpsychologie der Juden in Deutschland 1900–1930," 229–261; Zadoff, *Von Berlin nach Jerusalem und zurück*.

27. *Nemini parcetur*: No one will be spared.

28. Gerhard Scholem, late summer/autumn 1918, in Scholem, *Tagebücher*, 2:378. It is not improbable that Gershom Scholem was familiar with Kafka's parable "Before the Law" (1915).

29. Susman, *Das Buch Hiob und das Schicksal des jüdischen Volkes* [1946]; Sachs, *In den Wohnungen des Todes* [1947]; Wolfskehl, *Hiob oder die vier Spiegel* [1950].

30. Döblin, *Berlin Alexanderplatz*, 111; Mückain, "Erzählung als Heilung," 191.

31. Werner Scholem to Betty Scholem, partially censored letter dated 15 Nov. 1934, IPW, Nachlass Scholem.

32. Goddard and Glendinning, *Reni and the Brownshirts*, 18; interview with Edith Capon, PRG; Betty Scholem to Gershom Scholem, 18 Sept. 1933, in Scholem and Scholem, *Mutter und Sohn im Briefwechsel*, 329.

33. Interview with Edith Capon, PRG; Goddard and Glendinning, *Reni and the Brownshirts*, 18; Gershom Scholem to Betty Scholem, 7 Nov.1933, and Betty Scholem to Gershom Scholem, 20 June and 9 and 10 July 1933, in Scholem and Scholem, *Mutter und Sohn im Briefwechsel*, 348–349, 310, 316–318.

34. Kfar ha-Noar Ben-Shemen was founded in 1927 by the German Zionist Siegfried Lehmann.

35. Gershom Scholem to Betty Scholem, 22 June and 19 Oct. 1933, and Betty Scholem to Gershom Scholem, 4 July 1933, in Scholem and Scholem, *Mutter und Sohn im Briefwechsel*, 310, 338–339, 315; Emmy Scholem to Betty Scholem, 27 Sept. 1933, INL, Archive G. Scholem.

36. Betty Scholem to Gershom Scholem, 28 May and 18 Sept. 1933, in Scholem and Scholem, *Mutter und Sohn im Briefwechsel*, 304, 329; Käthe Scholem to Werner Scholem, with comments from Reinhold Scholem and Betty Scholem, 22 July 1933, as well as Erich Scholem to Werner Scholem, 24 Aug. 1933, IPW, Nachlass Scholem.

37. On this, see the survey by Erich Fromm from 1929/1930: *Arbeiter und Angestellte am Vorabend des Dritten Reiches*, 178; Brückner, *Psychologie und Geschichte*, 93–95; Usborne, "The New Woman and Generational Conflict," 137; Werner Scholem to his mother-in-law and daughters, 23 Nov. 1933, IPW, Nachlass Scholem.

38. Beschluss des Reichsgerichts in der Strafsache Hüffner u. Gen., 23 Nov. 1933, and Emmy Scholem to Landesgerichtsdirektor Dr. Zimmer, examining magistrate at the Reich Court, 29 June 1934, IPW, Nachlass Scholem; Prozessunterlagen des Volksgerichtshofes gegen Frida Hüffner, BAB SAPMO; Antrag auf Grund des Bundesergänzungsgesetztes Emmy Scholem, NLA, vol. 1, appendix 1, "Schilderung des Verfolgungsvorganges," 7 Apr. 1954, p. 2; Emmy Scholem to Betty Scholem, 4 Oct. 1933, INL, Archive G. Scholem; Betty Scholem to Gershom Scholem, 5 Nov. 1933, in Scholem and Scholem, *Mutter und Sohn im Briefwechsel*, 345.

39. Betty Scholem to Gershom Scholem, 5 Nov. 1933, in Scholem and Scholem, *Mutter und Sohn im Briefwechsel*, 345; Werner Scholem to Emmy Scholem, 20 Dec. 1933, IPW, Nachlass Scholem; interview with Edith Capon, PRG; Maiwald and Mischler, *Sexualität unter dem Hakenkreuz*, 105–106; Przyrembel, *"Rassenschande,"* 87.

40. Przyrembel, *"Rassenschande,"* 92; Werner Scholem to Emmy Scholem, 20 Dec. 1933, IPW, Nachlass Scholem; Dreyer, *Die zivilgerichtliche Rechtsprechung des Oberlandesgerichts Düsseldorf in der nationalsozialistischen Zeit*, 124–128.

41. Werner Scholem to Emmy Scholem, 20 Dec. 1933, and to his mother-in-law and his daughters in Hanover, 23 Nov. 1933, IPW, Nachlass Scholem.

42. Werner Scholem to Emmy Scholem, 20 Dec. 1933, and to his mother-in-law and his daughters, 23 Nov. 1933, IPW, Nachlass Scholem; Scholem, "In eigener Sache."

43. Werner Scholem to Emmy Scholem, 20 Dec. 1933, and to Betty Scholem, 6 Sept. 1934, IPW, Nachlass Scholem.

44. In 1946, Neye declared under oath that he had never been a member of the NSDAP. He repeated this assertion in the 1950s several times after he had become the rector of Humboldt University. Werner Scholem to Walther Neye, 14 Dec. 1933, IPW, Nachlass Scholem; Kleibert, *Die Juristische Fakultät*, 59–70.

45. Goddard and Glendinning, *Reni and the Brownshirts*, 33; interview with Edith Capon, PRG; Werner Scholem to Emmy Scholem, 20 Dec. 1934, IPW, Nachlass Scholem.

46. The following depiction is based on the interview with Edith Capon, PRG.

47. *Berliner Adreßbuch 1933*, 872; Emmy Scholem to Landesgerichtsdirektor Dr. Zimmer, 29 June 1934, IPW, Nachlass Scholem; Betty Scholem to Gershom Scholem, 7 June 1933, 12 Aug. 1934, 1 and 5 Oct. 1935, in Scholem and Scholem, *Mutter und Sohn im Briefwechsel*, 305–307, 366, 399, 401; Goddard and Glendinning, *Reni and the Brownshirts*, 19.

48. Peter Lübbe, "Einleitung," and Ruth Fischer, "Flight from Nazism," in Fischer and Maslow, *Abtrünnig wider Willen*, 6–7, 466; Emmy Scholem to Werner Scholem, 9 Sept. 1935, IPW, Nachlass Scholem.

49. Emmy Scholem to Reinhold Scholem, May 1934, and to Gershom Scholem, 16 Aug. 1934, and Jewish Refugee Committee to Gershom Scholem, 19 Nov. 1937, INL, Archive G. Scholem; report by Gerhart Friedländer, as related in Goddard, "Erinnerungen," chap. 2,

version 3, PRG; Betty Scholem to Gershom Scholem, 6 Mar. 1934, in Scholem and Scholem, *Mutter und Sohn im Briefwechsel*, 353; Deutscher, *Der verstoßene Prophet*, 256–260; Broué, *Trotzki*, 2:931–932; Keßler, *Arthur Rosenberg*, 183; German Jewish Aid Committee, "While You Are in England: Helpful Information and Guidance for Every Refugee."

50. Prozessunterlagen des Volksgerichtshofes gegen Frida Hüffner, BAB SAPMO; Betty Scholem to Gershom Scholem, 6 Mar. 1934, in Scholem and Scholem, *Mutter und Sohn im Briefwechsel*, 353.

51. Betty Scholem to Gershom Scholem, 6 and 20 Mar., 8 Apr., and 14 May 1934, in Scholem and Scholem, *Mutter und Sohn im Briefwechsel*, 353–354, 356–358, 361; Emmy Scholem to Reinhold Scholem, May 1934, INL, Archive G. Scholem; Gershom Scholem to Walter Benjamin, 11 Apr. 1934, in Benjamin and Scholem, *Correspondence*.

52. Possibly this happened on 25 Oct. 1933, when Hitler held an election speech in the Kuppelhalle in Hanover. Goddard, "Erinnerungen," chap. 2, version 3, and chap. "A Hitler Youth," PRG; Goddard and Glendinning, *Reni and the Brownshirts*, 36–37; Arndt, "Linden und der Nationalsozialismus"; Rabe, *Linden*, 40.

53. Werner Scholem to Betty Scholem, 13 July 1934, IPW, Nachlass Scholem; Goddard, "Erinnerungen," chap. "Leaving," PRG; Goddard and Glendinning, *Reni and the Brownshirts*, 41–43.

54. Betty Scholem to Gershom Scholem, 17 July 1934, in Scholem and Scholem, *Mutter und Sohn im Briefwechsel*, 361–362; Werner Scholem to Betty Scholem, 13 July 1934, IPW, Nachlass Scholem.

55. Werner Scholem to Emma Wiechelt, 3 Aug. [1934], IPW, Nachlass Scholem.

56. Betty Scholem to Gershom Scholem, 12 Aug. 1934, in Scholem and Scholem, *Mutter und Sohn im Briefwechsel*, 367; Goddard and Glendinning, *Reni and the Brownshirts*, 41, 44; interview with Edith Capon, PRG.

57. Interview with Renee Goddard, 18 June 2006, PMZ; Sandra Kirsch, *Emigration als Herausforderung*.

58. The Bourtanger Moor was a bog in which the Lingen prison in Emsland was located.

59. The newspaper in question is probably that of the Jewish alpine association, namely, the *Nachrichten des Alpenvereins Donauland und des Deutschen Alpenvereins Berlin*. Werner Scholem to Reinhold Scholem, 22 June 1934, and to Betty Scholem, 2, 13, and 27 July, 25 Oct., and 29 Nov. 1934, IPW, Nachlass Scholem; Betty Scholem to Gershom Scholem, 12 Aug. 1934, in Scholem and Scholem, *Mutter und Sohn im Briefwechsel*, 367.

60. Werner Scholem to Betty Scholem, 27 July and 11 Aug. 1934, IPW, Nachlass Scholem; Betty Scholem to Gershom Scholem, 12 Aug. 1934, in Scholem and Scholem, *Mutter und Sohn im Briefwechsel*, 367.

61. Emmy Scholem to Reinhold Scholem, May 1934, to Gershom Scholem, 16 Aug. 1934, and to Betty Scholem, 16 Oct. 1934, INL, Archive G. Scholem; Werner Scholem to Emmy Scholem, 29 Jan. 1935, IPW, Nachlass Scholem; Betty Scholem to Gershom Scholem, 17 July 1934, in Scholem and Scholem, *Mutter und Sohn im Briefwechsel*, 361–363; Antrag auf Grund des Bundesergänzungsgesetztes Emmy Scholem, NLA, appendix 1, "Schilderung des Verfolgungsvorganges," 7 Apr. 1954, p. 3.

62. Werner Scholem to Emmy Scholem, 29 Jan. 1935, IPW, Nachlass Scholem.

63. Jewish Refugee Committee, London, to Gershom Scholem, 19 Nov. 1937, INL, Archive G. Scholem; Goddard, "Erinnerungen," chap. "England," PRG; Emmy Scholem to Reinhold Scholem, May 1934, INL, Archive G. Scholem; Betty Scholem to Gershom and his

wife Escha Scholem, 5 and 14 Oct. 1935, in Scholem and Scholem, *Mutter und Sohn im Briefwechsel*, 402, 405; Jaffe and Roth, "Bentwich," 381.

64. Betty Scholem to Gershom Scholem, 26 Sept., 23 and 30 Oct. 1933, 20 Mar. and 4 Dec. 1934, in Scholem and Scholem, *Mutter und Sohn im Briefwechsel*, 330–331, 339–343, 355, 375; Werner Scholem to Emmy Scholem, 20 Dec. 1933, IPW, Nachlass Scholem.

65. Werner Scholem to Edith Scholem, 20 Sept. 1935, and to Betty Scholem, 27 July, 6 Sept., 4 and 25 Oct., 15 Nov. and 29 Dec. 1934, IPW, Nachlass Scholem.

66. Werner Scholem to Betty Scholem, 6 Sept. and 25 Oct. 1934, and 15 Feb. 1935, IPW, Nachlass Scholem; Antrag auf Grund des Bundesergänzungsgesetztes Emmy Scholem, NLA, vol. 1, appendix 1, "Schilderung des Verfolgungsvorganges," 7 Apr. 1954, p. 2.

67. Werner Scholem to Betty Scholem, 29 Nov. 1934, and to Emmy Scholem, 20 Dec. 1934, IPW, Nachlass Scholem; Betty Scholem to Gershom Scholem, 1 Oct. 1935, and to Escha Scholem, 5 Oct. 1935, in Scholem and Scholem, *Mutter und Sohn im Briefwechsel*, 399, 402.

68. Betty Scholem to Gershom Scholem, 17 July and 12 Aug. 1934, in Scholem and Scholem, *Mutter und Sohn im Briefwechsel*, 361–362, 366–367; Emmy Scholem to Landesgerichtsdirektor Dr. Zimmer, 29 June 1934, and to Heinrich Reinefeld, 30 Jan. 1935, IPW, Nachlass Scholem; Werner Scholem to Betty Scholem, 27 July 1934, IPW, Nachlass Scholem; Emmy Scholem to Gershom Scholem, 16 Aug. 1934, INL, Archive G. Scholem.

69. Goddard, "Erinnerungen," chap. "England," PRG; Betty Scholem to Escha Scholem, 5 Oct. 1935, in Scholem and Scholem, *Mutter und Sohn im Briefwechsel*, 402; Peter Lübbe, "Einleitung," in Fischer and Maslow, *Abtrünnig wider Willen*, 7–15, and appendix, 627.

70. Gefangen-Buch-Nummer 1873 (in Moabit his number was 1660); Betty Scholem to Gershom Scholem, 20 Aug. 1934, in Scholem and Scholem, *Mutter und Sohn im Briefwechsel*, 368; Werner Scholem to Betty Scholem, 6 and 20 Sept. 1934, IPW, Nachlass Scholem.

71. Between 1933 and 1935, thirty-six executions were carried out with a hatchet at Plötzensee; starting in 1937, prisoners were again executed with the guillotine. Oleschinski, *Gedenkstätte Plötzensee*, 16–17; Werner Scholem to Betty Scholem, 6 Sept. 1934, IPW, Nachlass Scholem.

72. Ernst Torgler (1893–1963), a KPD politician, served as the chairman of the KPD faction in the Reichstag starting in 1929; in 1933 he was one of the defendants in the Reichstag fire trial. Werner Scholem to Emmy Scholem, 20 and 29 Dec. 1934, IPW, Nachlass Scholem.

73. Werner Scholem to Betty Scholem, 13 July 1934, and to Emma Wiechelt, 3 Aug. [1934], IPW, Nachlass Scholem.

74. During the years 1934–1939, most trials held in the People's Court were against oppositionists, of whom 70 percent were linked to KPD organizations. Marxen and Schlüter, *Terror und "Normalität,"* 4–5, 11, 15–22; Wagner, *Der Volksgerichtshof im nationalsozialistischen Staat*, 22, 34–37, 79, 107–109; Betty Scholem to Gershom Scholem, 17 July 1934, in Scholem and Scholem, *Mutter und Sohn im Briefwechsel*, 362.

75. Werner Scholem to Betty Scholem, 13 July 1934, IPW, Nachlass Scholem; Büchner, *Danton's Death*, 7, 69.

76. Betty Scholem to Gershom Scholem, 17 July and 12 Aug. 1934, in Scholem and Scholem, *Mutter und Sohn im Briefwechsel*, 361–362, 366; Werner Scholem to Emma Wiechelt, 3 Aug. [1934], and to Betty Scholem, 27 July 1934, IPW, Nachlass Scholem.

77. Betty Scholem to Gershom Scholem, 20 Aug. 1934, in Scholem and Scholem, *Mutter und Sohn im Briefwechsel*, 368; Beschluss, 17 Sept. 1934, Prozessunterlagen des Volksgerichtshofes gegen Frida Hüffner, BAB SAPMO.

78. Emmy Scholem to Landesgerichtsdirektor Dr. Zimmer, 29 June 1934, and Werner Scholem to the family in Hanover, 19 Dec. 1933, IPW, Nachlass Scholem; interview with Edith Capon, PRG.

79. All references to the Hansa cell in secondary literature originate from the work of Michael Buckmiller and Pascal Nafe, whose sources are the documents in the trial against Werner Scholem. Buckmiller and Nafe, "Die Naherwartung des Kommunismus," 75.

80. In 1925, Werner Scholem headed the information department of the KPD and was responsible for the press and other publicly accessible materials; in the meantime, the KPD used the news headquarters in creating its own intelligence agency, which he had nothing to do with. Kaufmann et al., *Der Nachrichtendienst der KPD*, 109–110, 142.

81. According to her own testimony, Marie Luise von Hammerstein was already a Communist before she met Werner Scholem; this she wrote on 8 August 1985 to Peter Lübbe. Peter Lübbe, "Einleitung," in Fischer and Maslow, *Abtrünnig wider Willen*, 12.

82. Werner Scholem's Reichstag mandate did indeed terminate in May 1928, and he left the Leninbund about the same time. Emmy Scholem to Landesgerichtsdirektor Dr. Zimmer, 9 July 1934, IPW, Nachlass Scholem.

83. Buckmiller and Nafe, "Die Naherwartung des Kommunismus," 60–81, esp. 75–76.

84. Bergbauer and Schüler-Springorum,*"Wir sind jung, die Welt ist offen,"* 126.

85. Statement by Gustav Burg (König), 16 Dec. 1936, RGASPI Sign. F. 495, op. 205, d.6222, parts of which are printed in Enzensberger, *The Silence of Hammerstein*, 221–226; Müller, "Hitlers Rede vor der Reichswehr- und Reichsmarineführung," 79–81, 83, n. 28; Stoecker, *Handbuch der Kommunistischen Reichstagsfraktion*, 92; Weber and Herbst, *Deutsche Kommunisten*, 630.

86. On this, see the statement by Roth's friend Herbert Wehner, cited in Müller, *Die Akte Wehner*, 282–284; RGASPI Sign. F. 495, op. 205, d.6222 and op. 74, d.124. Bl.15, cited in Müller, "Hitlers Rede," 80, 86–87, 89; Kaufmann et al., *Der Nachrichtendienst der KPD*, 229–230, 291, 421.

87. Kaufmann et al., *Der Nachrichtendienst der KPD*, 289–299; Wirsching, "'Man kann nur den Boden germanisieren,'" 524; Volk, *Pattern for World Revolution*, 167; RGASPI Sign. F. 495, op. 205, cited in Müller, "Hitlers Rede," 84, 88; Grundmann, *Der Geheimappart der KPD im Visier der Gestapo*.

88. Buckmiller and Nafe, "Die Naherwartung des Kommunismus," 77–78; Enzensberger, *The Silence of Hammerstein* 435; Kluge, *Die Lücke, die der Teufel läßt*, 25–26.

89. Emmy Scholem to Gershom Scholem, 16 Aug. 1934, INL, Archive G. Scholem; and to Werner Scholem, 9 Jan. 1935, IPW, Nachlass Scholem; Werner Scholem to Emmy Scholem, 20 Dec. 1934, IPW, Nachlass Scholem.

90. Such as Jäger, "Hammerstein-Fragen," 3; Betty Scholem to Gershom and Escha Scholem, 11 May 1935, in Scholem and Scholem, *Mutter und Sohn im Briefwechsel*, 388.

91. Drobisch and Wieland, *System der NS-Konzentrationslager*, 27; Ernst Torgler was released in 1935.

92. Werner Scholem to Betty Scholem, 20 Sept. 1934, IPW, Nachlass Scholem.

93. Fieber, *Widerstand in Berlin gegen das NS-Regime 1933 bis 1945*, 127–128; Werner Scholem to Betty Scholem, 6 Sept. and 25 Oct. 1934, Heinrich Reinefeld to Emmy Scholem, 23 Oct. 1934, and Emmy Scholem to Heinrich Reinefeld, 26 Oct. and 28 Nov. 1934, IPW, Nachlass Scholem.

94. According to this law, any act of high treason perpetrated before this date could not be prosecuted. Betty Scholem to Gershom Scholem, 19 Nov. and 4 Dec. 1934, in Scholem

and Scholem, *Mutter und Sohn im Briefwechsel*, 372, 375; Werner Scholem to Betty Scholem, 29 Nov. 1934, IPW, Nachlass Scholem.

95. Prozessunterlagen des Volksgerichtshofes gegen Frida Hüffner, BAB SAPMO, Beschluss 21 June 1933, and Beschluss 18 Oct. 1934, documents of the pretrial investigation as well as the main trial; Emmy Scholem to Landesgerichtsdirektor Dr. Zimmer, 29 June 1934, IPW, Nachlass Scholem.

96. Prozessunterlagen des Volksgerichtshofes gegen Frida Hüffner, BAB SAPMO, 22, 66–68.

97. Ibid., 75–76; Heinrich Reinefeld to Emmy Scholem, 7 Dec. 1934, IPW, Nachlass Scholem.

98. The term "agitprop," agitation and propaganda, was originally a Communist coinage; Weber and Herbst, *Deutsche Kommunisten*, 507; Prozessunterlagen des Volksgerichtshofes gegen Frida Hüffner, BAB SAPMO, 67–68.

99. Prozessunterlagen des Volksgerichtshofes gegen Frida Hüffner, BAB SAPMO, 67–68, testimony by Willi Walter, 18 Apr. 1933.

100. Ibid., report from 19 Apr. 1933, 1–3. Hugo (not Walter) Wenzel was surprisingly set free in May 1934 for want of evidence against him; Jendretzky was arrested in the spring of 1934 and sentenced in September to three years imprisonment. Weber and Herbst, *Deutsche Kommunisten* 344, 858.

101. Prozessunterlagen des Volksgerichtshofes gegen Frida Hüffner, BAB SAPMO, 82. All of these documents appear to have been lost or destroyed.

102. Werner Scholem to Emmy Scholem, 13, 21, and 29 Jan., 7 and 15 Feb. 1935, and Emmy Scholem to Heinrich Reinefeld, 30 Jan. 1935, IPW, Nachlass Scholem.

103. Werner Scholem to Emmy Scholem, 7 and 15 Feb. 1935, IPW, Nachlass Scholem.

104. Ibid.

105. Ibid., 2 Mar. 1935.

106. Häusler et al., "Die Eröffnung des Friesenberghauses," 90–93; Kundt, " 'Juden und Mitglieder der Sektion Donauland unerwünscht' "; Betty Scholem to Gershom Scholem, 12 Mar. 1935, in Scholem and Scholem, *Mutter und Sohn im Briefwechsel*, 381.

107. Prozessunterlagen des Volksgerichtshofes gegen Frida Hüffner, BAB SAPMO, 2, 12–14, 31–32, 34; Betty Scholem to Gershom Scholem, 12 Mar. 1935, in Scholem and Scholem, *Mutter und Sohn im Briefwechsel*, 380–381.

108. In 1934, only 5.5 percent and thus relatively few of the cases tried before the People's Court ended in acquittal. Prozessunterlagen des Volksgerichtshofes gegen Frida Hüffner, BAB SAPMO; Marxen and Schlüter, *Terror und "Normalität,"* 18.

109. Betty Scholem to Gershom Scholem, 12 and 29 Mar. 1935, in Scholem and Scholem, *Mutter und Sohn im Briefwechsel*, 380–381, 384.

110. The fates of the brothers are so similar that the East German literary critic I. M. Lange confused their biographies in a manuscript written around 1960. Lange, "Mein Freund Walter Benjamin," 181; quote taken from a letter by Gershom Scholem to Walter Benjamin, 29 Mar. 1935, in Benjamin and Scholem, *Correspondence*, 157; Scholem, *Walter Benjamin*, 242; Gershom Scholem, "Ahnen und Verwandte Walter Benjamins," 45; Walter Benjamin to Gershom Scholem, 14 Jan. 1926, in Benjamin, *Gesammelte Briefe*, 3:109; Benjamin, *Georg Benjamin*, 50.

111. Walter Benjamin to Gershom Scholem, 7 and 25 May 1933, and 20 May 1935, in Benjamin and Scholem, *Correspondence*, 54, 160–161, quote on 46; Hilde Benjamin, *Georg Benjamin*, 210–213, 318–340.

112. Werner Scholem to the family, 10 Apr., 1 May, and 7 Sept. 1935, IPW, Nachlass Scholem; Antrag auf Grund des Bundesergänzungsgesetztes Werner Scholem, NLA, Anlage 1. Likewise, the lawyer Hans Litten, who arrived in Lichtenburg from the concentration camp Sonnenburg in the fall of 1935, asked his mother for "something for the heart," meaning news about good friends and their children. Litten, *Eine Mutter kämpft gegen Hitler*, 133.

113. Werner Scholem to the family, 17 May 1935, and Emmy Scholem to Werner Scholem, 20 May and 2 June 1935, IPW, Nachlass Scholem.

114. Dietrich, *Konzentrationslager Lichtenburg*, 35, 38–40, 42–43; Erfahrungsbericht von Dr. Ludwig Bendix, Gedenkstätte KZ-Dachau, 8, 44–55; Litten, *Eine Mutter kämpft gegen Hitler*, 94, 168–174.

115. Bendix was brought to Lichtenburg in the fall of 1935 and released from Dachau in 1937. He wrote his report in Palestine for a publication competition that had been announced in August 1939 by scholars at Harvard University. Erfahrungsbericht von Dr. Ludwig Bendix, Gedenkstätte KZ-Dachau, 6–18; Karlauf, "'So endete mein Leben in Deutschland,'" 24–30.

116. Werner Scholem to Emmy Scholem, 20 June 1935, IPW, Nachlass Scholem.

117. It is unclear why she speaks here of sixteen years; probably she was referring to 1921 when he was executive editor of the *Rote Fahne*; from 1923 to 1926 he wrote ever less often for the paper. Betty Scholem to Gershom Scholem, 18 Sept. and 1 Oct. 1935, in Scholem and Scholem, *Mutter und Sohn im Briefwechsel*, 396, 398.

118. Goebbels, diary entry from 14 July 1924, in *Tagebücher*, 102–103; Goebbels, "Welt-Bolschewismus ohne Maske," 2.

119. Goebbels, "Wesen, Methoden und Ziele der Propaganda," in *Reden*, 248.

120. Betty Scholem to Escha Scholem, 5 Oct. 1935, in Scholem and Scholem, *Mutter und Sohn im Briefwechsel*, 400–401; and to Emmy Scholem, 31 Oct. 1935, IPW, Nachlass Scholem; see also Bergbauer, Fröhlich, and Schüler-Springorum, *Denkmalsfigur*, 278–280.

121. Werner Scholem to Emmy Scholem, 20 July, 5 and 21 Aug. 1935, IPW, Nachlass Scholem; Erfahrungsbericht von Dr. Ludwig Bendix, Gedenkstätte KZ-Dachau, 80–81.

122. Erinnerungsbericht von Prof. Dr. Friedrich Kaul, Gedenkstätte KZ Lichtenburg, 1–3; Erfahrungsbericht von Dr. Ludwig Bendix, Gedenkstätte KZ-Dachau, 19–20, 65–78.

123. Werner Scholem to Emmy Scholem, 20 July 1935 and 5 Dec. 1936, Betty Scholem to Emmy Scholem, 11 Oct. 1936, and Canada, Department of the Secretary of State, to Emmy Scholem, 15 Apr. 1935, IPW, Nachlass Scholem.

124. Emmy Scholem to Betty Scholem, 30 Apr. 1935, INL, Archive G. Scholem; Betty Scholem to Gershom and Escha Scholem, 11 May, 5 and 14 Oct. 1935, in Scholem and Scholem, *Mutter und Sohn im Briefwechsel*, 388, 400–401, 404–405.

125. Betty Scholem to Gershom and Escha Scholem, 11 May, 5 and 14 Oct. 1935, in Scholem and Scholem, *Mutter und Sohn im Briefwechsel*, 388, 400–401, 404–405; Werner Scholem to Emmy Scholem, 10 Apr. 1936, IPW, Nachlass Scholem; quote taken from Gershom Scholem to Walter Benjamin, 18 Dec. 1935, in Benjamin and Scholem, *Correspondence*, 172–173.

126. Gershom Scholem wrote that "at the time when the final decision had to be made, it came to light that a list existed of people who could be freed only with Goebbels's permission and that the Gestapo had known all the time that my brother was on this list." According to the Goebbels biographer Peter Longerich, it is not highly probable that such a list existed, at least not in the form mentioned by Scholem. Information provided in writing by Peter

Longerich, 1 Feb. 2012, PMZ; Gershom Scholem to Walter Benjamin, 19 Apr. 1936, in Benjamin and Scholem, *Correspondence*, 177; Werner Scholem to Emmy Scholem, 24 Mar., 5 Apr., 5 May, 1 and 15 July, and 1 Aug. 1936, IPW, Nachlass Scholem.

127. The trip did not happen because Emmy was experiencing health problems and went instead to take the waters in Gräfenberg in the fall. Werner Scholem to Emmy Scholem, 15 July, 1 Aug., 20 Sept., 21 Oct. and 11 Dec.1935, as well as 3 Sept. 1936, IPW, Nachlass Scholem.

128. Betty Scholem to Emmy Scholem, 11 Oct. 1936, IPW, Nachlass Scholem.

129. Erfahrungsbericht von Dr. Ludwig Bendix, Gedenkstätte KZ-Dachau, 22, 26–30, 47–48.

130. In the *Jauchegrube* [the latrine detail] he also worked alongside another Berlin lawyer, Friedrich Kaul, who later became a famous legal scholar and participated in the Auschwitz trial as a joint plaintiff and representative of the victims living in the GDR. Erinnerungsbericht von Prof. Dr. Friedrich Kaul, Gedenkstätte KZ Lichtenburg, 1–3; Erfahrungsbericht von Dr. Ludwig Bendix, Gedenkstätte KZ-Dachau, 55–56.

131. Erfahrungsbericht von Dr. Ludwig Bendix, Gedenkstätte KZ-Dachau, 112–115; Erinnerungsbericht von Prof. Dr. Friedrich Kaul, Gedenkstätte KZ Lichtenburg, 1–3; Werner Scholem to Emmy Scholem, 1 and 6 Feb. 1937, IPW, Nachlass Scholem; Betty Scholem to Gershom Scholem, 20 Feb. 1937, in Scholem and Scholem, *Mutter und Sohn im Briefwechsel*, 425. Strenth Through Joy (Kraft durch Freude, KdF) was a large state-operated leisure organization in Nazi Germany.

132. Werner Scholem was brought to Dachau with the number 11390 and the label "Jude pol." Jüdische Häftlinge, Scholem Werner, Gedenkstätte KZ-Dachau; Erfahrungsbericht von Dr. Ludwig Bendix, Gedenkstätte KZ-Dachau, 117; Erinnerungsbericht von Prof. Dr. Friedrich Kaul, Gedenkstätte KZ Lichtenburg, 1–3; Litten, *Eine Mutter kämpft gegen Hitler*, 224; Carlebach, *Tote auf Urlaub*.

133. Erfahrungsbericht von Gerhard Pintus, sent on by Gershom Scholem to Emmy Scholem, 25 Aug. 1939, IPW, Nachlass Scholem; Erfahrungsbericht von Dr. Ludwig Bendix, Gedenkstätte KZ-Dachau, 67.

134. Federn reported many times about Werner Scholem in Buchenwald, but he had contacted Emmy Scholem beforehand and asked for her permission to do so. Emmy Scholem to Ruth Fischer, 22 Jan. and 23 Feb. 1962, Houghton Library, Ruth Fischer Archive; the reports by Ernst Federn are found in "In Memoriam: Werner Scholem," 120, as well as in Kuschey, *Die Ausnahme des Überlebens*, 357, 361–363, 489; Benedikt Kautsky, *Teufel und Verdammte*, 116; Carlebach, *Tote auf Urlaub*, 24; on Carlebach, see the affidavits by Benedikt Kautsky, 4 May 1951, in Schafranek, *Zwischen NKWD und Gestapo*, 203.

135. *Die Jobsiade* by Karl Arnold Kortum is a satirical epic poem that appeared in 1784 with the title *Leben, Meynungen und Thaten von Hieronymus Jobs dem Kandidaten, und wie Er sich weiland viel Ruhm erwarb auch endlich als Nachtswächter zu Sulzburg starb*. Werner Scholem to Emmy Scholem and the family, 13 Feb., 2 Apr. , 19 June, 14 and 18 July 1937, IPW, Nachlass Scholem; Betty Scholem to Gershom Scholem, 16 July 1937, in Scholem and Scholem, *Mutter und Sohn im Briefwechsel*, 430.

136. Portmann and Wolf, *"Ja, ich kämpfte,"* 27, 34–39, 44–47; Komintern Aktenbestand "Interbrigaden," Dossier 542-2-147, cited in ibid., 68; Nelles, "The Foreign Legion of the Revolution"; Collado Seidel, *Der Spanische Bürgerkrieg*, 35–39; Sittig-Eisenschitz, "An den Fronten des Spanischen Bürgerkriegs," 58–59. Isak Aufseher and Emmy Scholem

corresponded again from November 1946 until June 1947; however, the planned wedding never came to pass, probably because he already had a wife and child and did not end up getting a divorce. Isak Aufseher to Emmy Scholem, IPW, Nachlass Scholem.

137. Betty Scholem to Edith Scholem, 14 June 1937, IPW, Nachlass Scholem; and to Gershom Scholem, 4 Aug., 17 Nov. and 6 Dec. 1937, in Scholem and Scholem, *Mutter und Sohn im Briefwechsel*, 434, 437–438, 442; Jewish Refugee Committee, London, to Gershom Scholem, 19 Nov. 1937, INL, Archive G. Scholem; Goddard, "Erinnerungen," chap. "War," PRG.

138. Hans Behrend to Emmy Scholem, 20 Sept. 1937, IPW, Nachlass Scholem; Erfahrungsbericht von Gerhard Pintus, 25 Aug. 1939, IPW, Nachlass Scholem; Betty Scholem to Gershom Scholem, 26 Oct., 17 Nov., and 6 Dec. 1937, and 5 Jan. 1938, in Scholem and Scholem, *Mutter und Sohn im Briefwechsel*, 435, 438, 442, 446.

139. Werner Scholem to Emmy Scholem, 13 Feb., 4 Mar., 19 June, and 28 Aug. 1938, IPW, Nachlass Scholem.

140. From the report of another prisoner, Betty Scholem learned in the fall of 1938 that her son was doing relatively well because he was said to "have inside duty and supervision." This is highly unlikely because nothing like this is noted in the records of the concentration camp. Betty Scholem, "November. Die Kennkarte. Schmuck und Silber," 533; receipt certifying that Werner Scholem was delivered to Buchenwald concentration camp, ITS; Erfahrungsbericht von Gerhard Pintus, 25 Aug. 1939, IPW, Nachlass Scholem; Betty Scholem to Gershom Scholem, 25 Oct. 1938, in Scholem and Scholem, *Mutter und Sohn im Briefwechsel*, 452; Kautsky, *Teufel und Verdammte*, 245–256; reports by Ernst Federn in "In Memoriam: Werner Scholem," 118–120; Bunzol, *Die Leben des Buchenwaldhäftlings Alfred Bunzol 738*, 127; Hackett, *Der Buchenwald-Report*, 224–225; Niethammer, *Der "gesäuberte" Antifaschismus*, 523.

141. Stein, "Buchenwald—Stammlager," 332–333; Kautsky, *Teufel und Verdammte*, 30, 129–135; reports by Ernst Federn in Kuschey, *Die Ausnahme des Überlebens*, 549, and in "In Memoriam: Werner Scholem," 118–120; Karl Fischer also wrote that he had met Werner Scholem in Buchenwald "as a supporter of the IV International" (cited in "In Memoriam: Werner Scholem," 117).

142. Werner Scholem to the family, 2 Oct. 1938, IPW, Nachlass Scholem; Kautsky, *Teufel und Verdammte*, 184–185, 191–192.

143. Betty Scholem received similar reactions from the Jewish Refugee Committee in London and Norman Bentwich personally. Werner Scholem to the family, 2 Oct. 1938, IPW, Nachlass Scholem; Betty Scholem to Gershom Scholem, 27 Sept., 25 Oct. and 13 Nov. 1938, and 24 May 1939, in Scholem and Scholem, *Mutter und Sohn im Briefwechsel*, 448–449, 452, 454, 473.

144. According to a letter from the German embassy in Paris to the German foreign office, dated 16 Aug. 1934, Ruth Fischer planned a press campaign in the *Manchester Guardian*; however, all that ever appeared was the article "Coming Trial of Herr Scholem," *Manchester Guardian*, 22 Dec. 1934, 13. Fischer and Maslow, *Abtrünnig wider Willen*, 577–578; Ruth Fischer to Morgan Philips Price, 20 Jan. 1937, IPW, Nachlass Scholem; *De la Révolution de Lénine à la contre-révolution de Staline*, ISC.

145. Emmy Scholem to Karl Korsch, 4 Nov. 1938, Arthur Rosenberg to Emmy Scholem, 18 Nov. 1938, and Edith Scholem to Consul General Geist, 9 Jan. 1939, IPW, Nachlass Scholem; Mirjam Zadoff, "'. . . der lebendige Beweis für ihre Greuel,'" 39–41.

146. Betty Sara Scholem to the Camp Commandant, 2 Feb. 1939, ITS; and Betty's letters from 25 Jan. and 21 Feb. 1939, IPW, Nachlass Scholem; Sophie Scholem to the Concentration Camp Buchenwald, 5 Apr. 1933, and Hans Hirsch to Emmy Scholem, 5 May 1939, IPW, Nachlass Scholem; Betty Scholem to Gershom Scholem, 15 Feb., 4 Mar., 9 and 24 May 1939, in Scholem and Scholem, *Mutter und Sohn im Briefwechsel*, 460, 463, 469, 472.

147. Werner Scholem to Sophie Scholem, 4 June 1939, IPW, Nachlass Scholem; Hans Hirsch and Sophie Scholem to Emmy Scholem, 9 June 1939, IPW, Nachlass Scholem; Kurt Grossmann, *Emigration*, 134–137, 148; letters dated 4 and 18 May 1939, IfZ, Korrespondenz K. Grossmann.

148. Letters dated 7 and 27 May, and 1, 5, and 6 June 1939, IfZ, Korrespondenz K. Grossmann; London, *Whitehall and the Jews*, 67–68; Betty Scholem to Edith Scholem, 1 Mar. 1941, and Hans Hirsch to Emmy Scholem, 24 June 1939, IPW, Nachlass Scholem.

149. Hans Hirsch to Emmy Scholem, 21 Aug. 1939, IPW, Nachlass Scholem; Erfahrungsbericht von Gerhard Pintus, 25 Aug. 1939, IPW, Nachlass Scholem.

150. As Hans Hirsch recalled, Werner Scholem no longer received any news from his wife once the war started, which is why these months would have been "very overshadowed" by the silence. Käthe Schiepan was murdered in Theresienstadt concentration camp. Betty Scholem to Edith Scholem, 1 Mar. 1941 IPW, Nachlass Scholem; and to Gershom Scholem, 27 Mar. 1940, in Scholem and Scholem, *Mutter und Sohn im Briefwechsel*, 486; Käthe Schiepan to her cousin Max Borchardt and her sister Betty Scholem, 17 June 1941, in Scholem and Scholem, *Mutter und Sohn*, 536–538; Gershom Scholem to Walter Benjamin, 15 Dec. 1939, in Benjamin and Scholem, *Correspondence*, 262.

151. *Völkischer Beobachter*, 30 Oct. 1936 and 7 Jan. 1937, cited in Benz, *"Der ewige Jude,"* 65–73.

152. Belting, *Faces*, 55–58; Heimann-Jelinek, "Zur Geschichte einer Ausstellung," 131–145.

153. Letters by Siegrid Dominik, Jewish prisoner, Scholem Werner, Gedenkstätte KZ-Dachau.

154. Goebbels probably made use of him also for a newspaper and radio campaign on the "criminals of Buchenwald"; on this point, see Kautsky, *Teufel und Verdammte*, 189; Werner Scholem to Emmy Scholem, 20 Oct. 1935, IPW, Nachlass Scholem; Erfahrungsbericht von Dr. Ludwig Bendix, Gedenkstätte KZ-Dachau, 20; report by Ernst Federn in "In Memoriam: Werner Scholem," 120.

155. "16 Tage Moabit: Erlebnisse in Untersuchungshaft von Nr. 1621," *Berliner Illustrirte*, evening edition, 27 Oct. 1933, evening edition, supplements 1 and 2.

156. This is what Ruth Fischer related to Hans Magnus Enzensberger, in Enzensberger, *The Silence of Hammerstein*, 433–434; Ruth Fischer to Franz Jung, 18 Aug. 1960, in Fischer and Maslow, *Abtrünnig wider Willen*, 335.

157. Maslow as quoted in Peter Lübbe, "Einleitung," in Fischer and Maslow, *Abtrünnig wider Willen*, 11–12.

158. Maslow sent the finished manuscript to the London publisher Unwin & Allen; the novel was finally published in 2011. Ruth Fischer to Franz Jung, 18 Aug. 1960, in Fischer and Maslow, *Abtrünnig wider Willen*, 335.

159. Arkadi Maslow, "Die Tochter des Generals," Houghton Library, Ruth Fischer Archive, folder 3, p. 57; Arkadi Maslow to his stepson Gerhart Friedländer, 28 Dec. 1934, in Fischer and Maslow, *Abtrünnig wider Willen*, 53–59.

160. Arkadi Maslow, "Die Tochter des Generals," Houghton Library, Harvard University, Ruth Fischer Archive, folder 1, pp. 15–18, 26; folder 2, pp. 43–44; Mosse, "German Socialists and the Jewish Question," 127, 134.

161. Maslow, "Die Tochter des Generals," folder 1, pp. 27–29; folder 2, pp. 30–36, 38, 43–48; folder 3, pp. 55–57; folder 8, p. 5.

162. Ibid., folder 4, p. 1; folder 5, pp. 26–27; folder 7, pp. 10–11; folder 9, p. 6; folder 10, p. 6; folder 11; on Paul Vogt, see Hans Mommsen, "Der Reichstagsbrand und seine politischen Folgen," 367.

163. Ruth Fischer to Franz Jung, 18 Aug. 1960, in Fischer and Maslow, *Abtrünnig wider Willen*, 335; Franz Jung to Joachim Störig, 18 Apr. 1961, and to Carola Weingarten, 25 Dec. 1960, and to Artur Müller, 10 Feb. 1962, in Jung, *Briefe*, 702, 789, 847.

164. Franz Jung, "Betr. Hammerstein," 1242–1245, 1253; Enzensberger, *Hammerstein oder der Eigensinn*, 434–435.

165. Berit Balzer, "Nachwort," in Maslow, *Die Tochter des Generals*, 322, 394–395.

166. Gershom Scholem to Ernst Jünger, 8 Apr. 1975, INL, Archive G. Scholem.

Epilogue

1. Betty Scholem to Gershom Scholem, 10 Nov. 1940, in Scholem and Scholem, *Mutter und Sohn im Briefwechsel*, 493–494; David, *The Patron*, 309–310.

2. Scholem and Scholem, *Mutter und Sohn im Briefwechsel*, 496 n. 4.

3. Betty Scholem to Gershom Scholem, 27 Sept. 1940, in Scholem and Scholem, *Mutter und Sohn im Briefwechsel*, 491–492; Betty Scholem to Emmy Scholem, 18 Sept. 1940, IPW, Nachlass Scholem.

4. Gershom Scholem, undated diary entry, INL, Archive G. Scholem; Noam Zadoff, " 'Zion's Self-Engulfing Light,' " 275–279. Usually the abbreviation used in German for concentration camps was KZ or KL (*Konzentrationslager*).

5. Betty Scholem to Edith Capon, 1 Mar. 1941, and to Emmy Scholem, 6 Dec. 1945, IPW, Nachlass Scholem.

6. Death certificate dated 11 Sept. 1940, in Antrag auf Grund des Bundesergänzungsgesetzes Werner Scholem, NLA; Fragebogen der Effektenkammer Konzentrationslager Buchenwald, Einlieferungsschein Werner Scholems, as well as "Liste der verstorbenen Kameraden vom Bezirk Berlin-Brandenburg," 22 Nov. 1947, ITS; Klaus Drobisch to Walter Hammer, 28 Oct. 957, IfZ, Walter Hammer Archiv.

7. One of these acts of retaliation was the murder of the Jewish Communist resistance fighter Rudi Arndt in May 1940. Kautsky, *Teufel und Verdammte*, 20, 24.

8. Hördler and Jacobeit, *Lichtenburg*, 91.

9. Holm, *Stimmen aus Buchenwald*, 68; Porträtfotographie von Johann Blank, Archiv des Konzentrationslagers Buchenwald; Kautsky, *Teufel und Verdammte*, 38–9, 116; Kogon, *Der SS-Staat*, 19.

10. Kogon, *Der SS-Staat*, 119.

11. Ernst Federn, as quoted in "In Memoriam: Werner Scholem," 118; and in Kuschey, *Die Ausnahme des Überlebens*, 512–514.

12. Ernst Federn, as quoted in "In Memoriam," 119.

13. Gershom Scholem to Dina Waschitz, 2 Aug. 1981, in Scholem, *Briefe*, 3:240.

14. Compare with the story of Ernst Heilmann, in Bergbauer, Fröhlich and Schüler-Springorum, *Denkmalsfigur*, 278–280.

15. Benedikt Kautsky mentions this in connection with the murder of Rudi Arndt; see "Eidesstattliche Erklärung von Benedikt Kautsky vom 4.5.1951," in Schafranek, *Zwischen NKWD und Gestapo*, 201–208, here 204.

16. Gershom Scholem to Irmgard and Arthur Scholem, 12 Nov. 1980, in Scholem, *Briefe*, 3:220.

17. Renee Goddard to Gershom Scholem, 17 Dec. 1971 and 25 Mar. 1980, INL, Archive G. Scholem.

18. Gershom Scholem to David Scholem, 24 Nov. 1980, in Scholem, *Briefe*, 3:224; Betty Scholem to Emmy Scholem, 18 Sept. 1940, IPW, Nachlass Scholem.

19. Betty Scholem to Gershom Scholem, 27 Sept. 1940, in Scholem and Scholem, *Mutter und Sohn im Briefwechsel*, 492; Goddard, "Erinnerungen," chap. "Prologue und War," PRG.

20. Betty Scholem to Gershom Scholem, 27 Sept. 1940, in Scholem and Scholem, *Mutter und Sohn im Briefwechsel*, 492; Goddard, "Erinnerungen," chap. "Prologue und War," PRG. A total of about 14,000 people were interned on the Isle of Man then. Chappell, *Island of Barbed Wire*, 74.

21. *Kindertransport* (children's transport) was the informal name of a series of rescue efforts that brought thousands of refugee Jewish children to Great Britain from Nazi Germany between 1938 and 1940. In 1939, 25,000 German refugees under the age of twenty-five were in England, the majority of whom were Jews. Schröder and Herzberg, "Zur Geschichte der Organisation," 193; Goddard, "Erinnerungen," chap. "War," PRG.

22. Goddard, "Erinnerungen," chap. "Renee's Story Continued," PRG.

23. Goddard, "Erinnerungen," chap. "Prologue," PRG.

24. Fania Scholem, as cited in Ozick, "The Fourth Sparrow," 148.

25. Zadek, *My Way*, 146–147, 160, 166–167, 315.

26. "'I Am a Camera'—Isherwood's Berlin at the New Theater," 3; Howald, "Renee Goddard"; interview with Renee Goddard, 10 Jan. 2008, PMZ.

27. Interview with Renee Goddard, 10 Jan. 2008, PMZ.; Emmy Scholem to Gershom Scholem, 20 Feb. 1954, INL, Archive G. Scholem

28. Edith Capon to Fania Scholem, 1983, INL, Archive G. Scholem; interview with Edith Capon, PRG; Goddard, "Erinnerungen," chap. "Edith's Story," PRG.

29. Gershom Scholem to Edith Capon, 23 July 1963, and to Renee Goddard, 17 Aug. 1967, INL, Archive G. Scholem; and to Reinhold Scholem, 14 Nov. 1977, in Scholem, *Briefe*, 3:162.

30. Scholem, "November. Die Kennkarte. Schmuck und Silber," 535; interview with Renee Goddard, 18 June 2006, PMZ; Betty Scholem to Edith Capon, 1 Mar. 1941, IPW, Nachlass Scholem.

31. Betty Scholem to Emmy Scholem, Renee Goddard, and Edith Capon, 18 Sept. 1940, 1 Mar. 1941, 21 Oct. 1945, and 6 Dec. 1945, IPW, Nachlass Scholem; Gershom Scholem, diary entries from 15 and 27 May 1946, INL, Archive G. Scholem.

32. Heinz Wiegel-Hackebeil, who worked for a large publishing house and had married, was naturalized at the same time under the name Henry Newton. "List of Aliens"; Antrag auf Grund des Bundesergänzungsgesetzes Emmy Scholem, NLA, vol. 1, Eidesstattliche Erklärung von Henry Newton, 17 Feb. 1955; Betty Scholem to Emmy Scholem, 18 Sept. 1940, IPW, Nachlass Scholem; and to Gershom Scholem, 27 Sept. 1940, in Scholem and Scholem, *Mutter und Sohn im Briefwechsel*, 492.

33. Emmy Scholem to Erich Fried, 23 Dec. 1953, ÖNB, Nachlass Erich Fried; and to Gershom Scholem, 15 Apr. 1952 and 20 Feb. 1954, INL, Archive G. Scholem.

34. Her address in Bad Wimpfen was Goethestraße 7. Emmy Scholem to Gershom Scholem, 3 Oct. 1958, INL, Archive G. Scholem.

35. Weber and Weber, *Leben nach dem "Prinzip links,"* 279; Weber and Herbst, *Deutsche Kommunisten*, 692–694; Alexandra Ramm-Pfemfert to Karl and Ellen Otten, 24 Feb. 1959, in Ranc, *Alexandra Ramm-Pfemfert*, 475–476, 183.

36. Antrag auf Grund des Bundesergänzungsgesetzes Emmy Scholem, NLA, vol. 1, letter dated 8 July 1954, 2; as well as various medical reports and the verdict of 13 May 1959, 4.

37. Emmy Scholem to Gershom Scholem, 3 July 1964, 1 May 1966, 7 Feb. and 27 Apr. 1967, INL, Archive G. Scholem; Jüdisches Seniorenheim Hannover, Lola Fischl Haus; Quast, *Nach der Befreiung*, 97–99, 190–193.

38. Emmy Scholem to Gershom Scholem, 7 Feb. and 4 Apr. 1967, 26 Jan. 1968; Lina Schädler to Gershom Scholem, 12 Feb. 1968, INL, Archive G. Scholem.

39. On this, see the five-part series published in 1967 in the magazine *Der Spiegel* on the topic of anti-Semitism and right-wing radicalism by Peter Brügge, "Rechts ab zum Vaterland."

40. Emmy Scholem to Gershom Scholem, 18 Feb and 12 Apr. 1968, INL, Archive G. Scholem.

41. Scholem, *From Berlin to Jerusalem*, 31.

42. Emmy Scholem to Gerhard Scholem, 3 Dec. 1968, IPW, Nachlass Scholem; Renee Goddard to Fania and Gershom Scholem, 10 June 1970 and 25 Mar. 1980; Edith Capon to Gershom Scholem, 4 May 1970, INL, Archive G. Scholem; Gershom Scholem to Renee Goddard, 22 June 1980, in Scholem, *Briefe*, 3:207; Zadoff and Zadoff, "From Mission to Memory."

43. Ben-Rafael, *Jewish Identities*, xix–xx.

44. Gershom Scholem to the newspaper *Ha-Boker*, 14 Aug. 1959, as quoted in Gorny, "Forward," xi.

45. Gorny, "Foreword," xvi.

46. Völter, *Judentum und Kommunismus*, 31.

47. Diner and Frankel, "Jews and Communism," 8; Talmon, *Israel Among the Nations*, 1.

48. Gerrits, "Jüdischer Kommunismus," 234–244; Adam Kirsch, "The End of the Jewish Left."

49. Gerrits, "Jüdischer Kommunismus," 246–247, 253; Grab, "Sozialpropheten und Sündenböcke."

50. Deutscher, "The Non-Jewish Jew"; Shore, "Children of the Revolution," 61; Biale, *Not in the Heavens.*

51. Grebing, "Jüdische Intellektuelle in der deutschen Arbeiterbewegung," 26–30.

52. The original edition was published in 1957 in Hebrew.

53. Gershom Scholem, *Sabbatai Sevi*, xi.

54. Ibid., xii–xiii.

55. Zadoff and Zadoff, "From Mission to Memory."

56. Scholem and Biale, "The Threat of Messianism," 22; Scholem and Tsur, "An Interview," 25–26; Gershom Scholem, "Zionism—Dialectic of Continuity and Rebellion," 295–296.

57. On this, see also Mendes-Flohr, "Im Schatten des Weltkrieges," 31.

58. Mann, *Geschichte und Geschichten*, 186–189.

59. Slezkine, *The Jewish Century.*

60. Gershom Scholem, "Memory and Utopia in Jewish History," 162.

61. Werner Mosse,"Die Krise der europäischen Bourgeoisie und das deutsche Judentum," 11.

62. Gershom Scholem, "On the Social Psychology of Jews in Germany, 1900–1930," 26.

63. Alfred Laurence to Gershom Scholem, 6 Apr. 1981, in Scholem, *Briefe*, 3:454 n. 1.

64. Boehlich, "Ein Jude aus Deutschland," 464, first published in the *Frankfurter Rundschau* on 25 Feb. 1982.

BIBLIOGRAPHY

Archival Sources

Archiv des Konzentrationslagers Buchenwald
Porträtfotographie von Johann Blank, Sign. 074.014.
British General Register Office
Record Edith Elisabeth Charlotte Capon (1918–1988).
Bundesarchiv Berlin
Akten der Reichskanzlei: Weimarer Republik (online edition).
http://www.bundesarchiv.de/aktenreichskanzlei/1919–1933/0000/index.html.
Stiftung Archiv der Parteien und Massenorganisationen der DDR
Anträge an das Orbüro, Sign. RY 1/I 2/4/35.
Bericht an EKKI, 19 Oct. 1925, Sign. RY 1/I 2/706/14.
Berichte zur innerparteilichen Lage 1926, Sign. RY 1/I 2/705/22.
Berlin-Brandenburg-Lausitz II, Sign. RY 1/I 3/1–2/14.
Berlin-Brandenburg-Lausitz, Bezirksparteitag 20 June 1923, Sign. RY 1/I 3/1–2/2.
Bezirkskonferenzen Schlesien, Sitzung des Bezirksausschusses 6 May 1924, Sign. RY 1/I 3/7/9.
3. [Dritte] Tagung des Zentralausschusses der KPD, 18–19 Oct. 1924, Sign. RY 1/I 2/1/23, Fiche 1, 3.
Erklärung von Scholem, Katz und Rosenberg, Zentralausschuss der KPD, 5. [Fünfte] Tagung, 9–10 May 1925, Sign. RY 1/I 2/1/25, Fiche 9.
Lagebericht des Polizeipräsidiums Berlin, Sign. R 1507/1063 k.
Material über Ultralinke, Sign. RY 1/I 2/3/65, Fiche 1–4.
Orbüro unter Scholem, 1924, Sign. RY 1/I 2/4/60.
Parteikonferenz der KPD, 31 Oct.–1 Nov. 1925, Sign. RY 1/I 1/2/4, Fiche 1, 2, 5, 7, 10, 11, 14.
Parteikonferenzen Pommern, Sign. RY 1/I 3/3/11.
Plenartagung des ZK , 6–7 Aug. 1925, Sign. RY 1/I 2/1/28.
Plenartagung des ZK, 23–24 Aug. 1925, Sign. RY 1/I 2/1/31.
Plenartagung des ZK, 29 Oct. 1925, Sign. RY 1/I 2/1/33.
Plenartagung des ZK, 5 Nov. 1926, Sign. RY 1/I 2/1/49.
Politbüro-Dokumente zur Ultralinken, Sign. RY 1/I 2/3/64.
Politbüro-Sitzungen I, Sign. RY 1/I 2/3/4.
Politbüro-Sitzungen II, Sign. RY 1/I 2/3/2.
Protokoll der Sitzung der Zentrale mit den Vertretern der Berliner Bezirksleitung, 5 Apr. 1923, Sign. RY 1/I 2/2/3.

Protokoll des KPD-Bezirksparteitages, 20 and 21 Jan. 1923, Sign. RY 1/I 3/1-2/2; RY 1/I 3/1–2/16.

Prozessunterlagen des Volksgerichtshofes gegen Frida Hüffner Sign. R 3017/13 J 195/ 33; VGH/Z-H 531; NJ 13903, vols. 1–15.

Rede Scholems beim Jugendkongress in Leipzig, 15 May 1924, Schriftwechsel mit Massenorganisationen, Sign. RY 1/I 2/3/177.

Rede Scholems in der Sitzung der Zentrale mit Bezirkssekretären, 4 Sept. 1924, Sign. RY 1/I 2/2/4.

Rede Scholems, Zentralausschuss der KPD, 5. Tagung, 9–10 May 1925, Sign. RY 1/I 2/1/25, Fiche 5.

Rundschreiben der Linken Kommunisten (Ruhrgebiet) 1925, Sign. RY 1/I 3/18–19/ 15.

Rundschreiben von Scholem und Rosenberg, 15 Apr. 1925, Sign. RY 1/I 2/3/65.

Schreiben an die Parteizentrale, 24 June 1922, Schriftwechsel mit Massenorganisatio-nen, Sign. RY 1/I 2/3/177.

Schreiben von Scholem, Katz und Rosenberg an die Zentrale, 3 May 1925, Sign. RY 1/I 2/3/65.

Spitzelbericht einer Versammlung der Linken Kommunisten, 27 Oct. 1927, Berlin-Brandenburg Lausitz VI, innerparteiliche

Auseinandersetzungen, Sign. RY 1/I 3/1–2/64.

Tätigkeitsbericht des Orbüro, 10 Apr.–1 Oct. 1924, Sign. RY 1/I 2/4/24.

Werner Scholem an die "Erwachende Jugend" 1922, Sign. RY 1/I 2/707/54.

10. [Zehnter] Parteitag Berlin, 12–17 July 1925, Sign. RY 1/I 1/1/19, Fiche 3.

Gedenkstätte KZ-Dachau, Archiv

Aktennr. 931: Erfahrungsbericht von Dr. Ludwig Bendix.

Aktennr. 4490: Jüdische Häftlinge, Scholem Werner.

Gedenkstätte KZ Lichtenburg Prettin, Archiv

Erinnerungsbericht zur Lichtenburger Häftlingszeit von Prof. Dr. Friedrich Kaul, Inven-tarnr. 289.

Houghton Library, Harvard University, Ruth Fischer Archive

Arkadi Maslow. "Die Tochter des Generals, ein bisher unveröffentlichter Roman." Type-script, sign. bMS Ger 204–2776; microfilm sign. 08–9851.

Correspondence with Emmy Scholem, 1961, sign. bMS Ger 204 (797).

Institut für Politische Wissenschaft Hannover, Leibniz Universität Hannover

Nachlass Emmy und Werner Scholem.

Institut für Zeitgeschichte, Archiv

Martin Broszat, Einleitung zum Vortrag von Gershom Scholem am 15. März 1973, Sign. D 562.

Walter Hammer Archiv, Sign. ED 106.

Korrespondence K. Grossmann, Paris und New York, mit O. Wollenberg, London, betr.: Demokr. FlüFürsorge 1939–1940, Sign. ED 201/3, Akzn. 4435/70.

International Instituut voor Sociale Geschiedenis, Amsterdam

Bernstein, Eduard. "Die Ostjuden in Deutschland." Sign. E Bernstein A 79.

International Tracing Service, Arolsen

Archive Fond Werner Scholem, Sign. 098/65.

Instituto di Studi sul Capitalismo Genua
De la Révolution de Lénine à la contre-révolution de Staline. Les Brochures du Groupe International (marxistes-léninistes), Copenhagen/Paris 1937, sign. Tros-063.
Israeli National Library, Archive Gershom Scholem
Arc. 41599: Correspondence.
Arc. 41599/265: Diaries.
Israeli National Library, Library Gershom Scholem
Die Blau-Weiße Brille (1915–1916), 1–3.
Niedersächsisches Landesarchiv–Hauptstaatsarchiv Hannover
Antrag auf Grund des Bundesergänzungsgesetztes zur Entschädigung für Opfer der Nationalsozialistischen Verfolgung, Emmy Scholem Sign.: Nds. 110 W Acc. 14/99 no. 107351, vols. 1 and 2.
Antrag auf Grund des Bundesergänzungsgesetztes zur Entschädigung für Opfer der Nationalsozialistischen Verfolgung, Werner Scholem Sign.: Nds. 110 W Acc. 14/99 no. 107352.
Österreichische Nationalbibliothek, Literaturarchiv
Nachlass Erich Fried: Emmy Scholem an Erich Fried, 23 Dec. 1953.
Private Archive Renee Goddard
"Erinnerungen von Renee Goddard" (unpublished, unpaginated manuscript).
Photo album of Werner Scholem.
Interview with Edith Capon, undated.
Private Archive Mirjam Zadoff
Interview with Susanna Capon, 17 June 2006.
Interviews with Renee Goddard, 18 June 2006, 9 and 10 Jan. 2008.
Stadtarchiv Braunschweig
Birth record [Geburtenbucheintrag] of Emma Johanne Wilhelmine Rock, Sign. #4007/1896 (E34:G94); Sign. #4447/1970 St. A. Hannover.
Stadtarchiv Halle
Adreßbuch des Saalkreises, 1920.
Universitätsarchiv Göttingen
Matrikelschein Werner Scholem.
Universitätsarchiv Halle
Matrikelschein Werner Scholem.
Universitätsarchiv der Humboldt Universität Berlin
Eintrag Werner Scholem.

Films and Audio Plays

Linden: Ein Arbeiterlied; Erinnerung an eine Gegenwart. Film by Wolfgang Jost and Winfried Wallat, 1991.
Goddard, Renee, and Robin Glendinning. *Edith's Story*. BBC, 25 February 2010.
———. *Reni and the Brownshirts: The Childhood of Renee Goddard*. TX Radio 4, 18 June 2002. Transcript. Bristol, 2002.

Books and Articles

Abraham, Karl. *Psychoanalytische Studien II*. Frankfurt, 1971.
"Achtung Manöver! Der Sinn der neuen kommunistischen Taktik." *Der Vorwärts* 42, no. 519 (1925).

Angress, Werner T. "Juden im politischen Leben der Revolutionszeit." In Werner E. Mosse and Arnold Paucker, eds., *Deutsches Judentum in Krieg und Revolution, 1916–1923*, 137–315. Tübingen, 1971.

———. *Die Kampfzeit der KPD, 1921–1923*. Düsseldorf, 1973.

Arndt, Heiko. "Linden und der Nationalsozialismus: Endzeitstimmung und beginnender Terror 1932/33." Accessed 10 March 2017. http://www.lebensraum-linden.de/internet/page.php?site = 902000292&typ = 2&rubrik = 902000001.

Aschheim, Steven E. *Beyond the Border: The German-Jewish Legacy Abroad*. Princeton, N.J., Oxford, 2007.

———. "German Jews Beyond 'Bildung' and Liberalism: The Radical Jewish Revival in the Weimar Republic." In Steven E. Aschheim, *Culture and Catastrophe: German and Jewish Confrontations with National Socialism and Other Crises*, 31–44. London, 1996.

———. *Scholem, Arendt, Klemperer: Intimate Chronicles in Turbulent Times*. Bloomington, Ind., 2001.

"Ausgeschlossene Reichstagsabgeordnete." *Der Vorwärts* 43, no. 525 (1926).

Baedeker, Karl. *Hannover und die deutsche Nordseeküste: Braunschweig, Kassel, Münster; Handbuch für Reisende*. Leipzig, 1921.

Bahne, Siegfried. "Zwischen 'Luxemburgismus' und 'Stalinismus': Die 'Ultralinke' Opposition in der KPD." *Vierteljahrshefte für Zeitgeschichte* 9, no. 4 (1961): 359–383.

Barkai, Avraham. "Jüdisches Leben in seiner Umwelt." In Michael A. Meyer and Michael Brenner, eds., *Deutsch-jüdische Geschichte in der Neuzeit*, vol. 4, *Aufbruch und Zerstörung, 1918–1945*, 50–73. Munich, 2000.

———. "Politische Orientierung und Krisenbewußtsein." In Michael A. Meyer and Michael Brenner, eds., *Deutsch-jüdische Geschichte in der Neuzeit*, vol. 4, *Aufbruch und Zerstörung, 1918–1945*, 102–124. Munich, 2000.

Barouch, Lina. "Sprache zwischen Klage und Rache: Gershom Scholems frühe Schriften zur Sprache." *Münchner Beiträge zur Jüdischen Geschichte und Kultur* 1, no. 2 (2007): 48–55.

Bayerlein, Bernhard H., Leonid G. Babicenko, Fridrich I. Firsov, and Aleksandr Ju. Vatlin. *Deutscher Oktober 1923: Ein Revolutionsplan und sein Scheitern*. Berlin, 2003.

Bebel, August. *Antisemitismus und Sozialdemokratie*. Berlin, 1893.

Belting, Hans. *Faces: Eine Geschichte des Gesichts*. Munich, 2013.

Benjamin, Hilde. *Georg Benjamin: Eine Biographie*. Leipzig, 1977.

Benjamin, Walter. *The Correspondence of Walter Benjamin, 1910–1940*. Edited and annotated by Gershom Scholem and Theodor W. Adorno. Translated by Manfred R. Jacobson and Evelyn M. Jacobson. Chicago, London, 1994.

———. "Denkbilder." In *Gesammelte Schriften*, 4 (1): 316–348. Edited by Tillman Rexroth. Frankfurt a. M., 1972.

———. *Gesammelte Briefe*. Vol. 2, *1919–1924*, and vol. 3, *1925–1930*. Edited by Christoph Gödde and Henri Lonitz. Frankfurt a. M., 1996.

———. *Moscow Diary*. Edited by Gary Smith. Cambridge, Mass., 1986.

Benjamin, Walter, and Gershom Scholem. *Briefwechsel, 1933–1940*. Edited by Gershom Scholem. Frankfurt a. M., 1980.

———. *The Correspondence of Walter Benjamin and Gershom Scholem, 1932–1940*. Edited by Gershom Scholem. Translated by Gary Smith and Andre Lefevere. New York, 1989.

Ben-Rafael, Eliezer, ed. *Jewish Identities: Fifty Intellectuals Answer Ben-Gurion*. Leiden, 2002.

Benz, Wolfgang. *"Der ewige Jude": Metaphern und Methoden nationalsozialistischer Propaganda*. Berlin, 2010.

Berg, Meike. *Jüdische Schulen in Niedersachsen: Tradition, Emanzipation, Assimilation; Die Jacobson-Schule in Seesen (1801–1922); Die Samsonschule in Wolfenbüttel (1807–1928)*. Cologne, Weimar, Vienna, 2003.

Bergbauer, Knut, Sabine Fröhlich, and Stefanie Schüler-Springorum. *Denkmalsfigur: Biographische Annäherung an Hans Litten, 1903–1938*. Göttingen, 2008.

Bergbauer, Knut, and Stefanie Schüler-Springorum. *"Wir sind jung, die Welt ist offen . . .": Eine jüdische Jugendgruppe im 20. Jahrhundert*. Exhibition catalog. Berlin, 2002.

Berger, Alfred. "Deutschland." In *Jüdisches Lexikon*, vol. 4, col. 1443. Berlin, 1930.

Berger-Barzilai, Joseph. *Ha-Tragedyah shel ha-mahpekhah ha-Sovyetit* [The tragedy of the Soviet Revolution]. Tel Aviv, 1968.

Berghahn, Volker R. "Structuralism and Biography: Some Concluding Thoughts on the Uncertainties of a Historiographical Genre." In Volker R. Berghahn and Simone Lässig, eds., *Biography Between Structure and Agency: Central European Lives in International Historiography*, 234–250. Oxford, New York, 2008.

Bericht über die Verhandlungen des III. (8.) Parteitages der Kommunistischen Partei Deutschlands: Leipzig vom 28.1. bis 1.2.1923. Published by the Zentrale der Kommunistischen Partei Deutschlands. Berlin, 1923.

Bericht über die Verhandlungen des IX. Parteitages der Kommunistischen Partei Deutschlands: Frankfurt/M. vom 7. bis 10.4.1924. Published by the Zentrale der Kommunistischen Partei Deutschlands. Berlin, 1924.

Bericht über die Verhandlungen des X. Parteitages der Kommunistischen Partei Deutschlands: Berlin vom 12. bis 17.7.1925. Published by the Zentrale der Kommunistischen Partei Deutschlands. Berlin, 1926.

Berliner Adreßbuch 1933. Vol. 1. Berlin, 1932.

"Berufsberatung." *Kladderadatsch* 77, no. 14 (1924): 215.

Biale, David. *Gershom Scholem: Kabbalah and Counter-History*. Cambridge, Mass., London, 1982.

———. *Not in the Heavens: The Tradition of Jewish Secular Thought*. Princeton, N.J., 2011.

"Bisher 448 Abgeordnete gewählt." *Vossische Zeitung*, 5 May 1924, evening edition, no. 213, 1–2.

Bloch, Ernst. *The Spirit of Utopia*. Translated by Anthony A. Nassar. Stanford, Calif., 2000.

Blüher, Hans. "Die Untaten des bürgerlichen Typus." In Kurt Hiller, ed., *Das Ziel: Aufrufe zu tätigem Geist*, 9–36. Munich, Berlin, 1916.

Boehlich, Walter. "Ein Jude aus Deutschland: Nach Gershom Scholems Tod." In Gershom Scholem, *Briefe*, vol. 3, *1914–1982*, 463–464. Edited by Itta Shedletzky. Munich, 1999.

Boehm, Max Hildebert. "Vom jüdisch-deutschen Geist." In *Preußische Jahrbücher* 162 (1915): 404–420.

Bois, Marcel. "Im Kampf gegen Stalinismus und Faschismus: Die linke Opposition der KPD in der Weimarer Republik (1924–1933)." In Kora Baumbach et al., *Strömungen: Politische Bilder, Texte und Bewegungen; Neuntes DoktorandInnen-Seminar der Rosa-Luxemburg-Stiftung*, 86–109. Berlin, 2007.

———. *Kommunisten gegen Hitler und Stalin: Die linke Opposition der KPD in der Weimarer Republik; Eine Gesamtdarstellung*. Essen, 2014.

Bourdieu, Pierre. "Die biographische Illusion." In Pierre Bourdieu, *Praktische Vernunft: Zur Theorie des Handelns*, 75–82. Translated by Hella Beister. Frankfurt a. M., 1998.

Braun, Christina von. *Stille Post: Eine Andere Familiengeschichte*. Berlin, 2008.

Brauneck, Manfred. *Die rote Fahne: Kritik, Theorie, Feuilleton, 1918–1933*. Munich, 1973.

Brecht, Bertolt. "Typus des intellektuellen Revolutionärs." In Bertold Brecht, *Gesammelte Werke*, vol. 20. Edited by Suhrkamp Verlag in collaboration with Elisabeth Hauptmann. Frankfurt a. M., 1967.

Breithaupt, Wolfgang. *Volksvergiftung, 1914–1918: Dokumente der Vorbereitung des 9. November 1918*. Berlin, Leipzig, 1925.

Brenner, Michael. "From Self-Declared Messiah to Scholar of Messianism: The Recently Published Diaries Present Young Gerhard Scholem in a New Light." *Jewish Social Studies* 3, no. 1 (1996): 177–182.

———. *Jüdische Kultur in der Weimarer Republik*. Munich, 2000.

———. "A Tale of Two Families: Franz Rosenzweig, Gershom Scholem and the Generational Conflict Around Judaism." *Judaism* 42, no. 3 (1993): 349–361.

———. "Wie jüdisch war die jüdisch-intellektuelle Kultur der Weimarer Republik?" In Wilfried Barner and Christoph König, eds., *Jüdische Intellektuelle und die Philologie in Deutschland*, 131–140. Göttingen, 2001.

Brock, Peter. "Confinement of Conscientious Objectors as Psychiatric Patients in World War I Germany." *Peace & Change* 23, no. 3 (1998): 247–264.

Broué, Pierre. *Die deutsche Linke und die russische Opposition, 1926–1928*. Cologne, 1989.

———. *Léon Sedov, fils de Trotsky, victime de Staline*. Paris, 1993.

———. *Trotzki: Eine politische Biographie*. 2 vols. Cologne, 2003.

Brückner, Peter. *Psychologie und Geschichte: Vorlesungen im "Club Voltaire," 1980/81*. Berlin, 1982.

Brügge, Peter. "Rechts ab zum Vaterland." *Der Spiegel*, nos. 17–21 (1967).

Brüninghaus, Marc. *Unterhaltungsmusik im Dritten Reich*. Hamburg, 2015.

Buber, Martin. *Briefwechsel aus sieben Jahrzehnten*. Vol. 1, *1897–1918*. Edited by Grete Schaeder et al. Heidelberg, 1972.

———. *Die Geschichten des Rabbi Nachman*. Frankfurt a. M., 1906.

———. *Die Legende des Baalschem*. Zurich, 1908. Repr., Zurich, 1955.

———. "Die Revolution und wir." *Der Jude* 3, nos. 8–9 (1918/1919): 345–347.

———. "Die Tempelweihe: Rede gehalten am 19.12.1914." In Martin Buber, *Die jüdische Bewegung: Gesammelte Aufsätze und Ansprachen; Erste Folge, 1900–1914*, 229–242. Berlin, 1920.

Buber-Neumann, Margarete. *Kriegsschauplätze der Weltrevolution: Ein Bericht aus der Praxis der Komintern, 1919–1943*. Stuttgart, 1967.

Büchner, Georg. *Danton's Death; Leonce and Lena; Woyzeck*. Translated by Victor Price. Oxford, 1988.

Buckmiller, Michael, and Klaus Meschkat, eds. *Biographisches Handbuch zur Geschichte der Kommunistischen Internationale: Ein deutsch-russisches Forschungsprojekt*. Berlin, 2007.

Buckmiller, Michael, and Pascal Nafe. "Die Naherwartung des Kommunismus—Werner Scholem." In Michael Buckmiller et al., eds., *Judentum und politische Existenz: Siebzehn Porträts deutsch-jüdischer Intellektueller*, 60–81. Hanover, 2000.

Bunzol, Alfred. *Die Leben des Buchenwaldhäftlings Alfred Bunzol 738*. Bad Langensalza, 2011.

Carlebach, Emil. *Tote auf Urlaub: Kommunist in Deutschland; Dachau und Buchenwald, 1937–1945*. Bonn, 1995.

Carsten, Francis L. "Arthur Rosenberg: Ancient Historian into Leading Communist." In Walter Laqueur and George L. Mosse, eds., *Historians in Politics*, 315–327. London, Beverly Hills, Calif., 1974.

Chappell, Connery. *Island of Barbed Wire: Internment on the Isle of Man in World War Two.* London, 1984.

Collado Seidel, Carlos. *Der Spanische Bürgerkrieg: Geschichte eines europäischen Konflikts.* Munich, 2006.

"Coming Trial of Herr Scholem: Mistaken Identity?" *Manchester Guardian*, 22 December 1934, 13.

Danzer, Doris. *Zwischen Vertrauen und Verrat: Deutschsprachige kommunistische Intellektuelle und ihre sozialen Beziehungen (1918–1960)*. Göttingen, 2012.

Das Gedenkbuch des Bundesarchivs für die Opfer der nationalsozialistischen Judenverfolgung in Deutschland (1933–1945). Online edition, 2007. http://www.bundesarchiv.de/geden kbuch/index.html.de.

Dathe, Uwe. "Jena—eine Episode aus Gershom Scholems Leben." *Zeitschrift für Religionsund Geistesgeschichte*, no. 1 (2008): 73–78.

David, Anthony. *The Patron: A Life of Salman Schocken, 1877–1959*. New York, 2003.

Deleuze, Gilles, and Félix Guattari. *Kafka, für eine kleine Literatur*. Frankfurt a. M., 1976.

"Der 'Fall Gumbel.'" *Abwehrblätter* 35, nos. 11–12 (1925): 54.

Deutscher, Isaac. "The Non-Jewish Jew." In Tamara Deutscher, ed., *The Non-Jewish Jew and Other Essays*, 25–41. New York, 1968.

———. *Der verstoßene Prophet: Trotzki, 1929–1940*. Stuttgart, 1963.

Dietrich, Werner. *Konzentrationslager Lichtenburg*. Prettin, 2002.

Diner, Dan, and Jonathan Frankel. "Jews and Communism: The Utopian Temptation." Introduction in Dan Diner and Jonathan Frankel, eds., *Dark Times, Dire Decisions: Jews and Communism*, 3–12. Studies in Contemporary Jewry 20. Oxford, 2004.

Dittmann, Wilhelm. "Deutsche Arbeiter in Russland." *Freiheit*, no. 358, 31 August 1920.

———. "Wahrheit über Russland." *Freiheit*, no. 360, 1 September 1920.

Döblin, Alfred. *Berlin Alexanderplatz: The Story of Franz Biberkopf*. Translated by Eugene Jolas. London, 2004.

Dohrn, Verena, and Gertrud Pickhan. *Transit und Transformation: Osteuropäisch-jüdische Migranten in Berlin, 1918–1939*. Göttingen, 2010.

Dokumente und Materialien zur Geschichte der Arbeiterbewegung. Vol. 8. Berlin, 1975.

Drechsler, Hanno. *Die sozialistische Arbeiterpartei Deutschlands (SAPD): Ein Beitrag zur Geschichte der deutschen Arbeiterbewegung am Ende der Weimarer Republik*. Meisenheim am Glan, 1965.

Dreyer, Martin. *Die zivilgerichtliche Rechtsprechung des Oberlandesgerichts Düsseldorf in der nationalsozialistischen Zeit*. Göttingen, 2004.

Drobisch, Klaus, and Günther Wieland. *System der NS-Konzentrationslager, 1933–1939*. Berlin, 1993.

Duker, Abraham. *Jews in World War I: A Brief Historical Sketch*. New York, 1939.

Eckart, Wolfgang U., and Christoph Gradmann. "Medizin." In Gerhard Hirschfeld, Gerd Krumeich, and Irina Renz, eds., *Enzyklopädie Erster Weltkrieg*, 210–219. Paderborn, 2009.

Eloesser, Arthur. "Zweimal: Die meuternden Matrosen." *Vossische Zeitung*, 1 September 1930, evening edition, no. 411.

Engels, Friedrich. *Der Ursprung der Familie, des Privateigentums und des Staates*. Berlin, 1973.

Enzensberger, Hans Magnus. *The Silences of Hammerstein: A German Story*. Translated by Martin Chalmers. London, New York, Calcutta, 2009.

Etzemüller, Thomas. *Die Romantik der Rationalität: Alva und Gunnar Myrdal – Social Engineering in Schweden*. Bielefeld, 2010.

Falkenberg, Rudolf, ed. *Geschichte der deutschen Arbeiterjugendbewegung, 1904–1945*. Dortmund, 1973.

Fieber, Hans-Joachim. *Widerstand in Berlin gegen das NS-Regime 1933 bis 1945: Ein biographisches Lexikon*. Vol. 6. Berlin, 2003.

Fischer, Ruth. *Stalin and German Communism: A Study in the Origins of the State Party*. With a new introduction by John C. Leggett. New Brunswick, N.J., 2006.

———. "Trotsky in Paris" [1933]. In Ruth Fischer and Arkadij Maslow, *Abtrünnig wider Willen: Aus Briefen und Manuskripten des Exils*, 499–519. Edited by Peter Lübbe. Munich, 1990.

Fischer, Ruth, and Arkadij Maslow. *Abtrünnig wider Willen: Aus Briefen und Manuskripten des Exils*. Edited by Peter Lübbe. Munich, 1990.

Flachowsky, Soeren, and Holger Stoecker, eds. *Vom Amazonas an die Ostfront: Der Expeditionsreisende und Geograph Otto Schulz-Kampfhenkel (1910–1989)*. Cologne, Weimar, Vienna, 2011.

Flechtheim, Ossip K. *Die KPD in der Weimarer Republik*. Hamburg, 1986.

Foitzik, Jan. "Das kommunistische Intellektuellenmilieu in der Weimarer Republik: Redakteure der Roten Fahne." In Michel Grunewald, ed., *Das linke Intellektuellenmilieu in Deutschland, seine Presse und seine Netzwerke (1890–1960)*, 227–249. In collaboration with Hans Manfred Bock. Bern, 2002.

Friedländer, Elfriede [Ruth Fischer]. *Sexualethik des Kommunismus: Eine prinzipielle Studie*. Vienna, 1920.

Fritsch, Theodor. *Handbuch der Judenfrage: Eine Zusammensetzung des wichtigsten Materials zur Beurteilung des jüdischen Volkes*. Hamburg, 1928.

Fromm, Erich. *Arbeiter und Angestellte am Vorabend des Dritten Reiches*. Translation and introduction by Wolfgang Bonß. Stuttgart, 1980.

Gay, Peter. "Der berlinisch-jüdische Geist: Zweifel an einer Legende." In Peter Gay, *Freud, Juden und andere Deutsche: Herren und Opfer in der Modernen Kultur*, 189–206. Hamburg, 1986.

———. *Die Republik der Außenseiter: Geist und Kultur in der Weimarer Zeit, 1918–1933*. Frankfurt a. M., 1987.

Geller, Jay Howard. "From Berlin and Jerusalem: On the Germanness of Gershom Scholem." *Journal of Religious History* 35, no. 2 (2011): 211–232.

———. "The Scholem Brothers and the Paths of German Jewry, 1914–1939." *Shofar: An Interdisciplinary Journal of Jewish Studies* 30, no. 2 (2012): 52–73.

German Jewish Aid Committee, ed. *While You Are in England: Helpful Information and Guidance for Every Refugee* [London, 1933–1939].

Gerrits, André W. M. "Jüdischer Kommunismus: Der Mythos, die Juden, die Partei." In *Jahrbuch für Antisemitismusforschung*, 14:243–264. Berlin, 2005.

————. *The Myth of Jewish Communism: A Historical Interpretation.* Brussels, 2009.

Gershom Scholem (1897–1982): Commemorative Exhibition on the Fifth Anniversary of His Death and the Installation of His Library at the JNUL. Exhibition catalog (Hebrew and English). Edited by Margot Cohn and Rivka Plesser. Jerusalem, 1988.

Geyer, Martin H.: "Korruptionsdebatten in der Zeit der Revolution 1918/19: Der Fall 'Sklarz,' das Pamphlet 'Der Rattenkönig' und die (Ab-)Wege des politischen Radikalismus nach dem Ersten Weltkrieg." In Heidrun Kämper, Peter Haslinger, and Thomas Raithel, eds., *Demokratiegeschichte als Zäsurgeschichte: Diskurse der frühen Weimarer Republik*, 331–356. Berlin, 2014.

————. *Verkehrte Welt: Revolution, Inflation und Moderne, München, 1914–1924.* Göttingen 1998.

Gillerman, Sharon. "The Crisis of the Jewish Family in Weimar Germany." In Michael Brenner and Derek J. Penslar, eds., *In Search of Community: Jewish Identities in Germany and Austria, 1918–1933*, 176–199. Bloomington, Ind., 1998.

Gilman, Sander. *Jewish Self-Hatred: Anti-Semitism and the Hidden Language of the Jews.* Baltimore, 1990.

Goebbels, Joseph. *Reden, 1932–1945.* Edited by Helmut Heiber. Bindlach, 1991.

————. *Tagebücher.* Vol. 1, *1924–1929.* Edited by Ralf Georg Reuth. Munich, Zurich, 2008.

————. "Welt-Bolschewismus ohne Maske: Kernstück der Rede des Dr. Goebbels auf dem Reichsparteitag in Nürnberg 1935." Fichtebundblätter no. 791. Hamburg [1935].

Gorny, Joseph. "Foreword." In Eliezer Ben-Rafael, ed., *Jewish Identities: Fifty Intellectuals Answer Ben-Gurion*, xi–xvii. Leiden, 2002.

Grab, Walter. "Sozialpropheten und Sündenböcke: Juden in der deutschen Arbeiterbewegung 1840 bis 1933." In Julius H. Schoeps, ed., *Juden als Träger bürgerlicher Kultur in Deutschland*, 357–378. Stuttgart, Bonn, 1989.

Graf, Rüdiger. *Die Zukunft der Weimarer Republik: Krisen und Zukunftsaneignung in Deutschland, 1918–1933.* Munich, 2008.

Grebing, Helga. *Geschichte der deutschen Arbeiterbewegung: Von der Revolution 1848 bis ins 21. Jahrhundert.* Berlin, 2007.

————. "Jüdische Intellektuelle in der deutschen Arbeiterbewegung zwischen den beiden Weltkriegen." *Archiv für Sozialgeschichte* 37 (1997): 19–38.

————. "Jüdische Intellektuelle und ihre Politische Identität in der Weimarer Republik." In *Helga Grebing zum 75. Geburtstag: Mitteilungsblatt des Instituts für Soziale Bewegungen*, no. 34 (2005): 11–23.

————. "Der Typus des linken Intellektuellen in der Weimarer Republik." In Daniela Münkel and Jutta Schwarzkopf, eds., *Geschichte als Experiment: Studien zu Politik, Kultur und Alltag im 19. und 20. Jahrhundert*, 15–24. Frankfurt, New York, 2004.

Grossmann, Atina. *Reforming Sex: The German Movement for Birth Control and Abortion Reform, 1920–1950.* New York, Oxford, 1995.

Grossmann, Kurt R. *Emigration: Geschichte der Hitler-Flüchtlinge, 1933–1945.* Frankfurt a. M., 1969.

Grotjahn, Alfred. *Erlebtes und Erstrebtes: Erinnerungen eines sozialistischen Arztes.* Berlin, 1932.

Grundmann, Siegfried. *Der Geheimapparat der KPD im Visier der Gestapo—das BB-Ressort: Funktionäre, Beamte, Spitzel und Spione.* Berlin, 2008.

Gumbel, Emil Julius. *Vier Jahre politischer Mord.* Heidelberg, 1980.

Hackett, David A., ed. *Der Buchenwald-Report: Bericht über das Konzentrationslager Buchenwald bei Weimar.* Munich, 2002.

"'Hängt die Judenkapitalisten auf': Ruth Fischer als Antisemitin." *Der Vorwärts* 40, no. 390 (1923).

Hasenclever, Walter. *Der Sohn.* Stuttgart, 1994.

Häusler, Otto, et al. "Die Eröffnung des Friesenberghauses." *Nachrichten der Sektion "Donauland" des Deutschen und Österreichischen Alpenvereins,* no. 133 (1932): 90–93.

Heid, Ludger. *Maloche—nicht Mildtätigkeit: Ostjüdische Arbeiter in Deutschland, 1914–1923.* Hildesheim, Zurich, New York, 1995.

———. *Oskar Cohn: Ein Sozialist und Zionist im Kaiserreich und in der Weimarer Republik.* Frankfurt, New York, 2002.

Heimann-Jelinek, Felicitas. "Zur Geschichte einer Ausstellung: Masken; Versuch über die Schoa." In Fritz Bauer Institut, ed., *"Beseitigung des jüdischen Einflusses . . .": Antisemitische Forschung, Eliten und Karrieren im Nationalsozialismus,* 131–145. Frankfurt, New York, 1999.

Hepp, Michael, ed. *Die Ausbürgerung deutscher Staatsangehöriger 1933–45 nach den im Reichsanzeiger veröffentlichten Listen.* Vol. 2, *Namensregister.* Munich, New York, London, Paris, 1985.

Hiller, Kurt, ed. *Das Ziel: Aufrufe zu tätigem Geist.* Munich, Berlin, 1916.

Hirschinger, Frank. *"Gestapoagenten, Trotzkisten, Verräter": Kommunistische Parteisäuberungen in Sachsen-Anhalt, 1918–1953.* Göttingen, 2005.

"Hitlerisazia shel germania." *Davar,* 10 March 1933, 1.

Holm, Kirsten, ed. *Stimmen aus Buchenwald: Ein Lesebuch.* Göttingen, 2002.

Hördler, Stefan, and Sigrid Jacobeit, eds. *Lichtenburg: Ein deutsches Konzentrationslager.* Berlin, 2009.

Hortzschansky, Günter, et al. *Ernst Thälmann: Eine Biographie.* Berlin, 1980.

Howald, Stefan. "Renee Goddard: 'Wo sie war, passierte etwas.'" *WOZ Die Wochenzeitung,* 12 November 2009. http://www.woz.ch/0946/renee-goddard/wo-sie-war-passierte-etwas.

"'I Am a Camera.' Isherwood's Berlin at the New Theater." *Manchester Guardian,* 13 March 1954, 3.

"In Memoriam: Werner Scholem." *Die Internationale* 17 (1981): 117–120.

Die Internationale: Zeitschrift für Praxis und Theorie des Marxismus 7, nos. 2–3 (1924): 124–134.

Jacobson, Eric. *Metaphysics of the Profane: The Political Theology of Walter Benjamin and Gershom Scholem.* New York, 2003.

———. "Theories of Justice, Profane and Prophetic: Scholem on the Bolshevik Revolution." In Joseph Dan, ed., *Gershom Scholem (1897–1982): In Memoriam,* 2:59–76. Jerusalem, 2007.

Jaffe, Benjamin, and Cecil Roth. "Bentwich." In Michael Berenbaum and Fred Skolnik, eds., *Encyclopaedia Judaica,* 3:381. Detroit, 2007.

Jäger, Lorenz. "Hammerstein-Fragen: Das Leck." *Frankfurter Allgemeine Zeitung,* 26 March 2008, 3.

Jahr, Christoph. "Desertion." In Gerhard Hirschfeld et al., *Enzyklopädie Erster Weltkrieg,* 435–437. Paderborn, 2009.

Janiszewski, Bertram. *Das alte Hansa-Viertel in Berlin.* Norderstedt, 2008.

Jay, Martin. "Anti-Semitism and the Weimar Left." *Midstream* 20, no. 1 (1974): 42–50.

Jüdisches Seniorenheim Hannover, Lola Fischl Haus. Geschichtlicher Rückblick. Accessed 10 March 2017. http://www.lola-fischel-haus.de.

Judt, Tony, and Timothy Snyder. *Nachdenken über das 20. Jahrhundert.* Munich, 2013.

Jung, Franz. "Betr. Hammerstein: Der Kampf um die Eroberung der Befehlsgewalt im deutschen Heer 1932–1937." In Petra Nettelbeck and Uwe Nettelbeck, eds., *Schriften und Briefe,* 2:1237–1253. Bad Salzhausen, 1981.

———. *Briefe, 1913–1963: Werke 9/1.* Edited by Sieglinde Mierau and Fritz Mierau. Hamburg, 1996.

Jünger, Ernst. "Siebzig Verweht V." In Ernst Jünger, *Sämtliche Werke,* vol. 22, *Späte Arbeiten: Verstreutes; Aus dem Nachlass,* 9–214. Stuttgart, 2003.

———. "SP. R. Drei Schulwege." In Ernst Jünger, *Sämtliche Werke,* vol. 22, *Späte Arbeiten: Verstreutes; Aus dem Nachlass,* 731–769. Stuttgart, 2003.

Jünger, Ernst, and Gershom Scholem. "Briefwechsel, 1975–1981." *Sinn und Form: Beiträge zur Literatur* 61, no. 3 (2009): 293–302.

Jütte, Robert. *Lust ohne Last: Geschichte der Empfängnisverhütung von der Antike bis zur Gegenwart.* Munich, 2003.

Kafka, Franz. "Brief an den Vater." In Franz Kafka, *Hochzeitsvorbereitungen und andere Prosa aus dem Nachlaß,* 162–223. Edited by Max Brod. Frankfurt a. M., 1953.

Karlauf, Thomas. " 'So endete mein Leben in Deutschland': Der 9. November 1938." In Uta Gerhardt and Thomas Karlauf, eds., *Nie mehr zurück in dieses Land: Augenzeugen berichten über das Novemberpogrom 1938,* 11–33. Berlin, 2009.

Kauffeldt, Rolf. "Zur jüdischen Tradition im romantisch-anarchistischen Denken Erich Mühsams und Gustav Landauers." *Bulletin des Leo Baeck Instituts* 69 (1984): 3–28.

Kaufmann, Bernd, Eckhard Reisener, Dieter Schwips, and Henri Walther. *Der Nachrichtendienst der KPD, 1919–1937.* Berlin, 1993.

Kaufmann, Hans. "Gründung des Deutschen Alpenvereins Berlin." *Abwehrblätter* 35, nos. 11–12 (1925): 51–52.

Kautsky, Benedikt. *Teufel und Verdammte: Erfahrungen und Erkenntnisse aus sieben Jahren in deutschen Konzentrationslagern.* Zurich, 1946.

Kautsky, Karl. *Die soziale Revolution.* Berlin, 1911.

Kayser, Rudolf. "Der jüdische Revolutionär." *Neue jüdische Monatshefte,* no. 5 (1919): 96–98.

Kaznelson, Siegmund, ed. *Juden im deutschen Kulturbereich: Ein Sammelwerk.* Berlin, 1962.

Kerff, Willy. *Karl Liebknecht: 1914 bis 1916. Fragment einer Biographie.* Berlin, 1967.

Kerr, Alfred. "Bleibt unverwirrt." *Das Zeit-Echo: Ein Kriegstagebuch der Künstler* 1, no. 4 (1914/1915): 41–42.

———. *Mein Berlin: Schauplätze einer Metropole.* Berlin, 1999.

Kershaw, Ian. "Biography and the Historian: Opportunities and Constraints." In Volker R. Berghahn and Simone Lässig, eds., *Biography Between Structure and Agency: Central European Lives in International Historiography,* 27–39. Oxford, New York, 2008.

Keßler, Mario. *Arthur Rosenberg: Ein Historiker im Zeitalter der Katastrophen (1889–1943).* Cologne, Weimar, Vienna, 2003.

———. *Heroische Illusion und Stalin-Terror: Beiträge zur Kommunismus-Forschung.* Hamburg, 1999.

———. "Die KPD und der Antisemitismus in der Weimarer Republik." *UTOPIE kreativ* 173 (March 2005): 223–232.

———. *Ruth Fischer: Ein Leben mit und gegen Kommunisten (1895–1961)*. Cologne, Weimar, Vienna, 2013.

———. *Die SED und die Juden—zwischen Repression und Toleranz: Politische Entwicklungen bis 1967*. Berlin, 1995.

Kinkead-Weekes, Mark. "Writing Lives Forwards: A Case for Strictly Chronological Biography." In Peter France and William St Clair, eds., *Mapping Lives: The Uses of Biography*, 235–252. Oxford, 2002.

Kirsch, Adam. "The End of the Jewish Left." *Tablet Magazine*, May 2012. http://www.table tmag.com/jewish-arts-and-culture/books/99711/the-end-of-the-jewish-left.

Kirsch, Sandra. *Emigration als Herausforderung: Eine Studie zu Einbindungs- und Ablösungsprozessen von aus dem nationalsozialistischen Deutschland emigrierten Kindern und Jugendlichen*. Frankfurt a. M., 2010.

Kirsten, Wulf, and Holm Kirsten, eds. *Stimmen aus Buchenwald: Ein Lesebuch*. Göttingen, 2002.

Kistenmacher, Olaf. "Vom 'Judas' zum 'Judenkapital': Antisemitische Denkformen in der Kommunistischen Partei Deutschlands der Weimarer Republik, 1918–1933." In Matthias Brosch, Michael Elm, Norman Geißler, Brigitta Elisa Simbürger, and Oliver von Wrochern, eds., *Exklusive Solidarität: Linker Antisemitismus in Deutschland; Vom Idealismus zur Antiglobalisierungsbewegung*, 69–86. Berlin, 2007.

Kleibert, Kristin. *Die Juristische Fakultät der Humboldt-Universität zu Berlin im Umbruch: Die Jahre 1948–1951*. Berlin, 2010.

Kluge, Alexander. *Die Lücke, die der Teufel läßt: Im Umfeld des neuen Jahrhunderts*. Frankfurt a. M., 2003.

Kogon, Eugen. *Der SS-Staat: Das System der deutschen Konzentrationslager*. Munich, 1988.

Kollontaj, A[lexandra]. *Die neue Moral und die Arbeiterklasse*. Berlin, 1920.

"Kommunisten und Hindenburgwahl." *Der Vorwärts* 42 (31 May 1925).

"Die kommunistische Verlustliste." *Der Vorwärts* 43, no. 536 (1926).

König, Gerhard, and Inge König. *Das Polizeipräsidium Berlin-Alexanderplatz: Seine Geschichte, seine Polizei, seine Häftlinge (1933–1945)*. Berlin, 1997.

Konzentrationslager Buchenwald, 1937–1945. Permanent exhibition catalog. Göttingen, 1999.

Kroll, Thomas. *Kommunistische Intellektuelle in Westeuropa: Frankreich, Österreich, Italien und Großbritannien im Vergleich (1945–1956)*. Cologne, Weimar, Vienna, 2007.

Kundt, Klaus. "Juden und Mitglieder der Sektion Donauland unerwünscht." *Gedenkstättenrundbrief* 117 (2004): 19–28.

Kuschey, Bernhard. *Die Ausnahme des Überlebens: Ernst und Hilde Federn; Eine biographische Studie und eine Analyse der Binnenstruktur des Konzentrationslagers*. 2 vols. Gießen, 2003.

Landauer, Gustav. "Sind das Ketzergedanken?" In Martin Buber, ed., *Der werdende Mensch*, 120–128. Potsdam, 1921.

Lange, I. M. "Mein Freund Walter Benjamin: Mit einer Vorbemerkung von Erdmut Wizisla." *Sinn und Form. Beiträge zur Literatur* 65, no. 2 (2013): 175–188.

Langels, Otto. *Die ultralinke Opposition der KPD in der Weimarer Republik*. Frankfurt a. M., 1984.

Laschitza, Annelies. *Im Lebensrausch, trotz allem: Rosa Luxemburg; Eine Biographie*. Berlin, 1996.

———. *Die Liebknechts: Karl und Sophie—Politik und Familie*. Berlin, 2007.

Lässig, Simone. "Biography in Modern History—Modern Historiography in Biography." In Volker R. Berghahn and Simone Lässig, eds., *Biography Between Structure and Agency: Central European Lives in International Historiography*, 1–26. Oxford, New York, 2008.

———. *Jüdische Wege ins Bürgertum: Kulturelles Kapital und sozialer Aufstieg im 19. Jahrhundert*. Göttingen, 2004.

Lessing, Theodor. *Der jüdische Selbsthaß*. Berlin, 1930.

Liepach, Martin. *Das Wahlverhalten der jüdischen Bevölkerung in der Weimarer Republik*. Tübingen, 1996.

"List of Aliens to Whom Certificates of Naturalisation Have Been Granted by the Secretary of State." *London Gazette*, 22 April and 23 August 1949.

Litten, Irmgard. *Eine Mutter kämpft gegen Hitler*. Rudolstadt, 1984.

London, Louise. *Whitehall and the Jews, 1933–1948: British Immigration Policy and the Holocaust*. Cambridge, 2000.

Longerich, Peter. *Joseph Goebbels: Biographie*. Munich, 2010.

Löwe, Heinrich. "Feinde ringsum!" *Jüdische Rundschau* 32 (1914): 343–344.

Luban, Ottokar. "Die Auswirkungen der Jenaer Jugendkonferenz 1916 und die Beziehungen der Zentrale der revolutionären Arbeiterjugend zur Führung der Spartakusgruppe." *Archiv für Sozialgeschichte* 11 (1971): 185–223.

Ludendorff, Erich. *Kriegführung und Politik*. Berlin, 1923.

Luisenstädtisches Realgymnasium in Berlin. *Bericht über das Schuljahr 1914–1915*. Berlin, 1915.

Luxemburg, Rosa. "Diskussion." In Iring Fetscher, ed., *Marxisten gegen Antisemitismus*, 141–150. Hamburg, 1974.

———. *Letters from Prison: With a Portrait and a Facsimile*. Translated by Eden Paul and Cedar Paul. Berlin, 1921.

Maiwald, Stefan, and Gerd Mischler. *Sexualität unter dem Hakenkreuz: Manipulation und Vernichtung der Intimsphäre im NS-Staat*. Munich, 2002.

Mallmann, Klaus-Michael. "Gehorsame Parteisoldaten oder eigensinnige Akteure? Die Weimarer Kommunisten in der Kontroverse: Eine Erwiderung." *Vierteljahrshefte für Zeitgeschichte* 47, no. 3 (1999): 401–415.

———. *Kommunisten in der Weimarer Republik: Sozialgeschichte einer revolutionären Bewegung*. Dortmund, 1996.

Mann, Golo. *Geschichte und Geschichten*. Frankfurt a. M., 1961.

———. "Rede, gehalten beim Jüdischen Weltkongreß in Brüssel am 4.8.66." In Abraham Melzer, ed., *Deutsche und Juden, ein unlösbares Problem: Reden zum Jüdischen Weltkongreß 1966*, 35–52. Darmstadt, Frankfurt a. M. 1966.

Marxen, Klaus, and Holger Schlüter. *Terror und "Normalität": Urteile des nationalsozialistischen Volksgerichtshofs, 1934–1945; Eine Dokumentation*. Düsseldorf, 2004.

Maslow, Arkadij. *Die Tochter des Generals*. Edited and with an afterword by Berit Balzer. Berlin, 2011.

Materna, Ingo. "9. November 1918—der erste Tag der Republik: Eine Chronik." *Berlinische Monatsschrift* 4 (2000): 139–146.

Maurois, André. "Die Biographie als Kunstwerk." In Bernhard Fetz and Wilhelm Hemecker, eds., with the assistance of Georg Huemer and Katharina J. Schneider, *Theorie der Biographie: Grundlagentexte und Kommentar*, 83–97. Berlin, 2011.

Mendes-Flohr, Paul. *Divided Passions: Jewish Intellectuals and the Experience of Modernity.* Detroit, 1991.

———. "Im Schatten des Weltkrieges." In Michael A. Meyer and Michael Brenner, eds., *Deutsch-jüdische Geschichte in der Neuzeit,* vol. 4, *Aufbruch und Zerstörung, 1918–1945,* 15–36. Munich, 1997.

Mergel, Thomas. *Parlamentarische Kultur in der Weimarer Republik: Politische Kommunikation, symbolische Politik und Öffentlichkeit im Reichstag.* Düsseldorf, 2002.

Merkl, Peter H. "The Corruption of Public Life in Weimar Germany." In Henry Friedlander und Sybil Milton, eds., *The Holocaust: Ideology, Bureaucracy, and Genocide,* 63–68. Millwood, N.Y., 1980.

Meyer, Reinhard Friedrich. *Bibliographie der Privatdrucke Reinhold und Erich Scholems, 1920–1931.* http://meyerbuch.wordpress.com/2009/10/25/bibliographie-der-privatdrucke-reinhold-erich-scholems-1920–1931/.

Meyer-Leviné, Rosa. *Im Inneren Kreis: Erinnerungen einer Kommunistin in Deutschland, 1920–1933.* Edited and introduction by Hermann Weber. Cologne, 1979.

Miller, Susanne. *Burgfrieden und Klassenkampf: Die deutsche Sozialdemokratie im Ersten Weltkrieg.* Düsseldorf, 1974.

Mlynek, Klaus. "Hannover in der Weimarer Republik und im Nationalsozialismus, 1918–1945." In Klaus Mlynek und Waldemar R. Röhrbein, eds., *Geschichte der Stadt Hannover,* vol. 2, *Vom Beginn des 19. Jahrhunderts bis in die Gegenwart,* 405–578. Hanover, 1994.

Molthagen, Dietmar. *Das Ende der Bürgerlichkeit? Liverpooler und Hamburger Bürgerfamilien im Ersten Weltkrieg.* Göttingen, 2007.

Mommsen, Hans. "Generationenkonflikt und politische Entwicklung in der Weimarer Republik." In Jürgen Reulecke, ed., *Generationalität und Lebensgeschichte,* 115–126. Munich, 2003.

———. "Der Reichstagsbrand und seine politischen Folgen." *Vierteljahrshefte für Zeitgeschichte* 12, no. 4 (1964): 351–413.

Mommsen, Wolfgang J. "Die deutsche Revolution 1918–1920: Politische Revolution und soziale Protestbewegung." *Geschichte und Gesellschaft* 4, no. 3 (1978): 362–391.

Mosse, George L. *German Jews Beyond Judaism.* Bloomington, Ind., 1985.

———. "German Socialists and the Jewish Question in the Weimar Republic." *Leo Baeck Institute Yearbook* 16 (1971): 123–151.

———. "Gershom Scholem as a German Jew." *Modern Judaism* 10, no. 2 (1990): 117–133.

———. *The Jews and the German War Experience, 1914–1918.* New York, 1977.

Mosse, Werner E. "Die Krise der europäischen Bourgeoisie und das deutsche Judentum." In Werner E. Mosse and Arnold Paucker, eds., *Deutsches Judentum in Krieg und Revolution, 1916–1923,* 1–26. Tübingen, 1971.

Mückain, Olaf. "Erzählung als Heilung: Alfred Döblins Roman 'Berlin Alexanderplatz'—zwischen Bannung, Katharsis und Lösung." In Andreas Hermes Kick and Günter Dietz, eds., *Verzweiflung als kreative Herausforderung: Psychopathologie, Psychotherapie und künstlerische Lösungsgestalt in Literatur, Musik, Film,* 175–209. Berlin, 2008.

Müller, Reinhard. *Die Akte Wehner: Moskau, 1937 bis 1941.* Reinbek b. Hamburg, 1994.

———. "Hitlers Rede vor der Reichswehr- und Reichsmarineführung am 3. Februar 1933: Eine neue Moskauer Überlieferung." *Mittelweg 36,* vol. 10, no. 1 (2001): 73–90.

"Die Nacht der Papierschlangen." *Vossische Zeitung,* 2 January 1933, evening edition, no. 2, p. 4.

Nelles, Dieter. "The Foreign Legion of the Revolution: German Anarcho-Syndicalist and Volunteers in Anarchist Militas During the Spanish Civil War." Accessed 10 March 2017. http://libcom.org/library/the-foreign-legion-revolution.

Nettl, Peter. *Rosa Luxemburg.* Cologne, Berlin, 1967.

"Die neuen Antisemiten." *Der Vorwärts* 40 (1923): 5.

"Neue Notverordnung in Sicht: Schärfste Maßnahmen zum Schutz des deutschen Volkes vor der kommunistischen Gefahr vom Reichstag angekündigt." *Vossische Zeitung*, 28 March 1933, evening edition, no. 100, 1–2.

Niethammer, Lutz, ed. *Der "gesäuberte" Antifaschismus: Die SED und die roten Kapos von Buchenwald.* Berlin, 1994.

Niewyk, Donald L. *The Jews in Weimar Germany.* New Brunswick, N.J., London, 2001.

Oleschinski, Brigitte. *Gedenkstätte Plötzensee.* Edited by Gedenkstätte Deutscher Widerstand Berlin. Berlin, 1994.

Ozick, Cynthia. "The Fourth Sparrow: The Magisterial Reach of Gershom Scholem." In Cynthia Ozick, *Art & Ardor: Essays*, 138–150. New York 1983.

Paschen, Joachim. *"Wenn Hamburg brennt, brennt die Welt: Der kommunistische Griff nach der Macht im Oktober 1923.* Frankfurt a. M., 2010.

Peters, Ulrich. *Wer die Hoffnung verliert, hat alles verloren: Kommunistischer Widerstand in Buchenwald.* Cologne, 2003.

Peukert, Detlev J. K. *Die Weimarer Republik: Krisenjahre der Klassischen Moderne.* Frankfurt a. M., 1987.

Pietzsch, Henning. *Die Fronterfahrung der deutschen Soldaten im Ersten Weltkrieg und ihre Ideologisierung zum "Fronterlebnis" in den zwanziger Jahren.* Stuttgart, 2005.

Pikarski, Margot. *Geschichte der revolutionären Berliner Arbeiterbewegung, 1933 bis 1939.* Berlin, 1978.

"Die Polizeiaktion im Landtag." *Die Rote Fahne* 6, no. 102 (1923): 1–2.

Portmann, Werner, and Siegbert Wolf. *"Ja, ich kämpfte": Von Revolutionsträumen, "Luftmenschen" und Kindern des Schtetls; Biographien radikaler Jüdinnen und Juden.* Münster, 2006.

Prager, Eugen. "Die erfreuliche Spaltung." *Freiheit*, no. 3, 14 September 1920, 282.

Prestel, Claudia T. "The 'New Jewish Woman' in Weimar Germany." In Wolfgang Benz et al., *Jüdisches Leben in der Weimarer Republik*, 135–156. Tübingen, 1998.

Protokoll der Konferenz der Erweiterten Exekutive der Kommunistischen Internationale, Moskau vom 12. bis 23.6.1923. Hamburg, 1923.

Protokoll der Konferenz der Erweiterten Exekutive der Kommunistischen Internationale, Moskau vom 21.3. bis 6.4.1925. Hamburg, 1925.

Protokoll der Konferenz der Erweiterten Exekutive der Kommunistischen Internationale, Moskau vom 17.2. bis 15.3.1926. Hamburg, 1926.

Przyrembel, Alexandra. *"Rassenschande": Reinheitsmythos und Vernichtungslegitimation im Nationalsozialismus.* Göttingen, 2003.

Pulzer, Peter. "Der erste Weltkrieg." In Michael A. Meyer and Michael Brenner, eds., *Deutschjüdische Geschichte in der Neuzeit.* Vol. 3, *Umstrittene Integration, 1871–1918*, 356–380. Edited by Steven M. Lowenstein, Paul Mendes-Flohr, et al. Munich, 1997.

———. "Die Jüdische Beteiligung an der Politik." In Werner E. Mosse and Arnold Paucker, eds., *Juden im Wilhelminischen Deutschland, 1890–1914*, 143–239. Tübingen, 1976.

Quast, Anke. *Nach der Befreiung: Jüdische Gemeinden in Niedersachsen seit 1945; Das Beispiel Hannover.* Göttingen, 2001.

Rabe, Bernd. *Linden: Der Charakter eines Arbeiterviertels vor Hannover.* Hanover, 1984.

Raithel, Thomas. *Das schwierige Spiel des Parlamentarismus: Deutscher Reichstag und französische Chambre des Députés in den Inflationskrisen der 1920er Jahre.* Munich, 2005.

Ranc, Julijana. *Alexandra Ramm-Pfemfert: Ein Gegenleben.* Hamburg, 2003.

Rebiger, Bill. "'Das Wesentliche spielt sich nicht auf der Leipziger Straße ab, sondern . . . im Geheimen'—Gershom Scholem und Berlin." *EAJS Newsletter* 16 (2005): 81–99.

Reichmann, Eva G. "Der Bewußtseinswandel der deutschen Juden." In Werner E. Mosse und Arnold Paucker, eds., *Deutsches Judentum in Krieg und Revolution, 1916–1923*, 511–612. Tübingen, 1971.

Reichsgesetzblatt. Part 1, 28 February 1933, no. 17.

"Reichstag Dispersed with Jeers: A Communist Day." *Manchester Guardian*, 28 May 1924, 9.

Reichstagshandbuch, 1924: 2. und 3. Wahlperiode 1924. Berlin, 1924.

Remarque, Erich Maria. *All Quiet on the Western Front.* Translated by A. W. Wheen. New York, 2013.

Reuter, Ernst. *Schriften, Reden*, vol. 2. Edited by Hans E. Hirschfeld and Hans J. Reichhardt. Berlin, 1973.

Reuter, Gerd. *KPD-Politik in der Weimarer Republik: Politische Vorstellungen und soziale Zusammensetzung der KPD in Hannover zur Zeit der Weimarer Republik.* Hanover, 1982.

Rosenberg, Arthur. *Entstehung und Geschichte der Weimarer Republik.* Edited and introduction by Kurt Kersten. Frankfurt a. M., 1988.

Rosenthal, Jacob. *"Die Ehre des jüdischen Soldaten": Die Judenzählung im Ersten Weltkrieg und ihre Folgen.* Frankfurt a. M., New York, 2007.

Roth, Joseph. *Der stumme Prophet.* Reinbek b. Hamburg, 1987.

Rüger, Ulrich. "Anfänge der psychoanalytischen Therapie in Berlin, 1900–1933: Karl Abraham und das Psychoanalytische Institut der 20er Jahre." In Hanfried Helmchen, ed., *Psychiater und Zeitgeist: Zur Geschichte der Psychiatrie in Berlin*, 239–255. Lengerich, 2008.

Rühle, Otto. *Die Sozialisierung der Frau.* Dresden, 1922.

Sachs, Nelly. *In den Wohnungen des Todes.* Berlin, 1947.

Samsonschule in Wolfenbüttel. *Realschule und Erziehungsanstalt mit Berechtigung für den einjährig-freiwilligen Militärdienst.* Wolfenbüttel, 1906.

Samsonschule (Realschule) zu Wolfenbüttel. *Berichte über die Zeit von Ostern 1907–1908 bis 1910–1911.* Wolfenbüttel, 1908–1911.

Samsonschule Wolfenbüttel (1786–1921). *Ausstellung aus Anlaß der 200. Wiederkehr des Gründungstages. Veröffentlichungen des Braunschweigischen Landesmuseums 46.* Wolfenbüttel, 1986.

Saß, Anne-Christin. "Ostjudendebatte." In Wolfgang Benz, ed., *Handbuch des Antisemitismus: Judenfeindschaft in Geschichte und Gegenwart*, vol. 4, *Ereignisse, Dekrete, Kontroversen*, 261–262. Berlin, Boston, 2011.

———. "Ostjuden-Erlass." In Wolfgang Benz, ed., *Handbuch des Antisemitismus: Judenfeindschaft in Geschichte und Gegenwart*, vol. 4, *Ereignisse, Dekrete, Kontroversen*, 262–263. Berlin, Boston, 2011.

Schafranek, Hans. *Das kurze Leben des Kurt Landau: Ein österreichischer Kommunist als Opfer der stalinistischen Geheimpolizei.* Vienna, 1988.

———. *Zwischen NKWD und Gestapo: Die Auslieferung deutscher und österreichischer Antifaschisten aus der Sowjetunion an Nazideutschland, 1937–1941.* Frankfurt a. M., 1990.

Schoeps, Hans Joachim. *Ungeflügelte Worte: Was nicht im Büchmann stehen kann.* Berlin, 1971.

Schoeps, Julius H. *Leiden an Deutschland: Vom antisemitischen Wahn und der Last der Erinnerung.* Munich, 1990.

Scholem, Betty. "Ex Oriente Lux." In Paul Mendes-Flohr, *Divided Passions: Jewish Intellectuals and the Experience of Modernity,* 109–116. Detroit, 1991.

———. "November. Die Kennkarte. Schmuck und Silber." In Betty Scholem and Gershom Scholem, *Mutter und Sohn im Briefwechsel, 1917–1946,* 531–535. Edited by Itta Shedletzky and Thomas Sparr. Munich, 1989.

Scholem, Betty, and Gershom Scholem. *Mutter und Sohn im Briefwechsel, 1917–1946.* Edited by Itta Shedletzky and Thomas Sparr. Munich, 1989.

Scholem, Gerhard. *See also* Scholem, Gershom. "Abschied: Offener Brief an Herrn Dr. Siegfried Bernfeld und gegen die Leser dieser Zeitschrift." *Jerubaal: Eine Zeitschrift der jüdischen Jugend* 1, no. 4 (1918/1919): 125–130.

———. "Dem Andenken Hermann Cohens, 5 Apr. 1918." In Gershom Scholem, *Tagebücher,* 2:189–190. Edited by Herbert Kopp-Oberstebrink et al. Frankfurt a. M., 2000.

———. "Bekenntnis über unsere Sprache" [1926]. In Stéphane Mosès, *Der Engel der Geschichte: Franz Rosenzweig, Walter Benjamin, Gershom Scholem,* 215–217. Frankfurt a. M., 1994.

———. "Der Bolschewismus" [1918/1919]. In *Tagebücher,* 2:556–558. Edited by Herbert Kopp-Oberstebrink et al. Frankfurt a. M., 2000.

———. "Ideologie." *Die Blau-Weiße Brille,* no. 3., Tevet 5676 [Dec. 1915/Jan. 1916]. Reprinted in *Tagebücher,* 1:299–300. Edited by Herbert Kopp-Oberstebrink et al. Frankfurt a. M., 1995.

———. "Jüdische Jugendbewegung." *Der Jude* 1, no. 12 (1916/1917): 822–825. Reprinted in *Tagebücher,* 1:511–517. Edited by Herbert Kopp-Oberstebrink et al. Frankfurt a. M., 1995.

———. "Jugendbewegung, Jugendarbeit und Blau-Weiss." In *Die Blau-Weiss Blätter (Führernummer): Monatsschrift für jüdisches Jugendwandern* 1, no. 2 (1917): 26–30. Reprinted in *Tagebücher,* 2:101–106. Edited by Herbert Kopp-Oberstebrink et al. Frankfurt a. M., 2000.

———. "Kleine Anmerkungen über Judentum" [Winter 1917/1918]. Reprinted in *Tagebücher,* 2:195–215. Edited by Herbert Kopp-Oberstebrink et al.. Frankfurt a. M., 2000.

———. "Laienpredigt." *Die Blau-Weiße Brille,* no. 2, Tishrei 5676 [Sept./Oct. 1915]. Reprinted in *Tagebücher,* 1:297–298. Edited by Herbert Kopp-Oberstebrink et al. Frankfurt a. M., 1995.

———. "Über Klage und Klagelied" [1917]. In *Tagebücher,* 2:128–133. Edited by Herbert Kopp-Oberstebrink et al. Frankfurt a. M., 2000.

Scholem, Gershom. "Ahnen und Verwandte Walter Benjamins." *Bulletin des Leo Baeck Instituts* 61 (1982): 29–55.

———. "Der Bolschewismus," in Scholem, *Tagebücher,* 2:556–558. Edited by Herbert Kopp-Oberstebrink et al. Frankfurt a. M., 2000. [Following the translation of Eric Jacobson, in *Metaphysics of the Profane,* 195–196. New York, 2003].

———. *Briefe.* 3 vols. Edited by Itta Shedletzky and Thomas Sparr. Munich 1994–1999.

———. *Briefe an Werner Kraft.* Edited by Werner Kraft. Frankfurt a. M., 1986.

———. *Das Buch Bahir: Ein Schriftdenkmal aus der Frühzeit der Kabbala; Auf Grund der kritischen Neuausgabe.* Leipzig, 1923.

————, ed. *The Correspondence of Walter Benjamin and Gershom Scholem, 1932–1940.* New York, 1989.

————. *"Es gibt ein Geheimnis in der Welt": Tradition und Säkularisation; Ein Vortrag und ein Gespräch.* Edited by Itta Shedletzky. Frankfurt a. M., 2002.

————. "95 Thesen über Judentum und Zionismus, 15. Juli 1918 anlässlich Walter Benjamins 26. Geburtstag." In *Tagebücher*, 2:300–306. Edited by Herbert Kopp-Oberstebrink et al. Frankfurt a. M. 2000.

————. *From Berlin to Jerusalem: Memories of My Youth.* Translated by Harry Zohn. Philadelphia, 2012.

————. "Memory and Utopia in Jewish History" [1946]. In Gershom Scholem, *On the Possibility of Jewish Mysticism in Our Time & Other Essays*, 155–166. Edited by Abraham Shapira. Jerusalem, 1977.

————. "Mihu Yehudi Bahalacha Uvasifrut." In Gershom Scholem, *Od Davar: Pirkei morasha uthiya.* Edited by Avraham Shapira. Tel Aviv, 1992.

————. "On the Social Psychology of Jews in Germany 1900–1933." In David Bronsen, ed., *Jews and Germans from 1860 to 1933: The Problematic Symbiosis*, 9–32. Heidelberg, 1979.

————. *Sabbatai Sevi: The Mystical Messiah, 1626–1676.* Translated by R. J. Zwi Werblowsky. Princeton, N.J., 1973.

————. *Tagebücher, nebst Aufsätzen und Entwürfen bis 1923.* 2 vols. Edited by Herbert Kopp-Oberstebrink, Karlfried Gründer, Friedrich Niewöhner, and Karl E. Grözinger. Frankfurt a. M., 1995, 2000.

————. *Von Berlin nach Jerusalem: Jugenderinnerungen; Erweiterte Ausgabe.* Frankfurt a. M., 1997.

————. "Vorwort." In Walter Benjamin, *Moskauer Tagebuch*, 9–15. Edited by Gary Smith. Frankfurt a. M., 1980.

————. *Walter Benjamin: The Story of a Friendship.* London, 1982.

————. "Zionism—Dialectic of Continuity and Rebellion: Interview" [April/July 1970]. In Ehud Ben-Ezer, ed., *Unease in Zion*, 263–296. New York, 1974.

————. "Zur Sozialpsychologie der Juden in Deutschland, 1900–1930." In Gershom Scholem, *Judaica 4*, 229–261. Edited by Rolf Tiedemann. Frankfurt a. M., 1984.

Scholem, Gershom, and David Biale. "The Threat of Messianism: An Interview with Gershom Scholem." *New York Review of Books* 27, no. 13 (1980): 22.

Scholem, Gershom, and Jörg Drews. ". . . *und alles ist Kabbala": Gershom Scholem im Gespräch mit Jörg Drews.* Munich, 1998.

Scholem, Gershom, and Muki Tsur. "An Interview." In Gershom Scholem, *On Jews and Judaism in Crisis: Selected Essays*, 1–48. Edited by Werner J. Dannhauser. New York, 1976.

Scholem, Werner. "Für die kommunistische Internationale." *Volksblatt: Sozialdemokratisches Organ für Halle und den Bezirk Merseburg* 31, no. 212 (1920): 2–3.

————. "In eigener Sache." *Volksblatt: Sozialdemokratisches Organ für Halle und den Bezirk Merseburg* 31, no. 215 (1920): supplement, 1.

————. "Das rote Herz Deutschlands." *Volksblatt: Sozialdemokratisches Organ für Halle und den Bezirk Merseburg* 31, no. 238 (1920): supplement, 1–2.

————. "Skizze über die Entwicklung der Opposition in der KPD." *Die Internationale* 7, no. 6 (1924): 122–134.

————. "Solidarität mit Sowjet-Rußland?" *Volksblatt: Sozialdemokratisches Organ für Halle und den Bezirk Merseburg* 31, no. 211 (1920): 2.

———. "Die Zukunft der Unabhängigen Sozialdemokratie." *Volksblatt: Sozialdemokratisches Organ für Halle und den Bezirk Merseburg* 31, no. 206 (1920): 5.

———. "Zur Organisationsfrage: Einige noch ungelöste organisatorische Fragen." *Die Internationale* 8 (1925): 65.

Scholem, Werner, Ruth Fischer, Wilhelm Schwan, and Hugo Urbahns. *Die Wahrheit über die Verhandlungen mit der deutschen Opposition in Moskau: Bericht der Genossen Urbahns, Ruth Fischer, Scholem und Schwan.* Berlin [1927].

Scholze, Siegfried. "Karl Liebknecht und die Jenaer Jugendkonferenz Ostern 1916." *Zeitschrift für Geschichtswissenschaft* 19, no. 5 (1971): 1016–1033.

Schröder, Karsten, and Hans Herzberg. "Zur Geschichte der Organisation." In Alfred Fleischhacker, ed., *Das war unser Leben: Erinnerungen und Dokumente zur Geschichte der Freien Deutschen Jugend in Großbritannien, 1939–1946*, 188–230. In collaboration with Holger Stoecker. Berlin, 1996.

Schüle, Annegret. *Trotzkismus in Deutschland bis 1933: "Für die Arbeitereinheitsfront zur Abwehr des Faschismus."* Cologne, 1989.

Schulze Wessel, Martin. " 'Loyalität' als geschichtlicher Grundbegriff und Forschungskonzept: Zur Einleitung." In Martin Schulze Wessel, ed., *Loyalitäten in der Tschechoslowakischen Republik, 1918–1938*, 1–22. Munich, 2004.

Schumacher, Kurt. "Nachklänge zum Parteitag." *Esslinger Volkszeitung*, 25 June 1924, 147.

Schumacher, Martin, ed. *M.d.R.: Die Reichstagsabgeordneten der Weimarer Republik in der Zeit des Nationalsozialismus; Politische Verfolgung, Emigration und Ausbürgerung, 1933–1945; Eine biographische Dokumentation.* Düsseldorf, 1991.

Schuster, Frank M. *Zwischen allen Fronten: Osteuropäische Juden während des Ersten Weltkrieges (1914–1919).* Cologne, Weimar, Vienna, 2004.

Schwilk, Heimo. *Ernst Jünger: Ein Jahrhundertleben; Die Biografie.* Munich, 2007.

"16 [Sechzehn] Tage Moabit: Erlebnisse in Untersuchungshaft von Nr. 1621." *Berliner Illustrierte*, 27 October 1933, night edition, supplements 1 and 2.

Seymour, Miranda. "Shaping the Truth." In Peter France and William St Clair, eds., *Mapping Lives: The Uses of Biography*, 253–266. Oxford 2002.

Shavit, Zohar. "On the Hebrew Cultural Center in Berlin in the Twenties: Hebrew Culture in Europe—the Last Attempt." *Gutenberg Jahrbuch 1993*, 371–380.

Shedletzky, Itta. "Auf der Suche nach dem verlorenen Judentum: Zur 'historischen Gestalt' Gershom Scholems." *Münchner Beiträge zur Jüdischen Geschichte und Kultur* 1, no. 2 (2007): 30–47.

———. "Einleitung." In Betty Scholem and Gerschom Scholem, *Mutter und Sohn im Briefwechsel, 1917–1946*, 7–12. Edited by Itta Shedletzky and Thomas Sparr. Munich, 1989.

Shore, Marci. "Children of the Revolution: Communism, Zionism, and the Berman Brothers." *Jewish Social Studies* 10, no. 3 (2004): 23–86.

Sieg, Ulrich. *Jüdische Intellektuelle im Ersten Weltkrieg: Kriegserfahrungen, weltanschauliche Debatten und kulturelle Neuentwürfe.* Berlin, 2008.

Silberner, Edmund. *Kommunisten zur Judenfrage: Zur Geschichte von Theorie und Praxis des Kommunismus.* Opladen, 1983.

Singer, Kurt. "Allgemeines zur Frage der Simulation." *Würzburger Abhandlungen aus dem Gesamtgebiet der praktischen Medizin* 16 (1916): 139–156.

Sinowjew, Grigori. "Zur Lage in der KPD." *Die Internationale* 7, no. 6 (1924): 239.

Sittig-Eisenschitz, Eva. "An den Fronten des Spanischen Bürgerkriegs." *Utopie Kreativ*, no. 69 (1996): 56–63.

Sitzungsberichte des Preußischen Landtags. Vols. 1–14. Berlin, 1922–1924.

Slezkine, Yuri. *The Jewish Century*. Princeton, N.J., 2004.

Smith, Gary. "Afterword." *October* 35 (1985): 136–146.

Spartakusbriefe. Vol. 1. Berlin, 1921.

Stalin, Joseph. "Die deutsche Revolution und die Fehler des Genossen Radek: Aus dem Bericht auf dem Plenum des Zentralkomitees der RKP(B), Moskau, Dienstag, 15. Januar 1924." In Bernhard H. Bayerlein et al., eds., *Deutscher Oktober 1923: Ein Revolutionsplan und sein Scheitern*, 443–450. Berlin, 2003.

———. "Über den Kampf gegen die Rechten und 'Ultralinken' Abweichungen: Zwei Reden in der Sitzung des Präsidiums des EKKI, 22. Januar 1926." In J. W. Stalin, *Werke*, vol. 8, *1926 Januar–November*, 1–9. Dortmund, 1976.

Stapel, Wilhelm. *Über das seelische Problem der Symbiose des deutschen und des jüdischen Volkes*. Hamburg, Berlin, Leipzig, 1928.

Stein, Harry. "Buchenwald—Stammlager." In Wolfgang Benz and Barbara Distel, eds., *Der Ort des Terrors: Geschichte der nationalsozialistischen Konzentrationslager*, vol. 3, *Sachsenhausen, Buchenwald*, 300–356. Munich, 2006.

Stevenson, Robert Louis. *The Letters of Robert Louis Stevenson*. 8 vols. Edited by Bradford A. Booth and Ernest Mehew. New Haven, Conn., 1994–1995.

Stoecker, Walter, ed. *Handbuch der Kommunistischen Reichstagsfraktion, 1928–1930*. Berlin, 1930.

Stokes, Kenneth Michael. *Paradigm Lost: A Cultural and Systems Theoretical Critique of Political Economy*. Armonk, N.Y., London, 1995.

Susman, Margarete. *Das Buch Hiob und das Schicksal des jüdischen Volkes*. 1946. Frankfurt a. M., 1996.

Talmon, Jacob L. *Israel Among the Nations*. London, 1970.

Toller, Ernst. *I Was a German: The Autobiography of a Revolutionary*. New York, 1991.

Traverso, Enzo. "Die Juden, der Sozialismus und die Arbeiterbewegung." In Elke-Vera Kotowski et al., eds., *Handbuch zur Geschichte der Juden in Europa*, vol. 2, *Religion, Kultur, Alltag*, 460–470. Darmstadt, 2001.

Treml, Martin. "Between Utopia and Redemption: Gustav Landauer's Influence on Gershom Scholem." In Paul Mendes-Flohr and Anya Mali, eds., *Gustav Landauer: Anarchist and Jew*, 82–91. In collaboration with Hanna Delf von Wolzogen. Berlin, Munich, Boston, 2015.

Triendl, Mirjam, and Noam Zadoff. "Ob mein Bruder Werner gemeint ist? Erinnerungen an einen Pazifisten." *Freitag*, 18 June 2004. http://www.freitag.de/politik/0426-erinnerung-pazifisten.

Triendl-Zadoff, Mirjam. *Nächstes Jahr in Marienbad: Gegenwelten jüdischer Kulturen der Moderne*. Göttingen, 2007.

———. "Der unsichtbare Bruder: Der Briefwechsel zwischen Gershom Scholem und Ernst Jünger." *Freitag*, 25 July 2009. http://www.freitag.de/kultur/0930-scholem-juenger-briefwechsel-kpd-holocaust.

———. "Werner Scholem." In Michael Berenbaum and Fred Skolnik, eds., *Encyclopaedia Judaica*, 18:159. Detroit, 2007.

Trotzki, Leo. *Tagebuch im Exil, mit einem Vorwort von Carola Stern*. Cologne, Berlin, 1960.

Tuchel, Johannes. *Konzentrationslager: Organisationsgeschichte und Funktion der "Inspektion der Konzentrationslager," 1934–1938*. Boppard am Rhein, 1991.

Tuchman, Barbara W. "Biography as a Prism of History." In Barbara Tuchman, *Practicing History: Selected Essays*, 80–90. New York, 1981.

"Umschau." *Im Deutschen Reich* 25 (1919): 369.

Usborne, Cornelie. "The New Woman and Generational Conflict: Perception of Young Women's Sexual Mores in the Weimar Republic." In Mark Roseman, *Generations in Conflict: Youth Revolt and Generation Formation in Germany, 1770–1968*, 137–163. Cambridge, 1995.

Verhandlungen des Reichstags, II. Wahlperiode 1924: Stenographische Berichte. Vol. 381. Berlin, 1924.

Verhandlungen des Reichstags, II. Wahlperiode 1925: Stenographische Berichte. Vol. 385 Berlin, 1925.

Verhandlungen des Reichstags, III. Wahlperiode 1924: Stenographische Berichte. Vol. 393. Berlin, 1928.

Verhandlungen des Reichstags, III. Wahlperiode 1924: Stenographische Berichte. Vol. 394. Berlin, 1928.

Volk, Karl [Ypsilon]. *Pattern for World Revolution*. Chicago, New York, 1947.

Völter, Bettina. *Judentum und Kommunismus: Deutsche Familiengeschichten in drei Generationen*. Wiesbaden, 2003.

Wagner, Walter. *Der Volksgerichtshof im nationalsozialistischen Staat, mit einem Forschungsbericht für die Jahre 1975 bis 2010 von Jürgen Zarusky*. Munich, 2011.

Walter, Eva. "'Meine Frau hat keine Zeit!' Frauen in der KPD während der Weimarer Republik." In Franz Mehring Gesellschaft, ed., *Demokratie und Arbeitergeschichte. Jahrbuch 2: Geschichtsschreibung–Medienkritik–Unterrichtsmaterialien*, 96–107. Stuttgart, 1982.

Wassermann, Jakob. *Mein Weg als Deutscher und Jude*. Berlin, 1921.

Weber, Hermann, ed. *Der deutsche Kommunismus: Dokumente*. Cologne, Berlin, 1964.

———. *Die Wandlung des deutschen Kommunismus*. 2 vols. Frankfurt a. M., 1969.

———. "Kommentar zu den Beiträgen von Eberhard Kolb und Andreas Wirsching." In Heinrich August Winkler, ed., *Weimar im Widerstreit: Deutungen der ersten deutschen Republik im geteilten Deutschland*, 141–149. Munich, 2002.

———. "Zu den Beziehungen zwischen der KPD und der Kommunistischen Internationale." *Vierteljahrshefte für Zeitgeschichte* 16, no. 2 (1968): 177–208.

Weber, Hermann, and Andreas Herbst. *Deutsche Kommunisten: Biographisches Handbuch, 1918 bis 1945*. Berlin, 2004.

Weber, Hermann, and Gerda Weber. *Leben nach dem "Prinzip links": Erinnerungen aus fünf Jahrzehnten*. Berlin, 2006.

Weidner, Daniel. *Gershom Scholem: Politisches, esoterisches und historiographisches Schreiben*. Munich, 2003.

Weiner, Hannah. "Gershom Scholem and the Jung Juda Youth Group in Berlin, 1913–1918." *Studies in Zionism*, 5, no. 1 (1984): 29–42.

Weininger, Otto. *Geschlecht und Charakter: Eine prinzipielle Untersuchung*. Vienna, Leipzig, 1903.

Weissenberg, S. "Der Anteil der Juden an der Revolutionsbewegung in Rußland." *Zeitschrift für Demographie und Statistik der Juden* 3, no. 1 (1907): 1–7.

Weißgerber, Ulrich. *Giftige Worte der SED-Diktatur: Sprache als Instrument von Machtausübung und Ausgrenzung in der SBZ und der DDR.* Berlin, 2010.

Weitz, Eric D. "Communism and the Public Spheres of Weimar Germany." In David E. Barclay and Eric D. Weitz, eds., *Between Reform and Revolution: German Socialism and Communism from 1840 to 1990,* 275–291. New York, Oxford, 1998.

———. *Creating German Communism, 1890–1990: From Popular Protests to Socialist State.* Princeton, N.J., 1997.

———. *Weimar Germany: Promise and Tragedy.* Princeton, N.J., 2007.

Wheeler, Robert. "German Labor and the Comintern: A Problem of Generations?" *Journal of Social History* 7, no. 3 (1974): 304–321.

———. "Die '21 Bedingungen' und die Spaltung der USPD im Herbst 1920: Zur Meinungsbildung der Basis." *Vierteljahrshefte für Zeitgeschichte* 23, no. 2 (1975): 117–154.

"Die widerrechtliche Verhaftung der Genossen Scholem, Sobottka und Rosi Wolfstein." *Die Rote Fahne* 6, no. 102 (1923): 9.

Winkler, Heinrich August. *Der Schein der Normalität: Arbeiter und Arbeiterbewegung in der Weimarer Republik, 1924 bis 1930.* Berlin, 1988.

———. *Der Weg in die Katastrophe: Arbeiter und Arbeiterbewegung in der Weimarer Republik, 1930 bis 1933.* Berlin, 1990.

———. *Von der Revolution zur Stabilisierung: Arbeiter und Arbeiterbewegung in der Weimarer Republik, 1918 bis 1924.* Berlin, 1985.

———. *Weimar, 1918–1933: Die Geschichte der ersten deutschen Demokratie.* Munich, 1993.

Wirsching, Andreas. "'Man kann nur den Boden germanisieren': Eine neue Quelle zu Hitlers Rede vor den Spitzen der Reichswehr am 3. Februar 1933." *Vierteljahrshefte für Zeitgeschichte* 49, no. 31 (2001): 517–555.

———. "'Stalinisierung' oder entideologisierte 'Nischengesellschaft'? Alte Einsichten und neue Thesen zum Charakter der KPD in der Weimarer Republik." *Vierteljahrshefte für Zeitgeschichte* 45 (1997): 449–466.

———. *Vom Weltkrieg zum Bürgerkrieg? Politischer Extremismus in Deutschland und Frankreich, 1918–1933/39: Berlin und Paris im Vergleich.* Munich, 1999.

Wobick-Segev, Sarah E. "Praying to Goethe and Other Misadventures of Three Jewish Children in Breslau." Paper presented at the conference "Cosmopolitanism, Nationalism, and the Jews of East Central Europe," Central European University, Budapest, 27–29 May 2007.

Wolfskehl, Karl. *Hiob oder die vier Spiegel.* Hamburg, 1950.

Woolf Virginia. "The Art of Biography." In Virginia Woolf, *The Death of the Moth and Other Essays,* 119–126. London, 1981.

Wreschner, Arthur. *Die Reproduktion und Assoziation von Vorstellungen: Eine experimentell-psychologische Untersuchung, 1. Teil.* Leipzig, 1907.

Wünsch, Falk-Rüdiger. *Neukölln: Alte Bilder erzählen.* Erfurt, 1998.

Wünschmann, Kim. "Cementing the Enemy Category: Arrest and Imprisonment of German Jews in Nazi Concentration Camps, 1933–8/9." *Journal of Contemporary History* 45, no. 3 (2010): 576–600.

Yerushalmi, Yosef Hayim. *Freuds Moses: Endliches und unendliches Judentum.* Berlin, 1991.

Zadek, Peter. *My Way: Eine Autobiographie, 1926–1969*. Cologne, 1998.

Zadoff, Mirjam. "Familienrevolution im Jahr 1933: Die deutsch-jüdischen Kommunisten Werner und Emmy Scholem im Briefwechsel." In Sylvia Asmus, Germaine Goetzinger, Hiltrud Häntzschel, and Inge Hansen-Schaberg, eds., *Briefeschreiben im Exil*, 175–187. Munich, 2013.

———. " ' . . . der lebendige Beweis für ihre Greuel': Arthur Rosenberg an Emmy Scholem am 18. November 1938." *Münchner Beiträge zur jüdischen Geschichte und Kultur* 7, no. 2 (2013): 33–41.

———. *Next Year in Marienbad: The Lost Worlds of Jewish Spa Culture*. Translated by William Templer. Philadelphia, 2012.

Zadoff, Mirjam, and Noam Zadoff. "From Mission to Memory: Walter Benjamin and Werner Scholem in the Life and Work of Gershom Scholem." *Journal of Modern Jewish Studies* 13, no. 1 (2014): 58–74.

Zadoff, Noam. *Gershom Scholem: From Berlin to Jerusalem and Back*. Waltham, 2018.

———. " 'Zion's Self-Engulfing Light': On Gershom Scholem's Disillusionment with Zionism." *Modern Judaism* 31, no. 3 (2011): 272–284.

Zetkin, Clara. "Die Intellektuellenfrage: Aus dem Referat auf dem V. Kongress der Kommunistischen Internationale." In Clara Zetkin, *Ausgewählte Reden und Schriften*, 3:9–56. Berlin, 1960.

Zilkenat, Reiner. "Das Schicksal von Werner Scholem." *Neues Deutschland*, 14 July 1990.

Zimmermann, Moshe. *Deutsche gegen Deutsche: Das Schicksal der Juden, 1938–1945*. Berlin, 2008.

———. *Die deutschen Juden, 1914–1945*. Munich, 1997.

———. "Zukunftserwartungen deutscher Juden im ersten Jahr der Weimarer Republik." *Archiv für Sozialgeschichte* 37 (1997): 55–72.

Zimmermann, Rüdiger. *Der Leninbund: Linke Kommunisten in der Weimarer Republik*. Düsseldorf, 1978.

"Zum Gruß!" *Kladderadatsch* 77, no. 23 (1924): 362.

Zweig, Arnold. "Der heutige deutsche Antisemitismus: Vier Aufsätze." *Der Jude* 5 (1920/1921): 451–459, and 557–565.

INDEX

ACKNOWLEDGMENTS

I would like to express my gratitude first and foremost to Renee Goddard née Renate Scholem, and to her daughter Leonie Mellinger and her niece, Susanna Capon.

My sincere thanks also go to my editor, Jerry Singerman. I am also grateful to David Ruderman, the editor of the Jewish Culture and Contexts series when this project first came to the Press, and the current series editor, Steven Weitzman, both of whom this book has to thank for its existence. Dona Geyer and Jeffrey M. Green did fine work on the translation.

I am indebted to friends and colleagues for their valuable comments and conversations over the course of several years, in particular Martin H. Geyer, Itta Shedletzky, Michael Brenner, Irene Götz, Saul Friedländer, Jens Malte Fischer, David N. Myers, Ute and Jürgen Habermas, Stefanie Schüler-Springorum, Ada Rapoport-Albert, John Efron, Knut Bergbauer, Julie Mell and Malachi H. Hacohen, Bettina Bannasch, Hiltrud Häntzschel, Peter Wieckenberg, Erna Weiss, Diana and Efraim Zadoff, Sebastian Panwitz, Susannah Haas, Laura Stadler, Johannes Börmann, and last but not least Huberta and Richard Triendl.

This book is dedicated to my family, my parents and siblings, and especially to my husband, Noam Zadoff, and our children, Amos Joel and Emilia Inbár.